DICTIONARY
OF
BRITISH
MILITARY
HISTORY

DICTIONARY
OF
BRITISH
MILITARY
HISTORY

A & C Black • London

www.acblack.com

First published in Great Britain in 2003
Second edition published 2006

A & C Black Publishers Ltd
38 Soho Square, London W1D 3HB

A CIP record for this book is available from the British Library

ISBN-10: 0 7136 7507 1
ISBN-13: 978 0 7136 7507 8

1 3 5 7 9 8 6 4 2

Text Production and Proofreading
Joel Adams, Heather Bateman, Irene Lakhani,
Daisy Jackson, Katy McAdam

This book is produced using paper that is made from wood grown in
managed, sustainable forests. It is natural, renewable and recyclable. The
logging and manufacturing processes conform to the environmental
regulations of the country of origin

Text typeset by A & C Black
Printed in Italy by Rotolito Lombarda

Introduction

The Dictionary of British Military History provides an overview of British land warfare from the Danish invasion of the 9th century to the present day. It aims to give the general reader or enthusiast a condensed account of significant figures and events – battles, campaigns and soldiers, together with the weapons they used throughout the ages. Such a huge span of military history cannot be covered in close detail, and this is not the purpose of the book. Rather it offers a basic reference to the milestones in the history of armed forces of the British Isles.

The book also includes entries on the development of the British Army from its formation in the 17th century to the present day – its structure, ranks, regiments, uniforms and medals. Because the Army has also fought in arenas overseas, accounts are included of its involvement in battles and campaigns in Europe, America, India, Africa and Asia. These are largely confined to those of significance in British history or those in which significant numbers of British soldiers were involved. For the sake of simplicity the phrase 'battle of' has been used to indicate any conflict, for example a siege.

Biographies focus mainly on the military activities of the individual concerned. The inclusion of more detailed biographies would make the book cumbersome and the information can be found elsewhere in more specialised texts. Biographies of some more prominent enemy leaders have been included for the sake of completeness.

In a work of this limited size and extensive range descriptions are inevitably concise: for example, for the sake of brevity I have given the context of a particular battle (the war or campaign it was part of) as an italic note at the start of the account of the battle.

Again in the interests of brevity and saving space, each article is extensively cross-referenced. Words highlighted in bold refer the reader to other main entries, making it possible to give the information on a particular topic economically, without resorting to repetition.

Covering such a wide panorama of history in a work of this size must involve a subjective element in the choice of topics to discuss and the weight given to them. However I hope that the reader will find the book a useful tool for background reference and general orientation in what is a vast and complex subject.

My thanks are due to David Gibbons and all who offered me comments and advice on many aspects of the book during its compilation and revision. Thanks are also due to Edmund Wright for his work in preparing this second edition.

George Usher

A

Abercromby, Ralph (1734–1801)
Abercromby was born in Menstrie, Clackmannanshire, and was educated at Rugby School before studying law at Edinburgh and Leipzig Universities. He joined the 3rd Dragoons (**King's Own Hussars**) (1756) and served in Europe during the **Seven Years' War**. He was elected MP for Clackmannanshire (1774–80) before returning to active service (1793) as a **major-general** in Flanders. In 1795–96 he led successful operations against the French in St. Lucia and Trinidad, then held commands in Ireland and Scotland (1797–99). In 1800 he was in command of the force sent to expel the French from Egypt. He led the successful Anglo-Turkish operation in the battle of **Alexandria** in which he was mortally wounded.

Abercromby, Robert (1740–1827)
He was the younger brother of Ralph **Abercromby**. He served as a volunteer in North America, and because of his gallantry at **Ticonderoga** (1758) he was appointed an **ensign** and then **lieutenant** in the 44th Foot (**East Essex Regiment**) (1759). He was present at the battles of **Niagara** and **Montreal** and was promoted to **captain** (1761). He retired (1763) on half pay but returned to America at the outbreak of the **American War of Independence** in which he served with distinction. He was appointed **major** in the 62nd Foot (**Wiltshire Regiment of Foot**) (1772); **lieutenant-colonel** in the 37th Foot (**North Hampshire Regiment of Foot**) (1773) and **colonel** of the 75th Foot (**Stirlingshire Regiment**) (1787). He went with his **regiment** to India (1788). He was promoted to **major-general** and governor and **commander-in-chief** in Bombay (now Mumbai) (1790). He served in India for nine years during which time he subdued the Rohillas and managed to control a mutiny of his officers. He contracted an eye infection and had to return home (1797). Abercromby was promoted to **lieutenant-general** (1797) and elected MP for Clackmannanshire (1798). He was made governor of Edinburgh Castle (1801) and **general** (1802). Because of his increasing blindness he saw no further active service and resigned his seat in Parliament (1802).

Aberdeen, battle of
(1644; *Civil War*) A force of 3,000 **Covenanters** led by Lord Burleigh met 1,500 Royalists, led by the Marquis of **Montrose** outside Aberdeen (13 September). The Covenanters were put to flight with heavy losses.

Abukir, battle of *See* Alexandria, battle of

Abu Klea, battle of
(1885; *Sudan War*) An expedition was sent from Cairo under the command of General Sir Garnet **Wolseley** to relieve General **Gordon** in **Khartoum**. From this expedition an 1,880-strong camel corps under General Sir Herbert **Stewart** advanced to the camel stop at Abu Klea where they encountered some 10,000 followers of the **Mahdi**. During the ensuing battle (17 January) the Sudanese were repelled with the loss of some 1,000 men. The Anglo-Egyptian casualties were 165. Stewart was mortally wounded and died from his wounds immediately after the battle. The corps reached the Nile two days later and now under Lord Charles Beresford moved up-river to Khartoum, but arrived two days too late (28 January) to save Gordon.

Abu Kru, battle of
(1885; *Sudan War*) After the battle of **Abu Klea** the column previously led by Sir Herbert **Stewart** and now under the command of Colonel Sir Charles Wilson moved

towards Khartoum and was attacked by the Sudanese at Abu Kru. The attack was beaten off and the column reached the Nile on the same day (19 January). They boarded two steamers and fought their way to Khartoum (28 January) only to find that the Sudanese had stormed the city two days earlier. Wilson was ordered to withdraw.

Abyssinian campaign (1868)

Sir Robert **Napier** led an expedition to Magdala in Abyssinia (now Ethiopia) to release British hostages, including a Captain Cameron, who were held there by King Theodore. Napier brought his own troops from India, including the **Cameronians**, the **Duke of Wellington's**, the **Sherwood Foresters** and the **King's Own Royal Regiment (Lancaster)**, and landed at Zoulah (2 January). The 672km (420 mile) march began on 25 January and Magdala was stormed on 13 April. King Theodore was found dead and the captives were released.

accoutrements

The personal equipment of a soldier other than uniform and weapon(s), e.g. a pack or belt

[From French, from *accoutrer* 'to clothe or equip']

Accra, battle of

1. (1824; *Ashanti War*) A force of 1,000 British troops, commanded by General Sir Charles **McCarthy**, was surrounded at Accra by 10,000 Ashantis. The British were routed and McCarthy killed.

2. (1825; *Ashanti War*) 400 British troops with 4,600 local auxiliaries defeated 15,000 Ashantis, forcing them to abandon their advance on Cape Coast Castle

accredited honours *See* **battle honours**

ACF *abbreviation of* **army cadet force**

Aclea, battle of

(851; *Danish Invasion of Britain*) The battle between King Ethelwulf of Wessex and the Danes fought at Aclea (now Oakley), south of the Thames. It was the West Saxon victory over the Danes during the reign of Ethelwulf that established Wessex as the premier kingdom in Britain.

active service unit

A military unit deployed in a battle area, in contrast to being held in reserve.
Abbreviation **ASU**

ADC *abbreviation of* **aide-de-camp**

adjutant

An officer who assists a superior officer, particularly in communicating orders. The term is most commonly applied to an officer, typically a **captain**, holding this post in an **infantry battalion**, or the equivalent units in the other arms of service.

[From Latin *adjutant-*, present participle of *adjutare* 'to keep on helping']

adjutant-general

The assistant and executive officer of a **general** and head of a department of the **general staff**

Adjutant General's Corps

The **corps** was formed (1992) by the amalgamation of the **Royal Army Pay Corps**, the **Women's Royal Army Corps** (*see* **women soldiers in the British Army**), the **Corps of Royal Military Police**, the **Royal Army Educational Corps**, the **Military Provost Staff Corps**, the **Army Legal Corps**, and staff clerks of the **Royal Army Ordnance Corps**. It acts as the personnel management department of the British Army.

Adwalton Moor, battle of

(1643; *Civil War*) The Parliamentary forces under Lord Fernando Fairfax and his son Sir Thomas **Fairfax** laid siege to York early in 1643. William Cavendish, Earl of Newcastle, led the Royalist forces to relieve the city. The two armies met at Adwalton (now Atherton) Moor near Bradford (30 June). The Parliamentarians were defeated, leaving the Royalists in control of all Yorkshire, except Hull.

AE *abbreviation of* **ammunition examiner**

Afghanistan (2001)

The war in Afghanistan has to be understood against a background of the civil unrest between the ruling Taliban and the Northern Alliance parties, the internal poverty, the international heroin trade based in the country, and above all international terrorism instigated by the religious leader Osama bin Laden and directed mainly at the USA (the bombing of the US embassies in Nairobi and Dar es Salaam on 8 August 1998 and the attack on the USS Cole in February 1999). The USA demanded that Osama bin Laden be handed over to the United Nations for trial. The United Nations imposed trade embargoes on Afghanistan if he were not handed over. The response by bin Laden and his extremist group, al-Qaeda, was the destruction of the Twin Towers of the World Trade Center in New York by two passenger aircraft that had been hijacked by al-Qaeda (11 September 2001). The invasion of Afghanistan by the Americans and British, with the aim of capturing bin Laden, was immediate, and with the aid of the Northern Alliance the capital Kabul was quickly captured, the Taliban removed, and the country brought more or less under military control. An interim administration was installed, but a democratic constitution was agreed in January 2004 and in October Afghanistan held its first ever direct presidential election. However, although al-Qaeda influence in Afghanistan has largely been broken, Osama bin Laden has not been captured, the warlords' power has not been fully curbed, and the Taliban has not been destroyed: initially driven back to the Afghan–Pakistan border, it has since waged a guerrilla war in southern Afghanistan. The new Afghan regime still depends for security on the presence of foreign troops. In December 2001 the UN established the International Security Assistance Force (ISAF) to assist the Afghan government; initially responsible for the capital, Kabul, and its surrounding area, its role now encompasses about half the country. In 2003 it was taken over by **NATO**. British troops have always formed part of ISAF, and its commanders have included the British major-general John McColl (2001–02) and lieutenant-general David Richards (from 2006).

Afghan Wars (1839–42, 1878–80)

In the 19th century the British attempted to maintain control over Afghanistan without direct military intervention, but their domination of the area was threatened by Russian intervention from the north and west. This threat was met by a series of expeditions by the British to ensure control in the region.

See also **Ahmed Khel, battle of; Gandamak, battle of; Ghazni, battle of; Ghoaine, battle of; Jellalabad, battle of; Kabul, battle of; Kandahar, battle of; Khelat, battle of; Khojah, battle of; Maiwand, battle of; Peiwar Pass, battle of; Sherpur, battle of; East Essex Regiment of Foot; Elphinstone, William George Keith; Nott, William; Pollock, George; Roberts, Frederick Sleigh; Sale, Robert Henry**

AFV *abbreviation of* **armoured fighting vehicle**

agent

A regimental **paymaster** employed by the **colonel** of a **regiment**. A colonel had complete control of his regiment in the 17th and early 18th centuries and was also responsible for distributing the pay to the troops through his agent. The agent frequently transferred a large amount of the funds to his own pocket by various frauds.

See also **pay in the 17th and 18th centuries**

[From Latin *agent-*, present participle of *agere* 'to drive, lead, act or do']

Agincourt, battle of

(1415; *Hundred Years' War*) The renewed invasion of France by Henry V of England began with his conquest of Harfleur (22 September). The English army then moved towards Calais but the march was prevented by the flooding of the river Somme and by the French defences. This caused the English to move inland and to meet larger French forces under the constable, Charles d'Albret, and the marshal, Jean Boucicaut II, at Agincourt (25 October). Henry deployed his forces between two woods, thus cramping and reducing the effectiveness of the French superior numbers. At 11 a.m. the battle began with the British archers causing havoc in the French ranks and the French cavalry becoming bogged down in the mud. Two lines of French cavalry were repulsed but then the French camp-followers began to plunder Henry's baggage trains in his rear. Henry thought he was being attacked and consequently killed all the French prisoners. The third French cavalry charge was repulsed. There were some 7,000 French casualties out of 20,000 men with d'Albret killed and Boucicaut taken prisoner. The English lost some 1,600 men out of 6,000 men. The way was now open for Henry to reinforce the English base at Calais.

Agra, battle of
1. (1803; *Maratha Wars*) British forces commanded by General Gerard **Lake** besieged the fortress (4 October) defended by 6,000 troops in the citadel and seven **battalions** in the town. The latter force was attacked (10 October) and surrendered while the citadel surrendered (18 October) after a bombardment by British guns.

2. (1857; *Indian Mutiny*) The British **garrison** moved out to attack 10,000 rebels who were surrounding Agra (2 August). The Kotak contingent of the British force deserted to the rebels, and the British force had to take refuge in the fort. In October, a British force, commanded by Colonel William **Greathed**, attacked the rebels outside Agra. The rebels were put to flight.

Ahmadabad, battle of
(1780; *Maratha Wars*) The fortress garrisoned by 10,000 Arabs, Sind infantry and Marathas was stormed and taken by a British force, commanded by General Thomas **Goddard**

Ahmed Khel, battle of
(1880; *Afghan War II*) A British force moving to Ghazni was attacked by 3,000 Ghaznis. The attack was repulsed and 1,000 Ghaznis killed.

aide-de-camp
A staff officer who acts as a personal assistant to a senior officer. In modern times an ADC frequently wears an **aiguillette** as part of the uniform. In the 19th century an ADC wore a coat with distinguishing 'saw-edged' button loops. Up to the early 20th century the position of ADC was a privileged one and selection was largely under the personal control of the senior officer whom the ADC was to assist. Appointments were therefore often given as matters of family and political patronage.
Abbreviation **ADC**
[From French, 'camp assistant']

aigrette, egret
Heron feathers at the base of the plume worn by hussar officers
[From French, 'egret, heron']

aiguillette
A plaited cord ending in needles or points worn on the shoulder to distinguish several types of soldier. The original aiguillettes were short cords on the shoulder of a leather jacket used to attach the metal plates of armour. When armour was abandoned they were retained as attachments for sashes and a mark of rank. Later, they became a more elaborate form of decoration.
[From French, 'little needle']

Airborne Division, 1st *See* **Arnhem, battle of**

Aix-la-Chapelle, treaty of (18 October 1748)
The treaty made in Aix-la-Chapelle (now Aachen) concluded the War of the **Austrian Succession**. Virtually all the conquests were restored to both sides; the Pragmatic Sanction and the Prussian conquest of Silesia were acknowledged; the retention of the

British throne and the electorate of Hanover by the House of Hanover were reaffirmed and Palma, Piacenza and Guastelle in Italy were ceded to Spain.

Alamein *See* **El Alamein, battle of**

Alam Halfa, battle of

(1942; *World War II*) The battle which finally prevented Field Marshal **Rommel** from breaking through the British defences at **El Alamein** (31 August–6 September). The German **armoured divisions** were stopped mainly by attacks from the **artillery** and from the air. This was the first battle in which General Bernard **Montgomery** commanded the British 8th Army.

Albemarle, Duke of *See* **Monck, George**

Albuera, battle of

(1811; *Peninsular War*) While **Wellington** moved from Portugal towards Madrid along the northern route General William **Beresford** moved towards Badajoz in the south with 35,000 Spanish, Portuguese and British troops. He was attacked by 30,000 French troops, commanded by Marshal Nicolas **Soult**, at Albuera (16 May). Some of the Spanish troops fought ineffectively, but the British forced Soult to withdraw, having suffered 8,000 casualties. The British lost 4,000 killed, wounded and captured out of 9,000 men. Wellington was forced to re-group for an attack on Spain in the next year. The Allied forces were almost defeated but were saved by a forced march by the 7th Foot (**Royal Fusiliers**) from Badajoz. The battle was notable for the heroic defence of the **East Kent Regiment's colours** by Lieutenant Latham. It was at this battle that the 57th Foot (**West Middlesex Regiment**) earned the nickname 'the Die-Hards'.

Aldershot *See* **reforms after the Crimean War**

Alexander, Harold Rupert Leofric George (1891–1969)

Born at Caledon, Co. Tyrone, Ireland, Alexander was the second son of the Earl of Caledon. He was educated at Harrow and Sandhurst. During **World War I** he commanded a **battalion** of the **Irish Guards**. He was general **staff officer** Northern Command (1932–34) and then served on the **North-West Frontier** of India (1935). In 1940 he commanded the rearguard at Dunquerque (**Dunkirk**) and was the last man of the British forces to leave France. He was then appointed **GOC** Southern Command. In 1942 he was GOC in Burma (now Myanmar, see **Burma campaigns**) and then **commander-in-chief** Middle East (1942–43). He was in command of the invasion of Italy (1943) and was promoted to **field marshal** on the capture of Rome (1944) by which time he was also Supreme Allied Commander in the Mediterranean. At the end of the war he was appointed governor-general of Canada (1946–52) and then minister of defence in the Conservative government (1952–54).

Alexandria, battle of

(1801; *French Revolutionary Wars*) The British forces under General Ralph **Abercromby**, having landed at Abukir Bay, established a bridgehead which was counter-attacked at the battle of Alexandria (21 March). The French were repulsed, but Abercromby was mortally wounded. The **Gloucestershire Regiment** (28th Foot) gained distinction in repelling a superior number of French **grenadiers** and by the aid they gave to the 42nd Foot (**Black Watch**) who were surrounded.

Alford, battle of

(1645; *Civil War*) At the battle of Alford the Scottish **Covenanters** under General William **Baillie** were defeated by the Royalist forces under the Marquis of **Montrose**

Aligarh, battle of

(1803; *Maratha Wars*) The capture of the Maratha fortress of Aligarh by the Anglo-Indian forces under General Gerard **Lake** (28 August) led to the capture of Delhi (11 September) and of Agra (4 October)

Aliwal, battle of

(1846; *Sikh Wars*) The Anglo-Indian forces under Sir Harry **Smith** defeated the Sikhs at Aliwal on the banks of the Sutlej river 90 miles south-east of Lahore. A force of

10,000 defeated an army twice that size, largely by the use of cavalry. This was the first time that British **lancers** (see **Lancers, 16th**) had been deployed in a battle.

Alkmaar, battle of

(1799; *French Wars*) Anglo-Russian forces, commanded by the Duke of **York**, had been driven out of the Netherlands by the French. To redeem the situation 30,000 coalition troops moved against the French resulting in the indecisive battle of Alkmaar (2 October). The Allies took the town, but were besieged there by the French. After 14 days the duke signed the Convention of Alkmaar which allowed the withdrawal of Allied forces from the Netherlands on the release of French prisoners.

Allenby, Edmund Henry Hynman (1861–1936)

Educated at Haileybury and Sandhurst, he joined the **Inniskilling Dragoons**. He served in South Africa (1884–85, 1888) and in the **Boer War** (1899–1902). In **World War I** he commanded the 1st Cavalry Division (1914–15) and the 3rd Army (1915–17) which captured **Vimy Ridge**. He was appointed **commander-in-chief** of the Egyptian Expeditionary Force fighting against the Turks and entered Jerusalem (1917). He then routed the Turks at the battle of **Megiddo** (1918). He was promoted to **field marshal** and made high commissioner for Egypt (1919–25).

See also **Arras, battle of; Gaza, battles of**

alliance

The forces of two or more states joined together in conflict with a common enemy, e.g. the **Grand Alliance**.

See also **coalition**

allies

1. The forces of two or more states joined together in conflict with a common enemy
2. (1939–45; *World War II*) The armed forces of the countries at war with Germany, Italy and Japan, usually referred to as the Allies. They included the forces of the UK and the Commonwealth countries, the USA, the forces of the occupied European countries that had escaped the German occupation and, in the Far East, some Chinese forces.

Alma, battle of the

(1854; *Crimean War*) This battle was fought (20 September) to halt the British, French and Turkish advance on **Sebastopol** (now Sevastopol). Prince Aleksandr Menshikov, the Russian commander, deployed his forces to defend the heights on the south side of the river Alma, blocking the Allies' advance. The Allied attack was confused by wrangling between the British commander Lord **Raglan** and the French commander Marshal Armand de Saint-Arnaud. The Russians manoeuvred their men into a solid mass, reducing their efficiency, and were finally driven back. The Allies failed to exploit the resulting opportunity to attack the poorly defended Sebastopol, allowing the Russians to consolidate its defences. Saint-Arnaud died of cholera after the battle. The main British **regiments** involved were the 23rd Foot (**Royal Welch Fusiliers**), 7th Foot (**Royal Fusiliers (City of London Regiment)**), the 19th Foot (**Green Howards**) and the 95th Foot (**Derbyshire Regiment of Foot**).

Almanza, battle of

(1707; *War of the Spanish Succession*) The Anglo-Dutch-Portuguese forces under Viscount Galway were defeated by the French-Spanish forces under the Duke of **Berwick**. This ended the attempt to replace Philip V as king of Spain by Archduke Charles of Austria.

Alnwick, battle of

1. (1093; *English-Scottish Wars*) The counties of Cumberland and Westmorland had been annexed by William II (Rufus) of England. Malcolm III of Scotland responded by laying siege to Alnwick castle. The English sent a relief force that defeated the Scots (13 November). Malcolm and his eldest son Edward were killed.

2. (1174; *English-Scottish Wars*) William I (the Lion) of Scotland invaded Northumberland and laid siege to Alnwick castle. Henry II of England sent a relieving force that routed the Scots (13 June). William was captured and imprisoned in Normandy. He was released on his recognition of English hegemony over Scotland.

Alresford, battle of
(1644; *Civil War*) A Royalist force commanded by the Earl of Brentford and General Sir Ralph Hopton was defeated by the Parliamentarians, commanded by General Sir William Waller. The Parliamentarian losses were too heavy to allow them to follow up their advantage and the Royalists made an orderly retreat.

American War of Independence (1775–83)
The resentment of the 13 American colonies against the British government was fuelled by the Stamp Act (1765), the Boston Massacre (1770), the Boston Tea Party (1773) and the Intolerable Acts (1774). This led to battles between the colonial militia and the British troops at **Lexington** and **Concord**, Massachusetts (19 April 1775). The American Declaration of Independence was signed on 4 July 1776. The American victory at **Saratoga** (1777) ensured France's support for the American rebels. The persistent resistance of the American forces under General George **Washington** resulted finally in the surrender of the large British army at **Yorktown**, Virginia (1781), which effectively ended the war in America. But Britain was also involved with maritime wars that were exacerbated by the American Revolution. These were against France (from 1778), Spain (from 1779) and the Netherlands (from 1780). All these conflicts were concluded by the treaty of Versailles (1783), by which the independence of the United States was recognised, Florida and Minorca were ceded to Spain and the possessions in India were restored.

See also **Bemis Heights, battle of; Bennington, battle of; Brandywine, battle of; Brooklyn, battle of; Bunker Hill, battle of; Camden, battle of; Charleston, battle of; Cowpens, battle of; Danbury, battle of; Eutaw Springs, battle of; Fort Mercer and Fort Mifflin, battle of; Fort Washington, battle of; Freeman's Farm, battle of; Germantown, battle of; Gibraltar, battle of; Guilford Courthouse, battle of; King's Mountain, battle of; Lexington and Concord, battles of; Long Island, battle of; Minorca, battle of; Monmouth, battle of; Paoli, battle of; Paulus Hook, battle of; Quebec, battle of; Saratoga, battle of; Savannah, battle of; Stono Ferry, battle of; Stony Point, battle of; Ticonderoga, battle of; Trenton, battle of; Waxhaw Creek, battle of; Yorktown, siege of; Clinton, Henry; Cornwallis, Charles; Gage, Thomas; Howe, William, 5th Viscount Howe; Tarleton, Banastre; Washington, George**

Amherst, Jeffrey (1717–97)
Through the patronage of the Duke of Dorset, Amherst became an **ensign** in the Guards (1731) and ultimately was appointed **aide-de-camp** to the Duke of **Cumberland** in the Netherlands. He was promoted to **lieutenant-colonel** of the 15th Foot (**East Yorkshire Regiment**) by 1756. The Prime Minister, Pitt, recognised his ability and promoted him to **major-general** in command of an expedition to America (1758) where he became **commander-in-chief**. After the capture of **Montreal**, Amherst was appointed governor-general of British North America. On his failure to defeat the Indian chief Pontiac he returned to England (1763). He was made governor of Virginia (1768) and **colonel** of the 60th Foot (**King's Royal Rifle Corps**). In the same year he quarrelled with the king, but they were reconciled and Amherst was made colonel of the 3rd Foot (**East Kent Regiment**). He was appointed governor of Guernsey (1770) and a privy councillor (1772), and in the same year Lieutenant-General of Ordnance, effectively commander-in-chief of the army. He was created Lord Amherst (1776); promoted to **general** (1778); colonel of the 2nd Horse Grenadiers (1779) and then colonel of the 2nd Horse Guards (1782). He was valued chiefly as an adviser on the **American War**. In

1795 he resigned as commander-in-chief in favour of the Duke of **York** and was promoted to **field marshal** (1796).

Amiens, battle of

(1918; *World War I*) The Allied **commander-in-chief** Marshal Ferdinand **Foch** decided to attack the German salient which had been pushed towards Amiens and was threatening the Amiens-Paris railway. The attack was commanded by Sir Douglas **Haig**. The chief striking force in the centre was the 4th Army under Sir Henry **Rawlinson**. It consisted of 17 **divisions**, one American, five of the Canadian Corps, five of the Australian Corps and six British. The attack began on 8 August and, led by strong **tank** forces, had advanced nine miles by nightfall, farther and faster than previous British or French offensives. By 10 August the French 1st and 3rd Armies to the south had also pushed east. On 31 August the British 3rd Army under Sir Julian **Byng** and the British 1st Army under Sir Henry **Horne**, both to the north of the 4th Army, pushed eastward, and by 3 September the German forces under General Erich **Ludendorff** had been forced back to the **Hindenburg Line**. This was the turning point of the war on the **Western Front**.

ammunition technical officer

A **commissioned** or **non-commissioned officer** with particular expertise in explosives and various forms of ammunition.
Abbreviation **ATO**

Amoaful, battle of

(1874; *Ashanti War*) Major-General Sir Garnet **Wolseley** led a punitive expedition against the Ashantis under King Coffee. The 2,000 British troops met 10,000 Ashantis at Amoaful (31 January). The Ashantis were defeated and Wolseley destroyed their capital at Kumasi.

Anarchy, The (1135–54)

The reign of King Stephen of England. King Henry I died in 1135 without leaving a son to succeed him; his heir and chosen successor was his daughter, Matilda. The throne was seized by Stephen of Blois, Henry's nephew and the most powerful baron in England and Normandy, despite his oath to support Matilda. He was initially accepted but failed to give the strong leadership necessary to establish himself; worse, the favouritism he showed in attempting to build up a party of loyal barons alienated others. In 1138 the Scots invaded (see **Standard, battle of the**) and Matilda's half-brother, Robert, Earl of Gloucester, rebelled on her behalf. Matilda herself landed in England in 1139 and quickly gained control of most of the west. The high point of her fortunes was 1141 when, after the capture of Stephen at the battle of **Lincoln**, she had a realistic chance of making herself Queen. This opportunity was lost after the rout at **Winchester**, when Robert was captured; he was quickly exchanged for Stephen, who resumed his rule. The war descended into a desultory stalemate and there were no more major engagements. Matilda left England in 1148, but her son, the future Henry II, renewed the war when he invaded in 1153. Henry reached an agreement with Stephen, a broken man after the death of his son Eustace: Stephen was to remain King, but Henry was to succeed to the throne on his death (which occurred the next year). Stephen's reign was a time of lawlessness and disorder. The political divisions at the highest level reduced the King's ability to control the nobles, who were able to build up their independent power and to pursue their own interests through private warfare with impunity. Contemporary chronicles recorded the consequent suffering of the common people.

Anglo-French wars

There was ongoing aggression between the English and the French over several centuries, during which the English tried to maintain their hold on or to reconquer the dukedoms etc. that had been inherited by their kings from the time of the **Norman conquest of England**

anti-aircraft weapons

The first anti-aircraft (AA) weapon was the wagon-mounted Balloonkanone introduced by Krupps to shoot down balloons used by the French during the Siege of Paris (1870–71). During **World War I** anti-aircraft guns were usually modifications of existing army and navy weapons; purpose-built weapons followed later. Despite the formation of the Royal Air Force in 1918, ground anti-aircraft defences remained an Army responsibility through **World War II**. Prior to World War II sound locators, improved optical range-finders and other fire control equipment were developed, increasing the accuracy of the guns. Accuracy was further increased by the introduction of radar. In 1944 **proximity fuses** were introduced that greatly increased the effectiveness of anti-aircraft fire. After World War II surface-to-air missiles came into use. These are guided weapons, usually using radar or heat-seeking technologies which can be carried within the missile or may be controlled from ground stations. Such weapons have now entirely replaced the larger calibres of AA guns. However, their guidance systems can be impeded by increasingly sophisticated **electronic countermeasures** (*see* **electronic warfare**), Stealth technology, and other air-defence suppression capabilities; this in turn drives research into new less vulnerable guidance systems. Examples include the **Rapier Field Standard C** and **Starstreak High Velocity Missile** currently used by the British Army, both of which are designed to give battlefield AA protection; they operate over ranges under five miles at velocities over twice the speed of sound. Smaller calibre guns, roughly 12–30mm, often in multiple mounts, are still widely used for low-level AAA (anti-aircraft artillery, or 'triple A') tasks, especially against helicopters.

anti-tank weapons

The development of **tanks** during **World War I** naturally led to the development of anti-tank weapons. The first of these were simply new types of armour-piercing ammunition for existing **rifles** and **machine guns**; soon anti-tank rifles, generally single shot bolt-action weapons of about 12.5mm calibre, were also in use. Standard light **artillery** weapons could also be used in the anti-tank role. Anti-tank rifles were used into the early part of World War II, but were clearly obsolescent by then. By the time of World War II the increase in the thickness of tank **armour** had led to the development of purpose-built high-velocity anti-tank guns, often initially with a calibre of 37mm. These guns were fitted in tanks themselves and used against tanks from artillery-type mountings. Initially these guns fired solid shot ammunition which relied on kinetic energy to damage its targets. Larger and improved versions of this type of gun and ammunition remain the principal weapon of tanks into the 21st century. Since the later years of World War II many anti-tank weapons have used so-called 'shaped-charge' warheads which focus explosive power to defeat enemy armour. Tanks can fire such types of ammunition from their guns, and weapons using this type of ammunition have now entirely replaced the previous 'ground-based' anti-tank guns. Such weapons can be rocket launchers carried by a single person, introduced in World War II, or various types of missiles which can be launched by ground forces or from vehicles or aircraft. Modern guidance systems have made such weapons extremely accurate. The anti-tank weapons currently used by the British Army are the missile **Milan Portable Anti-Tank Guided Weapon** and the **Light Anti-armour Weapon**. They are due to be replaced by the **Javelin Light Forces Anti-tank Guided Weapon** and the **Next Generation Light Anti-tank Weapon**, respectively.

Antwerp, battle of

1. (1914; *World War I*) During August 1914 the Belgian forces of 150,000 men fell back on Antwerp under the German advance. To protect the German rear after the battle of the Aisne river, General Erich von **Falkenhayn** attacked Antwerp which fell after an artillery bombardment (9 October). King Albert I of Belgium moved his forces along the coast and met up with British forces under General Henry **Rawlinson** moving from Ostend to aid the Belgians. Both armies fell back on the Allied lines between Diksmuide and the North Sea.

See also **Ypres, battle of 1**

2. (1944; *World War II*) In August 1944 General **Eisenhower**, the supreme commander of the Allied Forces in Europe, decided that Field Marshal **Montgomery** should make a concerted attack on Antwerp. Consequently, the 2nd Army made a direct attack on Brussels (September 2nd) and moved rapidly to take Antwerp (3 September) with minimal damage to the docks. By 6 September they had crossed the Albert Canal, securing the port for use by the Allies.

ANZAC

The Australian and New Zealand Army Corps. These were the combined forces of Australia and New Zealand that played major roles in support of the UK during **World War I**. The Australian and New Zealand forces became separate entities in 1917 and the designation ANZAC was no longer used. The ANZACs played a heroic role in the **Gallipoli** campaign (1915), and their landing at Gallipoli is still remembered on ANZAC Day (25 April). ANZAC troops also saw notable service in France (1916), and their cavalry in the Middle East.

Anzio, battle of

(1944; *World War II*) By late 1943 the Allied advance on Rome had been blocked at the **Gustav Line**. The Allied commander of ground forces, Sir Harold **Alexander**, launched an amphibious attack (Operation Shingle) at Anzio, 70 miles behind the enemy lines (22 January). This VI Corps under General John Lucas consisted of the British 1st Infantry Division and the US 3rd Infantry Division. They failed to cut Highway 7 between Rome and Cassino. The German commander, Field Marshal Albert **Kesselring**, sealed off the beachhead with the German 14th Army (3 February). The Germans counter-attacked (16 February) with heavy artillery, but the beachhead held. A further attack was repulsed and the beachhead secured by 1 March. This then served as an advanced post from which the VI Corps could join the 5th Army's thrust on Rome. On 23 May the VI Corps, now under General Lucian Truscott, broke out, crossed Highway 7 and joined with the 5th Army which had broken through the Gustav Line. This joint army then moved on Rome.

Aong, battle of

(1857; *Indian Mutiny*) The mutineers were opposing the advance by British troops, commanded by General Sir Henry **Havelock**, on **Cawnpore** (now Kanpur) (15 July). The rebels were driven from their defensive position and the advance continued.

appointments

A place for displaying distinctions in a military unit, e.g. the **colours**, officers' **gorgets**, cross-belt plates, etc. When **battle honours** were awarded to a **regiment** they would be placed on the appointments

Aras, battle of

(1775; *Maratha Wars*) Raghunath Rao, who claimed the Peshwarship, was supported by 20,000 Maratha troops. He was opposed by 2,500 British troops, commanded by Colonel Keating, and a 25,000 strong force of Maratha chieftains. When the battle began (18 May) the troops of the Maratha chieftains fled. The British rallied and repulsed the Maratha troops.

arbalest *See* crossbow

Arcot, battle of

(1751; *British in India*) Mahomet Ali, the British candidate for the viceroyalty of the Deccan, was besieged in Trichinopoly (now Tiruchchirappalli) by French forces under the Marquis Joseph Dupleix. To relieve the pressure on Trichinopoly Robert **Clive** attacked Arcot with 200 European and 600 Indian troops (20 September) and took this capital of the pro-French Indian ruler. Dupleix moved to relieve Arcot with a force of some 16,000 men. Clive held out for 50 days before being relieved by a Maratha chieftain. The French power in India was checked and Mahomet Ali ascended the throne in 1752.

Ardennes, battle of

1. (1914; *World War I*) This was the first time that the French and German offensives had met head-on in World War I. The battle, a German victory, was fought on the east-central French border (20–24 August).

2. (1944–45; *World War II*) A massive counter-attack against the Allied advance by Marshal Gerd von **Rundstedt** (16 December) drove a 'bulge' in the Allied lines, surrounding Bastogne (20 December) and nearly reaching Celles (25 December). The British Field Marshal Sir Bernard **Montgomery**, commanding a combined Anglo-American force in the north, and the American General George **Patton**, commanding the American 3rd Army in the south, joined with the US 2nd Armored Division under General Ernest Harmon in the west to begin a counter-attack (3 January). By 9 February the original Allied line had been restored. Although the Allied advance had been delayed by some six weeks, the Germans had lost virtually all their reserve force (200,000 men, 600 tanks and assault guns and 1,500 aircraft) making the subsequent Allied advances on the Western and Eastern Fronts much easier.

See also **France 2**; **Germany**; *Also called* **Battle of the Bulge**

Argaon, battle of

(1803; *Maratha Wars*) Following the victory over the Maratha at **Assaye**, General Arthur Wellesley (**Wellington**) attacked the stronghold at Argaon (29 November). The Marathas were defeated, ending the Second Maratha War in central India.

Argyll and Sutherland Highlanders

The Argyll and Sutherland Highlanders (Princess Louise's) was founded (1881) by the amalgamation of the 91st (**Princess Louise's Argyllshire Highlanders**) Regiment of Foot and the 93rd (**Sutherland Highlanders**) Regiment of Foot. The new **regiment** was named Princess Louise's (Sutherland and Argyll Highlanders), changed (1882) to Princess Louise's (Argyll and Sutherland Highlanders) and to Argyll and Sutherland Highlanders (Princess Louise's) (1920). It merged (2006) with The Royal Scots, The Royal Highland Fusiliers, The King's Own Scottish Borderers, The Black Watch and The Highlanders (Seaforth, Gordons and Camerons) to form The Royal Regiment of Scotland.

Argyllshire Regiment of Foot *See* **Princess Louise's Argyllshire Highlanders**

Arikera, battle of

(1791; *British in India*) The British commander General Lord **Cornwallis** made a surprise attack on the troops of **Tipu Sahib** of Mysore encamped between Arikera and Seringapatam (13 May). The attack was foiled by heavy rain, but a second frontal attack routed the Mysore troops with the loss of 2,000 men. The British lost fewer than 500.

arm bands

A cloth band worn around the arm for identification. During the **Civil War** strips of cloth were worn around the arms to distinguish friend from foe during a period when all troops wore similar uniforms. During the **French Wars** (1792–1815) foreign troops attached to British units wore arm bands on their uniforms to avoid being taken for enemies. More recently, arm bands have been worn by soldiers carrying out special duties on a temporary basis when instant recognition is important. They usually show the initials of the duty being performed. Some troops such as military police wear arm bands permanently.

armes blanches

Swords and lances in contrast to firearms

[From French, literally 'white arms']

armour

1. Personal protection equipment. Metal armour had been associated with the Middle Ages, and gradually disappeared by the later 17th century with the increased efficiency of firearms and a need for free movement and light uniform, but the wearing of the **helmet, cuirass** and **gorget** continues for ceremonial uniforms into the 21st century. **World War I** saw personal armour being revived in the form of **steel helmets**, which, though they were by no means bullet-proof, gave the soldier a substantial degree of protection against fragments and shrapnel from **artillery** fire. Helmets have been a standard part of the soldier's combat equipment ever since. Light but robust modern ceramics and plastics are now increasingly used in helmets, flak jackets (see **bulletproof vest**), **body armour** and other types of protective clothing to enhance the safety of the 21st century soldier.
2. An armoured fighting vehicle. Since the introduction of the **tank** in World War I, 'armour' has come to be a shorthand term for those vehicles used in combat and protected against enemy fire by armour plate which was initially of steel but is now also often of other materials and other metals.
[From French *armure*, from Latin *armatura*, ultimately from *arma* 'weapons']

armoured car

A wheeled armoured vehicle, in contrast to the tank which has tracks. They are usually armed with a 20–90 mm gun and a machine gun. They tend to be unreliable on rough or slippery terrain, but are much faster than tanks on roads. They were used extensively during **World War II**.

armoured cart

A wooden structure that was effectively a small rectangular mobile fortress, used during the time of Henry VIII. It had a thick wood covering for the wheels and the horses and carried small cannon.

armoured division

A self-contained unit of **tanks** or other armoured vehicles capable of independent operation.
See also **division**

armoured fighting vehicle

Any vehicle that has bodywork made of protective material such steel plate and carries weapons such as **machine guns** or some form of **artillery**.
Abbreviation **AFV**

Armourers, Company of

Before the reign of Charles I, muskets were frequently damaged when repaired by unskilled workers. Charles laid down that no arms or armour were to be sold unless marked by the Company of Armourers' stamp.

armoury

Any place where arms or **armour** are kept

army

1. The armed forces of a country. The first regular paid army of a recognisably modern type in Britain was the **New Model Army** raised in 1645 by Oliver **Cromwell**. The regular army was disbanded by Charles II, leaving only the **Coldstream Guards** as his personal bodyguard. In 1689 the Bill of Rights dictated that control of the army passed from the sovereign to Parliament.
2. Any of a number of **corps** serving in a particular area or capacity, e.g. the 8th Army
[Via French *armée* from medieval Latin *armata*, ultimately from Latin *arma* 'weapons']

Army Air Corps

The Corps was formed in 1942 to co-ordinate the Glider Pilot Regiment and the **Parachute Regiment** and later (1944) the **Special Air Service Regiment**. It was disbanded (1950) but became active again (1957) overseeing the fixed-winged units of the Air Observation Post and Light Liaison units. Up to 1973 its members were specialists taken from other **regiments**, but since that date it has recruited its own members independently. Currently consisting of 21 squadrons and 8 flights, it is equipped primarily with helicopters that act in ground-support roles: observation and reconnaissance, direction of artillery fire, and direction of close air support.

Army Catering Corps
The corps formed (1941) from the Army School of Cookery, which had been established at Aldershot before **World War I**. Before 1941 each regiment was responsible for its own catering, with variable and generally poor standards. The formation of the Army Catering Corps saw an immediate improvement, but it was not until after **conscription** ended (1960) that the Corps consisted only of trained cooks and caterers. Initially under the control of the control of the **Royal Army Service Corps** (*see* **Royal Corps of Transport**), the Army Catering Corps became independent in 1965. It was absorbed into the **Royal Logistics Corps** in 1993.

Army Clothing Factory *See* reforms after the Crimean War

army corps *See* corps

Army Council *See* reforms after the Boer War

Army Legal Corps
The law as it affected the Army was administered by the uniformed branch of the Judge Advocate General's department. This was succeeded (1948) by the Army Legal Services Staff, which was re-named the Army Legal Corps (1978). In 1992 it was absorbed into the **Adjutant General's Corps** as the **Army Legal Services Branch**.

Army Legal Services Branch *See* Army Legal Corps

Army Medical Corps *See* Royal Army Medical Corps

Army Medical Services
An organisation that administers the **Royal Army Medical Corps**, the **Royal Army Veterinary Corps**, the **Royal Army Dental Corps** and **Queen Alexandra's Royal Army Nursing Corps**.

Army Nursing Service *See* Queen Alexandra's Royal Army Nursing Corps

Army Physical Training Corps
The Corps was founded (1860) as the Army Gymnastics Staff. It changed its title to the Army Physical Training Staff (1918) and to the Army Physical Training Corps (1940).

Arnhem, battle of
(1944; *World War II*) During the Allied advance through France and the Low Countries towards Germany, three divisions of airborne troops (two American and one British) were dropped to secure bridges over the lower Rhine (17 September). The operation was badly mismanaged and did not achieve all of its objectives following a German counter-attack (25 September). The (British) 1st Airborne Division of 10,095 lost 7,605 men during the operation.
See also **France 2**

Aroghee, battle of *See* Magdala, battle of

arquebus
The arquebus was invented in Spain and was the first gun to be used in a manner similar to the modern **rifle**. It was about 3½ feet long with a short stock, intended to be fired from the chest rather than the shoulder, and weighed about 12 pounds. The barrel was usually supported on a forked rod when firing. It had a variable bore and a range of about 200 yards (less than the **crossbow**), though it was not accurate at this distance. There was a **matchlock** firing mechanism. It was replaced by the **musket**.

Arras, battle of
(1917; *World War I*) The French General Robert **Nivelle** planned that the main 1917 French offensive would be aimed at the Aisne river. To draw the German reserves northwards prior to the attack Field Marshal Sir Douglas **Haig** launched an attack on Arras (9 April). North of Arras the Canadian Corps under General Henry **Horne**

stormed the ridge at **Vimy** while the Third Army under General Sir Edmund **Allenby** advanced in the south. The German commander, Baron Ludwig von Falkenhausen, brought in reserves and prevented any further advance even when the 5th Army under General Hubert **Gough** had been committed in the south. The British continued their abortive attempt to advance until 3 May, to divert German forces from the French attack in the south and Haig's later assault on **Ypres**.

arsenal

1. A stockpile of military equipment, or a building where this is stored

2. A factory or other facility that produces military hardware.

See also **Woolwich**

[Directly or via French from Italian *arzanale*, from Venetian Italian *arzana*, from Arabic *dar-(as-)sina'a* 'workshop, factory', referring to the Arsenale, the state dockyard of the Venetian Republic where its formidable navy was maintained]

artificers

During the early 18th century the raising of companies of specialist tradesmen was proposed, particularly for the settlement and defence of the colonies. The first such scheme materialised during the siege of **Gibraltar** (1779–83). In this period the **Royal Engineers** was a unit of officers only; the Royal Military Artificers were the engineer other ranks.

artillery

Any large gun served by a crew. The term originally meant provision of any type of weapon but now covers large guns and may include modern rocket-launchers and any weapon with a calibre of more than 15 mm. More precisely the term is confined to the larger weapons firing an unpowered missile.

There are various types of artillery. A **gun** is a long-barrelled piece of artillery, strictly speaking one which fires its projectile on a fairly flat trajectory and elevates the barrel to gain increased range, while a **howitzer** is a shorter-barrelled piece of less range, firing on an arched trajectory and depressing the barrel from its original elevated position to gain increased range. In the 18th century **mortars** were similar to howitzers, but could be of very large calibre. A modern mortar is a much lighter piece, usually capable of being carried by hand and operated by a crew of two. It has a short range and fires a missile in a trajectory nearing the vertical.

It is commonly accepted that the first British use of gunpowder weapons was at the battle of **Crécy** (1346), although it may have been earlier. The weapons would have been 'roundelades' or 'pots de fer', which were bottle-shaped and made of iron, firing arrow-shaped bolts.

Before the second half of the 19th century the artillery was made up of cannons, howitzers and mortars, all of them smooth-bore weapons, made of cast bronze, cast iron or wrought iron, and classified by the weight of the shot they fired. They were either mobile (horse artillery supporting the **cavalry** and foot artillery supporting the **infantry**) or static as in fortress or coastal defences. The mobile guns were mounted on two-wheeled carriages and towed by teams of horses while a support crew with ammunition, spare parts etc., accompanied the gun, sometimes on a wagon called a limber. Because of their short range (less than two miles) the guns were always deployed more or less in sight of the enemy. They were loaded by ramming black powder propellant down the barrel followed by the shot or other projectile. They were fired by applying a burning slow-match to a small hole at the breech-end. This produced an immense amount of black smoke and a tremendous recoil. The gun then had to be manhandled back into position and the barrel swabbed out with a wet sponge to extinguish any sparks. Most projectiles were solid round **shot** but explosive shells of various types and multiple sub-calibre projectiles like **canister** were also commonly used.

By the end of the 19th century various hydropneumatic systems had been developed which allowed the gun barrel to recoil along the top of the carriage and return to its original position. This eliminated the need to re-aim the gun after every shot was fired.

Breech loading had also been developed along with the fixing of the propellant and the projectile in a metal (usually brass) case called a shell. These innovations made loading easier and increased the rate of fire. During the 19th century barrels were also rifled and made of forged steel. The first British rifled field gun was used during the China War of 1860. The ammunition was later changed to a pointed cylindrical shape and fired by more efficient smokeless **nitrocellulose**-based propellant. The first breech-loading field gun was used in 1886 and the first fast-firing one in 1891. Artillery could now also be fired at an enemy that was out of sight.

At the start of **World War I** British artillery relied mainly on light shrapnel-type shells, effective against enemy troops in the open, but virtually useless in trench warfare. World War I saw all nations deploy many more larger-calibre guns and rely increasingly on high explosive and poison **gas** shells. Contrary to popular belief artillery and not the **machine gun** was the principal killer of World War I, and artillery remained the dominant arm during **World War II**, despite the development of **tanks** in the meantime.

Since World War II the distinction between guns and howitzers has been blurred, with modern weapons generally being able to fire at both high and low trajectories. Artillery is now defined as light, medium or heavy, depending on the calibre, with the light artillery supporting ground troops, and the medium and heavy artillery attacking troop concentrations and other installations in the rear. With the advent of the aircraft and the tank at the beginning of the 20th century, **anti-aircraft weapons** and **anti-tank weapons** were developed. Also since World War II, artillery that fires **rockets** has been developed and artillery guns have often been mounted on tracked or wheeled vehicles: the 155 mm **AS 90**, currently in service with the British Army, is a such a self-propelled gun.

[From French *artillerie* from Old French *artiller* 'to fortify, equip', from Latin *artillare* 'to make machines']

Artillery, Royal Regiment of

A permanent **regiment** of artillery was raised in 1716 when two companies of field artillery were established at Woolwich. Previously, a train of artillery had been raised for a particular campaign. This had proved inefficient in suppressing the Jacobite Rebellion of 1715 that was brought to a close before the artillery trains had been formed. In 1722 the two companies were amalgamated with the independent trains in Gibraltar and Minorca to form the Royal Regiment of Artillery. In 1801 the **Royal Irish Artillery**, which had been formed independently in 1755, was incorporated. A major weakness in artillery organisation throughout the 18th century was that the artillery was equipped and administered by the **Ordnance** and was therefore separate from the remainder of the army, which was responsible to the **War Office**. But in 1855 the Royal Regiment of Artillery became part of the Army, under the control of the War Office. In 1899 the regiment was organised into two separate branches, the **Royal Horse Artillery** and the **Royal Field Artillery** on the one hand, and the **Royal Garrison Artillery**, responsible for fixed, siege and mountain batteries. These distinctions were abandoned in 1924, but the Royal Horse Artillery retained its identity. A mounted battery of Royal Horse Artillery was re-formed for ceremonial duties in 1945 at the express wish of King George VI. This was called the Riding Troop RHA and was re-named the King's Troop RHA in 1947. Despite its name, the Royal Regiment of Artillery is currently a **corps** that consists of several regiments.

artillery train

The guns and wagons carrying the ammunition and equipment of an artillery unit

Artois-Loos, battle of

(1915; *World War I*) A coordinated attack by French and British forces in Artois. The French 10th Army under General Victor d'Urbal attacked **Vimy Ridge** (25 September) while the British 1st Army under General Sir Douglas **Haig** attacked **Loos** (using poison **gas** for the first time). The Allies' advances were checked by the Germans under

General Erich von **Falkenhayn**. The British assault petered out (8 October) followed by the French (15 October). This battle ended the fighting in northern France in 1915. The French lost 190,000 men, the British 60,000, while the defending Germans lost 178,000 men.

AS 90 *See* **artillery**

Ashanti War (1873)

There was increasing tension between the British on the coast and the Ashantis living inland, but the major conflict was triggered by a series of atrocities perpetrated by the Ashantis under King Coffee. **Wolseley** advanced from the coast of the Gold Coast (now Ghana) inland towards Kumasi. The Ashantis were defeated at the battles of **Amoaful** and Ordashu. The **Black Watch** and the **Royal Welch Fusiliers** were awarded battle honours in this campaign.

See also **Accra, battle of**

Ashdown, battle of

(871; *Danish Invasion of Britain*) The attack by the Danes on Wessex was checked by King Alfred at Ashdown (8 January)

Ashingdon, battle of (1016)

The battle was fought between Canute, the Danish king, and Edmund II (Ironside), king of England. Edmund was defeated, largely due to the defection of his brother-in-law Edric to the Danes (18 October). From the ensuing peace, Canute received lordship over all of England, except Wessex, over which Edmund still had control.

Asirghar, battle of

(1819; *Maratha Wars*) A strong Maratha garrison was besieged at Asirghar by a British force commanded by Sir John Malcolm and General John **Doveton** (18 March). The garrison was driven into the upper fort (21 March) and surrendered after a continuous bombardment (7 April).

Assam Light Infantry *See* **Queen Elizabeth's Own Gurkha Rifles (6th)**

assault rifle *See* **rifle**

Assaye, battle of

(1803; *Maratha Wars*) The forces of the Marathas were defeated by General Arthur Wellesley (**Wellington**) (23 September) at Assaye in Hyderabad. The British and allied forces suffered heavy losses of some 1,500 of their 4,000 troops. This was Wellington's first notable victory.

ASU *See* **active service unit**

Atbara, battle of

(1898; *Sudan War*) After the death of General **Gordon** at **Khartoum** (1885) the **Mahdi** controlled the Sudan. The increasing activity of France, Italy and Belgium in Africa made the British government decide to re-conquer the Sudan. The invasion under General Horatio Herbert **Kitchener** began in March 1896 with a force of 15,000 British and Egyptian troops. The advance was slow, consolidated by the laying of a railway. At Atbara, where the Atbara river joins the Nile, some 18,000 Sudanese were dug in. Kitchener's forces routed them, with a loss of 570 men to the Sudanese 6,000. Kitchener then proceeded up the Nile.

Atkins, Tommy

A typical British private soldier. Tommy Atkins was reputed to be a private soldier who served in the 23rd Foot (**Royal Welch Fusiliers**) although this is unlikely. General Sir Harry Calvert, who had served with the Fusiliers, became Adjutant-General at the **War Office** (1815) and drew up a specimen Army Pay Book. He filled in the blanks, as an example, with the particulars of Private Tommy Atkins, No. 6 Company, 1st Battalion, 23rd Regiment of Foot, born at Odiham, Hants. This was circulated to all units and Tommy Atkins passed into the English language.

ATO *See* **ammunition technical officer**

ATS *abbreviation of* **Auxiliary Territorial Service**. *See* **women soldiers in the British Army**

Auchinleck, Claude John Eyre (1884–1981)

Auchinleck passed out from **Sandhurst** and was commissioned (1904) in the 62nd Punjabis of the Indian Army. During **World War I** he took part in repelling the Turkish attack on the Suez Canal (1915). He served in Mesopotamia until the end of the war, and took part in the advance on Baghdad as **brigadier-general** of the 52nd Brigade. In 1927 Auchinleck attended the Imperial Defence College. As a **colonel** he returned to the Indian Staff College at Quetta as an instructor (1930–32) and took over command of the Pershaw Brigade (1933). For his competence in commanding operations against the upper Mohamands (1935) he was promoted to **major-general** and deputy chief of the general staff in India (1936). He was a key member of the Chatfield committee on the modernisation of the Indian Army (1938–39). He was posted home in 1940 and in July was promoted to GOC Southern Command. When the threat of invasion had passed he returned to India as **general** and **commander-in-chief**, India. Auchinleck then took over from **Wavell** as commander-in-chief in the Middle East (1941). After the defeat at **Tobruk** and the British retreat to **El Alamein** he was cautious about beginning a renewed offensive until the army was properly prepared. This annoyed Prime Minister Churchill who replaced Auchinleck by **Alexander**. Auchinleck returned to India where he was appointed commander-in-chief (1943) and was responsible for providing bases, troops etc., for the campaigns in **Burma** (now Myanmar). He was appointed **GCB** (1945) and **field marshal** (1946). The partition of India put stress on the Indian Army, and Auchinleck was criticised by the Indians for favouring Pakistan. The viceroy, Earl Mountbatten, asked him to resign (December 1947).

See also **Mersa-Matruh, battle of**

Auchmuty, Samuel (1756–1822)

Auchmuty's father was a rector in New York and when the **American War of Independence** began he supported the king as a volunteer and was rewarded with an ensigncy (1777) and lieutenancy (1778) in the 45th Foot (**Nottinghamshire (Sherwood Foresters) Regiment**). He went with his **regiment** to England and transferred to the 52nd Foot (**Oxfordshire Regiment of Foot**) with which he went to India (1783). He was promoted to **captain** in the 7th Foot (**Royal Fusiliers**) for his services and was made **brigade major** (1790) when he took part in the siege of **Seringapatam** (1792). Lord **Cornwallis** made him deputy quartermaster-general in Calcutta (now Kolkata) and **brevet** major (1794). Robert **Abercromby** promoted him to brevet **lieutenant-colonel** (1795) and Auchmuty became Abercromby's private secretary. He returned to England with Abercromby (1797) and was promoted to command the 10th Foot (**Royal Lincolnshire Regiment**) (1800). He then went to the Cape and was in command of a mixed force that was sent to Egypt. After the fall of **Alexandria** Auchmuty was made adjutant-general of the army in Egypt. He returned to England (1803) and was knighted. He was commandant of the Isle of Thanet (1803–06) and then went to South America (1806). After he captured **Buenos Aires** he was promoted to **brigadier-general**. When Buenos Aires was recaptured he attacked and took **Montevideo** which was later surrendered to the Spanish by General **Whitelocke**. Auchmuty was exonerated from any blame and was promoted to **major-general** (1808) and **colonel** of the 103rd Foot. He was appointed **commander-in-chief** in Madras (now Chennai) (1810) and was sent to Java to occupy the Dutch possessions. After a successful campaign he was created **KB** and made colonel of the 78th Foot (**Ross-shire Buffs**). In 1813 he handed over command to John Abercromby and returned to England. He was promoted to **lieutenant-general** and made **GCB** (1815). The peace of 1815 ended his active service. He was appointed commander-in-chief in Ireland (1821) and died while riding his horse.

Aughrim, battle of (1691)
After the battle of the **Boyne**, William III left the British troops in command of the Dutch General Godbert de **Ginkel**. He met the rebel forces under Patrick Sarsfield, Earl of Lucan, and the French general the Marquis de Saint Ruth at Aughrim (12 July). The Catholic army was routed, Saint Ruth was killed, and Lucan took refuge in Limerick.

Auldearn, battle of
(1645; *Civil War*) The royalist forces under the Marquis of **Montrose** routed a Scottish **Covenanter** force under General Sir John Urry at Auldearn (9 May)

Auray, battle of
(1364; *Hundred Years' War*) The siege of Auray by the English under John Chandos (29 September) was successfully maintained against the French relief forces under Charles de Blois and Bertrand du Guesclin. This caused Charles V of France to recognise the claim of John de Montfort that the Duchy of Brittany was an English possession.

Austrian Succession, War of the (1740–48)
On the death of the Holy Roman Emperor, Charles VI, his daughter Maria Theresa succeeded to his lands. Her claim was challenged by Philip V, king of Spain, Charles Albert, elector of Bavaria and Augustus III, king of Poland and elector of Saxony. At the same time Frederick II (the Great) of Prussia also claimed the province of Silesia, ruled by Maria Theresa. Frederick seized Silesia (1740–41) and the conflict escalated into the War of the Austrian Succession, with France, Spain and Bavaria allied to Prussia, and Britain, the Netherlands and Sardinia supporting Maria Theresa. The Prussians withdrew in 1742. The war spread to North America (**King George's War**), India and Italy. It was concluded by the Peace of **Aix-la-Chapelle** (now Aachen). Most of the territories except Silesia were restored and the rule of Maria Theresa guaranteed (the Pragmatic Sanction). Maria Theresa's husband was recognised as the Holy Roman Emperor, Francis I.

See also **Bergen op Zoom, battle of; Dettingen, battle of; Fontenoy, battle of; Lauffeld, battle of; Madras, battle of; Cumberland, Duke of (William Augustus)**

automatic pistol, automatic rifle
These weapons use either the recoil or the blowback from firing the bullet to remove the spent cartridge, reload and cock the weapon. Automatic weapons can be set to fire a single shot, or to continue firing whilst the trigger is pressed.
See also **pistol; rifle**

Auxiliary Territorial Service *See* **women soldiers in the British Army**

Avalanche, Operation *See* **Salerno, battle of**

axe
A tool with a short broad metal blade for chopping. During the 18th century axes were carried by **farriers** and **pioneers** as part of their equipment. Tomahawks (light axes) were also part of the equipment of the **Light Infantry** when they were formed in the American colonies. The axe has been the badge of the Pioneers since the 19th century. [From Old English *æx*]

Axholme, battle of
(1265; *Barons' Wars*) During the Second **Barons' War** in England, Simon de Montfort, son of Simon de Montfort killed at the battle of **Evesham**, took refuge at Axholme in Lincolnshire. He was defeated by Prince Edward (afterwards King Edward I) and fled overseas.

Azimghur, battle of
(1858; *Indian Mutiny*) A British column, commanded by Sir Edward Layard, routed 5,000 mutineers. Their leader, Kur Singh, was killed (15 April).

B

backing
A piece of black or coloured cloth set behind a badge on the headdress to increase its visibility. Backing was introduced on helmets around 1880.

Badajoz, battle of
(1812; *Peninsular War*) Badajoz was a stronghold barring the Allied advance into western Spain. It was besieged by **Wellington** in March, but it did not fall until 5 April. This opened the way to Spain and drove a wedge between the French armies in the north and south. It demonstrated the high casualties that could be sustained in a siege operation of this kind. In part in response to their losses, the attacking troops went on a prolonged rampage of looting and destruction after the city fell, much to the disgust and annoyance of Wellington.

Baden-Powell, Robert Stephenson Smyth (1857–1941)
Baden-Powell was born in London, the son of the Savilian Professor of Geometry at Oxford, and educated at Charterhouse. He joined the Army (1876) and served in India, Afghanistan, Ashanti (now in Ghana) and Matabeleland (now part of Zimbabwe). His most famous military achievement was the defence of **Mafeking** (now Mafikeng). He was promoted to **lieutenant-general** (1907). He is best known as the founder of the Boy Scouts (1908), now the Scouts. His book 'Scouting for Boys' (1908) advocated para-military training for youths to fit them for later military service to the nation.

badges
A means of identification to show rank, official position or association with something. Badges have been worn since the Middle Ages to identify noble families and their troops. Metal badges on headgear came into use during the reign of George I with the introduction of the portcullis on the caps of the **Honourable Artillery Company**. During the first half of the 18th century badges on other pieces of individual equipment were introduced, with collar badges and button badges being introduced later. **Rank badges** were developed for the infantry early in the 19th century and later in the same century for cavalry. A **chevron** was introduced as the badge for **non-commissioned officers** in 1802. Badges for drummers, trumpeters, buglers and pipers were introduced in the 19th century, while proficiency badges and badges of trades were introduced during the same period.

baggage train
The wagons carrying the equipment and reserve supplies of soldiers on the move. Baggage trains usually followed the main force and their loss was serious, as this meant that the troops were dependent on the personal equipment that they carried and possibly on foraging in the countryside for food.

Baghdad, battle of
(1917; *World War I*) General Sir Frederick Stanley **Maude**, the British commander, built up his forces at Basra and moved towards Baghdad (13 December 1916). He spent the next two months eliminating Turkish resistance south of the Tigris, forcing the evacuation of the fortress of **Kut-al-Imara** (25 February 1917). He moved up the river and out-manoeuvred the Turks, forcing their abandonment of their defences on the Diyala river without a major conflict. The Turkish army under General Halil Pasha then evacuated Baghdad (11 March) losing 9,000 men as prisoners.

bagpipes

A musical instrument consisting of a bag with several pipes sticking out of it that is held under the arm and played by blowing through one of the pipes. Scottish, Irish, Indian and Gurkha **regiments** use bagpipes to provide martial music. Other European armies such as the Polish also use bagpipes.

Bahur, battle of

(1752; *British in India*) In India, a French force of 2,500 was heavily defeated by 2,000 British troops and 4,000 Indian levies. The British were commanded by Major Stringer **Lawrence** and the victory determined that the Marathas entered the Seven Years' War on the side of the British.

Bailey bridge

A bridge made up of pre-constructed units which can be bolted together quickly. Bailey bridges are particularly useful in replacing bridges demolished by retreating enemy forces.

[After Sir D. Coleman Bailey (1901–85), the British engineer who invented it]

Baillie, William (fl.1640s)

A Scottish Covenanter **general**. Having trained in the service of the Dutch and Swedes, Baillie commanded the Covenanter forces in Scotland during the **Civil War**. Throughout the war he was engaged in skirmishes with the Marquis of **Montrose**, being defeated by him at the battle of **Alford**. He commanded the Scottish Parliamentary foot soldiers at the battle of **Marston Moor** and at the battle of **Preston**. After the defeat of the Royalists at Preston, he disappeared into obscurity.

Baird, David (1757–1829)

Baird became an **ensign** in the 2nd Foot (**Queen's Royal Regiment (West Surrey)**) (1772) and served at Gibraltar (1773–76). He was promoted to **lieutenant** (1778) and through the influence of Lord Macleod was promoted to **captain** in the 73rd Foot (later the 71st **Highland Light Infantry**). The **regiment** was sent to India (1780) where Baird was severely wounded and taken prisoner by **Haidar Ali**. He and the other officers were treated barbarously but were released (1784), when Baird had the bullet that caused his original wound removed from his thigh. He was promoted to **major** (1787) and returned home (1789). He purchased a lieutenant-colonelcy in the regiment (1790), returned to India (1791) and took part in the battle of **Seringapatam** (1792). He took Pondicherry from the French (1793) and was promoted to **colonel** (1795) in command of Tanjore. The regiment was ordered to return home but, on arrival in the Cape, Baird was requested to take command of the troops there as they had mutinied against their commander Sir David Dundas. He was promoted to **major-general** and stayed on in the Cape until 1798. He returned to India with the Scots Brigade and the 86th Foot (**Royal County Down Regiment**). When he arrived, Baird was given command of a **brigade** rather than the **division** to which his rank might have entitled him, which was given to Colonel Arthur Wellesley (**Wellington**). Baird then successfully stormed Seringapatam (1799). He was exhausted and was relieved by Wellesley who was also made governor of Seringapatam, a post to which Baird thought himself entitled. Baird then commanded the Indian corps sent to attack the French in Egypt. He landed at Cossier on the Red Sea (June 1801) and undertook the difficult march across the desert to the Nile. The troops arrived in time to take part in the capture of **Alexandria**. Baird became a popular hero at home and was made colonel of the 54th Foot (**West Norfolk Regiment of Foot**) by the king. He returned to India and saw that he had no hope of preferment over Wellesley, whose brother was governor-general. He gave up his command in disgust and returned home. He was knighted and promoted to **lieutenant-general** (1805) and given command of the army sent to recapture the Cape of Good Hope, where he was made governor. He was relieved of the post, having lent his troops for the capture of **Montevideo** – Baird was a scapegoat for the failure of the expedition. He returned home and was given command of the 1st Division of the force prepared to invade Denmark. He was wounded during the bombardment of

Copenhagen and returned home, becoming colonel of the 24th Foot (**South Wales Borderers**). He sailed from Cork (1808) with 10,000 men to reinforce Sir John **Moore's** army in Spain. He commanded the right wing at **Corunna** (now La Coruña) during which he lost his left arm. He returned home and never again held a field command. He was made a full **general** (1814); governor of Kinsale (1819); commander of the forces in Ireland (1820–22) and Privy Councillor and governor of Fort George (1829).

Baker rifle *See* rifle

balaclava

A tight-fitting knitted cap worn over the head and neck, leaving an opening in the front. It probably was introduced during the **Crimean War**, was popular with troops during **World War I** and **World War II** and is still in use.

[After the village of *Balaklava* in the Crimea, probably because it was worn by infantry in the campaign there]

Balaclava, battle of

(1854; *Crimean War*) During the Anglo-French siege of **Sebastopol** (now Sevastopol) their supplies came through the port of Balaclava. The Russians, under Prince Aleksandr **Menshikov**, launched a surprise attack on this base (25 October). General Lord **Raglan**, the British commander, deployed the 93rd Highlanders (**Sutherland Highlanders**) under General Sir Colin **Campbell** to stop the advance, which they did. Raglan ordered a counter-attack by the cavalry under General Lord **Lucan**. The **Heavy Brigade**, under Sir James **Scarlett** drove back the Russian cavalry. Then instead of using the **Light Brigade**, under General Lord **Cardigan**, to clear the way to Balaclava, they were instructed to attack Russian troops to the north. Instead they charged a strong force of Russian **artillery**, losing 113 killed and 134 wounded out of a force of 673. The reason for this blunder has never been clear, but it was probably due to the misinterpretation of an order given to a staff officer. The Allies retained Balaclava.

baldrick, baldric

A belt hung from the right shoulder to the left hip originally for carrying a sword, but later a drum was hung from it as well. Baldricks were worn until the 18th century.

balmoral

A flat woollen Scottish cap

[After the royal estate of *Balmoral* in Scotland]

Baltimore, battle of

(1814; *War of 1812*) A British force of 4,000, commanded by Major-General Robert **Ross**, landed under the protection of a naval bombardment to capture Baltimore. They were met by 3,200 Americans at Gadfly Wood. The Americans were driven from their position, but Ross was killed. The naval bombardment by Admiral Sir George Cockburn was ineffective, and the landing force was too small to attack the 13,000 militia actually entrenched around Baltimore. The British, now commanded by Colonel Arthur Brooke, withdrew.

See also **Fort McHenry, battle of**

Banbury, battle of

(1469; *Wars of the Roses*) The Yorkist King Edward IV, having married Elizabeth Woodville and formed an alliance with the Duke of Burgundy, alienated the Neville family, especially Richard, Earl of Warwick. In the spring of 1469, Edward left London and moved north to meet up with the Earls of Pembroke and Devon. Before he could do so, this force was routed by the rebels under Robin of Redesdale (26 July) at Edgcott, just north of Banbury. Pembroke and Devon were killed and Warwick, with the Duke of Clarence, crossed to Calais to force their will on Edward IV, who had fled there.

Banda, battle of

(1858; *Indian Mutiny*) A British force of some 1,000 men, commanded by General Whitlock, defeated 7,000 mutineers (19 April)

bandolier

1. In the 17th century, a sash-like belt used for carrying gunpowder cases. Each case contained sufficient powder for a single shot and was hung by a string from the bandolier. Twelve such cases were usually carried. A bag of shot was also hung at the lowest point.

2. A cartridge belt of various forms, but usually carried over the shoulder

bands

Up to 1749, **infantry** regimental bands were made up of civilians, paid for by the officers, but after this date they were replaced by regular soldiers subject to military discipline. The band consisted of 6–8 men led by a drum major and playing drums, clarinet, bassoon, hautbois (like an oboe) and sometimes the French horn. The fife was re-introduced about 1750, its use having been abandoned earlier in the century, so that eventually every battalion had its fife and drum band. In modern times **light infantry** and **rifle** regiments have bugle bands instead of fife and drums. The bugle was invented for the light infantry, doing away with the encumbrance of carrying drums, and originally used for passing commands to the regiment. Cavalry bands were similar to those of the infantry.

See also **regimental marches**; *Also called* **regimental bands**

Bangalore, battle of

(1791; *British in India*) The town was besieged by a British force commanded by Lord **Cornwallis** (5 March). In spite of **Tipu Sahib** making several attempts to relieve the town, it was taken by storm (21 March).

Bannockburn, battle of

(1314; *English-Scottish Wars*) After the death of Edward I (1307), Edward II gave up the war against the Scots. This allowed time for Robert I (the Bruce) to unite Scotland and force the English out of all the castles north of the Tweed, except Stirling and Berwick. When Robert laid siege to Stirling, Edward moved north with a relief force of 13,000 soldiers and 2,000 armoured knights. Robert met the attack (24 June) with 8,000 spearmen on a rise overlooking the Bannock burn, a tributary of the Forth. The English were routed, ending English hopes of gaining control over Scotland by force. Stirling castle fell to the Scots immediately and Berwick castle four years later.

BAOR *abbreviation of* British Army of the Rhine

bar

A second award of a **medal**. 'Tommy Atkins, MM and Bar' means that Atkins has been awarded the **Military Medal** on two occasions.

[From Old French *barre*]

barbed wire

Strong wire with pointed projections along its length, invented (1874) by an American, Joseph Gidden, for fencing farms. It was first used extensively for military fortifications during the Russo-Japanese War at the start of the 20th century. During **World War I** belts of barbed wire many metres deep and made of coil after coil of metal became a feature of every defensive position, especially on the **Western Front**. This use of barbed wire contributed to the largely static nature of the fighting on the Western Front, particularly in the first half of the war when **artillery** technology had not developed fuses and ammunition capable of destroying barbed wire defences effectively. Such developments, and the generally increasing accuracy and power of artillery, have meant that barbed wire has seen much less military use in **World War II** and thereafter, being regarded as a security measure rather than a real barrier to attack.

Barcelona, battle of

(1705; *War of the Spanish Succession*) An Anglo-Dutch force had taken Gibraltar (1704) and from there a fleet under Admiral Sir Cloudesley Shovell landed a force of 6,000 British soldiers, under the Earl of **Peterborough**, north of Barcelona (August 1705). This force took the hill of Montjuich, south of the city, which led to the surrender of the city (9 October). Archduke Charles (later Charles VI of the Holy Roman Empire) was proclaimed King Charles III of Spain.

Bardia, battle of

(1941; *World War II*) During the advance of the British XIII Corps from Egypt across Libya, General Sir Richard **O'Connor's** force surrounded the Italian 10th Army of 45,000 men, under Marshal Rodolpho Graziani at the port of Bardia (3 January). The 6th Australian Division bridged an anti-tank ditch, enabling the 7th Armoured Division to penetrate the defences. 40,000 Italians were captured or killed.

Barnard, Henry William (1799–1857)

Barnard was educated at Westminster and Sandhurst and was commissioned in the 1st Guards (**Grenadier Guards**) (1814). He served on the staff of his uncle, Sir Andrew Francis Barnard, during the occupation of Paris after the battle of **Waterloo** and then in Jamaica and Canada. He held various staff appointments at home and then went to the **Crimea** as a **major-general** (1854). He commanded a brigade of the 3rd Foot (**East Kent Regiment**) and was chief of staff under General **Simpson** until September 1855 after which he commanded the 2nd Division. On his return home he was given commands at Corfu, Dover and Shorncliffe before being sent to India (April 1857). He arrived at the beginning of the **Indian Mutiny** and led the attack on **Delhi**. He died of cholera 11 weeks before the city fell.

Barnet, battle of

(1471; *Wars of the Roses*) The Yorkist King Edward IV thrust towards London, held by the Lancastrians. The Duke of Clarence (the king's younger brother), who had been supporting the Lancastrians and the Earl of Warwick, defected to the king. In spite of this, Warwick moved out of London and met the Royalist forces at Barnet (14 April). In a confused battle in thick fog, Warwick was killed and the Lancastrians defeated.

Baronial War (1403–08)

A civil war in England and Scotland between Henry IV of England and the Percy family of Northumberland who tried to curb the power of the king. The Percys were aided by the Welsh led by Owen Glendower. The rebels were defeated at **Shrewsbury** and Henry Percy, Earl of Northumberland, was killed at **Bramham Moor** (1408) when the rebellion finally petered out.

Barons' Wars

1. (1215–17) The first Barons' War was brought about by the opposition to King John of England. It led initially to the issue of Magna Carta (1215). When this was repudiated by John later that year, the barons asked Louis, son of Philip II of France, to become king of England. However John's son became King Henry III (1216), and Louis, following defeats at **Lincoln** and Sandwich, relinquished his claim to the English throne by the treaty of Kingston-on-Thames (1217).
2. (1264–67) A revolt against Henry III was led by Simon de Montfort, Earl of Leicester, the king's brother-in-law. Montfort was killed at the battle of **Evesham** (1265) but the rebellion was not finally crushed for another two years.

Barossa, battle of

(1811; *Peninsular War*) The battle took place as part of the British attempt to relieve Cadiz. A 4,000-man British force commanded by General Thomas **Graham** defeated 9,000 French, commanded by Marshal Victor (5 March). The French lost some 5,000 killed and wounded, including two generals, while the British lost 50 officers and 1,160 men. A large Spanish force encamped nearby took no part in the action.

barracks

A building in which military personnel are accommodated. When barracks were first built, the accommodation was minimal with the troops sleeping in large dormitories. Barracks are now more comfortable with recreational facilities and small shops.

See also **Pitt's Reforms**

[From French *baraque*, Italian *baracca* or Spanish *baraca* 'soldier's tent, barracks']

barrel

The tube-shaped part of a gun

[Via Old French *barril* from medieval Latin *barriclus* 'small cask' because barrels used to be made from iron strips bound together with hoops, in the same way as a wine barrel]

Barrell's Regiment, Barrell's Blues *See* King's Own Royal Regiment (Lancaster)

basilisk *See* cannon

Bassein, battle of

(1780; *Maratha Wars*) The Maratha garrison was besieged by a British force commanded by General Thomas **Goddard** (13 November). The Maratha relieving force was defeated by Colonel Hartley at Duggar (10 December) and the garrison surrendered (11 December).

baton

A thin short staff carried as a symbol of office. Batons have been carried as a sign of command since Roman times but the first formal baton awarded in the British Army was by George IV to the Duke of **Wellington**. The badge of a **general** is now a baton crossed with a sword, and that of a **field marshal** is two crossed batons.

[Via French, from late Latin *bastum* 'stick']

battalion

A tactical military unit within a **regiment**, consisting of a headquarters and two or more **companies**. A battalion is usually commanded by a **lieutenant-colonel**. An infantry battalion at the time of the **Civil War** was about 1,200 men, which was necessary to give effective fire-power. As musketry became more effective the numbers were reduced, so that by 1700 the battalion was reduced to about 700 men, imitating Gustavus Adolphus of Sweden who introduced battalions of 400–500 men during the Thirty Years' War in the 17th century. They gave greater manoeuvrability than the huge squares of 3–4,000. This innovation was copied in the British Army, where the battalion size was down to 400–450 by the end of the 17th century. The equivalent force in the cavalry is the squadron.

See also **colonel; company; regiment**

[Via French, from Italian *bataglione* 'great battle', from late Latin *bat(t)uere* 'to beat']

battery

The smallest tactical unit of **artillery**, commonly composed of six or eight **guns** and their crews and support personnel (perhaps 200 men in all), towing and ammunition vehicles and horses

[Via Old French *baterie* from *batre* 'to beat', ultimately from late Latin *bat(t)uere* 'to beat']

battle dress

A comfortable combat uniform introduced into the British Army in 1937 after various experimental uniforms had been tried. It was feared that a uniform that resembled the overalls used until that time for dirty **barracks** duties would prevent men from feeling like soldiers and would remove pride in their appearance. Initially the battledress had no distinguishing marks (largely for security reasons) but various regimental badges and other forms of identification have gradually come into use.

battle group

A formation of troops, usually a small one, deployed for battle

battle honours

Officers and occasionally other ranks were given **medals** to commemorate a successful battle during the 18th century. The concept of battle honours for a **regiment** evolved from this so that by 1768 the 15th Light Dragoons (**King's Hussars (15th)**) noted their success at the battle of Emsdorf by wearing the name on their headdress and the honour on their regimental **colours**. Later they were worn on **accoutrements** of officers and attached to colours and regimental drums. Often the honours were not awarded until many years after the battle: e.g. **Tangier** (1662–80) was not awarded until 1910. So many battle honours were awarded after **World War I** that in 1922 it was ordered that regiments should have no more than 25 honours on their standards, guidons or colours, of which no more than 10 should be World War I honours. In 1956 a limit of 10 was applied to **World War II** honours and in 1958 a limit of two to honours received from the **Korean War**. When most of the existing regiments were amalgamated (1958–71) the new regiments were allowed to emblazon up to 40 honours on each of the Queen's and regimental colours. The honours that have been received but have not been chosen to be displayed on the colours are called **accredited honours**.

Battle of the Bulge *See* **Ardennes, battle of 2**

bay

A type of reddish-brown horse. The 2nd Dragoon Guards were mounted exclusively on this type of horse and so were called 'The Bays' (**Queen's Bays**).
[From Old French *bai*, from Latin *badius* 'chestnut-coloured']

bayonet

The bayonet was introduced to replace the **pike**. The original bayonet, introduced from France during the mid-16th century, was developed from the hunting knife and plugged into the barrel of the musket and designed to give the musketeer the ability to defend himself against cavalry charges and fight hand-to-hand even when his weapon was unloaded. This early bayonet evolved into a short sword that screwed into the barrel of the musket, but this also prevented the musket from being fired when the bayonet was fixed. This encumbrance was the direct cause of the rout of the English **regiments** at the battle of **Killiecrankie** (1689). After 1693 the bayonet was developed with a bent hilt which fitted onto the muzzle allowing the musket to be fired. The bayonet has survived in essentially this form into the 21st century, though hand-to-hand bayonet fighting (always rare even in the earliest times) has long been virtually unknown, with bayonets instead now being more likely to be used for domestic tasks by the soldier.
[From the French town of *Bayonne*, where it was supposedly invented]

bayonet belt

A belt worn over the shoulder to carry a bayonet. In the early 18th century the ordinary soldier wore a belt carrying both his sword and bayonet. Later in the century infantrymen stopped carrying swords and the bayonet was worn on a bayonet belt over the shoulder to which was attached a belt plate which usually carried the regimental **badge**. Since the 19th century a bayonet has usually been hung from the belt on a separate **frog**.

beachhead

A relatively small area of enemy coast that has been invaded and held to enable the main body of troops to land and be supplied

bearskin

A fur cap worn by the **Foot Guards**. Fur caps were authorised for the **grenadiers** in 1768 and when the 1st Foot Guards were named the **Grenadier Guards** after **Waterloo** (1815) all the men wore bearskins. Later the distinction was extended to all Foot Guards. (Note: a bearskin is not a 'busby'.)

Beaugé, battle of

(1421; *Hundred Years' War*) In spite of the Treaty of Troyes, the Orleanist French and Scottish forces began raiding English lands in the south of Normandy and Maine.

Thomas, Duke of Clarence, brother of Henry V, pursued the raiders, but his cavalry outdistanced his infantry and were routed at Beaugé in Anjou. Clarence was killed.

Beauséjour, battle of

(1755; *French and Indian War*) A force of 200 New Englanders and British regulars under Lieutenant-Colonel Robert **Monckton** and Lieutenant-Colonel John Winslow embarked from New Brunswick and seized St. John at the mouth of the St. John river. They then attacked the French fort of Beauséjour on the south-east coast. After a few days (19 June) the French surrendered so that by the end of June all the Bay of Fundy area was under British control.

Beda Fomm, battle of

(1941; *World War II*) After the fall of **Tobruk**, General Sir Richard **O'Connor** continued the British advance into Libya, the object of which was the capture of Benghazi. The 7th Armoured Division moved inland across the desert to reach Beda Fomm on the coast beyond Benghazi (5 February), thus cutting off the Italian retreat into Tripoli. The entire Italian army of 20,000 men surrendered; the British casualties were nine killed and 15 wounded. The victory at Beda Fomm ended the 500-mile drive of 10 weeks which annihilated the Italian 10th Army of 130,000 men, 400 tanks and 1,290 guns.

Bedford, battle of (1224)

Following the first Baron's War, Fawkes de Bréauté was outlawed (1224) for not accepting the terms of the peace signed at Kingston-on-Thames (1217). His brother William retaliated by imprisoning a royal justice in Bedford castle. Hubert de Burgh (later Earl of Kent) laid siege to the castle which surrendered (14 August) after two months. William was hanged and Fawkes allowed to go into exile.

Bedfordshire and Hertfordshire Regiment

The **regiment** was raised in 1688 as Colonel Douglas' Regiment of Foot, but Douglas was replaced on the accession of William III because of his adherence to James II. Colonel Hodges was given command of the regiment. In 1751 it became the 16th Regiment of Foot. The name was further altered to 16th (Buckinghamshire) Regiment of Foot (1782); 16th (Bedfordshire) Regiment of Foot (1809); Bedfordshire Regiment (1881); Bedfordshire and Hertfordshire Regiment (1919). The regiment has also been known as 'The Old Bucks' (from its previous association with Buckinghamshire), 'The Featherbeds' and 'The Peacemakers' (both from a long garrison duty served after the battle of **Dettingen**). It was amalgamated with the Essex Regiment (1958) to form the 3rd East Anglian Regiment.

Bedfordshire Regiment *See* Bedfordshire and Hertfordshire Regiment; West Yorkshire Regiment

BEF *abbreviation of* British Expeditionary Force

Belfast Regiment *See* Royal Sussex Regiment

Belmont, battle of

(1899; *Boer Wars*) A 3,000-strong Boer force occupying the hills near Belmont was attacked by 7 British **infantry battalions** and a **regiment** of **cavalry**. The frontal attack was successful, the British losing some 300 officers and men while the Boers suffered a similar number of casualties.

belt plate

A metal clip which replaced the buckle as a fastening for shoulder belts during the latter part of the 18th century. They were frequently decorated with insignia. They went out of general use after the **Crimean War**.

BEM *abbreviation of* British Empire Medal

Bemis Heights, battle of

(1777; *American War of Independence*) The second stage of the battle of **Saratoga**. The British defeat led directly to **Burgoyne's** surrender to the Americans.

Bengal European Light Cavalry, 2nd *See* Hussars, 20th

Bengal Infantry

The **regiment** was raised (1854) as the 3rd Bengal European Infantry in the army of the East India Company. It became part of the British Army establishment (1861) as the 107th (Bengal Infantry) Regiment. It was amalgamated with the 35th Foot to become the **Royal Sussex Regiment** in 1881.

Bengal Light Infantry *See* Queen Elizabeth's Own Gurkha Rifles (6th)

Bengal Sappers and Miners (1857)

A small party of the Bengal Sappers and Miners succeeded in blowing up the Kashmir Gate at Delhi, allowing the 52nd Light Infantry (**Oxfordshire Regiment of Foot**) to rush into the town. Most of the party were killed and Bugler Hawthorn was awarded a **Victoria Cross** for his part in the action.

See also **Delhi, battle of**

Bennington, battle of

(1777; *American War of Independence*) A British force under Sir John **Burgoyne** pushed southwards into America from Canada, becoming increasingly isolated through the failure of a multiple-pronged offensive. Supplies became critical. To alleviate the position, Colonel Friedrich Baum with 200 men moved east to attack the American supply depot at Bennington (11 August). This force was defeated by some 2,000 American militia under General John Stark (16 August). A second relief column, mostly Germans, was sent by Burgoyne to relieve the situation, but was met by American reinforcements. The British force, under Lieutenant-Colonel Heinrich Breymann, withdrew to the main British lines on the Hudson river. Thus Burgoyne's position at **Saratoga** became even more untenable.

Beresford, William Carr (1768–1854)

The illegitimate son of the 1st Marquis of Waterford, Beresford joined the army (1785) and served in Nova Scotia and Egypt. He was in command of the forces taking the Cape of Good Hope (1806) and at the battle of **Buenos Aires**. He was captured, but escaped and was appointed governor of Madeira. When recalled to active service he served with Sir John **Moore** at **Corunna** (now La Coruña), was chosen by General Sir Arthur Wellesley (**Wellington**) to reorganise the Portuguese Army, and was made a **marshal** (1809). He commanded the Portuguese troops at the battle of **Albuera** , then took part in the capture of **Badajoz** and was wounded at **Salamanca**. He left Portugal (1822) and was **Master-General of the Ordnance** (*see* **Ordnance, Board of**) in Wellington's government (1828–30).

beret

A soft flat hat. Berets were worn by Spanish troops in the early 19th century and then worn by the French. They were introduced into the British Army in 1924 as the black berets worn by the Tank Corps. Different coloured berets are now worn by different units, e.g. red berets are worn by the **Parachute Regiment**.

[Via French from late Latin *birrus*, 'hooded cloak']

Bergen op Zoom, battle of

1. (1747; *War of the Austrian Succession*) The British-Dutch-Austrian alliance had been defeated at **Lauffeld** and the French column under Count Ulrich von Löwendal moved quickly to besiege Bergen op Zoom (15 July). In spite of stubborn resistance by the British-Dutch garrison the town fell to the French (18 September).

2. (1799; *French Revolutionary Wars*) The French forces had been driven back in Germany, Switzerland and Italy, and to maintain this pressure another front was opened by a combined Anglo-Russian force of some 35,000 men at Bergen op Zoom. The French counter-attacked and while the British forces under the **Duke of York** held, the Russian flank collapsed, forcing the British to retreat north.

Berkshire Regiment of Foot

The **regiment** was raised (1755) as the 2nd Battalion of the 19th Regiment of Foot (**Green Howards**). It became a separate regiment (1758) as the 66th Regiment of Foot, and in 1782 the 66th (or Berkshire) Regiment of Foot. The regiment won battle honours when serving as marines under Nelson at the battle of Copenhagen (1801). Following amalgamation with the 49th in 1881 it became Princess Charlotte of Wales's (Berkshire) Regiment.

See also **Royal Berkshire Regiment (Princess Charlotte of Wales's)**

Berwick, Duke of (1670–1734)

The illegitimate son of James, Duke of York (later James II) and Arabella Churchill, sister of John Churchill, later 1st Duke of **Marlborough**. He was created Duke of Berwick (1687) and governor of Portsmouth (1688). He fled to France with James II and was present at the battle of the **Boyne**. He accepted the commission of **lieutenant-general** in the French Army (1693). During the War of the **Spanish Succession** he first served in Spain (1704) but then fought against the Huguenot rebels in Languedoc, capturing Nice (1706). For this he was made a marshal of France. He returned to Spain and recaptured Madrid from the Allies and defeated the British at the battle of **Almanza**. In 1714 he stormed Barcelona. He invaded Spain again in 1719, ending Philip V's claims to the regency of France. Berwick was killed by a cannon ball at the siege of Philippsburg during the War of the Polish Succession.

Also known as **Fitzjames, James**

Berwick upon Tweed, battle of

(1296; *English-Scottish Wars*) Edward I of England had been called in to arbitrate in the dispute over the Scottish crown. He found in favour of John Balliol (1292). Some of the Scottish nobles resented this intrusion into their affairs and formed an alliance with France (1295), at that time at war with England. Edward took this as an act of aggression and sacked Berwick (28 March). The population was slaughtered and the town reduced from a major commercial centre to a minor seaport. It was later made an English garrison.

Betwa, battle of

(1858; *Indian Mutiny*) A rebel force of 22,000 advanced to relieve the Rani of Jhansi besieged in her capital by 1,500 British and Indian troops commanded by Major-General Sir Hugh **Rose**. The rebels were beaten back with the loss of some 1,500 men.

BFA *See* **blank-firing attachment**

Bhurtpore, battle of

1. (1805; *Maratha Wars*) The city of Bhurtpore (now Bhurtpur) was garrisoned by 8,000 of the Rajah's troops and besieged by the British commanded by General **Lake** (4 January). Lake's artillery failed to reduce the city, as did four successive assaults by storm. Lake lost some 3,200 men and withdrew (21 April).

2. (1817; *Maratha Wars*) The city was besieged by Lord Combermere in support of the Rajah who had been expelled. After two months' bombardment, the city was taken by storm.

bicorn

A hat with two corners, worn by officers. The points were originally worn side-to-side over the shoulders and later fore-and-aft.

bill

A weapon resembling a spear with a short staff and a pointed head which had a blade or point to the side. It was still in use during the late 16th century but was gradually replaced by the **pike**.

[From Old English *bil*]

Bill of Rights (1689)

The act of parliament that embodied the terms of the Declarations of Rights, which William III and Mary II had accepted as a condition of being offered the throne after the Glorious Revolution of 1688. Among other provisions the act made it illegal for the monarch to raise a **standing army** in time of peace without the consent of Parliament. Parliament would then vote on the army's size and cost and control the discipline through the annual **Mutiny Act**.

Bingham, George Charles *See* **Lucan, Lord**[1]

Birdwood, William Riddell (1865–1951)
Birdwood was born in India and educated at Clifton College. He was commissioned in the **Royal Scots Fusiliers** (1883). He went to Sandhurst and was **gazetted** in the 12th Lancers and went to India (1885). He transferred to the 11th Bengal Lancers (1886) and saw active service. Birdwood was adjutant of the viceroy's bodyguard (1893–98) and was promoted to **captain** (1896). He then went to South Africa (1899) on the staff of the Natal Mounted Brigade. He took part in the battle of **Colenso** and the relief of **Ladysmith**, when he was wounded. From 1900–09 he was deputy assistant adjutant and then military secretary to **Kitchener**, with whom he went to India (1902). He was promoted to **colonel** (1905); made **brigadier-general** (1909) and **major-general** (1911). By 1912 Birdwood was secretary in the army department of the Indian government and a member of the legislative council. In 1914 he was given command of the Australian and New Zealand forces, known as **ANZACs**, sent to Egypt with the rank of **lieutenant-general**. He was sent to the **Dardanelles** to assess the position and decided that a naval bombardment alone would not be sufficient. This he reported to Kitchener (now Secretary of State for War). Ian **Hamilton**, rather than Birdwood, was given command of the Mediterranean Expeditionary Force, and then ignored Birdwood's advice against landing on the Helles beaches. Birdwood was then in command of the ANZAC forces during the **Gallipoli** campaign, subsequently commanded the ANZAC forces in France (1916) and in May 1918 commanded the 5th Army. He was promoted to **general** (1917). After the war, Birdwood commanded the Northern Army in India (1920–24) and was made Commander-in-Chief, India (1925), when he was promoted to **field marshal**. He retired in 1930.

Bishops' Wars (1639, 1640)
The first war began with a riot in Edinburgh when Charles I tried to enforce Anglicanism on the Scottish Church. The General Assembly of the Scottish Church, meeting in Glasgow, defied Charles who sent troops across the border. This came to nothing as Charles was forced, through lack of funds, to agree to the Pacification of Berwick (1639). Further unrest, and the Scots' intriguing with France, led Charles to call the Short Parliament (1640) to raise funds to invade Scotland. Funds were refused and Charles financed the expedition himself, having dissolved Parliament. The Scots seized Northumberland and Durham forcing Charles to call what later became known as the Long Parliament (1640) and thus precipitate the **Civil War**.
See also **Covenanters**

black powder
Gunpowder, a mixture of charcoal, potassium nitrate (saltpetre) and sulphur. This burns rapidly and consequently produces an explosion when ignited in a confined space. It probably originated in China during the 10th century, but may have been an Arab invention of the 13th century. When used as a propellant it produces a great deal of smoke and leaves a considerable residue in the gun barrel. Since the 1870s it has been superseded by other explosive compounds for most military uses.
See also **nitrocellulose**

Black Watch, The
The original **regiment** was raised (1739) from independent Highland regiments that were loyal to the Crown, by Lord Crawford, and was called the Earl of Crawford's Regiment of Foot (The Highland Regiment). It was designated the 42nd Foot (1749). From 1749–51 it was named from its **colonels** but in 1751 it became the 42nd Regiment of Foot; the 42nd (The Royal Highland) Regiment of Foot (1758); 42nd Royal Regiment of Foot (The Black Watch) (1861). The present regiment – The Black Watch

(Royal Highland Regiment) – is the senior Highland regiment and was formed by the amalgamation of the original regiment with the 73rd **Perthshire Regiment of Foot**. By 1936 the amalgamated regiment was called The Black Watch (Royal Highland Regiment). It saw service in the **Iraq War** near Baghdad before merging (2006) with The Royal Scots, The Royal Highland Fusiliers, The King's Own Scottish Borderers, The Argyll and Sutherland Highlanders and The Highlanders (Seaforth, Gordons and Camerons) to form The Royal Regiment of Scotland.

See also **Alexandria, battle of**; **Ashanti War**; **Ticonderoga, battle of**

Bladensburg, battle of

(1814; *War of 1812*) As part of the British offensive on the east coast of the USA a force of some 4,000 troops was taken up the Patuxent river in Maryland, in a fleet under Admiral George Cockburn. The force under General Robert **Ross** landed at Benedict from where, meeting no opposition, it moved towards Washington DC. A force of 6,000 American militia and regulars under General William H. Winder blocked the British advance at Bladensburg (24 August). After a minor skirmish, the Americans fled. The US President (James Madison) moved from Washington across the Potomac river and the British burnt a large part of Washington, including various public buildings around the Capitol. When the presidential residence was repaired it was painted white, becoming the White House. The next day the invaders sailed towards Baltimore.

blanco

A material, introduced about 1835 as a substitute for whiting, and used for cleaning equipment

[From French *blanc* 'white']

blank-firing attachment

An attachment to **small arms** or **artillery** enabling it to fire a projectile that does not hold a **bullet** or **warhead**.

Abbreviation **BFA**

Blenheim, battle of

(1704; *War of the Spanish Succession*) The Duke of **Marlborough** invaded Bavaria interposing Allied forces between the French on the Upper Danube and Vienna. The French were massed near the village of Blenheim at the confluence of the Danube and the Nebel. Louis William I of Baden-Baden was deployed to besiege Ingolstadt, while Marlborough with General Lord John **Cutts** and Prince Eugene of Savoy on his right with a force of 52,000 faced Marshal Comte Ferdinand de Marsin and Marshal Comte Camille de Tallard with a force of 60,000 which hinged on Blenheim (15 August). The morning's fighting was indecisive, but in the afternoon Marlborough threw his force of 8,000 Allied cavalry across the Nebel, forcing the French cavalry into the Danube. This trapped the French infantry in Blenheim, forcing Tallard to surrender. Tallard was taken prisoner; Vienna was saved and Bavaria was knocked out of the war.

blockhouse

A relatively small fortress, often made of timber, placed in a strategic defensive position or as an outpost. Blockhouses were used as command posts during the second **Boer War**.

Bloemfontein, battle of

(1900; *Boer Wars*) After defeating the Boers at **Paardeberg** (27 February) the way was open for the British forces under General Lord **Roberts** to carry out an all-out offensive on the Orange Free State. Roberts marched on Bloemfontein, which fell (31 March). Kroonstad fell (12 May) and all resistance was crushed by 24 May. The Orange Free State was annexed by Britain.

Blore Heath, battle of

(1459; *Wars of the Roses*) The Yorkists, under Richard, Duke of York, had defeated the Lancastrian King Henry VI at **St Albans** (1455), which led to an uneasy truce. But in 1459 at Blore Heath in Staffordshire, a group of Yorkist knights commanded by the Earl of Salisbury attacked a group of Lancastrian foot soldiers (22 September), who were defeated, allowing Salisbury to move south to join with Richard's main army.

Blücher, Gebbard Leberecht von (1742–1819)

Blücher was born at Rostock and served in the Swedish Army (1756–58) and then in the Prussian cavalry (1760–70). He was dismissed for insubordination and returned to his estates. He rejoined the army (1787) as a major and fought against the French, notably though without success in Prussia's catastrophic defeat of 1806. When Prussia rose against the French (1813), Blücher took command in Silesia. By January 1814 he had crossed the Rhine and entered Paris (31 March 1814). When **Napoleon** returned (1815) Blücher was defeated at Ligny, but appeared late in the day to secure **Wellington's** victory at **Waterloo**.

Also known as **Prince of Wahlstatt**

Blueberg, battle of

(1806; *French Wars*) A British force of 6,600 men commanded by General David **Baird** landed at Saldanha Bay (South Africa) (8 January) and was attacked by a French-Dutch force, commanded by General Janssens, from Cape Town. His opponents were defeated and Baird occupied Cape Town.

blue clothing

Blue was considered to be the royal colour and was worn by 'Royal' **regiments** up to the reign of William III, when the newly-formed regiments also wore blue. The red coat was introduced during the reign of Queen Anne, though regiments entitled to use the distinction 'Royal' in their names normally retained blue as their **facing** colour. George I re-introduced the blue uniform for the **artillery** and later in the 18th century it was worn by the **light dragoons**. The colour was kept by **hussars** and **lancers** up to the last days of full **dress**. Infantry officers wore blue frock coats for undress and scarlet for full dress.

Blues and Royals

Part of the **Household Cavalry** formed (March 1969) by the amalgamation of the **Royal Horse Guards** (The Blues) and the **Royal Dragoons** (1st Dragoons). The Royal Horse Guards date from 1661 when Colonel Unton Crook's Regiment of Horse, which originated in the Parliamentary army, was taken into royal service under the Earl of Oxford. It was then known as the Earl of Oxford's Regiment of Horse or the Royal Regiment of Horse. The name was changed in 1685 to Royal Regiment of Horse (Guards). It did not change its designation from horse to **dragoon guards** when this alteration was made for the other regiments of horse. The nickname 'The Blues' was derived from the blue livery associated with the Earl of Oxford. In 1875 it became the Royal Horse Guards and in 1891 The Royal Horse Guards (The Blues). In 1991 the Blues and Royals amalgamated with the **Life Guards** but maintained it own identity and traditions.

Board of General Officers *See* **pay in the 17th and 18th centuries**

body armour *See* **armour**

Boer Wars

1. (1880–81) The Dutch Boers had settled in the Transvaal which had been annexed by the British in 1877. The Boers revolted and repulsed the British who then recognised the South African Republic (5 April 1881).

See also **Bronkhorst Spruit, battle of; Laing's Nek, battle of; Majuba Hill, battle of; Joubert, Petrus (Piet) Jacobus; Kruger, Stephanus Johannes Paulus**

2. (1899–1901) The discovery of gold in the Transvaal brought many settlers, largely British. Cecil Rhodes, prime minister of the British Cape Colony in the south, and the British South Africa Company of Southern Rhodesia (now Zimbabwe) in the north, sought to form a union of all South Africa. The **Jameson Raid** by a few British adventurers (1895–96) worsened relations between the Boers and the British and the tension mounted. The Orange Free State allied itself with the Transvaal and the Transvaal president, **Kruger**, declared war (12 October 1899). By July 1900 the British had defeated the Boers, despite a series of early Boer victories, but guerrilla warfare continued until the British commander General Lord **Kitchener** rounded up some 120,000 Boers into concentration camps. It was on the establishment of these camps that this term entered the English language. The Boer resistance collapsed and the Transvaal and Orange Free State became part of British South Africa by the treaty of Vereeniging (31 May 1902). The Union of South Africa was later established (1910).

See also **Belmont, battle of; Bloemfontein, battle of; Colenso, battle of; Farquhar's Farm, battle of; Johannesburg, battle of; Karee, battle of; Kimberley; Ladysmith, siege of; Mafeking, siege of; Magersfontein, battle of; Modder river, battle of; Paardeberg, battle of; Pieter's Hill, battle of; Reddersberg, battle of; Rietfontein, battle of; Sanna's Post, battle of; Senekal, battle of; Spion Kop, battle of; Stormberg, battle of; Vaal Krantz, battle of; Botha, Louis; Buller, Redvers Henry; Kitchener, Horatio Herbert; Roberts, Frederick Sleigh; Rundle, Henry Macleod Leslie; White, George Stuart; Wolseley, Garnet Joseph**

bolt

1. A mechanism that fits into the **breech** of a **rifle** enabling the **cartridge** to be fed into the barrel ready for firing. The bolt contains a spring-loaded firing pin. When the bolt is rotated and drawn back the firing pin is locked against its compressed spring. As the bolt is pushed forward it forces a cartridge from the spring-loaded magazine into the chamber and the gun is ready to fire. When the trigger is pulled the firing pin is released and fires the bullet. When the bolt is drawn back again an ejector mechanism at the end of it withdraws the spent cartridge from the chamber and ejects it. The bolt is pushed forward again and the process is repeated.

2. The short arrow fired by a **crossbow**

bombard

An early form of cannon. Bombards were introduced during the 15th century by the Turks. Essentially they were simple tubes of wrought or cast iron, or made of iron bars held together by hoops. Bombards were used exclusively for siege operations or static defence. They were dragged on sledges and had to be fixed on earth emplacements or log platforms. The earlier forms fired stone cannon balls, some of which weighed as much as 1,500 pounds while the guns themselves reached 19 tons. Firing was limited to about seven shots a day.

[From French *bombarde* 'cannon', ultimately from Latin *bombus*, Greek *bombos* 'booming sound']

bombardier

Originally the soldier in charge of a **bombard**, by 1844 it referred to a junior **non-commissioned officer** in the **artillery**. Originally bombardiers wore one **chevron** on the right arm but then (1920) wore two when the rank of corporal was abolished in the artillery.

[From French, from *bombarde* 'cannon', ultimately from Latin *bombus*, Greek *bombos* 'booming sound']

Bombay Light Infantry

The **regiment** was raised by the East India Company as the 2nd Bombay European Regiment of Foot. The name was changed twice and in 1861 the regiment was taken into the British Army as the 106th Bombay Light Infantry Regiment. In 1881 the regiment was amalgamated with the 68th (Durham) Light Infantry to form the **Durham Light Infantry**.

bomber

In World War I, a man who threw hand **grenades**

bomblet

A small bomb, especially one that is part of a larger unit such as a **cluster bomb**

booby trap
A hidden or disguised bomb or **mine** that is detonated on contact or by remote control

Boomplaats, battle of (1848)
After Britain had annexed Natal (1844), the authorities in the British Cape Colony developed a policy of expansion, claiming the territory between the Orange and Vaal rivers (1848). The Boers in the area under Andries **Pretorius** revolted. The rebels were defeated by a British force under the command of General Sir Harry **Smith** at Boomplaats. Great Britain set up the Orange River Sovereignty, but withdrew (1854), allowing the Boers to form the Orange Free State.

boots
A piece of leather footwear that also covers part of the leg. Full-length boots were worn by cavalry since earliest times while the light cavalry wore shorter boots. The infantry wore boots from 1823 when shoes were discontinued. The boots were worn alternately on either foot to equalise the wear; they were not made differently for left and right feet. Eyelet holes were introduced to take laces. There were various types of infantry boot issued until 1913 when a new pattern Army ankle boot was issued. A lighter-weight ankle boot was issued in 1932 and rubber-soled boots in 1963. Modern boots make use of artificial materials, such as nylon.

Border Regiment
This was formed (1881) by the amalgamation of the **Cumberland Regiment** and the **Westmorland Regiment**. It formed part of the **King's Own Royal Border Regiment** after a further amalgamation in 1959.

Boroughbridge, battle of (1322)
There was continued unrest after the second Baron's War. Because of Edward II's ineffective government, the barons were encouraged to strengthen their individual positions. Thomas, Earl of Lancaster, nephew of the king, and the Welsh Marcher lords tried to establish a strong foothold in the north. To prevent this, and to establish the position of the Despensers at court, Edward moved north with a force and defeated the Lancastrians at Boroughbridge as they moved to join their allies in Scotland (16 March). The Earl of Lancaster was captured and beheaded at Pontefract.

Bosworth, battle of
(1485; *Wars of the Roses*) The Yorkists, commanded by Richard III, were attempting to intercept a march on London by the Lancastrians, led by Henry Tudor, Earl of Richmond. The two armies met at Bosworth in Leicestershire. In the hand-to-hand combat that followed, Richard was killed and Sir William Stanley, who commanded a uncommitted force on the outskirts of the battle, moved in to support the Lancastrians. The Yorkists fled. Henry was later crowned Henry VII, thus establishing the Tudor dynasty.

Botha, Louis (1862–1919)
Botha grew up in the Orange Free State, South Africa, and helped to form the New Republic (1884) in what became northern Natal, which then joined the South African Republic (1888). He was elected to the Volksraad (parliament) in 1897. His views were moderate, advocating co-operation with the non-Boer settlers (mostly British). At the outbreak of the **Boer War** (1899) he rose rapidly in the Boer military hierarchy to command the southern forces that besieged **Ladysmith**. On the death of Petrus (Piet) **Joubert** (1900), Botha was appointed commandant-general of the Transvaal forces. In spite of his military talents he was forced to surrender at **Paardeberg** and lost Pretoria to the British. After this he conducted a guerrilla campaign but was forced to negotiate. After the war he was elected the first prime minister of the Transvaal (1907) and then first prime minister of the Union of South Africa (1910). His moderate views led to conflict with the nationalist Afrikaners, especially when he aided the British by invading and successfully conquering German South West Africa (now Namibia) in 1915. He took part in the Versailles Peace Conference (1919).

Bothwell Bridge, battle of

(1679; *Scottish Covenanters' Revolt*) The royalist forces commanded by Viscount **Dundee** which had been defeated by the **Covenanters** at the battle of **Drumclog** were reinforced by troops under the Duke of **Monmouth**. The combined force defeated the Covenanters (2 July) at Bothwell Bridge over the Clyde. Monmouth's clemency to the rebels gained him much respect locally.

Boulogne, battle of

(1544; *Anglo-French War*) Henry VIII of England and the Holy Roman Emperor Charles V wished to curb the increasing power of Francis I of France and planned a joint invasion of France. Henry crossed to the English base at Calais and moved south, capturing Boulogne on 14 September. Four days later Charles made a separate peace with France. The English held Boulogne until 1550 when they sold it back to France.

Bouvines, battle of (1214)

During the continuous hostilities that existed between England and France, King John of England organised a two-pronged attack on the forces of the French King Philip II Augustus. King John led an attack on Poitou, which collapsed, while a coalition force consisting of English under the Earl of Shrewsbury, troops of the Holy Roman Empire under Emperor Otto IV, and forces from the Low Countries under the Count of Flanders attacked Bouvines (27 July). The coalition forces were defeated, destroying the coalition itself and weakening John's position at home.

bowler hat

A black hat with a rounded top and a narrow brim. Bowler hats were often worn by volunteer soldiers in the late 19th and early 20th centuries. They were frequently embellished and formed a cheap military-looking headdress. In the early and mid-20th century, 'getting a bowler hat' was a euphemism used when an officer was compelled to retire.

[After William *Bowler*, a 19th century British hatter]

Boxer Rebellion (1900–01)

An uprising by the Chinese against European settlements in eastern China, particularly those of the English and the French. The Allied forces captured **Peking** (now Beijing) (14 August 1900), effectively suppressing the rebellion.

Boyne, battle of the

(1690; *Irish Resistance to William and Mary*) The deposed James II gained strength in Ireland thus compelling William III to redress the situation. He personally landed a force of 35,000 English troops at Carrickfergus and marched to meet the forces of James and Lord Lucan (Patrick **Sarsfield**) at their line held along the river Boyne (1 July, Old Style). James' forces were defeated and he fled to France. William's commander Duke Frederick von Schomberg was killed.

Braddock Down, battle of

(1643; *Civil War*) The Parliamentarians, commanded by General Ruthven, had occupied Liskeard, Cornwall, but as they were not sufficiently supported, they were heavily defeated by a Royalist force commanded by Sir Ralph Hopton

Bramham Moor, battle of

(1408; *Baronial War*) Henry Percy, Earl of Northumberland, was pardoned for his part in the battle of **Shrewsbury** (1403) against Henry IV, but had to flee to Scotland in 1405 following a further unsuccessful rebellion. In 1408 he assembled a small force and invaded England. He was defeated and killed (19 February) at Bramham Moor, Yorkshire, by an *ad hoc* force of Yorkshire knights led by the sheriff of York.

Brandywine, battle of

(1777; *American War of Independence*) Moving from New York (July), 15,000 British troops, commanded by General Sir William **Howe**, met an American force of 11,000 commanded by General George **Washington** at Chadd's Ford on Brandywine Creek about 25 miles from Philadelphia. The British won the battle, but Washington's forces were left virtually intact and he still had access to Philadelphia.

brassard
An arm band worn around the upper arm
[From French, from *bras* 'arm']

breastwork
A defensive wall, usually of earth, and often constructed quickly

breech
The back part of a gun behind the **barrel**.
See also **muzzle**

breech-loading
A gun that is loaded through the **breech** as opposed to through the **muzzle**.
See also **muzzle-loading**

Brémule, battle of
(1119; *Anglo-French War*) The defeat of the forces of Louis VI of France by those of Henry I of England at Brémule confirmed Henry's possession of Normandy

Bren gun
A British adaptation of a Czech light **machine gun**. It was first made in 1937 and was lighter and more accurate than the **Lewis gun**, which it replaced. It was gas-operated and air-cooled, weighing 19 pounds with a cyclic rate of fire of 520 rounds per minute. It was one of the principal British **infantry** weapons of **World War II** and subsequent versions (known from 1958 as the **L4**) continued in service until the 1990s.
[From the initial letters of *Brno* in the Czech Republic, where the design of the gun originated, and *Enfield* in Greater London, England, where it was made]

Brentford, battle of
(1642; *Civil War*) After the battle of **Edgehill** Charles I resumed his march on London. The Royalist forces met the Parliamentarian forces under Robert Devereux, 3rd Earl of Essex, at Brentford. A cavalry charge led by Prince Rupert defeated the Parliamentarians (12 November) but did not prevent their joining with the forces from London. This combined force met the Royalists at Turnham Green (15 November) causing them to turn away from London and Charles to withdraw to Oxford.

brevet rank
A superior nominal rank formerly given to an officer, but without extra pay. Hence a brevet **major** would have the status of a major but be paid as a **captain**. Brevet ranks were often awarded in the field for some outstanding feat and confirmed as a **substantive rank** later, as is still the case today.
[From French, 'little letter', from Old French *brief* 'letter']

brick dust
Used during the 18th century to polish brass fitments

bridgehead
An advanced position in enemy territory that is being held while awaiting the arrival of a main force. The term derives from its original meaning: a fortification on the end of a bridge nearest the enemy.

brigade
A fighting unit. Initially it was any large body of troops. Later a brigade was specified as several, at least two but seldom more than four, **battalions** or **cavalry regiments**. Two or more brigades, with other units, make up a **division**. Brigade is still used in this sense in the modern army. In the 18th and 19th centuries the term could also mean the unit of artillery now usually known as a **battery**.
[Via French from Italian *brigata* 'military company', from *brigare* 'to fight']

brigade major, brigadier major
The principal staff officer of a brigade

Brigade of Guards

The administrative body which oversees activities of the **Foot Guards regiments**

Brigade of Gurkhas *See* **Gurkhas, Brigade of**

brigadier

The officer commanding a **brigade**. Originally this was a brigadier-general. This rank was abolished (1918) and replaced by colonel-commandant, which was replaced (1928) by the rank of brigadier, which still exists. The brigadier-general's badge was a crossed baton and sword while that of the brigadier is a crown and three stars.

[From French, from *brigade* 'military company', from Italian *brigata*, from *brigare* 'to fight']

brigadier-general *See* **brigadier**

Brihuega, battle of

(1710; *War of the Spanish Succession*) After a series of setbacks in Spain, the Allies were confined to Barcelona. In 1710 James, Earl Stanhope, led an expedition to capture Madrid and replace Philip V by Archduke Charles of Austria (the future Holy Roman Emperor Charles VI). Having failed to take Madrid, the Allies fell back towards Barcelona and were attacked and defeated by a Franco-Spanish force under the Duc de Vendôme. From then on the Allies held only Barcelona, which was returned to Spain by the Treaty of Utrecht (1713).

British Army of the Rhine

The British 2nd Army under the command of Field Marshal **Montgomery** crossed the Rhine (1945) and began the occupation of Germany. Parts of the force stayed on in Germany after the end of the war and took control of one of the four sectors into which Germany was divided. (The other sectors were controlled by France, the USSR and the USA.) With the beginning of the Cold War and the formation of **NATO**, this force was transformed into Britain's permanent contribution to the defence of West Germany from Soviet and Warsaw Pact forces. Following the end of the Cold War (1989), it was disbanded in 1994 and replaced by the smaller **British Forces Germany**.

British Empire Medal

The Order of the British Empire for Meritorious Service was instituted (1922) when the Medal of the Order of the British Empire was discontinued. The BEM was awarded for meritorious service to those who were not of high enough rank to be appointed to the **Order of the British Empire** itself. Between 1958 and 1974 the BEM was awarded for gallantry, when crossed oak leaves were worn on the ribbon, but was then replaced by the **Queen's Gallantry Medal**. The British Empire Medal is no longer awarded in the UK.

Abbreviation **BEM**

British Expeditionary Force

The home-based British army formed as a result of the army reforms of 1908. Previously British forces destined to serve abroad were sent as individual units and organised into **brigades** at their destination. After signing a treaty with France to support her against a potential German invasion, it was thought there should be a ready trained and organised unit to oppose such aggression quickly. Originally the force consisted of six infantry divisions and one cavalry division. The force served in France during both **World War I** and **World War II**.

See also **Dunkirk, battle of**; *Abbreviation* **BEF**

British in India *See* **India**

broadsword

A heavy sword with a broad blade and cutting edge. The basket-hilted broadsword, with a hilt that covers the back of the hand, sometimes erroneously called the claymore, was favoured by several Scottish **regiments** in the early 18th century. Versions of this weapon have remained in ceremonial use.

Brock, Isaac (1769–1812)

Brock was born in Guernsey and educated at a school in Southampton and then by a French tutor in Rotterdam. He joined the 8th Foot (**King's Regiment (Liverpool)**), in which his brother had bought a **company**, as an **ensign** by purchase (1785). He purchased a lieutenancy (1790) and was **gazetted** as **captain** on half pay. He changed to the 49th Foot (**Princess Charlotte of Wales's Regiment**) (1791) and served in Jamaica and Barbados. Brock returned home (1793) on sick leave. By 1797 he had purchased a lieutenant-colonelcy. His **regiment** returned home and served with Sir John **Moore** in Holland (1799) and with the fleet at Copenhagen (1801). Brock went to Canada with his regiment (1802) where he single-handedly suppressed a dangerous conspiracy at Fort George. He returned home on leave (1805) but returned to his regiment (1806). He was commander in Quebec and then took command of the troops in Upper Canada (1810) where he conducted a successful campaign against the American General Hull (1812). He was promoted to **major-general** and created **KCB**. Brock was killed while leading his regiment and the York Volunteers against the Americans at **Queenston Heights**.

brodrick

A stiff peakless cap introduced for other ranks in 1902. It had a semi-circular piece of cloth in the front in the facing colour. It became obsolete for infantry in 1905, but was retained by the Royal Marine Light Infantry throughout World War I. The Foot Guards had their own pattern introduced in 1900.

[After Sir John *Brodrick* who was Secretary of State for War (1900–03)]

Bronkhorst Spruit, battle of

(1880; *Boer Wars*) This was the opening engagement of the First Boer War (20 December) when a British column of 259 men, commanded by Colonel Anstruther, was ambushed by 150 Boers commanded by **Joubert**. The British lost 155 killed or wounded and the Boers lost two killed and five wounded.

Brooke, Alan Francis (1883–1963)

Born at Bagnres de Bigorre, France, Brooke was educated abroad and then attended the **Royal Military Academy** at Woolwich (1900–02). He was commissioned in the **Royal Field Artillery** and served in Ireland (1902–06). He moved to India and transferred to the **Royal Horse Artillery** (1909). At the start of **World War I** he served in France in command of an ammunition column. In the later years of the war he held a succession of increasingly senior posts on **division** and **corps** artillery staffs. Between the two world wars he held a further succession of staff appointments including Commandant of the School of Artillery (1929–32) and Inspector of Artillery (1935–36). He commanded the 8th Infantry Brigade (1934–35) and was Director of Military Training at the **War Office** (1937–37). He was then appointed to command the Anti-Aircraft and Southern Commands. At the outbreak of **World War II** he assumed command of the II Army Corps and was largely responsible for the successful evacuation of the **British Expeditionary Force** from Dunquerque (**Dunkirk**). He was appointed Commander-in-Chief, Home Forces (1940) in anticipation of a German invasion. In December 1941 he was appointed Chief of the Imperial **General Staff**. For the remainder of the war his brilliant military, administrative and diplomatic skills were displayed in the development of a more professional army, in negotiations with the Americans and the Soviets and, by no means the least important, in restraining some of the wilder strategies advocated by Prime Minister Churchill. He was one of the Allies' greatest strategic planners and was made a baron (1945) and created Viscount Alanbrooke of Brookeborough (1946). He received 13 foreign honours, more than any other military commander.

Also known as **Viscount Alanbrooke**

Brooklyn, battle of

(1776; *American War of Independence*) A British force of 30,000 commanded by Sir William **Howe** completely defeated an American force of 11,000 commanded by General Putman (27 August)

Brown Bess

A nickname for the standard British **flintlock musket** of the mid 18th and early 19th centuries. The term covered various slightly differing designs, with different official names; all were ¾ inch calibre, could be fired roughly three times in a minute and were only truly accurate at perhaps 50 yards or less.

See also **percussion cap**

[Possibly from German *Buchse* 'gun', with 'brown' from the colour of the rustproof finish given to the barrel]

Brudenell, James Thomas *See* Cardigan, 7th Earl of

Brunanburh, battle of (937)

The battle against the Scots and their allies that established Athelstan, the king of Wessex and Mercia, as king of nearly all of what is now England

Brunswick percussion rifle *See* rifle

Brunswick Star

A badge embroidered on the front of the caps of grenadiers in the Foot Guards during the 18th century. It consisted of the combined crosses of St George and St Andrew mounted within the Garter and surrounded by a four-pointed radiating star. The reason for the name is not clear.

bucket

A leather case attached to the harness of a horse as a holster for a **rifle** or **carbine**

[From Anglo-Norman *buket*]

Buckinghamshire Regiment *See* West Yorkshire Regiment

Buck's Volunteers *See* King's Light Infantry

Buenos Aires, battle of

(1806; *French Wars*) British forces under Colonel William Carr **Beresford** landed, some 1,500 strong, on the coast of Argentina (27 June) with a view to taking Buenos Aires, then held by the Spanish. They were defeated and forced to surrender to an Argentinian force led by the French naval officer Santiago de Liniers. A second attempt was made by a force of 10,000 men from Montevideo (held by the British) led by General John **Whitelocke** but they were also forced to retreat.

buff

1. Strong leather made from buffalo or ox hide with a soft surface that does not chafe the wearer. It was used to make the coat worn under the **cuirass** during the 17th century. The leather was also used to make sword belts and musket straps, or any other belt that had to bear a heavy weight.

2. A pale colour. Buff leather was frequently whitened so that buff **facings** such as those of the 13th Light Dragoons (**Hussars, 13th**) were in fact white. Buff waistcoats and breeches worn during the 18th century were pale in colour, not made of buff.

[From French *buffle* 'buffalo']

Buffs, The *See* East Kent Regiment

bugle

A long metal horn curled over to make a shorter instrument. Those carried by cavalry were circular and those used by the infantry were oval.

[Directly or via Old French from Latin *buculus*, diminutive of *bos* 'ox']

bugler

A person who plays a **bugle**. A bugler in the British Army is also a **drummer** and wears a drum on the upper arm as his insignia. The drum was not used for battle calls by

British **rifle regiments**, and their buglers wear a stringed horn as their insignia. This has also been the badge of riflemen since 1800.

Bulawayo, battle of (1893)

The chief of the Matabeles, Lobengula, had granted a safe passage to the South African Company through Matabeleland to Southern Rhodesia (now Zimbabwe), but he then led a revolt against the British, resulting in the British attack on Bulawayo, the Matabele capital (23 October). The rebels were massacred by the British machine-gun fire and Bulawayo was occupied (4 November).

Bulge, Battle of the *See* **Ardennes, battle of 2**

Buller, Redvers Henry (1839–1908)

Buller was born in Devon, educated at Eton and was commissioned as an **ensign** in the 60th Foot (**King's Royal Rifle Corps**) (1858). He was promoted to **lieutenant** (1862) and joined the 4th Battalion in Quebec. By 1870 he had been promoted to **captain** and took part in the Red river expedition. Buller entered the **Staff College** (1871) and then went to **Ashanti** (now in Ghana) with Sir Garnet **Wolseley** where he distinguished himself and was promoted to **brevet major** and **CB** (1874). He served on the headquarters staff (1874–78) and then in South Africa. He was made brevet **lieutenant-colonel** (1878). Buller took part in the Kaffir Wars and the **Zulu War**, when he was present at the battle of **Ulundi**. He returned home (1879) and was **aide-de-camp** to the Queen, promoted to **colonel** and created **CMG**. He was appointed to the staff in Scotland but by 1881 was back in South Africa as chief of staff to Sir Evelyn **Wood**. He returned home at the end of the year. In 1882 he was chief of intelligence to Wolseley in Egypt. Buller then commanded the 1st Infantry Brigade (1884) and took part in the battles of **El Teb** and Tamai. He was promoted to **major-general** (1884) and was chief of staff at the relief of **Khartoum** (1885) where his skilled retreat averted a disaster. He was made **KCB** and returned to England as a civilian to restore law and order in Kerry, Ireland. His success was instrumental in his being made under secretary for Ireland. His sympathies were with the Irish people so he returned to military duties as Quartermaster-General (1887–90), commander at Aldershot (1888–89) and Adjutant-General (1890–97). During this time he declined the post of Commander-in-Chief, India, was made **GCB** (1894) and promoted to **general** (1896). While at the **War Office** (1887–97) Buller showed that he was an excellent administrator when preparing the Army for the **Boer War**. In October 1899 Buller took command in South Africa but was not successful, his forces being defeated in several battles in 'Black Week' (December 1899). He returned home (1900) and resumed command at Aldershot. His appointment was criticised in the press as the new policy was to appoint those who would command the troops in war to command them in peacetime. Buller was aggrieved and made an indiscreet speech at a public lunch in London. He was removed from his command and not employed again. Buller died at Crediton, Devon, where he was buried with full military honours.
See also **Colenso, battle of**

bullet

A metal projectile fired from a **pistol**, **rifle** or **machine gun**. Originally bullets were spherical and made of lead and were rammed down the barrel of a muzzle-loading **musket** to be fired by a separate charge of **black powder**. The development of rifling of small arms gave the bullet a spin during firing which added to its accuracy and range, but also meant that an elongated pointed bullet was aerodynamically superior to the round ball. Such bullets began being developed about 1825 but as they had to fit tightly into the barrel, they were difficult to load into a muzzle-loading gun. The problem was overcome by Claude-Etienne Minié who developed (1849) a soft lead bullet which fitted easily into the rifle barrel but which had a cavity in the base in which was placed a conical plug. When the shot was fired the discharge forced the plug forward thus expanding the bullet to fit tightly into the rifling. By the 1860s the **percussion cap** was in general military use. By the end of the century **nitrocellulose** had replaced black

powder as the propellant and the way was open for the development of the modern bullet. This consists of a cartridge case containing the propellant with the bullet fixed in the front end and the percussion cap at the other. When the percussion cap is struck by the firing pin of the gun it detonates, firing the propellant. The rapid expansion of gases forces the bullet at a high velocity down the barrel of the gun.
[From French *boulet* 'small ball']

bulletproof vest
A sleeveless garment reaching to the waist. It is made of fabric and filled with various bullet-resistant materials.
Also called **flak jacket**

Bunker Hill, battle of
(1775; *American War of Independence*) The American **colonel** William Prescott attempted to fortify Bunker Hill which overlooked the British-held town of Boston. The British general Thomas **Gage** sent a force of 2,300 troops under Major-General William **Howe** to displace the Americans. The British advance was repelled twice, but the third attempt was successful at the cost of 1,000 British and 450 American casualties. The British troops were so depleted that they were unable to attack the Dorchester Heights which also overlooked Boston, allowing General George **Washington** to occupy them (March 1776), thus forcing the British to evacuate Boston. This was the first significant American victory of the war.

Burgoyne, John (1722–92)
Educated at Westminster School, Burgoyne joined the Army in 1740. He eloped (1743) with the daughter of the Earl of Derby and lived in France (1747–56). He served in the **Seven Years' War** and was captured at Valencia de Alcántara (1762). He sat as a Tory MP and then went to America (1774) and fought at **Bunker Hill** (1775). He then led an expedition from Canada (1777) and took **Ticonderoga**, but later surrendered to General **Gates** at **Saratoga**. He crossed the House and became a Whig and was **commander-in-chief** in Ireland (1782–83). Burgoyne was also a playwright of some reputation producing 'The Maid of the Oaks' (1775) and 'The Heiress' (1786).
See also **Bennington, battle of**

Burlington Heights, battle of
(1813; *War of 1812*) A British force of 1,000, commanded by Colonel Proctor, was attacking the Americans holding Burlington Heights. They were attacked by another American force under General Clay. The Americans initially broke Proctor's line, but he rallied his force which routed Clay with the loss of 1,000 men.

Burma campaigns
1. (1824–85) Three campaigns from India through which the British gained control of Burma (now Myanmar). They were led by General Sir Archibald **Campbell** (1824–26); General Sir Henry **Godwin** (1852–53) and General Harry **Prendergast** (1885).
See also **Kamarut, battle of**; **Kemendine, battle of**; **Kokein, battle of**; **Godwin, Henry Thomas**; **Prendergast, Harry North Dalrymple**
2. (1942; *World War II*) The Japanese seized Thailand (December 1941) enabling them to threaten Burma (now Myanmar) from the east. General Tomoyuki Yamashita took Singapore and the Japanese 15th Army attacked Burma (16 January). By 20 February the 17th Indian Division had been forced back to the Sittang river, so that Rangoon was threatened. Further north the 1st Burma Division moved to Toungoo to defend the northbound route to Mandalay. General Sir Harold **Alexander** took over the defence of Burma from General T.J. Hutton (5 March). Rangoon was evacuated (9 March) and upper Burma was threatened. The Japanese continued their advance into upper Burma where the US General Joseph Stilwell commanded the 5th and 6th Chinese armies. By 31 March Toungoo had fallen and by 28 April Lashio, the southern terminus of the Burma Road, was lost, cutting the last overland route to China. Mandalay fell on 1 May; some 8,600 wounded were evacuated to India by air while the remainder of the

Allied forces struggled back overland some 250 miles to cross the Assam border by 17 May.

3. (1943–45; *World War II*) It was necessary to open the overland supply route to China, so the Allies launched an offensive against the Japanese in Burma (December 1943). The US General Stilwell led his two Chinese divisions towards Myitkyina followed by US engineers under the command of General Lewis Pick who constructed the Ledo (later Stilwell) Road to join the Burma Road over 300 miles away. The British XV Corps attacked along the coast towards Akyab, while the Chindits, under the British General Orde **Wingate** carried out a guerrilla war behind the Japanese lines. The Japanese launched a major offensive against the British 14th Army, under General William **Slim**, at **Imphal**. Although isolated the British held on, helped by air supplies, preventing the Japanese approach to India. The offensive was broken and the siege relieved (22 June 1944). To the north Stilwell captured the airfield at Myitkyina (17 May) and the town itself (3 August). Stilwell was relieved of his command (19 October). The Allies under General Sir Oliver **Leese** resumed their advance. Slim moved from the west and north-west, while Daniel Sultan (who had taken over part of Stilwell's command) attacked from the north. These forces joined (16 December) and pushed on to Mandalay. The Chinese forces moved down the Burma Road and recaptured Lashio (7 March 1945), reopening the supply route. Mandalay fell to Slim's 14th Army (20 March) and Prome and Pegu fell (2 May). Rangoon was taken by an amphibious assault by the British XV Corps (3 May). Admiral Lord Louis Mountbatten was Commander-in-Chief South East Asia during the campaign.

Burma Gallantry Medal
The award was instituted (1940) to reward any member of the forces in Burma for gallantry which did not merit the **Victoria Cross**, **Military Cross**, or **Empire Gallantry Medal**. Awarded on the recommendation of the Governor of Burma, it became obsolete on Burmese independence (1948).

Burma Madras Infantry *See* **Princess Mary's Own 10th Gurkha Rifles**

busby
A fur cap originally worn by **hussars** and horse **artillery** but now worn by the **Royal Engineers** and **Royal Corps of Signals** in full dress. The term does not apply to the **bearskins** worn by the **Foot Guards**.
[After W. *Busby* of the Strand, London, who supplied the fur caps for hussars (1805)]

bush hat
A soft broad-brimmed hat usually with a dent in the top, and worn with one side of the brim turned up. It was worn during **World War II** by troops serving in hot climates.

bush shirt
A tunic-like shirt with pockets on the hips and buttoning down the front. It was worn either inside or outside the trousers by troops serving in hot climates during **World War II**.

Bussaco, battle of
(1810; *Peninsular War*) **Napoleon** was hoping to secure his hold on Spain and drive the British out of Portugal. To protect Lisbon, General Lord **Wellington** constructed a fortified line on the heights of Torres Vedras (1808–10). The French, commanded by Marshal André Masséna, forced Wellington to pull back to the heights of Bussaco, 125 miles north-east of Lisbon. Masséna, with 60,000 troops, attacked Wellington's 50,000 troops and was repelled (27 September). Wellington fell back to Torres Vedras and harried the French throughout the winter. Masséna withdrew, leaving Portugal free and giving Wellington time to organise an offensive in the following year.

buttonhole
A small sewn hole in clothing through which a button can be pushed. The various types of button used in the Army are legion, but the buttonholes themselves also developed some significance. Buttonholes in uniforms needed strengthening to avoid being cut by

the sharp buttons. The holes were strengthened with braid or lace with the braid developing in regimental patterns and colours. Later holes and buttonholes were worn in pairs.

Buxar, battle of

(1764; *British in India*) Mir Kasim, the Nawab of Bengal, led a revolt against the British (1763), seizing Patna on the Ganges. A British and local force under Major Hector **Munro** defeated the rebels (23 October) at Buxar, 77 miles west of Patna. Mir Kasim fled and British control of Bengal was restored.

Byland, battle of

(1322; *English-Scottish Wars*) After a three-year truce Robert I (the Bruce) of Scotland invaded England, and Edward II of England marched from Boroughbridge to meet him. The English were forced to retreat to Byland, near York, where they were defeated by the Scots (14 October). This defeat forced Edward finally to recognise the independence of Scotland.

Byng, Julian Hedworth George (1862–1935)

Byng was commissioned in the 10th Hussars (**Royal Hussars (Prince of Wales's Own)**) (1883) and served in the **Sudan** (1884) and South Africa (1899–1902). He commanded the IX Army Corps at **Gallipoli** (1915), the Canadian Army Corps at the capture of **Vimy Ridge** (1917) and the 3rd Army (1917–18) in the battle of **Ypres** (1917) and on the defensive against the German attacks in the spring of 1918. He commanded the first large-scale use of tanks at the battle of **Cambrai** (1917). He was appointed Governor-General of Canada (1921–26) and commissioner of the Metropolitan Police (1928–31).

See also **Amiens, battle of**

C

cadre

A skeleton military unit, but one still keeping its structure of commissioned and non-commissioned officers. Such a unit can be quickly expanded to full strength on mobilisation or to replace casualties in war. In **World War I**, e.g., a proportion of a unit's personnel would routinely be 'left out of battle' to enable the unit to be reconstituted as an effective entity in the event of heavy casualties.

[Via French, 'frame', from Italian *quadro* 'framework', from Latin *quadrum* 'square']

Caen, battle of

(1944; *World War II*) This city in **Normandy**, France, was the focus of much of the fighting that immediately followed the D-Day landings in 1944. Before the invasion began General **Montgomery**, commanding the Allied ground forces, had planned for his British and Canadian formations to capture the city in the very early stages of the campaign. This would force the Germans to deploy the bulk of their **tank** units to defend against the threat of further advances in this sector, thus enabling the Americans to break out of the Normandy beachhead further to the west. In fact Caen was not captured until 9 July, more than a month after D-Day. At the time and in later histories Montgomery was much criticised for his failure to take the city as quickly as he had originally intended, but it is also true that the fierce fighting which developed around Caen did absorb most of the German tank forces and make the American breakout easier, as Montgomery had intended.

Calais, battle of

1. (1346–47; *Hundred Years' War*) Following the battle of **Crécy** Edward III of England moved north and laid siege to Calais (4 September 1346). The garrison suffered severely and ultimately six leading citizens offered themselves as ransom for the people of the town. They were spared on the intervention of Edward's Queen Philippa. The city capitulated (4 August 1347) and remained as an English possession until 1558.

2. (1558) After the end of the Hundred Years' War, Calais had remained as an English possession even though the rest of France had been lost. When Mary I of England married Philip II of Spain, England was forced to support the Spanish Hapsburgs against the Valois kings of France. The French Army attacked Calais. Mary refused to support the garrison with men or money and it fell (6 January).

Calcutta, battle of

(1756; *Seven Years' War*) The new ruler of Bengal, Surajah Dowlah, although not wishing to become embroiled in the British-French power struggle in India, decided to reinforce his own status by attacking the British in Calcutta (now Kolkata) (16 June). The British residents fled by boat, leaving 100 men to defend Fort William. The fort surrendered (20 June). Of those captured, 146 were imprisoned in a cell 18 ft by 15 ft in size (The Black Hole of Calcutta). By morning only 23 were alive. In January 1757 Robert **Clive** re-took Calcutta.

See also **Arcot, battle of**; **Plassey, battle of**

Calicut, battle of (1790)

9,000 Mysore troops under their leader Hussein Ali occupied a strong defensive position in front of Calicut (10 December). It was attacked and carried by a British force of one European and two native **regiments** commanded by Colonel James **Hartley**. Hussein Ali was captured.

caliver
An early 'lightweight' musket that could be aimed and fired without being rested on a stand

caltrop
A metal ball with four spikes protruding from it in such a way that when the ball is on the ground one spike always faces upwards. They were thrown on the ground to prevent potential **cavalry** charges, and are now used occasionally to puncture the tyres of vehicles.
[Variant of obsolete *calcatrippe* 'thistle']

Cambrai, battle of
(1917; *World War I*) After the conclusion of the Third Battle of **Ypres**, Field Marshal **Haig** resolved to launch a new offensive in northern France using the substantial **tank** forces which had by then been assembled and which it had not been possible to deploy on the very muddy Ypres terrain. The 3rd Army commanded by Sir Julian **Byng** attacked the Germans at Cambrai (20 November). Instead of the usual artillery bombardment the attack was spearheaded by 324 tanks – the first time that massed tanks had been used in any battle. The advance stalled by nightfall along the St. Quentin canal, due in part to the mechanical failure of many of the tanks. The German General Erich **Ludendorff** ordered a counter-attack (30 November), which was successful, and by the end of the battle all the early British gains had been lost. The British incurred 37,000 casualties and the Germans 30,000.

Cambrai-St. Quentin, battle of
(1918; *World War I*) This was part of a huge pincer movement by the Allies that led to the final defeat of the German Army and the end of the war. An American-French force began an attack from the south, and the following day a force under Field Marshal **Haig** began an offensive from the west and north. The British 1st Army commanded by Sir Henry **Horne**, the 3rd Army commanded by Sir Julian **Byng**, the 4th Army commanded by Sir Henry **Rawlinson** and the French 1st Army commanded by General Marie Debeney attacked the northern sector (1st and 3rd Armies) on 27 September and the western sector (4th and French 1st) on 29 September. The line of the St. Quentin canal fell under heavy artillery and tank attack and the town of Cambrai was captured on 1 October. The **Hindenburg Line** collapsed and the Germans fell back to the Selle river.

Cambridge, 1st Duke of (Adolphus Frederick) (1774–1850)
The seventh son of George III. He served in the Hanoverian army and with the British army in the Low Countries, where he was severely wounded. He was a privy councillor (1802) and was made a **field marshal** (1813).

Cambridgeshire (1st) Regiment of Foot
The **regiment** was raised (1689) by Viscount Castleton as Lord Castleton's Regiment of Foot. By 1698 it was Colonel Saunderson's Regiment of Foot, in which year it was disbanded. It was re-raised (1702) as Colonel Saunderson's Regiment of Marines. The name changed with its **colonel** until it became General Willis's Regiment of Foot (1714). Again the name was changed with the colonel until 1751 when it became the 30th Regiment of Foot. In 1782 the regiment was called the 30th (1st Cambridgeshire) Regiment of Foot. In the reorganisation of 1881 it amalgamated with the 59th to become the **East Lancashire Regiment**.

Camden, battle of
(1780; *American War of Independence*) After the fall of Charleston to the British (May), the American commander General Horatio **Gates** attacked the British at Camden (16 August). The American force of 3,400 was surprised north of Camden by a British force of 2,200 commanded by Lord **Cornwallis**. The Americans suffered

some 2,000 casualties and the British 324. This defeat ruined Gates's career and opened the way for a British invasion of North Carolina. Subsequent attacks and guerrilla harassment forced the British to destroy and evacuate Camden (May 1781).

Cameron, Alan (1753–1828)

Cameron was born at Erracht, Inverness-shire, and gained a local reputation as an athlete. He volunteered for service in the **American War of Independence** and was taken prisoner. He broke his ankle when trying to escape and was released (1784). He returned to Erracht. In 1793 he was issued letters of service to raise a corps of Highlanders, which he did with ease – the 79th or Cameronian Volunteers (**Queen's Own Cameron Highlanders**). The **regiment** served in Flanders (1795) and Cameron was **gazetted** as **lieutenant-colonel** (1796) when the regiment took part in the capture of **Martinique**. The regiment was decimated by disease and was amalgamated with the 42nd Highlanders (**Black Watch**). Cameron returned to Scotland and recruited a new 79th. This regiment took part in the expedition to the Helder, in which Cameron was wounded. The 79th also fought in the battle of **Alexandria**. In 1804 Cameron was gazetted as **colonel** of the 79th, and took possession of Copenhagen after the siege (1807). In 1808 Cameron was made **brigadier-general** in Sir John **Moore's** army and took part in Moore's campaigns in Sweden and Portugal. He played a prominent part in the battle of **Talavera** and campaigned until the battle of **Bussaco**, after which he was invalided home. He was promoted to **major-general** (1810) and **lieutenant-general** (1819). In 1815 he was awarded the KCB. He died at Fulham.

See also **Queen's Own Cameron Highlanders**

Cameron Highlanders, Queen's Own *See* **Queen's Own Cameron Highlanders**

Cameronian Regiment of Foot

The **regiment** was raised (1689) as the Earl of Angus's Regiment of Foot, but was always known as the Cameronians. The title was changed with the **colonel** up to 1751 and then it was called the 26th Regiment of Foot. This was altered (1782) to the 26th (or Cameronian) Regiment of Foot. In 1881 it was amalgamated with the 90th Light Infantry Regiment, Perthshire Volunteers, to form The Cameronians (Scottish Rifles).

Cameronians, The (Scottish Rifles)

The **regiment** was formed (1881) by the amalgamation of the 26th **Cameronian Regiment of Foot** and the 90th Light Infantry Regiment, **Perthshire Volunteers**. In 1968 it was disbanded, but continued to exist as a **Territorial Army** unit until 1997.

See also **Abyssinian campaign**

camouflage

Efforts to conceal military equipment, personnel and installations, and thereby gain some tactical advantage, have been known since the earliest days of warfare. On the other hand, military heraldry and the early military uniforms of the 17th and 18th centuries were designed in part to make troops in the field conspicuous, both to present a formidable appearance to the enemy and to make their locations and identities clear to their own commanders. As missile weapons increased in range, accuracy and destructiveness and as, notably in the 20th century, with the introduction of aircraft and other technical means, reconnaissance methods developed, concealment became more important. Less conspicuous dark green uniforms were originally introduced for specialist **rifle** units in response to experience gained fighting against irregulars during the **American War of Independence**. Such units were established on a permanent basis during the wars against Revolutionary France. The traditional **red coats** of most of the infantry **regiments** in the army were, however, last worn in action as late as the Egyptian campaign of 1882. They were replaced by less conspicuous **khaki** combat clothing, which had first seen widespread use during the **Indian Mutiny**. Since then increasingly elaborate camouflage schemes have been introduced for all military equipment and for the combat uniforms of all personnel. For example, the **Combat 95**

Clothing System, currently used in the British Army, takes the camouflage principle beyond visible light by seeking to limit infrared reflection and thermal signature.
[From French, from *camoufler* 'to disguise', from Italian *camuffare*]

Campbell, Archibald (1769–1843)

Campbell joined the 77th Foot (**East Middlesex Regiment of Foot**) (1787) and sailed for India (1788). He was promoted to **lieutenant** (1791) and was present at the first siege of **Seringapatam**. He served at the reduction of Cochin (1795) and of the Dutch factories in Ceylon (now Sri Lanka) (1796). During the second **Mysore War** he was present at the battle of Seedaseer and the fall of Seringapatam. He was promoted to **captain** of the 67th Foot (**South Hampshire Regiment of Foot**) but transferred to the 88th (Connaught Rangers) so that he could stay in India. His health broke down and he returned to England. He was promoted to **major** in the short-lived 6th Battalion of Reserves (1804) and was stationed in Guernsey. Campbell transferred to the 71st **Highland Light Infantry** (1805) and served in Scotland and Ireland (1805–08). In 1808 he joined the 1st Battalion of his **regiment** in the Peninsula and served at the battles of **Roliça** and **Vimiero** and with Sir John **Moore** at **Corunna** (now La Coruña). He was selected by **Wellington** to assist **Beresford** in reorganising the Portuguese army and was promoted to **lieutenant-colonel** (1809). Campbell fought at **Bussaco** as **colonel** and as **brigadier-general** commanding the 6th and 18th Portuguese Regiments at Arroyo dos Molinos and **Albuera**. He was present at **Vitoria**, the Pyrenees and at the **Nivelle**. He served at Bayonne until the end of the war. He was knighted and made **aide-de-camp** to the Prince Regent (1814) and created **KCB** (1815). Campbell was made a Portuguese **major-general** (1816) but gave up his Portuguese commission and returned to England (1820). He was made lieutenant-colonel of the 38th Foot (**Staffordshire (1st) Regiment of Foot**) whom he joined at the Cape and sailed for India. From here he commanded an expedition into **Burma** (now Myanmar). He landed in Rangoon (1824). At the end of the war (1826) Campbell was made **GCB** and received a pension of £1,000 from the directors of the East India Company. He served as civil commissioner in Burma (1826–29) and returned home. He was created a baronet (1831) and was lieutenant-governor of New Brunswick (1831–37). He was promoted to **lieutenant-general** (1838). He was colonel of the 95th Foot (**Derbyshire Regiment of Foot**) (1829–34), of the 77th Foot (1834–40) and of the 62nd Foot (**Wiltshire Regiment of Foot**) (1840).

Campbell, Colin (1792–1863)

Born in Glasgow, the son of a carpenter named McIver, he took the name Campbell from his uncle, Colonel John Campbell. He was **gazetted ensign** (1808) and **captain** (1813). He fought in the **Peninsular War** and was twice wounded, and then served in the USA (1814). He served a long period of garrison duty in Gibraltar and the West Indies. In 1837 he was promoted to **lieutenant-colonel** of the 98th Foot (**Princess Louise's Argyllshire Highlanders**). He was awarded the **CB** for his part in the China campaign (1842) and a **KCB** for his part in the second **Sikh War** (1848–49). At the outbreak of the **Crimean War** (1854) he was given command of the Highland Brigade and took a crucial part in the battle of the **Alma**. He was in command of the troops that formed the 'thin red line' at the battle of **Balaclava**. He was awarded the **GCB** and made Inspector-General of Infantry (1856). At the outbreak of the **Indian Mutiny** he took command of the troops in India and relieved **Lucknow** and **Cawnpore** (now Kanpur). He was created Baron Clyde (July 1858). He returned home and was promoted to **field marshal** (1859). He died at Chatham and was buried in Westminster Abbey.

Campbell, John, 4th Earl of Loudoun (1705–82)

Campbell joined the army (1727), was appointed governor of Stirling Castle (1741) and was made **aide-de-camp** to the king (1743). At the outbreak of the **Jacobite Rebellion** he raised the 54th Foot in support of the king. The 54th was disbanded (1749) and Campbell was appointed **colonel** of the 30th Foot (**Cambridgeshire (1st)**

Regiment of Foot) (1749–70); he was also colonel-in-chief of the 60th Foot (**King's Royal Rifle Corps**) (1755–57). He was appointed captain-general and governor-in-chief of Virginia and **commander-in-chief** of the British forces in America (1756). Because of his dilatory behaviour and inaction he was recalled and replaced by **Amherst**. In 1762 he was appointed second in command of the British forces in Portugal under Lord Tyrawley. He was colonel of the 3rd Foot (**East Kent Regiment**) (1770–82) and governor of Stirling and Edinburgh castles (1763–82).

camp follower
A civilian who was officially or unofficially attached to a group of soldiers, whether a **regiment** or smaller unit. Camp followers included some wives, prostitutes and various petty traders who sold goods to the troops.

canister
One of the principal types of ammunition fired by **artillery** throughout the horse and musket era. In effect, a canister round was similar to a modern shotgun cartridge, with a number of small balls held together inside a container. On firing, the container would burst and the contents would spread apart. Canister was therefore a devastating weapon against formed bodies of enemy troops, though it was only effective at short ranges of a maximum of perhaps 300 yards. Canister rounds could be fired both by **cannon** and **howitzers**, the two principal types of artillery weapon in use in the period. Canister rounds continued to be produced for artillery up to and including **World War I**.
Also called **case shot**
[From Latin *canistrum*, from Greek *kanastron* 'wicker basket']

cannon
An artillery piece. Up to the 17th century, a cannon was a specific size of gun shorter and more mobile than the **culverin**. Later the term came to refer to an artillery piece in general, and especially those guns designed to fire on a fairly flat trajectory, as distinct from **howitzers** and **mortars** which usually lobbed their projectiles toward the enemy.
[Via French *canon* from Italian *cannone* 'large tube']

cannonball
A spherical missile fired from **muzzle-loading cannon**. Originally they were made of stone but later of cast iron.
See also **artillery**

canteen
A water container, or the combination of cooking pot, plate and cutlery, carried by an individual soldier
[Via French *cantine* from Italian *cantina* 'cellar']

cap
A form of headgear without a brim, in contrast to a hat which has a brim. A cap may have a peak and can be of many shapes.
[From late Latin *cappa* 'hood, hooded cloak']

cap comforter
A khaki tubular woollen scarf which was worn pulled down over the head particularly by troops during **World War I**

Cape Town, battle of
(1806; *French Wars*) The Dutch settlement of Cape Town came under French control after the Netherlands had capitulated to France. After the renewal of the war against France, Britain sent out an expeditionary force to capture Cape Town (1805). A force of 6,000 men commanded by General Sir David **Baird** took the town from a combined Dutch-French force and it remained in British hands even after the treaty of 1815.

captain
During the 16th century each group of **infantry** was commanded by a captain. Later, a captain commanded a single infantry **company** or cavalry **troop** and the rank was

below that of a **field officer**. In the early 19th century the rank was indicated by a single **epaulette** on the right shoulder. Captains now wear three stars on both shoulders.
[Via Old French *capitain* from late Latin *capitaneus* 'chief', from Latin *caput* 'head']

carabinier, carabineer, carbinier
A soldier armed with a **carbine**, usually a **dragoon**.
See also **Royal Scots Greys**

caracole
In the 17th or early 18th century, a **cavalry** manoeuvre relying on firepower rather than a mounted charge to break an enemy formation. To perform this manoeuvre a **regiment** formed in mass lines just out of range of the enemy's guns. Each rank then rode forward in turn, discharged their pistols and then rode to the rear to re-load. In the early 18th century, more able commanders like Marlborough realised that a determined cavalry charge was more likely to be effective and the caracole tactic became obsolete.
[From French *caracoler*, from *caracol(e)* 'snail's shell, spiral']

Carbiesdale, battle of
(1650; *Civil War*) After his defeat at **Philiphaugh**, the Marquis of **Montrose** fled to France. He returned to Scotland (1650) to rally the Royalists against the Commonwealth and landed in Caithness with 1,500 men. Few Scots supported him and his troops were routed at Carbiesdale (25 April). Montrose was betrayed and captured and hanged at Edinburgh (21 May).

carbine
A short-barrelled and light **musket** or **rifle**. It was probably introduced during the 16th century and was chiefly used as a **cavalry** weapon because its reduced length made it easier to handle on horseback. By the 18th century carbines were sometimes carried by officers, artillery soldiers and other 'non-infantry' personnel. It has been replaced in modern armies first by the **submachine gun** (e.g. the **Sten gun**) and then by the automatic rifle which is now the usual personal weapon of all troops.
[From French *carabine*, from *carabin* 'mounted musketeer']

carbinier *See* **carabinier**

Cardigan, 7th Earl of (1797–1868)
Educated at Christ Church, Oxford, Brudenell entered the army (1824) and purchased promotion to become a **lieutenant-colonel** in the **15th Hussars** (1832). He quarrelled with his officers and was forced to give up his command (1834). By family influence he obtained command of the 11th Light Dragoons, renamed as the 11th Hussars (1840). He inherited his father's title and fortune (1837) and spent some £10,000 a year on making his **regiment** the smartest-dressed in the army. He fought a duel with one of his officers (Captain Harvey Tuckett) but retained his command, being promoted to **major-general** (1854). He was appointed commander of the **Light Brigade** under his brother-in-law Lord **Lucan** at the outbreak of the **Crimean War** and was its commander at the Charge of the Light Brigade. Because of the dramatic nature of this incident he became extremely popular with the British public (though his military abilities were very limited) and on his return to the UK he was made Inspector-General of Cavalry. He died from injuries sustained when falling from his horse.
Also known as **Brudenell, James Thomas**; *See also* **Balaclava, battle of**

Cardwell reforms
A series of changes introduced to the Army by Edward Cardwell, Viscount Cardwell of Ellerbeck (1813–86), while he was Secretary of State for War (1868–74) during the Gladstone administration. Previously there had been a lack of co-ordination between the Army's **Commander-in-Chief** and the **War Office**. By his **War Office Act** (1870) Cardwell brought all Army administration under the control of the Secretary of State for War with three departments: military (with the Commander-in-Chief as its head), supply and finance, all housed in the War Office. Other changes included the abolition of flogging as a military punishment during peace time (1868); the reduction of the

army enlistment term from 12 years to 6 years on the active list and 6 years in the reserves (1870) – which was designed to encourage enlistment; and the abolition of the **purchase system** for officers' **commissions** (1871). The reforms continued when Hugh Childers was Secretary of State for War: a regular programme of trooping seasons and regulation of periods of duty abroad (1881); every **regiment** to have a distinctive badge (1881); regularising the facings for the uniforms of **infantry** regiments (except the 'Royal' ones) – i.e. the English ones were white, Scottish yellow, and Irish green (1881). Previous single-battalion infantry regiments were joined to form the 1st and 2nd battalions of a new regiment, with a county title; the county's **Militia** became the 3rd Battalion of the appropriate regiment and Volunteers were given a territorial title. Brigade districts were reduced to Regimental districts. The main purpose of this was to have one battalion of a regiment serving overseas with the other at home to train recruits and provide reinforcements. Although there were numerous exceptions in practice this system was generally followed in peacetime up to the onset of **World War II**.

Carleton, Guy (1724–1808)

Carleton joined the Earl of Rothe's Regiment (later 25th Foot **King's Own Scottish Borderers**) (1742) as an **ensign** and was promoted to **lieutenant** (1745). By 1757 he was **lieutenant-colonel** in the 1st Foot (**Royal Scots**). He took part in the Battle of **Louisburg** (1758) and was made lieutenant-colonel of the 72nd Foot (**Duke of Albany's Highlanders**) and in the same year quartermaster-general and **colonel** in America. He was wounded at the capture of **Quebec** (1759). He acted as **brigadier-general** at the siege of Belleisle (1761), was raised to the rank of colonel in the army (1762), and served at the siege of **Havana** at which he was wounded. Carleton was appointed lieutenant-governor of Quebec (1766) and then acting governor. He returned to England (1772) and by May 1722 was promoted to **major-general**. Carleton then steered the Quebec Bill through parliament. This allowed Roman Catholics there the free practice of their faith. He was appointed governor of Quebec (1775) and defended the town successfully in the **American War of Independence**. Carleton quarrelled with Lord George Germaine (**Sackville**) and demanded his own recall to Britain after which he was appointed governor of Charlemont (Ireland) (1778–1808). He was recalled to America as **commander-in-chief** (1782) and did much to conciliate the Americas. He returned home (1783). He was made colonel of the 84th Foot (**York and Lancaster Regiment**) (1782–83) and was again appointed governor of Quebec (1786–96). Carleton was created Baron Dorchester (1786). He was appointed colonel of the 15th Dragoons (**King's Hussars (15th)**) (1790) and raised to the rank of **general** in the army (1793). He became colonel of the 27th Dragoons (1801) and of the 4th Dragoons (**Queen's Own Hussars**) (1802). After his return from America he lived in retirement. He died at Stubbings, near Maidenhead.

Carlisle, battle of

(1745; *Jacobite Rebellions*) Carlisle was besieged by the Jacobites (9 November) and defended by the Westmorland militia and a few regular soldiers commanded by Colonel Durand. The Jacobites opened fire (13 November) and after little resistance the garrison surrendered (14 November).

cartouche

A **cartridge**. The term also referred to the box formerly used to carry cartridges and worn on a shoulder strap by cavalry and mounted officers.

[Via French from Italian *cartoccio* 'paper cornet', from *carta* 'paper']

cartridge

The cartridge was adopted for military use during the 17th century by King Gustavus Adolphus of Sweden. It consisted of a measured amount of powder enclosed with the ball in a cloth bag. Its use ensured consistent performance of the **musket** which was also easier to load, increasing the rate of fire to one round a minute. Later the cartridge might be made of various types of waxed or greased paper and in modern times it is usually metal.

See also **rifle**

[Alteration of French *cartouche*, from Italian *cartoccio* 'paper cornet', from *carta* 'paper']

cartridge belt

A belt to hold **cartridges** either singly or in groups in separate pouches. It was usually worn over the shoulder.

cartridge box

In the 18th and 19th centuries the **cartridge** box was worn over the shoulder or on a waist band. It had a heavy flap which would keep the cartridges dry (important since the cartridges would be made of cloth or paper), but that could be easily lifted.

case shot *See* **shot**

Cassino, battle of

(1944; *World War II*) The Allied advance in Italy was brought to a standstill (17 January) when it reached the defensive **Gustav Line** which hinged on Monte Cassino in the Rapido valley, thus blocking the advance on Rome. The US 5th Army, commanded by Lieutenant-General Mark Clark, and the British 8th Army, commanded by Lieutenant-General Sir Oliver **Leese**, were opposed by the German 10th Army commanded by General Heinrich von Vietinghoff. Despite heavy bombing attacks, repeated Allied attempts to take Cassino were repulsed for several months. The Allies mounted a further major offensive (11–12 May), Cassino fell (18 May) and the advance on Rome was renewed.

Castella, battle of

(1813; *Peninsular War*) A force of 17,000 Allied troops, commanded by General Sir John Murray, defeated 15,000 French, commanded by Marshal Suchet (13 April). The Allies lost some 600 men and the French 800, although Murray claimed 3,000 French casualties.

Castillon, battle of

(1453; *Hundred Years' War*) By the end of 1451 the English had been driven out of France (except Calais), but when Aquitaine rose against French rule, Henry VI sent the Earl of Shrewsbury (John Talbot) to Bordeaux to support the uprising (1452). Shrewsbury moved up the Dordogne river to attack the French who were besieging Castillon (17 July). The English were cut down by artillery fire, and Shrewsbury was killed. This battle ended the **Hundred Years' War**.

Castlereagh's Reforms

Viscount Castlereagh (1769–1822) was Minister for War and Foreign Secretary during the **French Wars** (1792–1815). Before these wars the army relied on pressed men as regular soldiers and on volunteers and a militia for home defence. There were no means of ensuring an adequate striking force or for maintaining its strength overseas. Castlereagh offered a bounty for transferring from the militia (a volunteer force) to the regular army, thus raising 25,000 men. He then instituted a ballot system that raised 38,000 men for the militia that would be reinforcements for the regular army. He then introduced compulsory service in the militia thus raising 350,000 men for home defence. Thus at the beginning of the **Peninsular War** the British Army had 110,000 regulars abroad with 105,000 at home, 65,000 general militia and 390,000 local militia and volunteers.

cavalry

A military force mounted on horseback. They were of immense value in the formalised battles of earlier times, especially in breaking through weakened enemy lines. They also functioned efficiently as reconnaissance units, being able to keep out of range of enemy weapons and to move quickly. With the advent of rapidly firing small arms and **machine guns**, by **World War I** cavalry charges became suicidal. Horses were abandoned in favour of armoured fighting vehicles and by the 1950s there were no cavalry units in the British Army that had horses other than for ceremonial duties.

In the cavalry the **regiment** was and is both the principal administrative body and a tactical unit, roughly comparable to an **infantry battalion**. Regiments were and are subdivided into **squadrons** and then into **troops**. In the 17th and early 18th century mounted regiments were in two categories: horse and **dragoons**. Later cavalry was divided into heavy and light categories. The principal role of heavy cavalry was to deliver decisive charges in battle; light cavalry were intended more for reconnaissance and skirmishing work. In the British Army the heavy cavalry were the **Household Cavalry**, the various **dragoon guards** regiments (those formerly known as 'horse') and the dragoon regiments (who had gradually lost their original function as mounted infantry); light cavalry regiments were **light dragoons** who later became known as either **hussars** or **lancers**. The distinction between heavy and light cavalry is preserved to some extent in the modern army with the former heavy regiments tending to be equipped with main battle tanks and the hussars and lancers having lighter reconnaissance vehicles.

In part because they were in a sense the descendants of the lordly medieval knights and in part because of the greater expense of equipping and maintaining a cavalryman and his horse, the officers in cavalry units in the British and other armies tended to be drawn more exclusively from the ranks of the nobility and the very rich than officers in other types of units. This is still the case, though to a reduced extent in the present-day army. It was also alleged at times, notably in **World War I** when the British Expeditionary Force in France was commanded by Sir Douglas **Haig** (a cavalryman), that cavalry officers were unduly favoured for promotion to senior posts because of their social position rather than their military talents.

[Via French from Italian *cavalleria* 'mounted militia', from *cavallo* 'horse', from Latin *caballus*]

Cawnpore, battle of
(1857; *Indian Mutiny*) When the Indian Mutiny broke out in May 1857 at Meerut, Nana Sahib, Dandhu Panth, took command of 3,000 rebel sepoys at Cawnpore (now Kanpur). He laid siege to the city (6 June). The small garrison held out until 26 June when they were promised safe conduct away from the city by boat down the Ganges. However, the mutineers opened fire killing almost all the men; one boat escaped. The women and children were taken prisoner and massacred when a relief column commanded by General Sir Henry **Havelock** approached the city (15 July). After this massacre and after he had relieved **Lucknow**, Sir Colin **Campbell** relieved Cawnpore (6 December), routing a force of 25,000 rebels with the loss of only 99 men.

CB *See* **Order of the Bath**

CBE *See* **Order of the British Empire**

CBW *abbreviation of* **chemical and biological weapons**

Cetshwayo, Cetewayo (1826?–84)
Cetshwayo was born near Eshowe, now in South Africa. He became ruler of Zululand (1873) and vigorously opposed the British incursions into his territory. His forces defeated the British at **Isandlwana**. After his defeat at **Ulundi** he presented his case in London, where he met Queen Victoria, and part of his kingdom was restored (1883). In spite of this he was driven out by the anti-royalist faction of his own people.

CGC *See* **Conspicuous Gallantry Cross**

CGM *abbreviation of* **Conspicuous Gallantry Medal**

chaco, chako, chakot *another spelling of* **shako**

chain shot *See* **shot**

Chalgrove Field, battle of
(1643; *Civil War*) A minor skirmish outside Oxford at which the Royalist **cavalry** under Prince **Rupert** routed the Parliamentarian cavalry. Its importance lies in the fact that John Hampden, a prominent Parliamentarian leader, was mortally wounded and

that this rebuff led Robert Devereux, 3rd Earl of Essex, the Parliamentarian commander, to abandon plans to besiege Oxford, the king's headquarters.

Challenger
Two generations of **tank** that have been the main battle tank of the British Army since the 1980s. The **Challenger 1**, introduced in 1983, had a crew of four, a 120mm main gun and a maximum speed of 37 mph. Its most noticeable feature was its early use of **Chobham armour**. Despite various technical problems it was used in the **Gulf War** (1991). These problems were addressed in the **Challenger 2**, which was introduced in 1998 with a similar, though updated, specification. It has seen service in **Kosovo** and in the **Iraq War** (2003).

Chanda, battle of
(1818; *Maratha Wars*) Chanda, the chief stronghold of the Rajah of Nagpur, was besieged by a British force commanded by Colonel Adams (9 May). The fort was taken after a two-day bombardment during which 500 of the 3,000 defenders were killed.

chaplain-general *See* **reforms of the Duke of York**

charge
1. An attack at the gallop by a force of **cavalry** against enemy troops that uses the shock of impact to disrupt, and hopefully break, the enemy formation. A cavalry charge had to be made at the correct moment to be effective, usually when the target had already been weakened. If it failed, the cavalry could not easily regroup and were themselves vulnerable.
2. A propellant such as **gunpowder** for a shot, **cannonball** or in a **shell** or **cartridge**

Charleston, battle of
(1780; *American War of Independence*) The British Lieutenant-General Sir Henry **Clinton** with 10,000 men laid siege to Charleston (13 April). After a heavy bombardment the American commander Major-General Benjamin Lincoln surrendered. Clinton returned to New York, leaving **Cornwallis** with 8,000 men to pacify Georgia.

Chelsea Hospital *See* **pay in the 17th and 18th centuries**

Chelsea pensioners
550 old or disabled soldiers who have no families or homes. They live in the Royal Hospital at Chelsea which was founded by Charles II and designed by Sir Christopher Wren (1692).

chemical and biological weapons
Lethal chemicals and microorganisms used as weapons of war.
Abbreviation **CBW**

chemical warfare
The use of lethal chemicals as weapons of war. The chemicals used are commonly organophosphate nerve agents first produced by Germany during **World War II**, although not used at that time. The more volatile of these, such as sarin, function as quick-acting respiratory poisons, while the less volatile, such as VX, act as contact poisons. They are all liquids. These agents can be loaded into bombs or **artillery** shells, or sprayed from vehicles. The effectiveness of these weapons depends largely on atmospheric conditions, and while unprotected troops are very vulnerable, protected troops are less vulnerable to chemical warfare than they would be to conventional artillery or air attack.
See also **gas**

Cheriton, battle of
(1644; *Civil War*) The Royalist forces, commanded by General Lord Ralph Hopton, were defeated at Cheriton (29 May) by the Parliamentarians commanded by General Sir William Waller. Hopton withdrew to Cornwall while Waller moved on Oxford.

Chernaya river, battle of

(1855; *Crimean War*) The Sardinians, commanded by Marchese di la Marmora, had joined the Allies east of Sebastopol (now Sevastopol). During August, the Russians, commanded by Prince Mikhail Gorchakov, led a sortie of three divisions out of Sebastopol. This was repulsed by the combined Sardinian, British and French force and was the last attempt made by the Russians to break out of Sebastopol.

Cheshire Regiment

The **regiment** was raised (1689) as the Duke of Norfolk's Regiment of Foot. The name changed with its **colonels** until 1751 when it was designated the 22nd (or the Cheshire) Regiment of Foot, and in 1881, the Cheshire Regiment, and it still exists under this name. The regiment won its oak-leaf and acorn badge at the battle of **Dettingen** when a detachment of the 22nd Foot defended George II, who was standing under an oak tree, against an attack by French cavalry. The king instructed that the regiment should wear oak-leaves as a memento. This they do on the anniversary of the occasion. The regiment was also the main force at the battle of **Meanee**. In 2007 it is due to unite with The Worcestershire and Sherwood Foresters Regiment, and The Staffordshire Regiment, to form The Mercian Regiment.

Chesterfield, battle of

(1266; *Barons' Wars*) The rebel barons' forces led by the Earl of Derby were defeated by Royalist troops commanded by Henry of Almaine (15 May). Derby was captured. This was the last major encounter of the Second Barons' War.

chevron

A 'V' with the points upwards or downwards. In the British Army, chevron badges were first introduced to mark a **non-commissioned officer** (NCO) with long service. In 1803 they were introduced as a badge of rank for NCOs. A **sergeant-major general** and quartermaster-sergeant wore four, a **sergeant** three and a **corporal** two. Some **regiments** wore them with the points upwards, but in 1803 it was decreed that the points should be worn downwards. Originally chevrons were worn on the upper arm, but after 1869 the sergeant-major's chevrons were worn on the lower sleeve with the points upwards. These have been replaced by a crown in the same position. Chevrons are also called **stripes** but they should not be confused with long service stripes which are worn on the left forearm, as were similar wound stripes during wartime.
[From French, 'rafter, chevron']

chief-of-staff

The senior officer of each of the armed forces, e.g. Army Chief-of-Staff

Childers' Reforms *See* **Cardwell reforms**

Chilianwala, battle of

(1849; *Sikh Wars*) The Anglo-Indian army commanded by General Sir Hugh **Gough** failed in its assault on the Sikhs at **Ramnagar** so it moved up the Chenab river and subsequently met a Sikh army of 40,000 at Chilianwala (14 January). Although Gough drove back the Sikhs, his casualties were so great as to preclude his pursuing them. During the encounter the 24th Foot (**South Wales Borderers**), a single battalion regiment, was nearly exterminated.

Chindits *See* **Wingate, Orde Charles**

Chippewa river, battle of

(1814; *War of 1812*) The first battle of the 1812 war in which British troops fought against American regulars. 3,500 Americans commanded by General Jacob Brown crossed the Niagara and took Fort Erie (3 July). The British under General Phineas Raill, who was serving under General Gordon **Drummond**, fell back to the Chippewa river. Brown ordered an attack by a **brigade** commanded by General Winfield Scott (5 July) which broke the British lines.

Chizai, battle of
(1372; *Hundred Years' War*) The French, commanded by Bertrand du Guesclin, laid siege to Chizai. They were engaged by the English, commanded by Thomas Hampton. The English were defeated and the French captured the town, enabling them to gain Saintonge and Poitou.

Chobham armour
A type of armour plating developed at the Fighting Vehicles Research and Development Establishment (near Chobham Common, Surrey) in the 1960s. Composed of layers of metal plates and ceramic blocks arranged in a specific matrix, it offers very good protection against high-explosive anti-tank ammunition. It is used in the British **Challenger** tank.

choking agent *See* gas

cholera belt
A flannel belt worn by troops serving in China and the Far East during the later 19th and early 20th century. It was worn under the outer garments in the belief that it would help prevent cholera.

Cholmondeley's (Colonel Cholmondeley's Regiment of Foot) *See* **Northamptonshire Regiment of Foot**

Chrysler's Farm, battle of
(1813; *War of 1812*) The American General James Wilkinson moved 8,000 troops down the St. Lawrence river as part of an attack on Montreal. The flotilla stopped at Chrysler's Farm (10 November) and Wilkinson sent General John Boyd with 2,000 men to guard his rear. They were defeated by a British force of 800 commanded by Colonel J.W. Morrison. This contributed to Wilkinson's decision to go into winter quarters and encouraged the British to take the initiative, completely thwarting the Americans in New York State.

Churchill, John *See* **Marlborough, 1st Duke of**

CIE *See* **Order of the Indian Empire**

C-in-C *abbreviation of* **commander-in-chief**

Ciudad Rodrigo
(1812; *Peninsular War*) Ciudad Rodrigo was a Spanish fortress near the border with Portugal which played an important role in various campaigns of the war. It was captured by the French in 1810. In 1812 **Wellington's** northern route to Madrid was barred by the strongly held fortress. Having marched through winter conditions, Wellington invested the fortress (8 January) and made a final assault (19 January). The fortress was captured with the loss of 1,300 men.

Civil War (1642–51)
The friction between Charles I and his parliament was a power struggle. Charles held that the king ruled by 'divine right' to which Parliament was subject, and called on Parliament only when he needed to raise taxes. Parliament demanded a more democratic form of government. This led to open war (1642), with the Anglican bishops and church supporting Charles and the Presbyterians supporting Parliament. Initially Charles was strong in the north and west with Parliament being supported in the south east, including London. After the battle of **Naseby** (1645) Charles surrendered and was imprisoned on the Isle of Wight. He escaped and made an alliance with the Scots. **Cromwell** put down the Scottish resistance and Charles was executed (1649). Further opposition in Scotland and Ireland was crushed. The monarchy was abolished and a republic (the Commonwealth) established (1651). Cromwell died (1658) and the monarchy (Charles II) was restored in 1660.

See also **Aberdeen, battle of; Adwalton Moor, battle of; Alford, battle of; Alresford, battle of; Auldearn, battle of; Braddock Down, battle of; Brentford, battle of; Carbiesdale, battle of; Chalgrove Field, battle of; Cheriton, battle of; Cropredy**

Bridge, battle of; Drogheda, battle of; Dunbar, battle of; Edgehill, battle of; Grantham, battle of; Inverlochy, battle of; Kilsyth, battle of; Langport, battle of; Lansdowne, battle of; Lostwithiel, battle of; Marston Moor, battle of; Naseby, battle of; Newbury, battle of; Philiphaugh, battle of; Preston, battle of; Roundway Down, battle of; Stow-on-the-Wold, battle of; Tippermuir, battle of; Wexford, battle of; Worcester, battle of; Baillie, William; Cromwell, Oliver; Fairfax, Thomas; Monck, George; Newcastle, Earl of; Rupert, Prince; Bishops' Wars; New Model Army

Clifton's (Colonel Sir William Clifton's Regiment of Foot) *See* West Yorkshire Regiment

Clinton, Henry (1738?–95)

Clinton's father was governor of Newfoundland and then of New York. Clinton joined the New York **Militia**, and when his father went to England was **gazetted** as **lieutenant** in the **Coldstream Guards** (1751). He joined the 1st Foot Guards (**Grenadier Guards**) as **captain** and then was promoted to **lieutenant-colonel** (1760). He was appointed **aide-de-camp** to the Prince of Brunswick and promoted to **colonel** (1760). Clinton was appointed colonel of the 12th Foot (**Suffolk Regiment**) (1766) and made **major-general** (1772). In the same year he was elected MP for Boroughbridge and then MP for Newark (1774–84). He returned to America and distinguished himself at **Bunker Hill** when he was promoted to local **lieutenant-general** (1775) and to local **general** (1776). Clinton played a major part in the capture of New York (1776) and was promoted to lieutenant-general and made KB (1776). In 1778 Clinton became **commander-in-chief** of the forces in North America. He had differences with **Cornwallis** and after the fall of **Yorktown** resigned in favour of **Carleton** and returned home (1787). He was elected MP for Launceston (1790) and appointed governor of Limerick. He was appointed colonel-in-chief of the 84th Foot (**York and Lancaster Regiment**) (1778) and colonel of the 7th Light Dragoons (**Queen's Own Hussars (7th)**) (1779). He was promoted to general (1793) and made governor of Gibraltar (1794), where he died.

Clive, Robert (1725–74)

Born near Market Drayton, Shropshire, Clive was brought up by an uncle at Eccles, and joined the East India Company in Madras (now Chennai) (1743). He was captured by the French when they took the city (1746) but escaped. He was commander at the battle of **Arcot**, and returned to England in triumph. He returned to India (1755) as governor of Fort St. David. He took **Calcutta** (now Kolkata) after the incident of the Black Hole of Calcutta, captured the French settlement at Chandernagore, and finally defeated the Nawab of Bengal, Suraj Dowlah, at **Plassey**. Consequently he was sole ruler of Bengal on behalf of the East India Company (1757–60). He returned to England (1760) and was elected MP for Shrewsbury (1761). In 1761 he was elevated to the Irish Peerage. The affairs of the East India Company fell into disarray and Clive was sent back to India (1764) as governor and **commander-in-chief** of Bengal. He restored the company and enforced military discipline in the troops, returning home (1767) to face parliamentary censure of his handing of the Company's affairs. He was vindicated (1773) but committed suicide.

clothing

The garments worn by the common soldier, in contrast to the garments worn by officers known as **dress**. The earliest known comprehensive official designations of military uniforms were made in the clothing book of 1742 which described the uniforms of each **regiment**. The Clothing Warrant of 1751 dictated that the personal arms of the regimental **colonel** were no longer to appear on regimental badges etc. or **colours**. They were to be replaced by the royal cypher, the white horse of Hanover or the Garter Star with the regimental number. The colonel was responsible for buying uniforms for his regiment from money provided by the government and charged against the individual soldier's pay. An unscrupulous colonel could try to make a profit from the process;

there were many middle-men involved in supplying the army and corruption was rife; funds for clothing were never generous. The result was that the quality and condition of what the men had to wear was often poor, though a good colonel often spent large sums of his own in outfitting his men.

cluster bomb

A single bomb that is opened by a timing device or on impact to scatter several smaller bombs (**bomblets**) from inside it

CMG *See* **Order of St Michael and St George**

coalition

A union of two or more countries with a common purpose, which may involve the use of their combined forces. The USA and the UK formed a Coalition to fight in Iraq (2003) and Coalition forces remained in Iraq afterwards to restore infrastructure and help establish a new government.

See also **alliance**; **Iraq War**

[From medieval Latin *coalition-*, from Latin *coalit-*, past participle of *coalescere* 'to grow together']

coat

The outer garment of the soldier during the 17th century, replacing the shorter doublet of an earlier period. It was worn over a waistcoat and was not particularly substantial in warmth or wear. The **facings** were usually of a different colour that was revealed when the cuffs were turned up, the collars turned down or the lapels turned back. Different **regiments** had different colours for their facings. During the late 18th century, the coat was replaced by the **coatee**, which in turn was replaced by the **tunic** in 1855.

[From Old French *cote*]

coatee

A coat that is closed at the front and cut across the waist, leaving the tails as ornamental skirts behind. Coatees were worn in the late 18th century and early 19th century, and were replaced by the **tunic** in 1855.

Cobbe, Alexander Stanhope (1870–1931)

Cobbe was born in India and educated at Wellington and Sandhurst. He received a **commission** in the **South Wales Borderers** (1889) and was promoted to **lieutenant** (1892). He transferred to the India Staff Crops (1894) and was attached to the 32nd Sikh Pioneers. He served at Chitral (1895), in Nyasaland (now Malawi) (1899–1900) and with the Central African Regiment in Ashanti (1900) where he was wounded. He was promoted to **captain** (1900) and served in Somaliland (1902) where he was awarded the **Victoria Cross**. Cobbe held various staff appointments (1902–14), was **aide-de-camp** to the king and promoted to **brevet colonel** (1911). He was general staff officer of the Lahore Division in France (1914) and transferred to the Indian Corps (1915). Cobbe was promoted to **brigadier-general** and returned to India (1916) as director of training. In June 1916 he took command of the Meerut 7th Indian Division in Mesopotamia and was promoted to **major-general** (August 1916) in command of the III Indian Corps (December 1916–February 1917). He was promoted to **lieutenant-general** (1919). Cobbe was Military Secretary at the India Office (1919–20, 1921–22) and in 1922 was made colonel of the South Wales Borderers. He was promoted to **general** (1924), made aide-de-camp general to the king and appointed **GCB** (1928). From 1926–30 Cobbe was Commander-in-Chief Northern Command in India.

See also **Sharqat, battle of**

cockade

Originally a bunch of ribbons, later developing into an elaborate pleated decoration. Cockades were worn as a sign of national identity by troops during the 18th century. British troops wore black cockades. The **Black Watch** wore red for some time. Later they were used as rank badges; **field officers** wore pink or red, **captains** yellow and subalterns green.

[From French *bonnet à la coquarde* 'bonnet worn proudly', from obsolete *coquard* 'proud', from *coq* 'cock']

cocked hat

A hat with the brim turned up on both sides, developing from the original 17th century broad-brimmed military hat during the reign of William and Mary. When the third side was turned up it became a three-cornered cocked hat or **tricorn**. Later, the front cock was pushed up so high that it left only two corners at the sides, and the tricorn became the **bicorn**. This then developed into a flattened hat that could be carried under the arm. **Quartermasters** of the **Foot Guards** still wear cocked hats in full dress, as do officers of the **Chelsea pensioners**. The Pensioners themselves still wear tricorns.

coehorn, cohorn

A light **mortar** invented by Baron van Menno Coehorn, a Dutch engineer (1641–1704), and in service for many years afterwards

Colchester *See* **reforms after the Crimean War**

Coldstream Guards

The **regiment** was raised (1650) by Colonel George **Monck** at Newcastle by the amalgamation of five companies of Fenwick's Regiment and five companies of Hesilbridge's Regiment, and was called Colonel Monck's Regiment of Foot. When Monck was created Duke of Albemarle, the regiment was re-named the Duke of Albemarle's Regiment of Foot (1660) and then the Duke of Albemarle's Regiment of Foot Guards (1661). When Albemarle died (1670) the regiment was re-named the Coldstream Regiment of Foot Guards. This was in recognition of the march they made from Coldstream to London to ensure the restoration of Charles II. The name was changed to 2nd Foot Guards in 1782 and to the Coldstream Guards in 1855. It is the only regiment in the army that can trace a linear descent from the Commonwealth Army of the 17th century. It remains the second-ranking regiment of **Foot Guards**.

Colenso, battle of

(1899; *Boer Wars*) The Boers, commanded by General Louis **Botha**, held Colenso on the Tugela river. They were attacked by a British force commanded by General Sir Redvers **Buller** (15 December). The Boers held the position, inflicting over 1,000 casualties on the British, who withdrew. Many of the casualties were among the 14th and 66th Field Batteries that were ordered to advance against the entrenched Boers over open country. When they had run out of ammunition they were ordered to take cover and abandon their guns. Seven **Victoria Crosses** were won in later attempts to retrieve the guns in broad daylight. In fact, all but two of the guns were lost to the Boers. This was the third British defeat within a week and led to Buller being replaced by General Lord **Roberts**.

colonel

1. King Ferdinand of Spain introduced (1505) the colunela of 1,000–1,500 men organised as five **companies**, as a tactical formation. It was commanded by a 'cabo de colunela' or colonel. The colunela was the precursor of the modern **battalion** and **regiment**.

In the 16th and 17th centuries, the colonel of a regiment was not only its commander in action but also the person who had raised it for service and who was responsible for equipping and paying it and selecting its officers, among other functions. With the development of the **standing army** from the later 17th century, this role changed. By the mid-18th century, colonels were not expected to command their regiments in battle; this was a lieutenant-colonel's job. Colonelcies became honorary appointments, given e.g. to distinguished generals or members of the royal family. By the time of the **French Wars** (1792–1815) an individual could only hold one colonelcy. Colonels were paid, however, until the mid-19th century and could hope to make a profit out of the money the government gave them to clothe and equip their men; many, however, spent large sums of their own money on their regiments. For much of the period generals were paid only according to their half-pay for their own regimental rank, so a colonel's pay was a means of paying a general more than he would otherwise receive. Just as various reforms in the 19th century removed the colonel's financial role in the affairs of his regiment, so too were his responsibilities for selecting officers and similar matters taken away. The term 'colonel' is still used for a regiment's ceremonial head, usually a retired senior officer; and a regiment's **colonel-in-chief** is its patron, usually a member of the royal family.

2. An army rank, the most senior of the **field officer** grades, ranking immediately below the most junior **general officer**. Traditionally, a colonel was the commander of a regiment. When rank badges were introduced in 1810, colonels wore a crown and star on each **epaulette**. After the **Crimean War** the rank badge was transferred to the collar, and since 1881 they have been worn on the shoulder straps. A full colonel wears a crown and two pips while a **lieutenant-colonel** wears a crown and one pip.

[From obsolete French *coronel* (now *colonel*) from Italian *colonnello* from *colonna* 'column'; compare Spanish *colunela* 'column']

colonel-commandant *See* brigadier

colonel-in-chief *See* colonel

colours

A banner or flag formerly used in military operations to indicate the position of the commander and to form a rallying point for the troops during battle. In the British Army these flags or colours came to represent the **regiment** itself and would be carried by **ensigns** and guarded by selected **non-commissioned officers**. By the end of the 17th century, in addition to those of the regiment, every **infantry company** and every cavalry **troop** had its own colours. An infantry company usually had three colours, two for the two wings of musketeers and one for the pike-men. The latter were abandoned with the abolition of **pikes**. The company colours did not survive except in the regiments of **Foot Guards**. The Sovereign's Colours are occasionally presented to a regiment or other unit as a sign of special recognition and honour. The capture of the enemy's colours indicated their complete defeat and the loss of the regimental colours was the ultimate disgrace. Colours were not carried into battle after the battle of **Isandlwana** (1879).

colour sergeant

A rank introduced (1813) in recognition of meritorious service. There was then one in each **company**. When companies were amalgamated to form double companies under the **Cardwell reforms**, one of the colour sergeants became the **company sergeant-major** and the other **company quartermaster sergeant**.

Combat 95 Clothing System

The current standard for personal clothing in the British Army. Utilising developments in extreme sports and expeditionary wear, it seeks to provide suitable protection for any environment. As well as normal **camouflage**, it minimises infrared reflection and thermal signature to reduce the wearer's visibility to **thermal imagers**.

commander-in-chief

The officer in supreme command of a group of military forces. In theory the sovereign was and is the commander-in-chief of the British Army. However, military officers were appointed to a position of this, or a very similar, name throughout the period from 1660 to the **reforms after the Boer War**. The commander-in-chief did not normally hold a battlefield command but was based in the **Horse Guards** in London and responsible for most aspects of the army's administration. His principal civilian assistant for much of the 18th and the early 19th century was the Secretary at War, who was also usually a politician (and is not be confused with the Secretary of State for War, the cabinet member dealing with military policy). For much of the period the commander-in-chief did not control the whole military establishment; the **artillery** and **engineers** were controlled by the Board of **Ordnance**, e.g. Notable holders of the post

included the Duke of **Marlborough** and the Duke of **York**. Another royal duke, the deeply conservative Duke of Cambridge, held the post for most of the second half of the 19th century (1856–95), but it was abolished with the creation of a more professional **general staff** after the problems exposed by events of the **Boer War**.
See also **reforms after the Boer War**

commando

A soldier trained in guerrilla and hand-to-hand fighting and sabotage, as well as in conventional operations, or the unit to which the soldier belongs. Commando units originated in the early stages of **World War II** when so-called Independent Companies were established to carry out raids on enemy-held coasts. These units were greatly expanded as the war progressed, some of them being based on the Royal Marines and some being volunteers recruited from throughout the Army. A commando unit was about the size of a reinforced **company**. The commandos played an important part in the **Normandy** invasion and in other amphibious operations throughout the war. Army commandos were disbanded after the end of the war but the Royal Marine Commandos exist to the present day.
[From Portuguese, 'raiding party', from *commandar* 'to command']

command post

The temporary headquarters of a group of soldiers. It varies in size, depending on the number of troops involved, and is usually near the site of action.

commissariat

The department responsible for providing supplies to an army

commissary

An officer who was responsible for supplying requirements such as food and supplies. The Commissary for Artillery was responsible for the supplying of powder, shot and horses to pull the guns. These posts were frequently abused by fraudulent accounting.
[Via French *commissaire* from medieval Latin *commissarius* 'officer in charge']

commissary of musters

A person who was responsible for the immediate provisioning of the troops. To ensure that his men were properly provided for, an officer was often obliged to pay the commissary of musters considerable bribes out of his own pocket.
See also **commissary**; **pay in the 17th and 18th centuries**

commission

The authority given to an officer to function in that capacity. Officers of the rank of second lieutenant or above (or earlier, **ensign** or **cornet** and above) receive a commission in the sovereign's name. Under the **purchase system**, commissions in the army used to be paid for.
See also **Cardwell reforms**
[Via French from Latin *commission-*, from *commiss-*, past participle of Latin *committere* 'to put together']

Committee for Imperial Defence *See* reforms after the Boer War

Commonwealth alliances

Many British **regiments** and **corps** have alliances with their counterparts in Commonwealth countries which have been developed through their taking part in combined operations or training, or where they have a common history or traditions, or there is some personal relationship

company

The smallest administrative unit in the army. By the 18th century a company usually consisted of some 100–150 infantry under the command of a **captain**. The number of companies that make up a **battalion** has varied from ten, e.g., in the Napoleonic period to four in the modern era. The company is also a tactical formation and since the early

20th century has consisted of a headquarters and two or more **platoons**. The comparable body in the **artillery** is the **battery** and in the **cavalry**, the **troop**.

[From Anglo-Norman *compainie*, from late Latin *companion-* 'person who shares bread', from Latin *panis* 'bread']

company quartermaster sergeant
A sergeant attached to the **quartermaster's** department of a **company**

company sergeant-major
The senior **non-commissioned officer** of a **company**

Concord, battle of *See* **Lexington and Concord, battles of**

Congreve, William (1772–1828)
Congreve was an artillery officer who is most famous for the invention of the military **rocket** which he based on those used by the Indian prince **Haidar Ali** against the British (1792 and 1799). He is also credited with being the inventor of metal plating for warships (1805). On the death of his father (1814) he inherited the title and the post of Comptroller of the Royal Laboratory at Woolwich Arsenal. From 1818 he was MP for Plymouth.

conscientious objector
Someone who objects to warfare on grounds of conscience, often religious, and hence refuses to undertake military service. While such objectors have always been subject to various forms of discrimination by society in times of war, they only came into conflict with the state when military service was made compulsory: in Britain, when conscription was introduced in **World War I** and **World War II**. The ultimate penalty was imprisonment, but many conscientious objectors were willing to serve in noncombatant units, e.g. in medical teams.

conscript *See* **conscription**

conscription
Compulsory service in the armed forces by persons (conscripts) within a particular age group. Conscription was introduced in Britain during World War I (1916) but was ended in 1919. It was again introduced in July 1939, just before the beginning of World War II, but was ended in 1960, after which the forces were again all volunteers. Some people who were in a reserved occupation, e.g. skilled factory workers or coal miners, were not subject to conscription.

Also called **national service**

Conspicuous Gallantry Cross
A decoration instituted in 1993 that is awarded to all ranks for acts of conspicuous gallantry during active operations against the enemy. Ranking second after the **Victoria Cross**, it replaced the **Distinguished Conduct Medal**, the **Conspicuous Gallantry Medal** and (for gallantry) the **Distinguished Service Order**. It was first awarded in 1995.

Abbreviation **CGC**

Conspicuous Gallantry Medal
A medal instituted briefly in 1855, during the **Crimean War**, and then permanently from 1874. Primarily a naval decoration for non-commissioned ranks, it was also awarded to other services for acts of gallantry in action at sea. Its scope was extended to acts of gallantry in air combat from 1943. It was replaced by the **Conspicuous Gallantry Cross** in 1993.

Abbreviation **CGM**

constable
Originally the royal household's chief military officer, the position evolved into the rank of **field marshal**

[Via Old French *conestable* from late Latin *comes stabilis* 'count of the stable']

controller of army pay accounts *See* **pay in the 17th and 18th centuries**

Coote, Eyre (1726–83)

Coote was born in Ireland and had his early military service in Germany and Scotland in the 1745 **Jacobite Rebellion**. He sailed for India with the 39th Foot (**Dorsetshire Regiment of Foot**) (1754). He was a **captain** in the 39th (1755) and was present at the capture of **Calcutta** (now Kolkata), and at **Plassey** where he commanded the 3rd Division. In 1759 he was **gazetted lieutenant-colonel** of the 84th Foot (**York and Lancaster Regiment**) which was newly raised for service in India. Coote was then commander of the troops in Madras (now Chennai) and occupied **Wandiwash** (1759). He finally took command of the force that occupied **Pondicherry** (1761), ending the French power in India. Coote returned to England (1762). He was promoted to **colonel** (1765) and elected MP for Leicester (1768). In 1769 he was appointed **commander-in-chief** in Madras, but could not get on with the governor so returned home by the overland route through Egypt (1770). He was made colonel of the 27th Foot (1771) and was promoted to **major-general** (1775). Coote was elected MP for Poole (1774–80), made commander-in-chief of India (1777) and promoted to **lieutenant-general** (1777). He arrived in Calcutta (1779). He then defeated **Haidar Ali** at **Porto Novo** and again at Paramnakam. He continued the offensive until early 1782, but returned to Bengal suffering from ill-health. He died in Madras.

Cope, John (d. 1760)

Cope was a **cornet** in the **cavalry** (1707). He was **colonel** of the 39th Foot (**Dorsetshire Regiment of Foot**) (1730–32), of the 5th Foot (**Royal Northumberland Fusiliers**) (1732–37), of the 9th Dragoons (1737–41), and of the 7th Dragoons (**Queen's Own Hussars (7th)**) (1741–death). He was created **KB** and was MP for Queensborough (1722–27), for Liskeard (1727–34) and for Orford (1738–41). Cope was one of the **generals** in command of the troops sent to assist the Empress Maria Theresa (1742). He was promoted to **brigadier-general** (1735), **major-general** (1739) and **lieutenant-general** (1743). He was **commander-in-chief** of the British troops during the early stages of the 1745 **Jacobite Rebellion** and was exonerated for negligence following the Jacobite victory at **Prestonpans**. In 1751 he joined the staff in Ireland.

cordite

An explosive mixture of **nitrocellulose** and nitroglycerine. It was introduced by Nobel (1887) as Ballistite, which he patented. The British refused to recognise the patent and manufactured the propellant under the name of cordite. It was the standard propellant used in British ammunition in the two World Wars.

[From *cord*, because of its stringy appearance]

cornet

In the 18th and 19th centuries, the lowest rank of an officer in the **cavalry**. A cornet carried the cornet (flag) of the troop. The names of flags changed but the rank was retained until 1871 when it was abolished. A single star was worn as a badge of rank between 1855 and 1871.

[From French, 'small horn']

Cornwallis, Charles (1738–1805)

Cornwallis was born in London, the son of the 1st Earl Cornwallis. He was educated at Eton and was commissioned **ensign** in the 1st Foot Guards (**Grenadier Guards**) (1756). He then studied at the military academy in Turin. He was appointed **aide-de-camp** to the Marquis of **Granby** on the Continent and was promoted to **captain** in the 85th Foot (**King's Light Infantry**) (1759). Cornwallis was elected MP for Eye (1760) and made **lieutenant-colonel** of the 12th Foot (**Suffolk Regiment**) (1761). He was aide-de-camp to the king (1765) and **colonel** of the 33rd Foot (**Duke of Wellington's Regiment**) (1766). His career was mainly political but he was made constable of the Tower of London (1770) and promoted to **major-general** (1775). Cornwallis held various posts during the **American War of Independence**. He commanded the successful British operations in South Carolina in 1780–81, winning the battles of **Camden** and **Guilford Courthouse**. His surrender at **Yorktown** (1781) was decisive in Britain's defeat. In 1786 he sailed to **India** as governor-general and he reformed the civil and military services. Cornwallis returned home (1794) when he became **Master-General of the Ordnance** (*see* **Ordnance, Board of**) (1795). He was recalled to India, but did not go. Instead he was appointed Viceroy of Ireland where he suppressed a rebellion (1798). He resigned as viceroy and master-general (1801) because of King George III's refusal to allow Catholic Emancipation. In 1801 he was made commander of the eastern district and went to France to negotiate what was to become the treaty of Amiens (1802). In 1805 he was again asked to go to India as governor-general and **commander-in-chief**. He died at Ghazipore (October 1805) while on a peace mission.

See also **Fort Mercer and Fort Miffin, battle of**; **Fort Washington, battle of**

Cornwall Light Infantry

The **regiment** was raised (1702) as Colonel Edward Fox's Regiment of Marines, as a prototype of this type of fighting force. The name was changed with the colonels until 1713 when it was disbanded. It was re-formed (1715) as the 32nd Regiment of Foot and the name changed (1782) to the 32nd (or Cornwall) Regiment of Foot, and in 1858 to the 32nd (Cornwall) Light Infantry. It was present at **Lucknow** and **Cawnpore** (now Kanpur) in the **Indian Mutiny**.

Cornwall's (Colonel Henry Cornwall's Regiment of Foot) *See* **Royal Norfolk Regiment**

Cornwall's, Duke of, Light Infantry *See* **Duke of Cornwall's Light Infantry**

coronation blues

Full **dress** for **other ranks** was abolished during **World War I** but was restored as coronation blues for those taking part in the procession during the coronation of George VI (1937)

corporal

The rank below a **sergeant**. It had little significance in early times when corporals wore uniforms of the same quality as the men. Sergeants' uniforms were of superior quality. The rank was distinguished by braid or a shoulder knot. Two **chevrons** were introduced as a rank badge in 1803 and are retained today.

[Via French from Italian *caporale* 'of the head', from *capo* 'head', from Latin *caput*]

corps

1. A large military formation, usually of two or more **divisions** and numbering from 20,000 to 60,000 or more men. Corps of this sort were first widely used in warfare by **Napoleon** and, as their large size suggests, have only been formed by the British Army in major wars. In these wars, two or more corps might make up an 'army'.

Also called **army corps**

2. A unit similar to a **regiment** in such organisations as the **Royal Corps of Signals** or services such as the **Army Catering Corps**

[Via French from Latin *corpus* 'body']

Corps of Waggoners *See* **reforms of the Duke of York**

Corunna, battle of

(1809; *Peninsular War*) After **Napoleon** had invaded Spain in 1808, a British force commanded by Sir John **Moore** moved into Spain from Portugal towards Salamanca and Valladolid, intending to distract Napoleon's much larger army from overrunning the whole country. This aim was successful but the operation put Moore's army in considerable danger. Napoleon moved from Madrid (28 December 1808) and cut off Moore's communications with Portugal. This forced Moore to retreat towards the north-west coast of Spain through the Cantabrian Mountains where he was constantly harassed by the French, commanded by Marshal Nicolas **Soult**. Moore arrived at the port of Corunna (now La Coruña) (14 January) to find that the evacuating fleet had not arrived. Soult attacked (16 January) but was thrown back, allowing the remaining British troops to be evacuated (18 January). Moore was killed during the action.

County of Dublin Regiment
The **regiment** was raised (1793) by Colonel William Fitch as the 83rd Regiment of Foot. The name was changed (1859) to the 83rd (County of Dublin) Regiment of Foot. It amalgamated with the Royal County Down regiment in 1881 to become the Royal Irish Rifles (later the **Royal Ulster Rifles**).

court martial
A military court set up to try offences against military law. It is staffed and regulated by officers.

Covenanters
The Covenanters were Scottish Presbyterians who signed the National Covenant (1638) in which they pledged to maintain their forms of worship and religious liberty. After the signing the Scottish Assembly abolished the Anglican Church, protesting particularly against its episcopal government. This led to open warfare with Charles I in the Bishops' Wars of 1639 and 1642, which laid stress on Charles' finances and his relationship with the English Parliament and were one of the factors leading to the **Civil War**. In 1643 the Covenanters signed the Solemn League and Covenant and took part in the Civil War with the Parliamentarians. Charles I surrendered (1646) and in 1647 accepted the Solemn League and Covenant with its religious reforms. Charles II signed the Covenant (1650) and the Scots fought for him before his escape to France.
See also **Scottish Covenanters' Revolt**

covering fire
A discharge of firearms with the objective of either distracting enemy troops or keeping them pinned down so an assault can be made against them in relative safety

Cowpens, battle of
(1781; *American War of Independence*) The British were largely dominant in the south in spite of the American victory at **King's Mountain**. This dominance was reduced when an American force under General Daniel Morgan out-manoeuvred the British force commanded by Colonel Banastre **Tarleton** at Cowpens in South Carolina (17 January).

Coy *abbreviation of* **company.**

Craufurd, Robert (1764–1812)
Craufurd joined the Army (1779) as an **ensign** in the 25th Foot (**King's Own Scottish Borderers**), was promoted to **lieutenant** (1781) and became a **captain** in the 75th Foot (1783). He was deeply interested in military studies and fluent in German. He served in **India** (1790–92), was promoted to **major**, and became attaché to the Austrian army in the Netherlands and on the Rhine. He was promoted to **lieutenant-colonel** (1797) and served in Ireland (1798). He was then attached to the Austro-Russian army in Switzerland, and his unfavourable but accurate reporting of the mismanaged British expedition to the Helder ensured that he was passed over for promotion. He went on half pay and was elected as MP for East Retford (1801). His criticism of military policy made him enemies, but William Windham (War Secretary) obtained a colonelcy for him (1805) and he then took part in the abortive attack on **Buenos Aires** (1807). For this he was held blameless and was given a command of a **brigade** in the **Peninsular War** (1808) where he earned the nickname of 'Black Bob'. During the **Corunna** campaign he managed the retreat of the light brigades to Vigo admirably and returned to the Peninsula (1809) as a **brigadier**. In spite of an epic **forced march**, he missed the battle of **Talavera**. He was then given command (1809–12) of the newly formed Light Brigade (later Light Division) whose function was to serve as an advance or rear guard for the army and to provide skirmishing troops in battle. He trained his men to a remarkably high standard so that they were an effective force at **Bussaco** (1810), **Torres Vedras** (1810–11) and **Fuentes de Oñoro** (1811). He was promoted to **major-**

general (1811). He was killed at **Ciudad Rodrigo** (1812). Craufurd was one of **Wellington's** most able commanders.

See also **light infantry**; **Rifle Brigade, The**

Cravant, battle of

(1423; *Hundred Years' War*) A combined English and Burgundian force under the command of John of Lancaster, Duke of Bedford, encountered a combined French and Scottish force at Cravant (1 August). The French-Scottish force was defeated, due largely to the efficiency of the English **longbows**.

Crécy, battle of

(1346; *Hundred Years' War*) Edward III of England landed an invasion force in Normandy (12 July) and moved across the countryside pursued by Philip VI of France. The English turned to meet the French at Crécy (26 August). Due to some defect in their command structure the French attacked prematurely led by 4,000 Genoese **crossbow** men. They were decimated by the English **longbows**. The French cavalry then attacked and were treated similarly by the English longbows. By the end of the day the French had lost about 8,000 men and the English fewer than 100.

Crete, battle of

(1941; *World War II*) After the German 12th Army had taken Greece, 26,000 Allied forces evacuated to Crete. They were joined by a further 1,500 Allied reinforcements and 14,000 Greeks. Because the evacuation had been so precipitous, these forces were poorly supplied and communications were unreliable. After heavy bombing the Germans began to land parachutists and glider troops (20 May). By 27 May 22,000 German troops had landed, all on the north side of the island. The defenders, commanded by General Bernard **Freyberg**, fought back, but were forced to evacuate the island after an unrelenting attack on the ground and from the air. British codebreakers had learned many of the details of the German plan in advance of the attack but Freyberg was forbidden to redeploy his troops to take advantage of this information so that the wider gains from codebreaking were not put at risk. The British forces withdrew to Egypt. Most of the 13,000 Allied casualties were prisoners. The island surrendered on 31 May.

Crimean War (1853–56)

A war basically between Russia and Turkey, caused by Russia's claim to protect the Orthodox Christians throughout the Turkish Empire and the holy places in the Near East. Turkey rightly feared that these claims were an excuse to support Russian expansion in the region generally. Russia occupied the Turkish-controlled provinces of Wallachia and Moldavia on the Danube, and Turkey declared war (4 October 1853). Britain and France entered the war on the side of Turkey (1854), concentrating their offensive on the Crimean peninsula in the Black Sea. An indecisive peace was signed in Paris (30 March 1856).

See also **Alma, battle of the**; **Balaclava, battle of**; **Inkerman, battle of**; **Sebastopol, battle of**; **Campbell, Colin**; **Cardigan, 7th Earl of**; **Lucan, Lord[1]**; **Raglan, Lord**; **reforms after the Crimean War**

Cromwell, Oliver (1599–1658)

Cromwell was born in Huntingdon. His father was a local landowner, Justice of the Peace and an MP in one of Queen Elizabeth's parliaments. Cromwell was educated at the local grammar school and Sidney Sussex College, Cambridge, and was a Calvinist. He was elected MP for Huntingdon (1628) and Cambridge (1640). Like many of the lesser gentry, he became increasingly dissatisfied with the administration of Charles I. At the beginning of the **Civil War** he enlisted a troop of cavalry in Huntingdon that took part in the battle of **Edgehill**. During 1643 he gained a reputation as a military organiser and was given the rank of **colonel**. He insisted that his troops were well-behaved, well-trained and regularly paid. His successes at Gainsborough (28 July 1643), Winceby and Newark led to his promotion to governor of the Isle of Ely and to his persuading Parliament to create a new army which would be able to attack the

enemy. The **New Model Army** was commanded by Edward Montagu, 2nd Earl of Manchester, with Cromwell (with the rank of **lieutenant-general**) as second-in-command. After the defeat at Newbury, Cromwell quarrelled with Manchester whom he considered to be lethargic and slow. The quarrel was patched up, and it was agreed by Parliament that no member of either house should hold command in the army. Sir Thomas **Fairfax** took command of the army and insisted (1645) that Cromwell should be his second-in-command. Cromwell then fought at **Naseby** and **Langport** and took part in the siege of Oxford. After the war, Parliament wanted to disband the army. Cromwell, who thought that his men were being disgracefully treated, threw in his lot with his soldiers and left London (4 June 1647). Cromwell then acted as mediator between the army, Parliament and the King, but this came to nothing when the King fled to the Isle of Wight and opened negotiations with the Scots. Fairfax then ordered Cromwell into Wales to crush a rising and then he moved north and defeated the Scottish Royalists and those in northern England, his campaign culminating in the siege of Pontefract. Somewhat reluctantly, Cromwell signed the death warrant of Charles I. He was the first chairman of the Council of State of the new Commonwealth. He believed that the Catholics in Ireland had massacred the English settlers in 1641 and when they supported the Stuart cause conducted a ruthless campaign against them. Cromwell now turned against the Royalists in Scotland (1650) who were finally defeated at the battle of **Dunbar**. A year later Cromwell destroyed the army of Charles II at **Worcester**. This was his last military campaign, the rest of his life being devoted to politics.
See also **Drogheda, battle of**

Crook's (Colonel Unton Crook's Regiment of Horse) *See* Blues and Royals

Cropredy Bridge, battle of
(1644; *Civil War*) A Parliamentary force led by General Sir William Waller, moving from Kent to attack Royalist Oxford, was defeated at Cropredy Bridge near Banbury

crossbow
The bow most used during the Middle Ages and beyond. It first appeared in Europe (Italy) in the 10th century and its use continued into the late 15th century when it was replaced by the **arquebus**. The first recorded use of the crossbow in Britain was by the Normans at the battle of **Hastings** (1066). Originally it was made of wood, and consisted of a short bow fitted to a stock. The replacement of wood by wrought iron or mild steel helped give the weapon tremendous power, firing a short arrow (**bolt** or quarrel) some 300 yards with a force that would penetrate chain mail. Some mechanical aid was needed to draw the bow. In the earlier types, the foot was placed in a stirrup on the front of the stock and the bowstring attached to a hook on the belt. The soldier stood up, stretching the bowstring until it was hooked onto a trigger mechanism. The bolt was placed in a groove in the stock and fired by releasing the trigger. Later a winch mechanism was used to draw back the bowstring. Although powerful and accurate, the crossbow had a slow rate of fire. Its use was outlawed by the Church (1139) as being too barbarous a weapon for use against other Christians. (Its use against Moslems was permitted.) There were two types of crossbow, the arbalest and latch. The arbalest was the heavier weapon with the bow made of steel and brought into tension by a windlass mechanism that was attached to the string and carried separately. The latch was a lighter weapon usually made of wood and with a simple windlass.
See also **longbow**

Crusader, Operation *See* Sidi-Rezegh, battle of

CSI *See* Order of the Star of India

Ctesiphon, battle of
(1915; *World War I*) An Anglo-Indian army commanded by General Sir Charles **Townshend** had captured **Kut-al-Imara** and moved up the Tigris to attack Baghdad. They were met by a well-entrenched Turkish force at Ctesiphon about 20 miles from

Baghdad (22 November). The Allies were repulsed with a loss of 4,500 men from a force of 14,000, and fell back on Kut-al-Imara.

cuirass

A piece of body armour extending from the neck to the waist consisting of a breastplate and backplate joined by straps down the sides. The cuirass was worn by pikemen up to their demise by the end of the 17th century. In the **cavalry** the backplate was abandoned and replaced by a breastplate alone by 1675. The cuirass was worn on active service up to the later years of the 18th century. The **Life Guards** and **Royal Horse Guards** (*see* **Blues and Royals**) wore cuirasses for the coronation of George IV (1821) and they are still worn by the **Household Cavalry** on state occasions.

See also **armour**

[Via Old French *cuirace* from Latin *coriaceus* 'made of leather', from *corium* 'leather']

Culloden Moor, battle of

(1746; *Jacobite Rebellions*) Although they had defeated the Hanoverian forces at **Falkirk**, the Jacobite forces were still forced to retreat to the north. They tried to make a surprise attack on the Hanoverian forces, commanded by the Duke of **Cumberland**, near Inverness but were forced to accept a formal battle at Culloden (16 April). The Hanoverian artillery decimated the charging Scots, and when they fled the English cavalry chased and massacred them. This destroyed any hope of a Stuart restoration to the British throne, but earned Cumberland the name of 'Butcher' and the long-felt antagonism of the Scots.

culverin

An early type of long-barrelled **cannon**. It fired an 18-pound **shot**. Variants in differing sizes were the bastard culverin, royal culverin, and demiculverin, esmeril, falcon, falconet and rabinet. By the 18th century names of this kind had become obsolete, with cannon mainly being known instead simply by the weight of ball that they fired.

[From French *coulevrine*, from *couleuvre* 'snake', from Latin *colubra*]

Cumberland, Duke of (William Augustus) (1721–65)

Son of George II. He was commander of the Allied forces during the War of the **Austrian Succession** and was defeated by the French Marshal **Saxe** at the battle of **Fontenoy** (1745). He was recalled to put down the **Jacobite Rebellion** in Scotland and defeated the Scots at **Culloden Moor**. He returned to the Continent to be defeated by Saxe again at the battle of **Lauffeld** (1747). He suffered a further defeat during the **Seven Years' War** at the battle of **Hastenbeck**, in Hanover. As a result of this he signed a treaty promising to evacuate Hanover, one of his father's possessions. His father dismissed him and repudiated the agreement. His refusal to act as **commander-in-chief** unless Prime Minister Pitt resigned led to Pitt's temporary dismissal (1757).

Cumberland Regiment

The **regiment** was originally raised (1702) as Lord Lucan's Regiment of Foot. In 1747 it became the 34th Regiment of Foot and in 1782 the 34th (Cumberland) Regiment of Foot. It was known as 'The Cattle Reeves'. During the battle of Arroyo dos Molinos in the **Peninsular War** the regiment captured a large contingent of French troops and officers of high rank, and the **Border Regiment**, which was formed from the amalgamation of the Cumberland and **Westmorland Regiments**, still possesses the drums and drum-major's staff of the 34th French regiment. It had a laurel wreath on its badge which commemorated the part the regiment played in the retreat from **Fontenoy**.

Cunningham, Alan Gordon (1887–1983)

Cunningham was born in Edinburgh and educated at Cheltenham College and the **Royal Military Academy**, Woolwich. He was commissioned in the **Royal Artillery** (1906) and served on the **Western Front** throughout **World War I**. Cunningham served in the Straits Settlements (Malaysia) (1919–21) and then as an instructor at the Small Arms School, Netherhaven. He was promoted to **lieutenant-colonel** (1937) and attended the Imperial Defence College. He commanded the 1st Division, Royal Artillery (1937) and was promoted to **major-general** (1938). He commanded several infantry divisions and was then appointed general-officer-commanding, **East Africa** (1940) for the campaign to re-conquer Abyssinia (now Ethiopia), which he led successfully. **Auchinleck** then selected Cunningham to command the 8th Army in the desert, but he proved ineffective in this post and was defeated by **Rommel**. He returned home to become commandant of the **Staff College** and GOC Northern Ireland and Eastern Command. He was then appointed high commissioner and **commander-in-chief**, Palestine and high commissioner, Transjordan (1945–48). He was **colonel-**commandant of the Royal Artillery (1944–54).

See also **East Africa**

Cunningham's Dragoons *See* Queen's Own Hussars

Curragh *See* reforms after the Crimean War

Curragh Incident (1914)

Throughout the 19th and early 20th century many officers in the British Army were drawn from the Protestant Anglo-Irish gentry. When the British government proposed to give (the whole of) Ireland Home Rule, a number of officers stationed at the Curragh barracks near Dublin gave a written pledge that they would resign their commissions rather than obey orders to force the Ulster Protestants to accept Home Rule. The incident was shortly followed by the outbreak of **World War I** before the issues involved had been resolved.

See also **French, John Denton Pinkstone**

Cutts, John (1661–1707)

Cutts fought with William III at the battle of the **Boyne** and was commander at the siege of **Namur**. He served under **Marlborough** during the War of the **Spanish Succession** and was third in command at the battle of **Blenheim**.

CVO *See* Royal Victorian Order

D

dag

A small single-handed firearm introduced in 1544 as a **cavalry** weapon. It was a **wheellock** weapon derived from the **arquebus**.

[From French *dague* 'long dagger']

Dalyell, Thomas (1599?–1685)

Dalyell served as a **captain** under Major Robert Monro in Aberdeen and then in Ireland, where he was promoted to **colonel** commanding the garrison at Carrickfergus and controller of customs. As a Royalist he was banned from his native Scotland. He fought for King Charles II at the battle of **Worcester**, having been made a **major-general** of foot. He was taken prisoner and confined in the Tower of London, from where he escaped and ultimately joined Charles on the Continent. He served in the Russian Army but in 1666 was appointed **commander-in-chief** in Scotland where he was commissioned to raise a **troop** of horse with which he ruthlessly suppressed the Covenanters. He was created a privy councillor (1667) and was MP for his home town of Linlithgow (1678–death). In 1681 Dalyell was given a commission to enrol a **regiment** of **dragoons**, primarily to suppress the Covenanters.

See also **Royal Scots Greys**

Danbury, battle of

(1777; *American War of Independence*) The American forces had established a supply depot at Danbury, Connecticut. General Sir William **Howe** sent General William Tyron, who was also governor of New York, to destroy it. He landed 2,000 men at Fairfield (25 April) and, marching unopposed, destroyed the depot. The American General Benedict Arnold with 700 militia harassed the British until they re-embarked at Norwalk, gaining him the recognition he was seeking.

Danish invasion of Britain (837–1016)

During the 9th century Danes made several invasions of England, following a policy of territorial expansion. After 837 there was a large Danish army in Britain. They finally became established, leading to their gaining control over a large area in the east that was known as the Danelaw. In 1016 a peace was agreed by which a Danish state ruled by Canute was recognised by Edmund II (Ironside) of Wessex.

Dardanelles, battle of *See* **Gallipoli, battle of**

Dargai, battle of

(1897; *North-West Frontier*) The **Gordon Highlanders**, commanded by Colonel Mattias, stormed and took the heights of Dargai, 50 miles from Peshawar, which were held by a force of Afridis

DBE *See* **Order of the British Empire**

DCB *See* **Order of the Bath**

DCM *abbreviation of* **Distinguished Conduct Medal**

DCMG *See* **Order of St Michael and St George**

DCVO *See* **Royal Victorian Order**

D-Day *See* **Normandy**

decorations

A star, cross, or other device conferred as a mark of honour. Strictly speaking they rank higher than **medals**, and are commonly awarded for acts of bravery, or other distinguished service. A decoration would not be awarded simply for long service, good conduct, or for taking part in a particular campaign.

See also **medals**

Deeg, battle of

1. (1780; *Maratha Wars*) A British force of 6,000, commanded by General Fraser, attacked 14 battalions of Maratha infantry, cavalry, and 160 guns. The Marathas were routed, losing 87 guns, while the British suffered 643 casualties, including General Fraser who was killed.

2. (1804; *Maratha Wars*) The garrison of Maratha troops was besieged (11 December) by a British force commanded by General Lord Gerard **Lake**. It was bombarded for six days, and stormed (23 December). Over 100 guns were captured.

Defence (Committee) Council *See* **reforms after the Boer War**

defilade

A fortification designed to protect the occupants from cross-fire

Delhi, battle of

1. (1803; *Maratha Wars*) A British force of 4,500, commanded by General Lord Gerard **Lake**, attacked 19,000 Marathas of Scindia's army (11 September). The Marathas held a strong defensive position from which Lake drew them by feigning a retreat. He then turned and inflicted enormous casualties in a bayonet charge. The British lost some 400 killed.

2. (1804; *Maratha Wars*) A small British garrison was besieged in Delhi by 20,000 Marathas with 100 guns, commanded by Jeswunt Rao Holkar (7 October). After nine days' bombardment Holkar withdrew.

3. (1857; *Indian Mutiny*) The Indian rebels seized Delhi and killed all the Europeans. Sir Henry **Barnard** with 2,000 troops occupied a ridge overlooking the city (8 June) but the force was too small to attack. A contingent of reinforcements led by General John **Nicholson** marched 30 miles a day for three weeks from the Punjab and the combined force attacked Delhi (14 September). After 6 days of street fighting the city fell, but Nicholson was killed.

demobilise

To release troops from conscripted military service.

See also **conscription**

denims

The hard-wearing suits of overalls made of denim cloth which were worn instead of ordinary uniforms when soldiers were employed in fatigues or other dirty duties

depleted uranium

Uranium that contains less than the natural content of the isotope ^{235}U and that is therefore less radioactive than normal uranium. A by-product of nuclear fission, it has been available in countries with nuclear technology since the 1940s. Its very high density, similar to that of tungsten, makes it suitable for armour-piercing ammunition, in which it has been used since the 1970s. More recently it has also been used to strengthen vehicle armour. However, the long-term effects of its residual radioactivity and extreme toxicity make its use highly controversial.

Abbreviation **DU**

Derbyshire Regiment of Foot

The **regiment** was raised (1823) by Sir John Halkett as the 95th Regiment of Foot. The name was changed (1823) to the 95th (or Derbyshire) Regiment of Foot. In the reorganisation of 1881 it amalgamated with the 45th to become part of the **Sherwood Foresters**.

See also **Alma, battle of the**

detachment

A small group of troops separated from the main body to perform a particular military task.

See also **detail**

detail

A small group of troops set apart for a particular duty, e.g. as an escort or kitchen duties.

See also **detachment**

detonator

1. The part of a **cartridge** or **shell** that contains a substance such as mercury fulminate that explodes on striking, thus firing the main charge

2. A small charge that is inserted into a bulk of explosive and is fired electrically by a timing device or by remote control

Detroit, battle of

(1812; *War of 1812*) The invasion of Canada was the prime American objective of the war. The American General William Hull crossed the Detroit river (12 July) with 2,000 men. He moved as far as Windsor and then withdrew to Detroit where he surrendered to a Canadian force under General Isaac **Brock**. This gave the British control of the west of Lake Erie and Michigan County. Hull was court-martialled.

Dettingen, battle of

(1743; *War of the Austrian Succession*) The British forces moved from the Lower Rhine towards the Main valley to drive a wedge between the French and the Bavarians. The French Marshal Duc Adrien de **Noailles** trapped 35,000 British, Hanoverian and Hessian troops in a defile between Aschaffenburg and Hanau by placing 25,000 troops at their rear. The French cavalry to the front attacked prematurely (27 June) and were routed by a frontal attack from the Allied infantry, near the village of Dettingen. The attack was led by George II, the last time a British monarch personally led troops in the field. The French then withdrew all their troops west of the Rhine.

Devonshire and Dorset Regiment

The **regiment** was formed in May 1958 by the amalgamation of the **Devonshire Regiment** and the **Dorset Regiment** and was renamed the Devonshire and Dorset Light Infantry in 2005. It is due to unite with The Royal Gloucestershire, Berkshire and Wiltshire Light Infantry, The Light Infantry, and The Royal Green Jackets in 2007, to form The Rifles.

Devonshire Regiment

The **regiment** was raised (1685) by the Duke of Beaufort as the Duke of Beaufort's Musketeers. The name was changed in the same year to the Marquess of Worcester's Regiment of Foot when Beaufort's son took command. It was named after its **colonels** until it became the 11th Regiment of Foot (1751), in 1782 the 11th (or North Devonshire) Regiment of Foot and in 1881 the Devonshire Regiment. The regiment took part in the battle of **Salamanca** after which only 4 officers and 67 men remained alive.

Dieppe, battle of

(1942; *World War II*) An amphibious assault by Canadian troops and British **commandos** on the German-held French port of Dieppe (19 August). The force, aided by tanks, gained a foothold on the beach but suffered heavy casualties. The Canadians alone lost 900 killed and 2,000 prisoners. The Allies also lost 98 planes. Although the losses were heavy, valuable lessons were learnt which benefited the Allied forces in later amphibious operations.

Disbanding Act (1699)

The Act that limited the size of the **standing army** to 7,000 men, passed to curb William III's involvement in European wars

dispatches, mentioned in

A commendation for outstanding service, but not such as would qualify for the award of a **decoration** or **medal**. The term evolved from the long-standing custom, predating the award of medals, of naming those who had performed well in official reports sent home or to senior commanders. The term is sometimes contracted simply to a 'mention' or abbreviated as m-i-d.

Distinguished Conduct Medal

A medal instituted (1854) to reward troops in the **Crimea**. Replacing the Meritorious Service Medal of 1845, it was available to all ranks other than officers and was awarded for distinguished, gallant, and good conduct. Originally it was awarded on a quota basis to each **regiment** depending on the funds available to pay the annuity attached to it. It was replaced by the **Conspicuous Gallantry Cross** in 1993.
Abbreviation **DCM**

Distinguished Service Cross

A decoration instituted in 1901 as the **Conspicuous Service Cross** and renamed in 1914. It was awarded for gallant or distinguished naval service in face of the enemy. Originally confined to naval officers, it was extended in 1940 to members of the army or air force serving on board ship. In 1993 it became available to all ranks.
Abbreviation **DSC**

Distinguished Service Medal

The award was instituted (1914) as an award for acts of bravery that did not merit the **CGM**. Initially it was awarded to non-commissioned naval personnel, but during **World War II** it was extended to Army and RAF personnel serving on a ship. It was discontinued in 1993 when the **Distinguished Service Cross**, previously for officers only, became available to all ranks.
Abbreviation **DSM**

Distinguished Service Order

The Order was instituted in 1886 as an award made to officers below the rank of **major** who had been mentioned in dispatches for distinguished service under fire, or under conditions equivalent to service in actual combat. Before 1886 the only possible award to these officers was the **CB**, which was rarely given to junior officers. Since 1993 it has been awarded to all ranks for distinguished leadership; its other function, of marking personal gallantry, was taken over by the **Conspicuous Gallantry Cross**.
Abbreviation **DSO**

division

The smallest military formation that contains the arms and ancillary support necessary to carry out independent operations. Divisions have been formed by the British Army in wartime since the **French Wars** (1792–1815) and have been part of the army's peacetime organisation throughout the 20th century. A division is usually made up of 12,000–20,000 troops and is commanded by a **major-general**. Two or more divisions may be joined to form a **corps** when conducting a particular campaign. Divisions in turn are composed of two to four **brigades** and include combat troops of one or more categories from **infantry**, **cavalry** and **tanks**, plus **artillery**, **engineers** and other supporting services. The term is also used in the modern Army for administrative bodies containing a group of **regiments**. There is, e.g., a King's Division, a Light Division, and a Scottish Division.
[Via French from Latin *division-* from *divis-*, past participle of *dividere* 'to separate']

Dodecanese Islands, battle of

(1943; *World War II*) The British Prime Minister, Winston Churchill, decided that there was a need for Allied bases in the Aegean, close to the Balkans. In September

General Sir Henry Maitland-Wilson, commander in the Mediterranean, put a battalion of troops on each of the islands of Cos, Leros, and Samos. Between 3 October and 12 November the Germans drove out the Allies by amphibious assault, but particularly by the use of parachutists. About 1,000 Allied troops were evacuated but 3,000 were taken prisoner. Six destroyers and two submarines were also lost.

Dodowah, battle of (1826)

While the British were trying to maintain control in the Gold Coast (now Ghana), the Ashantis invaded Gold Coast Colony from the north and were driven off by a British force commanded by Colonel Purdon

Donauwörth, battle of

(1704; *War of the Spanish Succession*) The Duke of **Marlborough** decided to take the offensive against France and its allies and moved 52,000 men up the Rhine from the Netherlands (9 May), striking south-east to the Danube. He arrived at Donauwörth (1 July). Here he met a Bavarian force commanded by Count D'Arco, which had fortified a hill. The British made a frontal attack killing three-quarters of the Bavarian force. Marlborough then crossed the river to threaten Augsburg, thus ensuring the safety of Vienna. This action was a preliminary to the battle of **Blenheim**.

Dormer, James (1679–1741)

Dormer was appointed **captain** in the 1st Foot Guards (**Grenadier Guards**) (1700) and was wounded at **Blenheim**. He commanded the newly raised corps of Irish Foot in Spain and was present at Saragossa (now Zaragoza). He was taken prisoner and paroled. In 1715 he was commissioned to raise a **regiment** of **dragoons** in the south of England (**King's Hussars (14th)**). He commanded a **brigade** during the Jacobite rising in Lancashire. In 1720 he was appointed **colonel** of the 6th Foot (**Royal Warwickshire Fusiliers**) and made envoy extraordinary in Lisbon (1727). Dormer was promoted to **lieutenant-general** and colonel of the 1st Troop of Horse Grenadiers (1737) and made governor of Hull (1740).

Dormer's Dragoons *See* **King's Hussars (14th)**

Dorset Regiment

The **regiment** was formed (1881) by the amalgamation of the 39th **Dorsetshire Regiment of Foot** and the 54th **West Norfolk Regiment of Foot**. In 1958 a further amalgamation saw the regiment become part of the **Devonshire and Dorset Regiment**.

Dorsetshire Regiment of Foot

The **regiment** was raised (1702) as Colonel Richard Coote's Regiment of Foot. The name was changed with that of its **colonels** until 1751 when it became the 39th Regiment of Foot. In 1782 it was called the 39th (or East Middlesex) Regiment of Foot. The Dorsetshire connection was not made until 1807 when the regiment became the 39th (or Dorsetshire) Regiment of Foot.

See also **Gibraltar, battle of**; **Royal Sussex Regiment**

Double Company System *See* **Cardwell reforms**

Douglas's (Colonel Douglas's Regiment of Foot) *See* **Bedfordshire and Hertfordshire Regiment**

Doveton, John (1768–1847)

Doveton joined the 1st Madras light cavalry as a **cornet** (1785) and served with **Cornwallis** in India. He was promoted to **lieutenant** (1792) and again took part in the campaigns against **Tipu Sahib**. He was promoted to **captain** (1800), to **major** (1801) and to **lieutenant-colonel** (1804). In 1808 he commanded the expedition against Bhangash Khan and in 1813 was promoted to **colonel**. Doveton was then promoted to **brigadier-general** in command of the Hyderabad contingent (1814) which he brought to a high state of efficiency. He commanded the force that relieved Nagpur (1817), for which he received the **CB** (1818). He was made **KCB** (1819) and promoted to **major-**

general. He retired to Madras (now Chennai) (1820) and was promoted to **lieutenant-general** and made **GCB** (1837).
See also **Asirghar, battle of**

Doyle, John (1750?–1834)

Doyle intended to become a lawyer but was commissioned as an **ensign** in the 48th Foot (**Northamptonshire Regiment of Foot**) (1771). He was promoted to **lieutenant** (1773), joined the 40th Foot (**Somersetshire (2nd) Regiment of Foot**), and went to America. He distinguished himself at the battle of Brooklyn and was present at **Brandywine** and **Germantown**, where he was wounded. He helped Lord Rawdon raise the Loyal American Legion (105th Foot) in which Doyle was made **captain** and with which he served at **Charlestown**. He was promoted to **major** (1781) and by the end of the war (1783) he was a **major-general**. In 1783 Doyle was elected MP for Mullingar in the Irish House of Commons and was made Irish secretary for war (1796). In 1793 he raised the 87th Foot (**Royal Irish Fusiliers**) and went with the Earl of Moira to the Netherlands. In 1799 he resigned his seat and went as **brigadier-general** to Gibraltar and then to Minorca. He then went to Egypt with Sir Ralph **Abercromby** where he played a major part in the campaign. He was made major-general (1802) and private secretary to the Prince of Wales. In 1804 Doyle was appointed lieutenant-governor of Guernsey and made a baronet (1805). He was promoted to **lieutenant-general** (1808), and **KB** (1813). He left Guernsey (1805) when the staff was reduced, and was made governor of Charlmont (1818). He was promoted to **general** (1819).

drab

The original name for khaki when it was adopted as a service colour
[From Old French *drap* 'cloth']

dragon's teeth

Rows of pyramid-shaped concrete pillars about six feet high, built in rows as protection against tanks

dragoon guards

By the 1740s the **regiments** of horse (normal **cavalry** as distinct from **dragoons** who were mounted infantry) were considered to be too expensive and were therefore downgraded to a status similar to that of the dragoons. To distinguish them, and as a consolation, they were given the title dragoon guards and were paid a little more than dragoons. The 1st Regiment of Horse retained that title, later becoming the Royal Horse Guards and eventually the **Blues and Royals**; the 2nd–8th Regiments of Horse, respectively, became the 1st–7th Dragoon Guards. Three regiments were converted in this way in 1746 with others following later. They generally retained the **red coats** previously worn by the horse. Several regiments in the modern army still use the term dragoon guards as part of their titles.

Dragoon Guards, 1st

The **regiment** was raised (1685) as the 2nd Horse, becoming the 1st Dragoon Guards in 1746.
See also **King's Own Regiment of Horse**; **Warburg, battle of**

Dragoon Guards, 2nd *See* **Queen's Bays, The**

Dragoon Guards, 3rd *See* **Warburg, battle of**

Dragoon Guards, 4th

Part of the **Heavy Brigade** at the battle of **Balaclava**

Dragoon Guards, 5th *See* **Princess Charlotte of Wales's Dragoon Guards**

Dragoon Guards, 6th *See* **Warburg, battle of**

Dragoon Guards, 7th (Princess Royal's)

The **regiment** was raised (1688) as the 8th Horse or Earl of Devonshire's Regiment. It took part in the battle of **Dettingen** when its **colours** would have been lost except for the bravery of **Cornet** Richardson who, although severely wounded, held on to them until he was rescued. George II personally presented him with the colours as a reward. The regiment became the 4th Regiment of Horse (1751), the 7th (The Princess Royal's) Dragoon Guards (1788) and the 7th Dragoon Guards (Princess Royal's) (1921). It amalgamated (1922) with the **4th Royal Irish Dragoon Guards** to form the 4th/7th Dragoon Guards.

See also **Warburg, battle of**

dragoons

In the 17th century, dragoons were mounted infantry, men who manoeuvred on horseback but fought on foot. They were armed with **carbines** nicknamed 'dragons' from the flaming match used to fire them, hence the name dragoons. They were mounted on inferior horses and were paid less than the contemporary horse **regiments** (though these were later designated as **dragoon guards**). In the 18th century the mounted infantry role gradually became obsolete and the dragoons became pure **cavalry**, indistinguishable from the dragoon guards other than in the details of uniform. From the 1750s a tactical need was perceived for two distinct types of cavalry, 'heavy' for battlefield charges and 'light' for scouting and skirmishing. From then into the 19th century an increasing number of dragoon regiments were converted to the light cavalry role, initially being entitled **light dragoons** and later **hussars** and **lancers**. Several regiments remained simply as dragoons and were classed as heavy cavalry.

Dragoons, 1st

The **regiment** was raised (1685) by Sir John Lanier as the Queen's Regiment of Horse which was re-named (1714) the King's Own Regiment of Horse. The name was changed (1746) to the 1st (or King's) Regiment of Dragoon Guards and in 1920 to the **1st King's Dragoon Guards**. The 1st Queen's Dragoon Guards was formed (1959) by the amalgamation of the 1st King's Dragoon Guards and the **Queen's Bays** (2nd Dragoon Guards).

See also **Royal Dragoons**

Dragoons, 2nd *See* **Royal Scots Greys**

Dragoons, 3rd *See* **King's Own Hussars**

Dragoons, 4th *See* **Queen's Own Hussars**

Dragoons, 6th *See* **Hussars, 20th; Inniskilling Dragoons**

Dragoons, 8th *See* **King's Royal Irish Hussars**

Dragoons, 10th *See* **Royal Hussars (Prince of Wales's Own)**

Dragoons, 12th *See* **Royal Lancers, 12th (Prince of Wales's)**

Dragoons, 13th *See* **Hussars, 13th; Light Brigade**

Dragoons, 14th *See* **King's Hussars (14th)**

Dragoons, 15th *See* **King's Hussars (15th)**

Dragoons, 18th *See* **Royal Hussars (Queen Mary's Own)**

Dragoons, 19th *See* **Royal Hussars (Queen Mary's Own)**

Dragoons, 20th *See* **Hussars, 20th**

Draper, William (1721–87)

Draper was born in Bristol and became a fellow of King's College, Cambridge (1749). He became an **ensign** in Lord Henry Beauclerk's 48th Foot (**Northamptonshire Regiment of Foot**) (1744). He was present at **Culloden Moor** and was appointed **adjutant** in a **battalion** of the 1st Foot (**Royal Scots**). He went to Flanders with the 2nd Battalion and was promoted to **captain** (1749). In 1757 Draper was promoted to **lieutenant-colonel** and raised the 79th Foot for service in the East Indies. The **regiment** arrived in Madras (now Chennai) and Draper distinguished himself at Fort St. George. He became commander of the troops in Madras when Stringer **Lawrence** resigned (1759) but returned home through ill-health. He was appointed deputy quartermaster-general (1760) and then **colonel** (1762). He returned to Madras as

brigadier-general and commanded the expedition against **Manila**. He was made colonel of the 16th Foot (**Bedfordshire and Hertfordshire Regiment**) (1765). He was involved in a political scandal involving the ransom received from Manila and his exchange to be colonel of the 121st Foot, but he was completely exonerated. Draper was promoted to **lieutenant-general** (1777) and appointed lieutenant-governor of Minorca (1779). He returned home (1782) and retired to Bath.

dress
The uniform worn by officers, in contrast to the **clothing** worn by the **other ranks**. Full dress uniform is made for display and, while it was formerly worn during battles, it is now worn only on parades and ceremonial occasions. Undress uniform is more informal, having few trimmings and a more comfortable cut than dress uniform.
[From the verb to *dress*, from Old French *dresser* 'to arrange, prepare']

Dress Regulations
It was not until 1802 that there was any serious attempt to regularise officers' dress. A very short 'General Orders on Dress for Officers' was issued in 1811 and the 16-page 'Dress of General and Staff Officers' in 1816. The complete 'Dress Regulations' was produced in 1822, but this was a guide to tailors, as officers had to provide their own uniforms. There was no need for its general publication as **other ranks** were provided with uniform. In 1860 a series of booklets was published to cover dress and some equipment in the British Army, but this did not continue. More recently Dress Regulations for officers have appeared at intervals.

drill
Regular structured exercises aimed at instilling discipline into troops and teaching the handling of weapons. Until the 19th century, drill also taught the complex coordinated movements required of large bodies of men on the battlefield.

Drogheda, battle of
(1649; *Civil War*) A punitive attack on the Irish Catholics at Drogheda by Oliver **Cromwell** using 10,000 troops of the **New Model Army**. The town, defended by the Marquess of Ormond, James Butler, fell (11 September) and Cromwell massacred all the priests and friars. This brutality is remembered in Ireland to this day.

Drogheda Light Horse *See* **Royal Hussars (Queen Mary's Own)**

Drumclog, battle of
(1679; *Scottish Covenanters' Revolt*) The Scottish Covenanters, having gained no relief from the repressive measures of the Duke of Lauderdale, revolted. Viscount **Dundee** met the rebels, led by John Balfour, at Drumclog (11 June) where the Covenanters won a decisive victory.

drumhead court martial
A **court martial** that takes place on the field of action, and very soon after an offence has allegedly been committed. It used to be carried out around an upturned drum.

drum-major
The original function of the drum-major was to teach drumming, but this was extended to include recruitment and punishment. Drum-majors wore distinctive uniforms including a broad sash over the shoulder. In 1881 drum-majors were called sergeant-drummers and wore four reversed **chevrons**. The name drum-major was restored in 1928 but the chevrons were retained. The elaborate staff carried by a drum-major is said to be derived from the cane used for punishment. Now the drum-major is the officer who leads and directs a military band when it is marching.

drummer
A person who plays a drum. Since the 17th century drummers' uniforms had 'reversed facings'. The normal soldier wore a **red coat** with the **facings** determined by the choice of the **colonel**. Thus the drummer was dressed in the livery of the colonel with red collars and cuffs. In 1831 the 'reversed facings' were discontinued and the drummers were distinguished by lace or braid.

Drummond, Gordon (1772–1854)
Drummond joined the army as an **ensign** in the 1st Foot (**Royal Scots**) (1789). His promotion was rapid so that by 1794 he was **lieutenant-colonel** of the 8th Foot (**King's Regiment (Liverpool)**). He served in the Netherlands (1794–95) and then with Sir Ralph **Abercromby** in the West Indies (1795–96). He was promoted to **colonel** (1798) and again served under Abercromby in Minorca and in Egypt, where he took part in the capture of Cairo and **Alexandria** (1801). His **regiment** then went to Malta and Gibraltar. Drummond returned home and took command of a division in Jamaica as **major-general** (1805). He was transferred to the staff in Canada (1808) and was promoted to **lieutenant-general** (1811) and second-in-command to Sir George **Prevost**. He took a prominent part in the **American War of 1812**. Drummond was made **colonel** of the 97th Foot (**Earl of Ulster's Regiment of Foot**) (1814) before returning home (1815). He was promoted to colonel of the 84th Foot (**York and Lancaster Regiment**) (1819); of the 71st Foot (**Highland Light Infantry**) (1824); and of the 49th Foot (**Princess Charlotte of Wales's Regiment**) (1829). He was promoted to **general** (1825) and in 1846 he finally became colonel of the 8th Foot.
See also **Chippewa river, battle of; Fort Erie, battle of**

DSC *abbreviation of* **Distinguished Service Cross**

DSM *abbreviation of* **Distinguished Service Medal**

DSO *abbreviation of* **Distinguished Service Order**

DU *See* **depleted uranium**

Duchess of York's Own Regiment of Light Dragoons *See* King's Hussars (14th)

Duke of Albany's Own Highlanders (72nd Foot)
The **regiment** was raised (1778) by the Earl of Seaforth as Seaforth's Highlanders, 78th Regiment of (Highland) Foot. The name was changed to 72nd (Highland) Regiment of Foot (1786); 72nd Regiment of Foot (1809) and 72nd (or The Duke of Albany's Own Highlanders) (1823).
See also **Seaforth Highlanders, The**

Duke of Beaufort's Musketeers *See* Devonshire Regiment

Duke of Cambridge's Own *See* East Middlesex Regiment of Foot

Duke of Clarence's Regiment of Foot *See* Queen's Own Regiment

Duke of Cornwall's Light Infantry
The **regiment** was formed (1881) by the amalgamation of the 32nd (Cornwall) Light Infantry and the 46th (**South Devonshire**) Regiment of Foot. In 1959 it was amalgamated once more to form part of the **Somerset and Cornwall Light Infantry**.

Duke of Edinburgh's Own Gurkha Rifles (7th)
The **regiment** was raised (1902) as the 8th Gurkha Rifles. By 1907 it was called the 7th Gurkha Rifles and then became the 7th Duke of Edinburgh's Own Gurkha Rifles (1959). It became part of the **Royal Gurkha Rifles** in 1994.

Duke of Edinburgh's Regiment of Foot
The **regiment** was raised (1824) as the 99th (or Lanarkshire) Regiment of Foot, with the name changing (1874) to the 99th (Duke of Edinburgh's) Regiment of Foot

Duke of Edinburgh's Royal Regiment (Berkshire and Wiltshire)
The **regiment** was formed (1959) by the amalgamation of the **Royal Berkshire Regiment (Princess Charlotte of Wales's)** and the **Wiltshire Regiment of Foot**. It amalgamated with The Gloucestershire Regiment to form **The Royal Gloucestershire, Berkshire and Wiltshire Regiment** in 1994.

Duke of Lancaster's Regiment (King's, Lancashire and Border)
The **regiment** is due to be formed in late 2006 by the amalgamation of The King's Own Royal Border Regiment, The King's Regiment and The Queen's Lancashire Regiment

Duke of Norfolk's Regiment of Foot *See* Cheshire Regiment; Suffolk Regiment

Duke of Wellington's Regiment

The **regiment** was raised (1702) as the Earl of Huntingdon's Regiment of Marines. The name changed with its **colonels** until 1751 when it became the 33rd Regiment of Foot. In 1782 the name was again changed to 33rd (or 1st Yorkshire West Riding) Regiment of Foot, and in 1853 Queen Victoria gave permission for it to be called the 33rd (Duke of Wellington's Regiment) as it was **Wellington's** first regiment. It was the only British regiment named after someone not of the royal family. The first battalion has most recently seen service in the war in Iraq.

See also **Abyssinian campaign**

Duke of Wellington's Regiment (West Riding)

The **regiment** was formed (1881) by the amalgamation of the 33rd (**Duke of Wellington's Regiment**) and the **76th Regiment of Foot**. It is expected to unite with The Prince of Wales's Own Regiment of Yorkshire and The Green Howards to form The Yorkshire Regiment (14th/15th, 19th, and 33rd/76th Foot) in 2006.

Duke of York's Own *See* East Yorkshire Regiment

Duke of York's Rifle Corps *See* King's Royal Rifle Corps

Dunbar, battle of

1. (1296; *English-Scottish Wars*) Having taken **Berwick**, Edward I of England moved into Scotland and met a Scottish force commanded by the Earl of Athol at Dunbar (27 April). The Scots were defeated, with some 10,000 killed. The king of Scotland, John Balliol, abdicated (2 June) after the English had taken Edinburgh. Edward took the Scottish Coronation Stone, the Stone of Scone, to England and proclaimed himself king of Scotland.

2. (1650; *Civil War*) The Scots disliked the government of the English Commonwealth and proclaimed Charles II their king. **Cromwell** moved a force to Scotland and met the Scots, commanded by David Leslie, at Dunbar. The Scots out-manoeuvred Cromwell and forced the English into the town, occupying the surrounding hills. When the Scots came down into the town, Cromwell broke the attack, killing 3,000 and taking 10,000 prisoners. In spite of this defeat, the Scots crowned Charles king at Scone (15 January 1651). General **Monck** was one of Cromwell's commanders during this battle.

Dundee, Viscount (1649–89)

Graham served as a soldier of fortune in France and the Netherlands before returning to Scotland (1678) as a **captain** of **dragoons**. He was sent south to suppress the Presbyterian rebels but was defeated at **Drumclog** (1 June 1679). He took part in the defeat of the rebels at **Bothwell Bridge** (22 June 1679). He then moved to England and when William of Orange invaded England (1688) Graham became second-in-command of the Scottish army sent to aid James II and was created Viscount Dundee. James fled from England (December 1688) and Dundee returned to Scotland to rally forces in support of James. His force routed that of General Hugh Mackay at **Killiecrankie** (17 July 1689), but during the battle Dundee was mortally wounded.

Also known as **John Graham of Claverhouse**; **Bonnie Dundee**

Dunes, battle of the (1658)

A French army supported by 6,000 English troops from the **New Model Army** besieged the Spanish-held town of Dunkirk in May 1658. A relieving Spanish army, which included a contingent of exiled English royalists under the future King James II, was met in battle by most of the besieging army on 14 June. The Spanish took up positions on the sand dunes near the town, but were routed. Dunkirk surrendered the same day.

Also called **Dunkirk, battle of**

Dunkirk, battle of

1. *See* **Dunes, battle of the**

2. (1940; *World War II*) The rapid advance of the Germans through France and Flanders, especially by their Panzer (**tank**) **divisions**, hemmed in the **British Expeditionary Force** and the French 1st Army at Dunquerque (Dunkirk). In spite of heavy air attack and bombardment, 338,000 troops were evacuated to the UK. The evacuation was remarkable in its use of every available ship, even private yachts and other small vessels.

Durham Light Infantry

The **regiment** was formed in 1881 by the amalgamation of the 68th (Durham) Light Infantry and the 106th Bombay Light Infantry. The original Durham Light Infantry was raised (1756) as the 2nd Battalion of the 23rd Regiment of Foot, and became the 68th Regiment of Foot (1768). In 1782 the name changed to 68th (or the Durham) Regiment of Foot and in 1808 to the 68th (Durham) Light Infantry.

E

Earle, William (1833–85)

Earle was educated at Winchester and entered the army as an **ensign** in the 49th Foot (**Princess Charlotte of Wales's (or Hertfordshire) Regiment**) (1851). He was promoted to **lieutenant** (1854) and went to the **Crimea** where he was present at the **Alma**, **Inkerman** and **Redan**. He was promoted to **captain** (1855) and transferred to the **Grenadier Guards** (1856). In 1863 he was promoted to captain in the Guards, equivalent to **lieutenant-colonel** in the rest of the army, and was assistant military secretary in Gibraltar (1859–60); brigadier-major in Nova Scotia (1862) and military secretary to General Doyle in North America (1865–72). He was promoted to **colonel** (1868). Earle was then appointed military secretary to Lord Northbrook in India (1872–78). In 1880 he was made **major-general** and in 1882 went to Egypt in command of the garrison at Alexandria (1882–84). For the defence of Alexandria he was made **CB**. Earle was killed at **Kirbekan**.

Earl of Angus' Regiment of Foot *See* **Cameronian Regiment of Foot**

Earl of Barrymore's Regiment of Foot *See* **Somerset Light Infantry**

Earl of Bath's Regiment of Foot *See* **Royal Lincolnshire Regiment**

Earl of Crawford's Regiment of Foot *See* **Black Watch, The**

Earl of Donegal's Regiment of Foot *See* **Royal Sussex Regiment**

Earl of Dumbarton's Regiment of Foot *See* **Royal Scots**

Earl of Huntingdon's Regiment of Foot *See* **Somerset Light Infantry**

Earl of Huntingdon's Regiment of Marines *See* **Duke of Wellington's Regiment**

Earl of Leven's Regiment of Foot *See* **King's Own Scottish Borderers**

Earl of Mar's Regiment of Foot *See* **Royal Scots Fusiliers**

Earl of Oxford's Regiment of Horse *See* **Blues and Royals**

Earl of Peterborough's Regiment of Foot *See* **Queen's Bays, The**

Earl of Plymouth's Regiment of Foot for Tangier *See* **King's Own Royal Regiment (Lancaster)**

Earl of Seaforth's Regiment of Foot *See* **Duke of Albany's Own Highlanders (72nd Foot)**

Earl of Shrewsbury's Horse *See* **Princess Charlotte of Wales's Dragoon Guards**

Earl of Ulster's Regiment of Foot

The **regiment** was raised (1824) as the 97th (Earl of Ulster's) Regiment of Foot. The name remained unchanged until 1881 when it was amalgamated with the 50th to form the **Queen's Own Royal West Kent Regiment**.

East Africa

1. (*World War I*) German East Africa (the present Rwanda, Burundi and continental Tanzania) was invaded from India by the British (November 1914). This attack was repelled by the locally trained African forces commanded by Paul von Lettow-Vorbeck. The East African situation remained undecided until February 1916 when the British, under General **Smuts**, invaded from Nyasaland (now Malawi) in the south while the Belgians invaded from the west. Dar es Salaam fell to Smuts (September 1916) and the Belgians took Tabora in the same month. Von Lettow-Vorbeck moved south across Portuguese East Africa (now Mozambique) (November 1917) and back into German East Africa to invade Northern Rhodesia (now Zambia) (September 1918). He took Kasama (8 November 1918), but the armistice was signed on 11 November, ending the war in Europe, and von Lettow-Vorbeck surrendered on 25 November.

2. (*World War II*) When Italy entered the war (10 June 1940), British Somaliland (now the northern part of Somalia) was surrounded on three sides by the Italians who advanced at Berera (15 August 1940), forcing General Godwin-Austen to evacuate across the gulf to Aden. On 10 February 1941 General Sir Alan **Cunningham** marched north-east from Kenya with the 1st South African and 11th East African Brigades, while General William **Platt** led two Indian regiments, the 4th and 5th, east from the Sudan. On 1 May Haile Selassie, emperor of Ethiopia, re-entered his capital Addis Ababa and the Italian commander-in-chief, the Duke of Aosta, surrendered with 220,000 men.

East Anglian 3rd Regiment (16th/44th Foot)
The **regiment** was formed (1958) by the amalgamation of the Bedfordshire and Hertfordshire Regiment and the Essex Regiment. It later became part of the **Royal Anglian Regiment**.

East Anglian (1st) Regiment (Royal Norfolk and Suffolk)
The **regiment** was formed (1959) by the amalgamation of the Royal Norfolk Regiment and the Suffolk Regiment. It later became part of the **Royal Anglian Regiment**.

East Anglian (2nd) Regiment (Duchess of Gloucester's Own Royal Lincolnshire and Northamptonshire)
The **regiment** was formed (1960) by the amalgamation of the Royal Lincolnshire Regiment and the Northamptonshire Regiment. It later became part of the **Royal Anglian Regiment**.

East Devonshire Regiment
20th Foot. The **regiment** was in Italy (1805) and took part in the battle of **Inkerman**. The name was changed (1881) to the **Lancashire Fusiliers**.

East Essex Regiment of Foot
The **regiment** was raised (1741) as the 55th Foot by Colonel James Long and was known as Colonel James Long's Regiment of Foot. The title changed with the name of the **colonel** until 1748 when it became the 44th Regiment of Foot and then the 44th (or East Essex) Regiment of Foot. It formed part of the **Essex Regiment** from 1881. The 1st Battalion (44th Foot) was annihilated at **Gandamak** during the First **Afghan War** in 1842.

East Indies
(1941–42; *World War II*) To prevent the Japanese invasions in the Malay Archipelago (the East Indies), the islands lying between mainland Asia and Australia, the Allies set up a unified command of Australian, British, Dutch and American (ABDA) troops commanded by Sir Archibald **Wavell**. When Wavell arrived in Bandoeng, in Java, the Japanese already had dominance in the Philippines, Malaya and most of the archipelago, except Java (by 31 January 1942). By 24 February Bali and Timor were occupied. The Allied position was hopeless and Wavell dissolved the consortium (25 February) and flew to take command in India. The Dutch refused to concede defeat, and after the destruction of an Allied naval force (27 February–1 March) the Japanese were free to land in Java. On 9 March the Dutch General Hein ter Poorten surrendered.

East Kent Regiment
The **regiment** was raised (1665) by Colonel Robert Sydney. It was called the Holland Regiment as many of its members had served as trained bands fighting with the Protestants in Holland. It was known as Prince George of Denmark's Regiment of Foot

(3rd Foot) (1689) and as the 3rd (or The Buffs) Regiment of Foot (1751). There were several other changes of name resulting in The Buffs (Royal East Kent Regiment) (1935) and, following an amalgamation in 1965, the **Queen's Own Buffs, The Kent Regiment**. The original uniform was scarlet with buff facings. The regiment was also known as 'The Resurrectionists' (referring to its claim to be as old as the **Scots Guards**) and 'The Nutcrackers'. It claims the privilege of marching through the City of London with bayonets fixed.

See also **Albuera, battle of**

East Lancashire Regiment

The **regiment** was formed (1881) by the amalgamation of the 30th (**Cambridgeshire (1st)**) Regiment of Foot and the 59th (**Nottinghamshire (2nd)**) Regiment of Foot. It was known originally as the West Lancashire Regiment but the name was changed later in 1881 to the East Lancashire Regiment. By a later amalgamation it became part of the **Lancashire Regiment (The Prince of Wales's Volunteers)**.

East Middlesex Regiment of Foot

The **regiment** was raised (1787) as the 77th Regiment of Foot. The name was changed to the 77th (The East Middlesex) Regiment of Foot (1807) and to the 77th (East Middlesex) Regiment (Duke of Cambridge's Own) in 1876. It was amalgamated to become part of the **Middlesex Regiment** in 1881. The title East Middlesex was also used by the 39th Foot (**Dorsetshire Regiment of Foot**) 1782–1807.

East Norfolk Regiment of Foot *See* **Royal Norfolk Regiment**

East Suffolk Regiment of Foot *See* **Suffolk Regiment**

East Surrey Regiment

The **regiment** was formed (1881) by the amalgamation of the 31st **Huntingdonshire Regiment** and the 70th **Surrey Regiment**. In 1959 it became part of the **Queen's Royal Surrey Regiment**.

East Yorkshire Regiment

The **regiment** was raised (1685) as Sir William Clifton's Regiment of Foot. The name was changed with the **colonel** until 1751 when it became the 15th Regiment of Foot. In 1752 it was named the 15th (or the Yorkshire East Riding) Regiment of Foot, becoming the East Yorkshire Regiment (1881). In 1935 the name was changed to the East Yorkshire Regiment (Duke of York's Own). In 1958 it became part of the **Prince of Wales's Own Regiment of Yorkshire**. The regiment took part in the battle of **Blenheim** and in the capture of **Quebec**.

Eaton Hall *See* **Mons Officer Cadet School**

Edgehill, battle of

(1642; *Civil War*) The first battle of the Civil War. The Parliamentarians with 20,000 infantry and 5,000 cavalry under the command of Robert Devereux, 2nd Earl of Essex, met the Royalist army of similar size marching south from Nottingham at Edgehill in Warwickshire (23 October). The Royalist cavalry, commanded by Prince **Rupert**, routed the Parliamentary infantry, but the Royalist infantry, left unprotected, were then severely harassed, losing their cannon. Both sides withdrew, the battle undecided.

Edinburgh Regiment *See* **King's Own Scottish Borderers**

Edinburgh's Royal Regiment (Berkshire and Wiltshire), Duke of *See* **Duke of Edinburgh's Royal Regiment (Berkshire and Wiltshire)**

Edington, battle of

(878; *Danish Invasion of Britain*) The battle at which Alfred the Great defeated the Danish king Guthrum. This led to the Peace of Wedmore by which the Danes were limited to the lands roughly north of the Thames while Alfred retained the southern part of the country. This ensured the survival of the kingdom of Wessex from which the Saxons would ultimately expand.

EGM *abbreviation of* **Empire Gallantry Medal**

Eisenhower, Dwight David (1890–1969)

Eisenhower was born in Kansas, the son of a creamery worker. He attended the local high school at Abilene and then entered the US Military Academy at West Point. He was commissioned **second lieutenant** and sent to San Antonio, Texas, where he married. During **World War I** he commanded a **tank** training centre and then served in the Panama Zone (1922–24). He was selected to attend the Command and General Staff School at Fort Leavenworth, graduating in 1926. He was now a **major**. In 1928 he graduated from the Army War College, and served in France before becoming aide to US Army Chief of Staff General Douglas MacArthur (1933), with whom he went to the Philippines to assist in reorganising the army there. He was promoted to **lieutenant-colonel** and returned to the US (1939). He was made a full **colonel** (1941) and in the same year chief of staff of the 3rd Army. He was promoted to **brigadier-general** (September 1941) and in December 1941 Army Chief of Staff General George C. Marshall appointed Eisenhower to the Army's War Plans Division in Washington. He was promoted to **major-general** (March 1942) and appointed head of the Operations Division of the War Department. In June 1942 Marshall appointed him commander of the US troops in Europe. Eisenhower was promoted to **lieutenant-general** (July 1942) and made head of the Allied invasion of French **North-West Africa** (Operation Torch) (November 1942). In February 1943 he was promoted to **general** and directed the amphibious assault on **Sicily** and the Allied drive through Italy. In December 1943 Eisenhower was appointed supreme commander of the Allied Expeditionary Forces and went to London to prepare for the **Normandy** invasion. In December 1944 he was promoted to the newly created rank of general of the army. On his return to the USA (November 1945) he replaced Marshall as chief of staff. He left active service (May 1948) and became president of Columbia University. In 1950 President Truman appointed him supreme commander of **NATO**. He was the 34th President of the United States (1953–61).

El Alamein, battle of

1. (1942; *World War II*) After the fall of **Tobruk** the British 8th Army, commanded by General Sir Claude **Auchinleck**, fell back eastwards from Libya into Egypt pursued by **Rommel's** Panzer (**tank**) divisions of the Afrika Korps. Auchinleck set up a defensive position just west of El Alamein running south to the Qattara Depression. A battle took place (10–27 July) but was indecisive. It had stemmed the Axis advance and gave the British time to re-build the 8th Army. Because there was no absolute victory Auchinleck was relieved as Commander-in-Chief, Middle East, by General Harold **Alexander** with General Bernard **Montgomery** taking over command of the 8th Army.
2. (1942; *World War II*) By October 1942 the 8th Army had been reinforced and the second battle of El Alamein began with an 800-gun barrage (23–24 October). By 4–5 November the Axis withdrawal had begun – Tobruk (13 November), Benghazi (20 November) and Tripoli (23 January) were retaken. This was one of the decisive battles of the war.

electronic warfare

The utilisation of the electromagnetic spectrum in warfare. Electronic warfare falls into three main areas: (a) surveillance using radio, radar, infrared radiation, etc., to gather intelligence about the enemy's movements and intentions and specifically to identify potential targets and threats; (b) **electronic countermeasures** (ECM), or **electronic attack** (EA), which seeks to disrupt the enemy's surveillance, communications or other systems, e.g. by **jamming** (overloading detection systems with random or false information) or by powerful electromagnetic pulses that damage delicate electronic systems; and (c) **electronic counter-countermeasures** (ECCM), or **electronic protection** (EP), which seeks to defend against ECM by such techniques as rapidly changing radio transmission frequencies in a pseudo-random fashion to avoid jamming signals. The scope for ECM and ECCM is continually widening as military equipment becomes more reliant on sophisticated electronics and computers.

Eliott, George Augustus (1717–90)

Eliott was born at Stobs, Scotland, and educated at the University of Leyden and the French military academy at La Fère. He served as a volunteer in the Prussian Army and ultimately became a **cornet** in the 2nd Horse Grenadier Guards (2nd Life Guards) (1739). He served throughout the War of the **Austrian Succession**, including at the battles of **Dettingen** and **Fontenoy**. By 1754 he was a **lieutenant-colonel**, aide to George II (1756) and **colonel** of the 1st Light Horse (**King's Hussars (15th)**) (1759). He was noted for his care of the troops. He served in Cuba (1762) and bought estates from his share of the booty from the capture of **Havana**. Eliott was **commander-in-chief** in Ireland (1774–75) and was made governor of Gibraltar (1775) where he was in command during the siege (1779–82). He was created Lord Heathfield (1787).

Eliott's Light Horse *See* **King's Hussars (15th)**

elite troops

Special troops, such as light or **grenadier companies** or **light infantry**, trained for specialised operations rather than taking part in the main thrust of a battle. They were frequently given distinctive uniforms.

El Obeid, battle of

(1883; *Sudan War*) The Muslim leader in the Sudan, the **Mahdi**, revolted (1881–82) against Egyptian misrule. As Egypt was a protectorate of Great Britain, Sir William **Hicks** led an Egyptian expedition to put down the revolt. He met a rebel force at El Obeid, 220 miles south-west of Khartoum (1 November) where his army of about 10,000 men became trapped in a defile. After four days fighting, the whole force, including Hicks was killed. The battle strengthened the British government's resolve to withdraw from the Sudan.

See also **El Teb, battle of**

Elphinstone, William George Keith (1782–1842)

Elphinstone, whose father was a director of the East India Company, joined the army as an **ensign** in the 41st Foot (**Welsh Regiment**) (1804) and was a **captain** in the 93rd Foot (**Sutherland Highlanders**) by 1806. He transferred to the **Grenadier Guards** (1807) and to the 15th Light Dragoons (**King's Hussars (15th)**) (1810). He was promoted to **major** in the 8th West India Regiment (1811) and purchased a lieutenant-colonelcy in the 33rd Foot (**Duke of Wellington's Regiment**) (1813). He served with distinction at **Waterloo** and was made a CB. Elphinstone commanded his **regiment** until 1822 and then went on half pay. He was promoted to **colonel** and made **aide-de-camp** to the king (1825) and promoted to **major-general** (1837). In 1839 he was appointed to command the Benares **Division** of the Bengal Army and given command of the army at **Kabul** (1841). Elphinstone's poor health contributed to his mismanagement of this disastrous campaign. He was captured by the Afghans and died of dysentery in captivity.

See also **Afghan Wars**

El Teb, battle of

(1884; *Sudan War*) The increasing pressure of the rebels in the Sudan led the British government to withdraw the Anglo-Egyptian forces. One of the withdrawing columns was ambushed at El Teb, near Suakin on the Red Sea (4 February) and some 3,500 men were killed. At a second battle (29 March) the rebels were repulsed.

See also **El Obeid, battle of**

Empire Gallantry Medal

The Medal of the Order of the British Empire for Gallantry was instituted in 1922, with both civil and military divisions, to mark acts of gallantry. It became obsolete on the foundation of the **George Cross** in 1940, and all existing holders were obliged to exchange their decorations for the GC.

Abbreviation **EGM**

Enfield rifle *See* rifle

Enfield Small Arms Factory
The manufacture of small arms was in the hands of private contractors until 1802 when locks were made and firearms assembled at the Tower of London. In 1808 a factory was established at Lewisham for the production of locks and barrels. In 1800 a large number of walnut trees, the wood of which was used to make the stocks of rifles, had been planted at Waltham Abbey and nearby Enfield Lock. When the facilities at the Tower became too small, an arms factory was built at Enfield (1804). By the end of the **French Wars** (1792–1815) the making of all government small arms was transferred to Enfield, but it was not until the middle of the 19th century that the factory manufactured complete weapons. Up to this time the individual parts of firearms were made by small manufacturers and these parts were then assembled at Enfield.

engineers
The need for properly trained engineers was recognised early in the formation of the regular army. They had existed earlier when they were called trench-masters or pioneers; those working in fortresses were called surveyors. Charles I employed foreign engineers, especially Dutch, and these engineers were attached to the Board of **Ordnance**. Further engineers were employed if extra work was envisaged at home or abroad. At the end of the campaign they were discharged or put on half pay. The engineers held no military rank but by the early 18th century they were ranked as officers as regards the payment of prize money.

See also **artificers; Pitt's Reforms; reforms after the Crimean War; Royal Engineers, Corps of**

England, Richard (1793–1883)
England was born in Detroit and was educated at Winchester. He joined the army as an **ensign** in the 14th Foot (**West Yorkshire Regiment**) (1808). He was promoted to **lieutenant** (1809) and served in the Netherlands and Sicily. He was promoted to **captain** in the 60th Foot (**King's Royal Rifle Corps**) (1811) and exchanged to the 12th Foot (**Suffolk Regiment**) (1812). During 1815–18 he served in the army of occupation in France and during 1821–23 was **aide-de-camp** in Dublin. England was promoted to **major** in the 75th Foot (**Stirlingshire Regiment**) (1823) and **lieutenant-colonel** (1825). In 1833 the **regiment** went to the Cape where England was promoted to **brigadier-general** commanding the eastern front during the **Kaffir Wars**. He was promoted to **colonel** (1838). In 1839 he was transferred to the 41st Foot (**Welsh Regiment**) and commanded the Belgaum district of Bombay (now Mumbai) as brigadier-general. In 1841 he was made commander of the Bombay Division. He relieved General **Nott** at Kandahar and took part in the battle of **Khojah**. His conduct was criticised by Nott but in spite of this he was made **KCB** (1843). England gave up his command and settled in Bath. In 1849 he was given command of the Curragh Brigade and promoted to **major-general** (1851). He then commanded the 3rd Division in the **Crimea** where he was present at the battle of the **Alma**, took a prominent part at **Inkerman** and directed the attack on the **Redan**. He returned to Britain (1855) in poor health and saw no further active service. England was promoted to **lieutenant-general** and made **GCB**. He was made colonel of the 41st Foot and promoted to **general** (1877).

English-Scottish Wars (c. 1290 – c. 1550)
The struggle of the Scots to gain political independence from England and to establish their national identity lasted several centuries. The ruthlessness of the English campaigns and their determination to maintain dominance in Scotland was partly dictated by the continued Scottish alliance with France during this period.

See also **Hundred Years' War**

ensign

A banner or sign of office, or the officer who carried such a flag or banner. An ensign was the most junior commissioned officer in the **infantry**. This rank has now been replaced by **second lieutenant**.

See also **colours**

[From Old French *enseigne*, from Latin *insignia* 'badges']

epaulette

An ornamental piece of cloth worn on the shoulder. Epaulettes originated from the need to keep shoulder sashes or belts in position. They later became highly ornamented and by 1810 various crowns and stars were worn on them to indicate an officer's rank. They are still worn in this way to the present day in most working and dress uniforms, though not now in combat.

[From French *épaulette*, from *épaule* 'shoulder']

esmeril

A very light **culverin** weighing 200 pounds and 2.5 feet long. It had a 1 inch bore and fired a 0.3 pound projectile with an effective range of 200 yards.

Also called **rabinet**

espontoon *See* **spontoon**

Essex Regiment

The **regiment** was formed (1881) by the amalgamation of the 44th (**East Essex**) Regiment of Foot and the 56th (**West Essex**) Regiment of Foot. The regiment took part in the Khartoum expedition (1884). It amalgamated with the Bedfordshire and Hertfordshire Regiment (1958) to form the 3rd East Anglian Regiment.

European Regiment *See* **Bombay Light Infantry**

Eutaw Springs, battle of

(1781; *American War of Independence*) The American commander General Nathaniel Greene occupied the High Hills of the Santee river in South Carolina and from there moved against the British commanded by Lieutenant-Colonel Alexander Stuart at Orangeburg. The British fell back to Eutaw Springs to avoid being cut off from Charleston. Greene attacked (8 September) and the British were at first forced to retreat but defeated the Americans in a counter-attack. In spite of this victory, the British position in the south was severely jeopardised, and with **Yorktown** surrendering six weeks later, this was the last pitched battle of the war in the south.

Evesham, battle of

(1265; *Barons' Wars*) Simon de Montfort had led the rebel barons across the Severn at Worcester to meet up with his son's army, which, unknown to de Montfort, had been defeated at **Kenilworth**. The royalist army led by Prince Edward (later Edward I) caught up with the barons at Evesham (4 August). During the ensuing battle the rebel forces were massacred and de Montfort killed.

Experimental Corps of Riflemen *See* **Rifle Brigade, The**

Eyre, Vincent (1811–81)

Eyre joined the Military Academy at Addiscombe and was **gazetted** to the Bengal establishment (1829). In 1837 he was a **lieutenant** in the horse **artillery** and **commissary** of ordnance at Kabul (1839). He was wounded during the First **Afghan War** and he and his family were taken hostage. He was rescued and appointed commander of artillery at Gwalior (1844) where he improved the settlement. Having been home on leave he returned to India (1857). He served in Burma (now Myanmar) but returned to India as a **major** at the outbreak of the **Indian Mutiny**. He took part in the relief of **Lucknow**. He retired (1863) with the rank of **major-general**. During the Franco-Prussian War he organised an ambulance service under the **Red Cross**.

F

facings
The material used to line soldiers' coats from the 17th century onwards. When the cuffs, collar or skirts were turned back the facings were revealed. Facings in a variety of colours were worn by different **regiments** until 1881 when they were simplified to blue for Royal regiments, white for English and Welsh, yellow for Scottish and green for Irish. This was not a popular move and when the **Buffs** reverted to their buff facings, other regiments were allowed to change back to their traditional colours. When full **dress** for **other ranks** was largely abolished after **World War I** facings ceased to be a feature of uniforms, though in both earlier and modern times the facing colour has also featured as the background colour on each regiment's **colours**.

Fairfax, Thomas (1612–71)
Fairfax attended Cambridge University and fought with the Dutch against the Spanish (1629–31). He took part in the **Bishops' Wars** (1639 and 1640) against the Scots and was knighted (1640). He succeeded to his father's title of Baron Fairfax of Cameron in 1648. At the beginning of the **Civil War** he supported the Parliamentarians, commanding the **cavalry** in his native Yorkshire. In 1645 he was appointed **commander-in-chief** of the **New Model Army**. He hoped to establish a limited monarchy and refused to serve on the commission that condemned Charles I to death. He resigned as commander-in-chief (1650) over the proposed invasion of Scotland and retired from politics. He quarrelled with his friend **Cromwell** (1657) and after Cromwell's death (1658) helped **Monck** to restore parliamentary rule in the face of opposition from the army. He was a member of the parliament that invited Charles II to return to England (1660).

Falaise Gap, battle of
(1944; *World War II*) When the Allied forces began to break out of the **Normandy** beachhead very large German forces were trapped by a pincer movement performed by the US 1st and 3rd Armies on the one hand and the British 2nd and Canadian 1st Armies on the other. The Americans moved towards Falaise from the south and the British-led forces from the north (13 August). The only possible escape was to the east. The Germans were subjected to incessant artillery fire and air attacks; their escape route was blocked by 19 August. The fighting continued until 21 August, but the German armies in Normandy were destroyed.

falcon
A lightweight **culverin**. It weighed 800 pounds and was 6 feet long. It had a bore of 2.5 inches and fired a 3 pound shot over an effective range of 400 yards.
[From the custom of naming firearms after birds of prey]

falconet
A lightweight **culverin**. It weighed 500 pounds and was 3.7 feet long. It had a bore of 2 inches and fired a 1 pound shot over an effective range of 280 yards.

Falkenhayn, Erich Georg Anton Sebastian von (1861–1922)
Falkenhayn was a member of the Prussian general staff and served in the international expedition (1900) against the Boxers in China. He was Prussian minister for war (1913–15) and in 1914 also replaced General Helmuth von **Moltke** as chief of the general staff after Germany's failure to conquer France in 1914. Falkenhayn tried to balance Germany's priorities between the Western and Eastern Fronts and supporting

Austria-Hungary against Serbia. He came into conflict with **Hindenburg** and **Ludendorff**, then Germany's principal commanders in the war against Russia. In 1916 Falkenhayn prepared a massive new attack on the French at Verdun but was dismissed as chief of the general staff later in the year when this attack and other operations had not achieved decisive results. He was replaced by Hindenburg. Falkenhayn then commanded the German force which overran Romania before commanding the Central Powers' forces (mainly Turkish) against **Allenby** in Palestine (1917). He was replaced by General Otto Liman von Sanders and served in Lithuania (March 1918) until the end of the war.

Falkirk, battle of

1. (1298; *English-Scottish Wars*) After the English defeat at **Stirling Bridge**, and having established the support of France by marrying King Philip IV's sister, Edward I took the field against the Scots led by Sir William Wallace at Falkirk (22 July). The Scots were decimated by the English **longbows** and the subsequent **cavalry** charge. Wallace escaped but was captured in Glasgow (1305) and hanged, drawn and quartered at Tyburn (London).

2. (1746; *Jacobite Rebellions*) After Prince Charles Edward (Bonnie Prince Charlie) had invaded England he was forced to withdraw to Scotland due to lack of support. The harrying Hanoverian army was kept at bay by Lord George Murray. At Falkirk the army of 6,000 Scots turned on the Hanoverian force of similar size (17 January), breaking the Hanoverian lines and inflicting heavy losses. This temporarily preserved the Jacobite position in Scotland.

See also **Culloden Moor, battle of**

Falklands War (1982)

Argentina has long claimed sovereignty over the Falkland Islands though these have been administered by Britain since 1833. An Argentine force under the command of General Mario Benjamín Menéndez landed at Port Stanley in the Falklands (2 April) and occupied the islands, called the Malvinas by Argentina. The Argentinians also took control of South Georgia the next day. Britain sent a task force led by Rear-Admiral John Woodward from the UK to recover the islands. On 23 April a small force of Royal Marine **commandos** and the **Special Air Service Regiment** re-took South Georgia. British warships, including two aircraft carriers, established a 200-mile exclusion zone around the islands. Port Stanley airport was bombed (1 May); the Argentinian cruiser Belgrano was sunk by a submarine (2 May) and the British carrier aircraft gained air superiority over the islands. The Argentinian aircraft now had to operate at the extreme of their range from their home bases. The main assault force, commanded by Major-General Jeremy Moore, landed at San Carlos Water (21 May) and moved on from there to take the settlements of Darwin and **Goose Green**. Royal Marines, **Scots** and **Welsh Guards**, the **Parachute Regiment** and Gurkhas were among the **regiments** taking part. Later there was fierce fighting, particularly at Mount Tumbledown and Mount Longdon, on the approaches to the islands' capital, Port Stanley. Air attacks by the Argentinians achieved some successes, sinking the cruiser Sheffield and the container ship Atlantic Conveyor and damaging landing ships at Bluff Cove, all of these causing significant casualties. Port Stanley had been surrounded and would shortly have fallen when General Menéndez decided to surrender (14 June). Some 10,000 prisoners were taken but ultimately repatriated. The British forces lost some 250 dead, while the Argentinians lost at least 700.

FANY *abbreviation of* **First Aid Nursing Yeomanry**

Farquhar's Farm, battle of

(1899; *Boer Wars*) The garrison at **Ladysmith**, commanded by Sir George **White**, moved out in three columns to attack the Boer army commanded by **Joubert** (30 October). The left hand column detached to hold Nicholson's Nek was overwhelmed while a Boer attack on the right, and lack of heavy guns, forced White to retreat. The retreat was helped by the arrival of two heavy naval guns. The British lost 317 killed and wounded, with 1,068 missing. The Boer losses were light.

farriers
Soldiers that took care of the **cavalry** horses, especially their shoeing. They wore blue coats and wore a fur cap with a horse-shoe cap badge. They also wore leather aprons and carried axes, even on horseback. The special dress for farriers of cavalry of the line disappeared in the 19th century, but a similar ceremonial uniform is still worn by farriers of the **Household Cavalry**.

Farrington's (Colonel Farrington's Regiment of Foot) *See* **Worcestershire Regiment**

Farrukhabad, battle of
(1804; *Maratha Wars*) After being initially suppressed (1803), the Maratha chief Jaswant Ras Holkar renewed the war along the Upper Ganges. The rebels were met by a British force commanded by General Gerard **Lake**. The Marathas were routed with only two British soldiers killed.

fascines
Large bundles of brushwood or similar materials, tied together and used to fill ditches and construct batteries for guns

fatigue dress
Simple clothing worn for day-to-day duties when uniforms may get dirty. In the 18th century a long grey coat was worn. Later the soldiers' usual **red coat** was simply removed and a cloth cap worn instead of the hat. By the end of the century strong overalls or short jackets in white or a light colour were worn. From 1844 red fatigue jackets were worn by **infantry** and blue by the **cavalry**, while the **Foot Guards** and Highlanders continued to wear white. With the introduction of **khaki** everyday uniforms the specific fatigue dress disappeared, though **denims** and other types of overalls have been commonly used for potentially dirty work up to the modern era.

faulconet
A light cannon, firing a shot of just over 2.2 pounds

fencibles
Before 1663 the name applied to the local levies raised in Scotland, but by the 18th century the term was applied to troops raised specifically for the defence of Great Britain during wartime.
See also **trained bands**

Fenwick's Regiment *See* **Coldstream Guards**

Ferkah, battle of
(1896; *Sudan War*) A force of 9,500 Egyptian troops and a British horse battery, commanded by General **Kitchener**, made a surprise attack at night on 4,500 Mahdists commanded by Emir Hamada. The Mahdists were driven from their camp with the loss of 1,500 killed. 44 of the 62 emirs in the camps were killed and four captured. The Egyptians lost 20 killed and 81 wounded.

Ferozeshah, battle of
(1845; *Sikh Wars*) Having defeated the Sikhs at **Mudki**, General Sir Hugh **Gough** pressed into the East Punjab with 16,000 Anglo-Indian troops. He reached Ferozeshah (21 December) where he attacked some 50,000 entrenched Sikhs. The first assault failed, but the second was successful. 7,000 Sikhs were killed while Gough lost 694 killed and 1,721 wounded. This was one of the bloodiest battles of any in India.

Ferrybridge, battle of
(1461; *Wars of the Roses*) Edward of York had proclaimed himself Edward IV and marched north against the Lancastrian forces of Henry VI who were entrenched along the Aire river in western Yorkshire. The Lancastrian Lord Clifford at first repelled the attack by the Yorkist Lord Fitzwilliam, who was killed (28 March), but when Yorkist

reinforcements arrived they took the bridge. During the second attack Clifford was killed.

field dressing
An emergency first aid package carried by individual soldiers. They were first introduced during the **Crimean War** when they consisted of a calico bandage and pins. They were originally carried in the knapsack but then in the left-hand tunic pocket (1874). The first antiseptic field dressings were issued in 1884. The components changed and became more comprehensive. In **World War I** the field dressing was carried inside the tunic, and in **World War II** in a pocket on the right hand front of the **battle dress** trousers.

field gun
An **artillery** weapon designed for use in battles 'in the field' and therefore capable of being moved reasonably easily, as distinct from guns employed in fixed defences ('fortress guns') or those guns used to attack defended localities ('siege guns'). For much of the 19th and early 20th centuries the Royal **Artillery** was divided into two sections, a mounted branch which provided the field artillery, and a dismounted branch, the **Royal Garrison Artillery**.

Fielding's (Colonel Fielding's Regiment of Foot) *See* Welsh Regiment

field mark
During the 17th century forces on opposing sides could look very similar as there were no regular distinctive uniforms, so troops would use a distinctive mark, such as a bunch of leaves or a piece of cloth, to distinguish friend from foe

field marshal
The highest rank in the army. The rank has existed since 1736 and from the earliest times to the present has most often been awarded on an honorary basis to British and also foreign royalty. Particularly successful commanders have also received the rank as, in modern times, have army officers who have been Chiefs of the Defence Staff.
See also **constable**

field officer
Originally, an officer of the rank of **captain** and below who commanded troops in the field, in contrast to **staff officers** who had overall command of a battle or engagement. In the 17th century each **company** acted as an independent unit and was commanded by a **captain**, **lieutenant** and **ensign** who were field officers. As better co-ordination between companies became necessary, senior (staff) officers were created such as the **colonel** (of a **regiment**), **lieutenant-colonel** and **major**. Later, as their roles changed, the latter two became field officers.

fire
The command given to discharge an **artillery gun** or a personal weapon. It originates from the command 'Give fire' meaning to apply a slow match to the touch-hole of a **musket**.
[From Old English *fyr*]

fire master
The member of an artillery train who was responsible for manufacturing the explosives used to destroy bridges, city gates etc. He would have three or four assistants, who were called fire workers

fire worker *See* fire master

First Aid Nursing Yeomanry
A women's corps of mounted medical orderlies founded in 1909. Their function was to ride on to the battlefield, give first aid to the wounded and bring them back to hospital. In 1914 they became ambulance drivers and hospital nurses. The name was changed (1927) to the First Aid Nursing Yeomanry (Ambulance Car Corps) and to the

Women's Transport Service (FANY) in 1933. They later lost their connection with nursing and were absorbed into the ATS.
Abbreviation **FANY**

first lieutenant *See* **lieutenant**

First World War *See* **World War I**

Fitzjames, James *See* **Berwick, Duke of**

flak jacket *See* **bulletproof vest**

flame thrower
The modern flame thrower was invented during the 1900s by the German Richard Fiedler and was first used by the Germans against the Allies in 1915. The pattern of the flame thrower thereafter remained essentially unchanged, being a fuel tank or tanks, a container of compressed gas or some other means of spraying the flammable material, and some form of ignition. Flame throwers could be small enough to be carried and operated by one man or could be mounted in a vehicle, usually a modified **tank**. Even the largest types had a short range, usually less than 100 yards. They were used fairly extensively by British forces during **World War II** in attacks on fortified positions but are not employed by the present-day British Army.

Flanders
(1940; *World War II*) The German assault through the Netherlands and Belgium began (10 May) when their airborne troops captured two bridges over the Albert Canal, while the 6th Army of two **divisions** crossed the Meuse river at Maastricht. Liège fell (11 May) and by 20 May the combined French 1st Army and the **British Expeditionary Force** had been forced back across the Scheldt river. Meanwhile Marshal Gerd von **Rundstedt** had moved his army of 44 divisions southwards to the French frontier (12 May) establishing bridgeheads over the Meuse at Sedan. By 20–21 May the German Panzer (**tank**) divisions had smashed through the French Army to reach the coast at Abbeville. The French and British counter-attacks were repulsed and the Germans took Boulogne (23 May) and Calais (27 May). The Belgians surrendered (28 May) leaving the combined British and French forces to escape from Dunquerque (**Dunkirk**).

flank company
In the 18th and 19th centuries **infantry battalions** had **companies** of **light infantry** and **grenadiers** trained for special duties. These companies were referred to as flank companies because one took position on each flank of the battalion when it was drawn up in line ready for battle.

flash
1. The ribbon used to tie a **queue**, or pigtail. When the queue was abolished c.1808, the Welsh Fusiliers were abroad and continued to wear the flash as a ribbon worn at the back of the collar.
2. Cloth signs sewn on the uniform since World War I
3. The end of the ribbons shown below the turn-down of knee-length socks worn by Highland regiments and as part of tropical dress

Fleurus, battle of
(1690; *War of the Grand Alliance*) Louis XIV of France had overrun the Palatinate (1688) and the European powers that had formed the League of Augsburg reorganised as the Grand Alliance. Both Louis and the Grand Alliance rushed forces into the Spanish Netherlands (now Belgium). The armies met at Fleurus. Prince George Frederick of Waldeck commanded 40,000 Allied troops in a strong position behind a marsh, but was attacked frontally and by a pincer movement by the French troops commanded by the Marshal Duc de Luxembourg. The Allied army was smashed, with 5,000 killed and 8,000 taken prisoner; 48 guns and 150 **colours** were also lost.

flintlock
A firing system for firearms developed during the early 16th century. It replaced the **matchlock** and **wheellock**. A more advanced form of flintlock was developed in

France during the early 17th century. This consisted of a horizontal priming pan which was loaded with a small charge of gunpowder and was covered by a pan and striker (frizzen) made in one piece; in front of this was mounted a piece of flint. When the trigger was pulled the flint hit the striker which showered sparks onto the powder. This ignited and in turn ignited the main charge in the **barrel** which propelled the ball. This type of mechanism remained standard for all firearms until the invention of the **percussion cap** at the start of the 19th century.

Flodden, battle of

(1513; *English-Scottish Wars*) While Henry VIII was invading France, the Scots, led by King James IV, crossed the Tweed. The English army of 25,000, led by Thomas Howard, Earl of Surrey, out-flanked the Scottish army of 50,000 and forced them to attack at Flodden (9 September). The English **longbows** cut down the Scots spearmen and the English victory was completed by hand-to-hand fighting. James IV was killed. This was the last major battle won by the longbow.

Flügelman

The man on the wing of a **company** who was expected to move forward and demonstrate drill movements to the rest of the company
[From German *Flügelmann*, from *Flügel* 'wing']

Foch, Ferdinand (1851–1929)

Foch entered the French **artillery** training school (1873) and joined the War College (1885) where he became professor. By 1908 he was a **brigadier-general** and head of the school. He commanded a **division** (1911) and was put in command of the XX Army Corps at Nancy (1913). When **World War I** broke out (1914) he was within three years of retirement age but fought under **Joffre** in Lorraine. His tenacity in command of the 9th Army enabled Joffre to win the First Battle of the **Marne**. Joffre then sent him to coordinate the attacks of the British, French and Belgians at **Ypres**. During 1915–16 Foch commanded the Northern Army Group and in 1917 was appointed chief of the French War Minister's general staff when he advocated a single command of the Allied forces. This was not accepted by the British or the French high commands. The near-collapse of the separate British and French fronts in the face of the German offensives in the spring of 1918 proved Foch right and he was made **commander-in-chief** of the Allied forces on the Western and Italian Fronts. By improving the mutual support between the British and French forces he was able to hold the **Western Front** against the German General **Ludendorff** while awaiting the arrival of the Americans. On 18 July and 8 August Foch took the offensive and Germany asked for an armistice which was dictated by Foch at Rethondes (11 November 1918). He was created a marshal of France (6 August 1918). After the war he was honoured as a **field marshal** of Great Britain and of Poland. He was buried near **Napoleon** in the Church of Saint-Louis in the Invalides in Paris.

Fontenoy, battle of

(1745; *War of the Austrian Succession*) Louis XV of France concentrated his forces for a campaign in the southern Netherlands (now Belgium). The French forces commanded by Marshal Comte Maurice **Saxe** besieged Tournai with 50,000 men. The Allied forces commanded by the Duke of **Cumberland** moved to relieve the city and the two armies met at Fontenoy where Saxe had established a strong defensive position. The Allied column failed to force its way between the two redoubts and had to fall back with the loss of 7,000 men dead and wounded. Cumberland withdrew to Brussels and Tournai fell. This was the last battle that the British forces fought during the war, the army being recalled to put down the **Jacobite Rebellion** in Scotland.
See also **Border Regiment**

Foot, 1st *See* Royal Scots

Foot, 2nd *See* Queen's Royal Regiment (West Surrey)

Foot, 3rd *See* East Kent Regiment

Foot, 4th *See* King's Own Royal Regiment (Lancaster)

Foot, 5th *See* Royal Northumberland Fusiliers

Foot, 6th *See* marines; Royal Warwickshire Fusiliers

Foot, 7th *See* Albuera, battle of; Alma, battle of the; Royal Fusiliers (City of London Regiment)

Foot, 8th *See* King's Regiment (Liverpool); West Suffolk Regiment of Foot

Foot, 9th *See* Royal Norfolk Regiment

Foot, 10th *See* Royal Lincolnshire Regiment

Foot, 11th *See* Devonshire Regiment

Foot, 12th *See* Suffolk Regiment; Yorkshire North Riding Regiment of Foot (2nd)

Foot, 13th *See* Somerset Light Infantry

Foot, 14th *See* West Yorkshire Regiment

Foot, 15th *See* East Yorkshire Regiment

Foot, 16th *See* Bedfordshire and Hertfordshire Regiment

Foot, 17th *See* Royal Leicestershire Regiment

Foot, 19th *See* Green Howards, The; marines

Foot, 20th *See* marines; East Devonshire Regiment; Lancashire Fusiliers; South Hampshire Regiment of Foot

Foot, 21st *See* Royal Scots Fusiliers

Foot, 22nd *See* Cheshire Regiment; Dettingen, battle of

Foot, 23rd *See* Alma, battle of the; Atkins, Tommy; Durham Light Infantry; Royal Welch Fusiliers

Foot, 24th *See* Chilianwala, battle of; South Wales Borderers

Foot, 25th *See* South Wales Borderers

Foot, 26th *See* Cameronian Regiment of Foot

Foot, 27th *See* Inniskilling Regiment of Foot

Foot, 28th *See* Alexandria, battle of; North Gloucestershire Regiment

Foot, 29th *See* Worcestershire Regiment

Foot, 30th *See* Cambridgeshire (1st) Regiment of Foot

Foot, 31st *See* Huntingdonshire Regiment

Foot, 32nd *See* Cornwall Light Infantry; Duke of Cornwall's Light Infantry

Foot, 33rd *See* Duke of Wellington's Regiment

Foot, 34th *See* Cumberland Regiment; Border Regiment; marines

Foot, 35th *See* Royal Sussex Regiment

Foot, 36th *See* Herefordshire Regiment of Foot; marines

Foot, 37th *See* North Hampshire Regiment of Foot

Foot, 38th *See* Staffordshire (1st) Regiment of Foot; South Staffordshire Regiment

Foot, 39th *See* Dorsetshire Regiment of Foot

Foot, 40th *See* Somersetshire (2nd) Regiment of Foot

Foot, 41st *See* Welsh Regiment

Foot, 42nd *See* **Alexandria, battle of; Black Watch, The**

Foot, 43rd *See* **Monmouthshire Light Infantry; Oxfordshire and Buckinghamshire Light Infantry**

Foot, 44th *See* **Afghan Wars; East Essex Regiment of Foot; Essex Regiment**

Foot, 45th *See* **Nottinghamshire (Sherwood Foresters) Regiment**

Foot, 46th *See* **Duke of Cornwall's Light Infantry; South Devonshire Regiment of Foot**

Foot, 47th *See* **Lancashire Regiment of Foot**

Foot, 48th *See* **Northamptonshire Regiment of Foot**

Foot, 49th *See* **Princess Charlotte of Wales's (or Hertfordshire) Regiment**

Foot, 50th *See* **Queen's Own Regiment**

Foot, 51st *See* **Yorkshire West Riding (2nd) Light Infantry Regiment**

Foot, 52nd *See* **Oxfordshire Regiment of Foot; Queen's Own Regiment**

Foot, 53rd *See* **Shropshire Regiment of Foot; Yorkshire West Riding (2nd) Light Infantry Regiment**

Foot, 54th *See* **Monmouthshire Light Infantry; Oxfordshire Regiment of Foot; West Norfolk Regiment of Foot**

Foot, 55th *See* **East Essex Regiment of Foot; Shropshire Regiment of Foot; Westmorland Regiment**

Foot, 56th *See* **West Essex Regiment of Foot; West Norfolk Regiment of Foot**

Foot, 57th *See* **Albuera, battle of; West Middlesex Regiment**

Foot, 58th *See* **Alexandria, battle of; Northamptonshire Regiment; Rutlandshire Regiment; West Essex Regiment of Foot**

Foot, 59th *See* **Northamptonshire Regiment of Foot; Nottinghamshire (2nd) Regiment of Foot; West Middlesex Regiment**

Foot, 60th *See* **King's Royal Rifle Corps; Rutlandshire Regiment**

Foot, 61st *See* **Nottinghamshire (2nd) Regiment of Foot; South Gloucestershire Regiment**

Foot, 62nd *See* **Wiltshire Regiment of Foot**

Foot, 63rd *See* **Princess Charlotte of Wales's (or Hertfordshire) Regiment; West Suffolk Regiment of Foot**

Foot, 64th *See* **Staffordshire (2nd) Regiment of Foot**

Foot, 65th *See* **Yorkshire North Riding Regiment of Foot (2nd)**

Foot, 66th *See* **Royal Berkshire Regiment (Princess Charlotte of Wales's)**

Foot, 67th *See* **South Hampshire Regiment of Foot**

Foot, 68th *See* **Durham Light Infantry**

Foot, 69th *See* **South Lincolnshire Regiment**

Foot, 70th *See* **Surrey Regiment**

Foot, 71st *See* **Highland Light Infantry**

Foot, 72nd *See* **Duke of Albany's Own Highlanders (72nd Foot)**

Foot, 73rd *See* **Highland Light Infantry; Perthshire Regiment of Foot**

Foot, 74th (Highlanders)
The **regiment** was raised (1787) by Major-General Sir Archibald **Campbell** as the 74th (Highland) Regiment of Foot. By 1847 it was called the 74th (Highlanders) Regiment of Foot. It amalgamated with the 71st to become the **Highland Light Infantry** in 1881.

Foot, 75th *See* **Stirlingshire Regiment**

Foot, 76th

The **regiment** was raised (1787) by Colonel Thomas **Musgrave** as the 76th Regiment of Foot, for service in India, and at the expense of the East India Company. Up to 1812 it was also known as the Hindoostan Regiment. Its name remained unaltered. They were known as the 'Lambs' because of the white coats they wore.

Foot, 77th *See* **East Middlesex Regiment of Foot**

Foot, 78th *See* **Ross-shire Buffs**

Foot, 79th *See* **Queen's Own Cameron Highlanders**

Foot, 80th *See* **Gage, Thomas; Staffordshire Volunteers**

Foot, 81st *See* **Loyal Lincolnshire Volunteers**

Foot, 83rd *See* **County of Dublin Regiment; Loyal Lincolnshire Volunteers**

Foot, 84th *See* **York and Lancaster Regiment**

Foot, 85th *See* **King's Light Infantry**

Foot, 86th *See* **Royal County Down Regiment**

Foot, 87th *See* **Royal Irish Fusiliers**

Foot, 88th *See* **Campbell, Archibald**

Foot, 89th *See* **Princess Victoria's Regiment**

Foot, 90th *See* **Perthshire Volunteers**

Foot, 91st *See* **Princess Louise's Argyllshire Highlanders**

Foot, 92nd *See* **Gordon Highlanders**

Foot, 93rd *See* **Balaclava, battle of; Sutherland Highlanders**

Foot, 95th *See* **Abyssinian campaign; Alma, battle of the; Derbyshire Regiment of Foot; Sherwood Foresters; Rifle Brigade, The**

Foot, 96th

The 96th Regiment of Foot was raised (1824) to replace the original 96th (or the Queen's Own) Regiment of Foot which was raised (1798) and disbanded (1818). The 96th merged with the 63rd to become the **Manchester Regiment** in 1881.

Foot, 97th *See* **Earl of Ulster's Regiment of Foot**

Foot, 98th *See* **Princess Louise's Argyllshire Highlanders; Prince of Wales's Regiment of Foot**

Foot, 99th *See* **Duke of Edinburgh's Regiment of Foot**

Foot, 100th *See* **Gordon Highlanders**

Foot, 103rd *See* **Auchmuty, Samuel**

Foot, 104th *See* **McCarthy, Charles**

Foot, 105th *See* **Doyle, John; Madras Light Infantry**

Foot, 106th *See* **Bombay Light Infantry**

Foot, 107th *See* **Bengal Infantry**

Foot, 108th *See* **Madras Infantry**

Foot, 115th *See* **Hislop, Thomas**

Foot, 121st *See* **Draper, William**

Foot Guards

The foot **regiments** that are in personal attendance on the reigning sovereign. Since the 17th century they have worn the Royal livery of red and blue. There were three Foot Guards regiments (the **Grenadier Guards**, the **Coldstream Guards**, and the **Scots Guards**) from the 17th until the early 20th century, when two more (the **Irish Guards** and the **Welsh Guards**) were founded. The regiments have long been distinguished by

the arrangement of the buttons on their dress uniforms; those of the Grenadier Guards (the 1st Guards) are regular, the Coldstream Guards are in pairs, the Scots Guards in threes, the Irish Guards in fours and the Welsh Guards in fives. The Guards regiments have gained a reputation as elite fighting troops. They have also remained socially exclusive in their selection of officers and in recent years have been accused of racism because they have almost entirely avoided recruiting any non-white other ranks.
See also **Household Cavalry**

Foot Guards, 1st *See* **Grenadier Guards**

footsoldiers *See* **infantry**

forage cap
Originally, a simple cap worn by **cavalry** men when collecting forage for their horses, later the undress hat for the cavalry, whose headgear had become elaborate. It was usually round and stiffened and could have a peak. In 1898 the broad-topped peaked forage cap, based on a naval pattern, was introduced and is still worn.

forced march
A march undertaken at great speed, often over a long distance and under difficult conditions

Formigny, battle of
(1450; *Hundred Years' War*) The French King Charles VII had taken Rouen (1449) and forced the English back on Formigny. Of an English army of 5,000, some 4,000 were killed, thus ending the fighting in northern France.

Fort Erie, battle of
(1814; *War of 1812*) After the battle of **Lundy's Lane** the Americans withdrew to Fort Erie. The fort was besieged by a British army of 3,500 men commanded by General Gordon **Drummond** (2 August). The fort was bombarded (13–15 August) and a British assault repulsed. The British batteries were destroyed, either by an American assault or an accidental explosion, and the siege was lifted (21 September). On 5 November the Americans withdrew behind the Niagara Falls and Fort Erie was destroyed.

Fort McHenry, battle of
(1814; *War of 1812*) A British fleet of 10 ships sailed up Chesapeake Bay towards Baltimore and disembarked 4,000 men, commanded by General Robert **Ross** at the mouth of the Patapsco river about 14 miles from Baltimore (12 September). They were to attack Fort McHenry which protected Baltimore. This force was met by 3,200 American militia commanded by General John Striker in Godly Wood. The Americans were repulsed but Ross was killed. A bombardment of Fort McHenry failed (13 September) and the attack on Baltimore was abandoned. The failure of the attack on the fort is commemorated in the US national anthem 'The Star-Spangled Banner'.

Fort Mercer and Fort Miffin, battle of
(1777; *American War of Independence*) After repulsing the American attack at **Germantown**, General Sir William **Howe** needed to hold the Delaware river as a supply route to Philadelphia. The way was blocked by Fort Mercer, about 20 miles from Philadelphia. The initial attack (22 October) was repelled. Fort Miffin, just below Fort Mercer on Mud Island, was bombarded by a floating battery and warships (10–15 November) and the Americans abandoned the fort. General Lord Charles **Cornwallis** made a new assault on Fort Mercer, the position of which was now untenable and the Americans evacuated it (20 November).

Fort Sitabaldi, battle of
(1817; *Maratha Wars*) Fort Sitabaldi was attacked (24 November) by the Rajah of Nagpurm, Nappa Sahib, with 15,000 troops. The assault was repelled by the **garrison** of some 1,300 troops from Madras (now Chennai) and Bengal. This victory ended Nappa Sahib's uprising.

Fort Washington, battle of

(1776; *American War of Independence*) A force of 8,000 British and Hessian troops, led by General Lord Charles **Cornwallis** and Baron Wilhelm von Knyphausen, attacked the fort held by 3,000 Americans commanded by Colonel Robert Magaw. The position was indefensible and Magaw surrendered his entire force (16 November). Cornwallis then crossed the Hudson river and took the fort without resistance. The Americans then fell back across New Jersey.

Fowkes's (Colonel Fowkes's Regiment of Foot) *See* Monmouthshire Light Infantry

Fox's (Colonel Edward Fox's Regiment of Marines) *See* Duke of Cornwall's Light Infantry

France

1. (1940; *World War II*) After their victory in **Flanders** the German forces turned south and attacked France. The 140 German divisions, led by the Panzers (**tanks**) reached Rouen (9 June). By 12 June, the Marne had been crossed in two places and Cherbourg taken (18 June). To the east the Maginot Line was breached (14–15 June). Paris was declared an open city (11 June) and the French government moved to Tours and then to Bordeaux. The French surrendered at Compiègne (22 June).

2. (1944; *World War II*) After the Allied victory in the battles at **Falaise Gap** the US General George **Patton** pursued the Germans across northern France. By 16 August Dreux and Orleans were liberated as was Chartres (18 August). By 24 August Paris was liberated and the French General Charles de Gaulle set up the French headquarters there. Meanwhile to the north-east the Canadian 1st, British 2nd and US 1st Armies forced the Germans across northern France. The 21st Army Group commanded by Field Marshal Sir Bernard **Montgomery** drove through the Low Countries. Amiens fell (31 August), Brussels (3 September), Antwerp (4 September) and Bourges (9 September). The US 1st Army took Mons (3 September) and drove into Luxembourg. The US 3rd Army took Reims and Châlons and Verdun (1 September), and crossed the Moselle (7 September). Meanwhile the US 9th Army was taking the ports of Brittany. German resistance stiffened at the **Siegfried Line** and Marshal Gerd von **Rundstedt** was appointed German commander-in-chief. The invasion of southern France (called Operation Dragoon (Anvil)) began (15 August). After a parachute drop of 8,000 men the US 7th Army landed on the beaches between Cannes and Toulon and moved towards the Rhône Valley. The French II Corps then landed and took Toulon and Marseilles (28 August). The US VI Corps took Grenoble (24 August) and Lyons (3 September) linking up with Patton's 3rd Army at Sombernon.

See also **Ardennes, battle of**; **Arnhem, battle of**; **Caen, battle of**; **Germany**; **Normandy**

Freeman's Farm, battle of

(1777; *American War of Independence*) The first stage (19 September) of the battle of **Saratoga** at which the British advance on Albany was checked

French, John Denton Pinkstone (1852–1925)

French was educated at Eastman's Naval Academy, Portsmouth, and joined the Navy (1866). He left the Navy and joined the Suffolk Artillery Militia (1870). In 1874 he was **gazetted** in the 8th Hussars (**King's Royal Irish Hussars**) but soon transferred to the 19th Hussars (**Queen Alexandra's Own Hussars**). By 1883 he had been promoted to **major**. He was appointed **adjutant** of the Northumberland Hussars (1881) but went to Egypt (1884) in command of a detachment of the 19th Hussars. He took part in the retreat from **Khartoum** with distinction, and on his return home (1885) was promoted to **brevet lieutenant-colonel**. French was given command of the 19th Hussars (1888) and went to India as brevet **colonel** (1889). He returned home on half pay (1893) but was promoted to colonel and appointed an assistant adjutant-general at the **War Office** (1895). He wrote a new 'Cavalry Manual' and by 1898 was **major-general** in command of the 1st Cavalry Brigade at Aldershot. In September 1899 French went to

Natal in command of mounted troops under Sir George **White**. He remained in the Cape until 1902 when he was promoted to **lieutenant-general**. He was appointed **commander-in-chief** at Aldershot where he reformed army training. He was promoted to **general** (1907) and left Aldershot (1907) to become inspector-general of the forces when he reformed military manoeuvres. He succeeded Field Marshal Lord Nicholson as Chief of the Imperial General Staff (1912) and was promoted to **field marshal** (1913). He resigned over the **Curragh Incident** in support of his officers. In 1914 he went to France as commander-in-chief of the **British Expeditionary Force**. He proved to be a hesitant commander, being reluctant to commit his forces to the decisive first battle of the **Marne river** which halted and then threw back the German advance in September 1914. French resigned as commander-in-chief (1915) after the failure of the battle of **Loos**, though this may have been as much the fault of his replacement, **Haig**, as it was French's responsibility. He was created Viscount French (1916) and appointed Commander-in-Chief of Home Forces. As such he was in command of the forces that suppressed the Easter Rising in Ireland (1916). He was appointed lord-lieutenant of Ireland (1918) and an attempt was made on his life (1919). The Irish situation degenerated and French resigned (1921) and retired into private life. He was created Earl of Ypres (1922) and was made captain of Deal Castle (1923). He died at Deal.

See also **Kimberley**; **Ypres, battle of** 1; **Neuve-Chapelle, battle of**

French and Indian War (1754–63)

The American phase of the **Seven Years' War** in which the American colonial troops fought alongside the British against the French, Canadians and Indians. The climax was the battle of **Quebec**, and after the treaty of Paris (1763) the British were supreme in North America.

See also **Beauséjour, battle of**; **Louisbourg, battle of**; **Montreal, battle of**; **Niagara, battle of**; **Oswego, battle of**; **Quebec, battle of**; **Sainte Foy, battle of**; **Ticonderoga, battle of**; **Abercromby, Robert**; **Amherst, Jeffrey**; **Gates, Horatio**; **Montcalm, Louis Joseph, Marquis de**; **Wolfe, James**

French Revolutionary Wars *See* French Wars

French Wars (1792–1815)

These wars may be conveniently divided into the French Revolutionary Wars, during which France defended the newly-formed republic against the monarchies of Europe, which Britain joined in 1793, and which may be considered to have ended in 1801, and the Napoleonic Wars, which were concerned with the acquisition of territory and consolidating French influence. The Revolutionary Wars were fought against various coalitions of European powers who supported the deposed Louis XVI (executed 1793) and during which the French were largely victorious, except for **Napoleon's** failure in Egypt (1798). By the time Napoleon became first consul of France (1799), all effective military opposition to France was over and France was the dominant power on the Continent. The Peace of Amiens (1802) ended the fighting briefly but war between Britain and France was renewed in 1803. Invasion of Britain or Ireland had always been a threat during the 1790s, but this was removed after Nelson's victory at Trafalgar (1805). In 1804 Napoleon declared himself Emperor of France. From then until 1814 Britain was joined in fighting France at various times by Austria, Prussia, Sweden, Russia and Spain. Napoleon kept his domination over western and central Europe until 1812 and his disastrous invasion of Russia. Throughout the period Britain continued to expand its colonial markets which led to many battles against the French and others outside Europe. The **Peninsular War** fought by the Portuguese and British commanded by **Wellington** began the decline of French power, while Napoleon's disastrous invasion of Russia (1812–13) saw the beginning of the end of French dominance in Europe. A new anti-French coalition was formed (1813) and Napoleon was forced to withdraw west of the Rhine. France was invaded (1814) and Paris occupied later in the year. Napoleon abdicated (April 1814) and was exiled to the island of Elba. He returned to France (March 1815) and rallied a new army that was opposed by the forces of the seventh coalition (Great Britain, Russia, Prussia and Austria). The campaign was brief, ending in Napoleon's defeat at **Waterloo**. Napoleon abdicated (22 June 1815) and the Bourbon monarchy (Louis XVIII) was restored.

See also **War of 1812**

Freyberg, Bernard Cyril (1889–1963)

Freyberg was born in Richmond, Surrey, UK, but his family emigrated to New Zealand (1891) where he served in the Territorial Army. During **World War I** he took part in the retreat from **Antwerp** and in the **Gallipoli** campaign. He was awarded the **Victoria Cross** (1917) and was promoted to **brigadier-general** when he was 27. During 1917–18 he commanded the 29th Division. Freyberg held senior staff appointments in the UK and then was **major-general** commanding the New Zealand Expeditionary Force (1939–45) and commanded the Allied forces in **Crete** (1941). He then served in North Africa and Italy under **Montgomery** and **Alexander**. He was knighted (1942) and was appointed governor-general of New Zealand (1946–52). He was created a baron in 1951.

frizzen *See* **flintlock**

frog

1. The attachment of a sword or bayonet to a belt
2. A braid or cord loop going over a button or other fastening to keep a coat closed

Fuentes de Oñoro, battle of

(1811; *Peninsular War*) Having liberated Portugal, **Wellington** began to attack French-held Spain. He led the northern part of a two-pronged attack by taking 30,000 troops towards Almeida. Marshal André Masséna brought 30,000 men out of **Ciudad Rodrigo** to protect Almeida and met Wellington who was entrenched at Fuentes de Oñoro. The French attack (5 May) was repelled with a loss of 1,500 men by the Allies and 2,200 by the French. The French withdrew and the British took Almeida.

Fulford, battle of

(1066; *Norwegian Invasion of England*) In one year, King Harold II was faced with two invasions of England. The first came when the Norwegian King Harold III Hardrada and the former Earl of Northumberland (Tostig) sailed up the Humber and landed at Fulford (20 September). They were opposed by Edwin of Mercia and Morcar of Northumberland. The English were defeated and Harold II moved from London to counter-attack, meeting the Norsemen at **Stamford Bridge**. This northern campaign reduced the number of troops available for the battle of **Hastings** which took place in the following month.

full dress

The elaborate uniform worn on ceremonial occasions

fusilier, fusileer, fuzileer

A soldier armed with a fusil, which was a type of light-weight **flintlock musket** of the later 17th century. **Regiments** of fusiliers were formed to escort ammunition wagons and were the first regiments to be equipped with flintlocks. This was to reduce the potential danger of sparks given off by the then more usual **matchlock** muskets which could drift and explode the barrels of gunpowder. Once the whole army was equipped with flintlocks by the early 18th century, fusiliers had no special role and were only distinguished from standard **infantry** regiments by their name and the details of their uniforms. The name is still used in the titles of various regiments in the modern army.
[From French, from *fusil* 'musket']

fusillade

A coordinated and continuous firing of **small arms**
[From French, from *fusiller* 'to shoot', from *fusil* 'musket']

fuzee

A light **flintlock** carried by officers in the 18th century

G

Gage, Thomas (1721–87)

Gage was commissioned **lieutenant** (1741) in Colonel Cholmondeley's Regiment (48th Foot, later the **Northamptonshire Regiment of Foot**). He ultimately became **lieutenant-colonel** in the 44th Foot (**East Essex Regiment**) (1751) and went to America (1754). He raised a provincial **regiment** (80th Foot) and thanks to his campaigns the British dominance in Canada was assured. He was appointed governor of Montreal (1760), became a **major-general** (1761) and **commander-in-chief** of North America (1762), based in New York. The 80th Foot was disbanded and Gage was appointed **colonel** of the 22nd Foot (**Cheshire Regiment**). He became a **lieutenant-general** (1770) and returned home (1772). In 1774 Gage was appointed governor-in-chief and captain-general of Massachusetts and was based in Boston. His mismanagement of the situation has been said to have been the cause of the battle of **Lexington** and subsequently of **Bunker Hill**. He left America (1775) and ultimately became colonel of the 11th Dragoons. He was later made a full **general** (1782).

gaiters

Cloth coverings to protect soldiers' stockings and to prevent mud, etc., getting into their shoes, introduced at the end of the 17th century. They reached above the knee being fastened with a strap just below the knee. They were buttoned down the outside. They were usually white or grey, but the more practical black was introduced by 1760. They were last worn by infantry of the line in 1823 when breeches were replaced by trousers. From 1771 the light infantry wore gaiters that reached to the calf at the back of the leg. In 1862 short leather gaiters (half gaiters) were introduced for the light infantry. Initially these were worn under the trousers, and at the beginning of the 19th century Highland regiments worn them over their hose and shoes; they are still worn by some Scottish regiments. Gaiters were replaced in World War I by **puttees**. However, the modern British Army uses gaiters made from artificial waterproof materials.

gaiter trousers, gaiter trowsers

One-piece white cloth trousers fitting tight to the calf and buttoning up the outside, worn over the breeches to protect them. They were introduced in 1791.

gallantry, awards for *See* decorations; medals

Gallipoli, battle of

(1915–16; *World War I*) As the situation on the **Western Front** had reached a stalemate, it was decided after much debate to attack Constantinople (now Istanbul) in an attempt to knock Turkey out of the war and open a new supply route from the Western powers to Russia. A naval bombardment of the Dardanelles (18 March 1915) failed and the British and French determined to open this waterway into the Sea of Marmara by a land campaign. A force of 15,000 men commanded by General Sir Ian **Hamilton** landed (25 April) on the beaches of the north-west; 35,000 men commanded by Sir Aylmer Hunter **Weston** landed at Cape Hellas, and the **ANZAC Corps**, commanded by Sir William **Birdwood**, landed at Ari Burnu. Within a few days the Allied advance had been brought to a standstill. On 6 August a further 25,000 Allied troops were landed further north at Suvla Bay, but delayed their advance, allowing the Turks to bring up reinforcements. The stalemate continued until 22 November, when the Allies decided to withdraw. The withdrawal (20 December–9 January) was almost the only truly successful phase of the campaign, being completed with few losses. Out of 480,000 British and French troops landed at Gallipoli, some 250,000 became casualties.

galloper

An **aide-de-camp** or orderly officer of the late 19th century, so called because he carried messages and commands from the central command to the various parts of the battlefield

galloper gun

A light mobile cannon attached to an **infantry regiment** in the mid–late 18th century

Galway, Viscount *See* **Massue, Henri de**

Gandamak, battle of

(1842; *Afghan War I*) A British-Indian force of some 4,500 (the British element being largely the 44th (**East Essex Regiment**)), commanded by Major-General William **Elphinstone**, with a large number of camp-followers, was given a safe conduct to return from **Kabul** into India. The column was attacked constantly during the withdrawal and the last survivors were overwhelmed at Gandamak on 13 January by a large force of Afghans and virtually wiped out. A few men, women and children were taken hostage. A punitive expedition, led by General Sir George **Pollock**, relieved Jellalabad (16 April) and released the hostages in Kabul (15 September).

garrison

A permanent body of troops based in the **barracks** of a town
[From Old French *garison* 'fortification', from *garir* 'to defend']

gas

Poisonous gas used as a weapon against troops or civilians. Gas was first used as a weapon during **World War I** when the Germans used chlorine against the Russians in Poland (January 1915). The Germans used it again with greater effect against the British and French at **Ypres** (April 1915). British forces first used poison gas at the battle of **Loos**. The Germans then developed phosgene, a more lethal compound, and gas shells fired by artillery. Both sides developed **gas masks**. The Germans then introduced mustard gas, a blistering compound of carbon, hydrogen, sulphur and chlorine (1917). The German use of mustard gas was a major factor in limiting the success of British attacks during the Third Battle of Ypres in 1917. Poison gas was an unusually terrifying weapon though paradoxically it caused relatively few fatalities; many more victims were temporarily incapacitated but would recover and be able to return to military duty. Many, however, incurred permanent respiratory damage which caused considerable suffering to them in later life. There were relatively few fatalities. After World War I there was a universal revulsion against the use of gas as a weapon and attempts were made to ban it in the inter-war years. Although more potent gases such as nerve gases were developed with improved methods of delivery, they were not used during **World War II**. After World War II the USSR and Western nations including Britain maintained a substantial interest in the use of gas and chemical weapons and in the means of protecting against them. Britain is now party to international treaties which attempt to outlaw the development and use of such weapons but continues to be active in researching means of defence against them. The threat of their use by Iraq was a factor in the **Gulf War** (1990–91) and the **Iraq War** (2003).
See also **chemical warfare**

gas mask

A breathing device to protect the wearer from poisonous gases. It acts as a filter and does not replace oxygen, although some types may have an added oxygen supply. Typically the gas mask consists of a tight-fitting face piece with transparent eyepieces and a breathing valve to which is attached a replaceable filter. This filter typically contains finely ground charcoal (carbon) which adsorbs the poisonous gas, and soda-lime which neutralises any poisons released by the charcoal, and a filter screen to remove finely divided solids. The mask is tightly held to the head by straps. Such masks are effective only against true gases that attack the respiratory system. Agents dispersed as vapours such as mustard gas, and which attack through the skin, require protective clothing to be worn as well as gas masks. No single type of gas mask can protect against all toxic substances so military gas masks are made to counteract those substances most likely to be used in war by modifying the typical form.

Gate Pah, battle of

(1864; *Maori War*) A British force of 1,700 attacked the Maori stockade called Gate Pah (27 April). After a bombardment, 600 men forced an entry but were repulsed. The stockade was evacuated the next day with the loss of 30 Maoris dead or wounded. The British lost 112 dead or wounded.

Gates, Horatio (1728?–1806)

Gates was born at Maldon, UK, and served during the **French and Indian War** (1754–63) in America as a **major**. He returned to Britain but emigrated to what is now West Virginia (1772). He was made adjutant-general in the American Continental Army (1775) and took over the command in northern New York from General Philip Schuyler (1777). He forced the surrender of **Burgoyne** at the battles of **Saratoga** and was elected president of the Board of War. A plan to replace General George **Washington** by Gates collapsed and Gates returned to his command in New York. He was transferred to the south where he was defeated by Lord **Cornwallis** at the battle of **Camden**. After the war Gates moved to New York and served one term in the state legislature.

gatling gun

A type of **machine gun** invented (1862) by an American, Dr Richard Gatling. It consisted of a series of barrels revolving around a central axis with a single feeding and firing mechanism. It was fired by turning a handle. The gun was introduced to the British Army and Navy (1874) and was used during the Second **Afghan War** and various other colonial conflicts of the late 19th century. It was superseded before **World War I** by other types of machine gun.

Gaulauli, battle of

(1858; *Indian Mutiny*) A British column, commanded by Sir Hugh **Rose**, was attacked by 20,000 rebels under Tantia Topi (22 May). After their initial advantage a bayonet charge broke the rebels who fled with heavy losses.

Gaza, battles of

(1917; *World War I*) To extend the water pipeline and the railway which reached from the Suez Canal into Palestine, General Sir Archibald **Murray** sent a force, commanded by General Sir Charles Dobell, to attack Gaza (26 March). After an initial success, the arrival of Turkish reinforcements forced the British to withdraw. General Sir Edmund **Allenby** took over command in southern Palestine and was strongly reinforced by Australian, New Zealand (**ANZAC**) and Indian troops. The Turks held a line from Gaza to Beersheba. On 31 October the British attacked Beersheba forcing the Turks back on Gaza. On fear of being cut off, Gaza was evacuated (7 November) and the Turks fell back northwards towards Jerusalem. Allenby continued his advance; Jaffa was taken (16 November) and Jerusalem was outflanked. The British occupied Jerusalem (9 December) without a battle.

Gazala, battle of

(1942; *World War II*) Both the Axis army and the British attempted to take the offensive in North Africa, but the Axis commander, **Rommel**, struck first with a force of 113,000 men and 560 tanks (May). After fierce fighting the British 8th Army, commanded by Lieutenant-General Neil Ritchie and consisting of 125,000 men and 849 tanks, was defeated and forced to fall back into Egypt (21 June). **Tobruk** was

captured soon afterwards. The British lost some 88,000 men, including those captured in Tobruk, and the Germans lost some 60,000.
See also **El Alamein, battle of**

gazette
To publish an officer's appointment to a **substantive rank** in the 'London Gazette'
[Directly or via French from Italian *gazzetta*, Venetian dialect *gazeta de la novità* 'pennyworth of news']

GBE *See* **Order of the British Empire**

GC *abbreviation of* **George Cross**

GCB *See* **Order of the Bath**

GCIE *See* **Order of the Indian Empire**

GCMG *See* **Order of St Michael and St George**

GCSI *See* **Order of the Star of India**

GCVO *See* **Royal Victorian Order**

general
A military rank since 1576. Initially this was simply the title given to the commander of an army. When ranks became more formally established the unqualified 'general' became the second most senior **general officer** grade, below **field marshal** and above **lieutenant-general**, **major-general** and **brigadier-general** (in decreasing order of seniority). 'General' may also be used as an informal title for any of these ranks. In the modern Army, general, and its Royal Navy and Royal Air Force equivalents (admiral and air chief marshal), are sometimes referred to as 4-star ranks, as this is the insignia worn for such ranks in some other armed forces, though not in the British services.
[Via French from Latin *generalis* 'of the whole class', from *genus* 'race, kind']

general headquarters
The base of a major military operation under the command of the **commander-in-chief** or the officer in command of a particular operation in the field.
Abbreviation **GHQ**

general officer
Any officer above the rank of **colonel**

general officer commanding
A senior officer who is responsible for the general conduct of a war in a particular sphere, in contrast to the **commander-in-chief** and regimental and staff officers who are concerned with individual **regiments**. General officers hold the ranks of **major-general**, **lieutenant-general**, **general** and **field marshal**.
Abbreviation **GOC**

General Service Medal
The earliest war **medal**, issued in 1848 to end the long-standing grievance that **other ranks** had no form of recognition for their service. There were 29 clasps denoting service in particular battles or campaigns that could be awarded, one of the earliest being for the battle of Alexandria (1801). Previously the only standard medal had been a gold one for senior officers, though service in the battle of **Waterloo**, e.g., was rewarded with a special medal.

general staff *See* **reforms after the Crimean War; reforms after the Boer War**

General Willis's Regiment of Foot *See* **Cambridgeshire (1st) Regiment of Foot**

Geneva conventions
A series of international agreements signed between 1864 and 1949. They were inspired by the Swiss philanthropist Henri Dunant, who campaigned to alleviate suffering in wartime after witnessing the battle of Solferino (1859). The first convention (1864) governed the treatment of the wounded and the civilians treating them during times of conflict. This applied only to soldiers, but the second convention

(1906) extended the same protection to naval personnel. The third convention (1929) laid down rules for the humane treatment of prisoners of war; and the fourth (1949), in the wake of the extensive abuses of **World War II**, extended similar protection to civilians, as well as consolidating the pronouncements of the first three conventions. The Geneva conventions are closely connected to the **Red Cross** and to the **Hague conventions**.

Geneva cross

A plain red cross on a white ground, the reverse colours of the Swiss flag. New humanitarian laws of warfare were introduced (1864) and the Geneva cross was used to identify noncombatants involved in humanitarian and medical work. It is one of the symbols of the **Red Cross**.

George Cross

A decoration instituted (1940) as a reward for outstanding gallantry by civilians, but which can also be awarded to military personnel for similar acts that do not fall within the scope of a military award. For example, it is awarded to mark acts that, although showing extreme gallantry, were not committed in the face of the enemy and so are ineligible for the **Victoria Cross**.

Abbreviation **GC**

George II (1683–1760; reigned 1727–60)

The last British monarch to command troops in the field.

See also **Dettingen, battle of**

George Medal

A decoration instituted (1940) as a reward for bravery by civilians, but which can also be awarded to military personnel for similar acts that do not fall within the scope of a military award. It is the junior award to the **George Cross**.

Abbreviation **GM**

Germain, Lord George *See* **Sackville, George**

Germantown, battle of

(1777; *American War of Independence*) 11,000 American troops, commanded by General George **Washington**, attacked 9,000 British, commanded by General Sir William **Howe**, stationed at Germantown near Philadelphia (October 4). The attack was planned to take place from four directions but was too complicated and resulted in the Americans firing on each other in dense fog. The attack was repulsed with the loss of 535 British troops and about 1,000 Americans. The previous American victory at **Saratoga** and this demonstration of Washington's tactical ability played a part in persuading the French to enter the war against Britain.

Germany

(1945; *World War II*) After the decisive victory in the Rhineland, the American General Dwight **Eisenhower** (Supreme Allied Commander in the west) regrouped his forces to assault Germany. He commanded 85 **divisions** along the Rhine, consisting of 7 armies divided into 3 army groups. In the north Field Marshal Sir Bernard **Montgomery** commanded the Canadian 1st, the British 2nd and the US 9th; in the centre General Omar Bradley commanded the US 1st and US 3rd; in the south General Jacob Devers commanded the US 7th and the French 1st. This force was opposed by about 26 German divisions commanded by Field Marshal Albert **Kesselring**. The British 2nd Army began the attack at Wesel (23 March). By 4 May all the German forces in the north had surrendered to Montgomery. On 8 May Germany surrendered unconditionally.

Ghazni, battle of

(1839; *Afghan War I*) The near-impregnable Afghan fortress of Ghazni was garrisoned by a force of 3,000 commanded by Haider Khan. It was besieged by a British force commanded by General **Keane**. Lacking siege guns, Keane was forced to blow the main gate. The fortress was stormed (21 January) with the loss of 18 officers and 162 men killed and wounded. The Afghans lost 500 killed.

Ghoaine, battle of
(1842; *Afghan War I*) A British force, led by General Sir William **Nott**, moving from Kandahar to Ghazni was attacked by the Afghans who were heavily defeated, losing all their guns and baggage (30 August)

GHQ *See* **general headquarters**

Gibraltar, battle of
1. (1704; *War of the Spanish Succession*) The British and Dutch decided to take Gibraltar to tighten their control in the Mediterranean. An Allied fleet commanded by Admiral Sir George Rooke reached the Rock (23 July) and opened a bombardment, while 1,800 marines, commanded by Prince George of Hesse-Darmstadt, landed and took the fort.
2. (1779–83; *American War of Independence*) Spain joined France and the American colonies in their war against Britain (June 1779). Initially the French and Spanish maintained a loose blockade of Gibraltar but by September 1782 Gibraltar, commanded by General **Eliott**, was blockaded by 50 ships of the line, 10 floating batteries with 33,000 troops, and 300 pieces of artillery on land. The main attack began (9 September 1782) with a bombardment from the land, followed (13 September) by one from the floating batteries. These latter were destroyed by artillery fire or assault from gun-boats and the besieging army pulled back, hoping to starve out the garrison. Admiral Lord Richard Howe broke the blockade, bringing supplies that enabled the garrison to withstand the siege until the end of the war.

Gibson's (Colonel Gibson's Regiment of Foot) *See* **North Gloucestershire Regiment**

Ginkel, Godbert de (1630–1703)
Ginkel was born in Utrecht and trained for a military career. He came to England (1688) with William of Orange. He went to Ireland with William (now William III) (1690) and distinguished himself at the battle of the **Boyne** and at the first siege of **Limerick**. He was appointed general-in-chief of the Irish forces. During 1691 he commanded the campaign in Ireland, taking Athlone (30 June) and defeating the Marquis de Saint Ruth at the battle of **Aughrim** (12 July). He captured Galway (26 July) and took Limerick (3 October). Ginkel then moved to Dublin and returned to England (5 December). He was created Baron of Aughrim and Earl of Athlone (1692). In 1692 he accompanied William to the continent and at the renewal of war with France (1702) served under **Marlborough**. He was largely responsible for the capture of Kaiserswerth. Ginkel died in Utrecht after a short illness.

glaive *See* **guisarme**

Gloucestershire Regiment
The **regiment** was formed (1881) by the amalgamation of the 28th (**North Gloucestershire Regiment**) of Foot and the 61st (**South Gloucestershire Regiment**) of Foot. In 1994 it was merged with The Duke of Edinburgh's Royal Regiment (Berkshire and Wiltshire), to form **The Royal Gloucestershire, Berkshire and Wiltshire Regiment**.

GM *abbreviation of* **George Medal**

GOC *abbreviation of* **general officer commanding**

Goddard, Thomas (d. 1783)
Goddard was born in Wiltshire and commissioned in the 84th Foot (**York and Lancaster Regiment**) which was raised for service in India (1759). He took part in the battle of **Pondicherry**. When his **regiment** was disbanded (1763) Goddard took service as a **captain** with the East India Company and raised the 1st Battalion of the 7th Regiment, Bengal Infantry (Goddard's Battalion). By 1768 he had been promoted to **lieutenant-colonel** and was appointed commander of the troops at Lucknow (1776).

He was second-in-command to Colonel Leslie of the force sent from Bengal to assist the Bombay Army in the war against the **Marathas** (1779). Leslie died in the same year and Goddard was given complete command. For the next two years he conducted campaigns against the Marathas which led to a treaty (13 October 1781). Goddard was promoted to **brevet brigadier-general** and remained in India until 1783 when ill-health caused his return home. He died on the ship at the end of the journey.
See also **Ahmadabad, battle of**

Godwin, Henry Thomas (1784–1853)

Godwin entered the army (1799) as an **ensign** in the 9th Foot (**Royal Norfolk Regiment**). He served in Gibralta and the **Peninsular War**, in which he was made **brevet major**. In 1815 he was promoted to lieutenant-colonel of the 41st Foot (**Welsh Regiment**). The **regiment** went to India (1822) and to Burma (now Myanmar) (1824) and took part in nearly every action of the campaign. Godwin was further promoted to **colonel** (1837) and **major-general** (1846). In 1850 he was appointed a divisional commander in Bengal and was **commander-in-chief** during the Burma campaign (1852). He returned to India as commander of the Sirhind Division of the Bengal Army. He died in Simla.
See also **Burma campaigns 1**

Golden Rock, battle of

(1753; *British in India*) The French and Mysoris in Trichinopoly (now Tiruchchirappalli) occupied the strategic position of Golden Rock (7 August). They were dislodged by 1,500 British troops commanded by Major Stringer **Lawrence** and 5,000 Tanjore troops.

good conduct stripes

They were introduced in 1836 and were worn on the right arm, just above the cuff by **infantry** and just below the elbow by **cavalry**. After 1881 they were worn on the left forearm with the point of the chevron facing upwards.

Goorkha Light Infantry *See* Queen Elizabeth's Own Gurkha Rifles (6th)

Goose Green, battle of

(1982; *Falklands War*) The British intended to eliminate the Argentine garrisons at Darwin and Goose Green so as to clear their line of advance on Port Stanley. About 600 men of the 2nd Battalion, **Parachute Regiment**, commanded by Lieutenant-Colonel H. Jones, attacked some 1,700 Argentine troops. The Argentine defences were stormed with the loss of 18 killed, including Jones, and 35 wounded. The Argentine forces lost 250 killed, 150 wounded and 1,000 prisoners were taken; they were penned in a semi-circle around Goose Green and surrendered, after the 15-hour battle. Lieutenant-Colonel Jones was awarded a posthumous **Victoria Cross**.

Goraria, battle of

(1857; *Indian Mutiny*) A force of 5,000 rebels held a strong position which was attacked by a British column of 3,000 commanded by Brigadier Stuart (23 November). The initial attack failed but the rebels were dispersed on the following day with the loss of over 1,500.

Gordon, Charles George (1833–85)

Gordon was the son of an **artillery** officer and was commissioned in the **Royal Engineers** (1852). He served in the **Crimean War** and was promoted to **captain**. He volunteered for service in China and was present at the occupation of Peking (now Beijing) (October 1860). He went to Shanghai (May 1862) and in 1863 was given command of a 3,500-man peasant force defending the city against the Taiping rebels. This force, known as the 'Ever Victorious Army', played an important part in the suppression of the rebellion. He returned to England (1865) and was greeted as a national hero and called 'Chinese Gordon'. He commanded the Royal Engineers at Gravesend (1865–70) and in his spare time carried out philanthropic work amongst the poor. The khedive Ismail Pasha of Egypt appointed him governor of the province of

Equatoria in the Sudan (1873), and during this period he mapped the Upper Nile as far as the present Ugandan border (1874–76). He came back to England but returned as governor-general of the Sudan. During this period he suppressed rebellions and the slave trade. He returned to England (1880) through ill health. He then served in India, China, Mauritius and Cape Colony. He returned to the Sudan (1884) as governor-general to evacuate the Egyptian forces from Khartoum, which was threatened by the Sudanese rebels led by the **Mahdi**. Gordon arrived in Khartoum in February 1884 and the city came under siege (March 1884). The rebels broke into the city (26 January 1885) and Gordon was killed. The British public acclaimed 'Gordon of Khartoum' as a national hero and blamed the government for failure to relieve the siege. Later biographers believed that Gordon refused to evacuate the city when it was possible early in the siege.

Gordon Highlanders

The **regiment** was formed (1881) by the amalgamation of the 75th (**Stirlingshire**) Regiment of Foot and the 92nd (Gordon Highlanders) Regiment of Foot. The 92nd was raised (1794) by the Duke of Gordon as the 100th Regiment of Foot, known as the Gordon Highlanders. It was re-numbered the 92nd Regiment of Foot in 1798 and became the 92nd (Gordon Highlanders) Regiment of Foot in 1861. The regiment took part in the siege of **Delhi** and in the **Khartoum** expedition (1884). In 1994 it united with The Queen's Own Highlanders (Seaforth and Camerons) to form The Highlanders (Seaforth, Gordons and Camerons).

See also **Dargai, battle of**

Gore's Regiment of Dragoons *See* **Royal Hussars (Prince of Wales's Own)**

gorget

Originally a piece of armour protecting the throat, but later a crescent-shaped badge worn hung around the throat by officers when on duty. Its use was abolished in 1830.
[From Old French *gorgete*, from *gorge* 'throat']

Gothic Line

(1944–45; *World War II*) After the fall of Rome (4 June 1944) the Allied 15th Army Group, commanded by Sir Harold **Alexander**, pressed northward through Italy. Seven **divisions** of Allied forces were withdrawn to prepare an assault on southern **France**, while the Germans, commanded by Field Marshal Albert **Kesselring**, were reinforced by eight divisions. The Allies pushed forward slowly and by August 1944 reached the prepared defences of the Gothic Line which pivoted in the east on Rimini. Pisa fell (2 September) and Rimini (20 September). The assault on Bologna was repulsed and Kesselring managed to seal the breaches in the Gothic Line. This, with the coming of winter, prevented the Allies from concluding the Italian campaign.

See also **Po Valley, battle of**

Gough, Hubert de la Poer (1870–1963)

Gough received his **commission** in the 16th Lancers (1889) and served in India (1897) and in the **Boer War** (1899–1902). He commanded the 3rd Cavalry Brigade (1914) and was given command of the 5th Army on its formation (1916). He commanded large sections of the British forces in the battles of the **Somme** (1916) and **Ypres** (1917). His army was forced to withdraw (March 1918) and, although he contributed to the cessation of the German advance, Gough was blamed by the government for the temporary German success and he was removed. He retired (1922) with the rank of **general** and was awarded the **KCB** (1937).

See also **Arras, battle of**

Gough, Hugh (1779–1869)

Gough received his **commission** in the Limerick City Militia of which his father was **lieutenant-colonel** (1793), and after other commissions was **lieutenant** in the 78th Highlanders (**Ross-shire Buffs**) (1795). He was present at the capture of the Cape of Good Hope. He was transferred to the 87th Prince of Wales's Irish (**Royal Irish**

Fusiliers) and served in the West Indies until 1803. In 1803 he was given command of a **regiment** of Irish reserves formed in Somerset and was battalion major (1805). Gough then went to Spain (1808) where he was wounded at the battle of **Talavera**. For his services there he was promoted to lieutenant-colonel. His regiment fought at the battle of **Barossa** and at the defence of Tarifa (1811). Gough's battalion then moved to join **Wellington** at **Vitoria**. He was severely wounded at the **Nivelle** (1813), returned home and was knighted (1815). His battalion (the 2nd/87th) was disbanded (1817) and Gough was on **half pay** until 1819 when he was given command of the 22nd Foot (**Cheshire Regiment**) in Ireland (until 1826). He again retired, was made **major-general** (1830) and **KCB** (1831). In 1837 he was appointed to command the Mysore **Division** of the Madras Army and served in China. In 1843 Gough was promoted to Commander-in-Chief, India. He took a prominent part in the **Sikh Wars**. His tactics in India, although successful, were criticised and he returned home (1849). He was created a viscount (1849); **general** (1854); colonel-in-chief of the 60th Foot (**King's Royal Rifle Corps**) (1854) and **colonel** of the Royal Horse Guards (**Blues and Royals**) (1855) on the death of Lord **Raglan**. He received other honours and was made a **field marshal** (1862).

See also **Ferozeshah, battle of; Mudki, battle of; Ramnagar, battle of**

Graham, Thomas (1748–1843)

Having spent his early years as a gentleman on his estates in Leicestershire, on the death of his wife (1791) Graham went with Lord Hood's fleet and took part in the operations on shore at Toulon. On his return home he raised the **Perthshire Volunteers**. In April 1794 he was elected MP for Perth, but served with his **regiment** at Quiberon under the command of Sir John Doyle, and afterwards in Gibraltar. He distinguished himself at the capture of Minorca (1798), organised the defence of Messina (1798–99) and took part in the blockade of Malta (1799–1800). He was at home serving as an MP (1800–08) and then went to Sweden with Sir John **Moore** and was also with him at **Corunna** (now La Coruña). He was promoted to **major-general** (1809) and took part in the siege of Flushing. He was invalided home. In 1811 he was promoted to **lieutenant-general** and sent to relieve Cadiz. He defeated the French at **Barossa**, but after a dispute with the Spanish commanders joined **Wellington** (June 1811), taking part in the capture of **Ciudad Rodrigo** and was created KB. He commanded an army corps at **Badajoz** and at **Salamanca**. He commanded the left wing of 40,000 men at the battle of **Vitoria** and was wounded at Tolosa. His troops invested San Sebastian (July 1813) but failed to take it until 9 September. He crossed the border (7 October 1813) and established the British Army on French soil. He returned home through ill health but (November 1813) took command of the British troops in Holland. Here he won a victory at Merxem but failed to take Bergen-op-Zoom. Graham returned home (1814) and was created Baron Lyndoch of Balgowan. He was promoted to full **general** (1821); **colonel** of the 58th Foot (**Rutlandshire Regiment**) (1823), the 14th Foot (**West Yorkshire Regiment**) (1826) and the 1st Foot (**Royal Scots**) (1834). In 1829 he was appointed governor of Dumbarton Castle. In 1817 he founded the United Services Club in Pall Mall (London).

Granby, Marquis of (1721–70)

He was the eldest son of the 3rd Duke of Rutland and was educated at Eton and Trinity College, Cambridge. He was elected MP for Grantham (1741). He raised a **regiment** at Leicester (the 'Leicester Blues') (1745) of which he was **colonel**. The regiment was disbanded after the battle of **Culloden** but Granby retained his rank as colonel in the army. He was re-elected MP for Grantham and served with the army in Flanders (1747). He was then elected MP for Cambridgeshire (1754), which seat he held until his death. Granby was promoted to **major-general** (1755) and **colonel** of the Horse Guards (1756). At the beginning of the **Seven Years' War** he commanded a **brigade** of **cavalry**. He was promoted to **lieutenant-general** (1759) and took a prominent part in the battle of **Minden**. For his mis-handling of the battle, the **commander-in-chief**,

George **Sackville**, was court-martialled and Granby was appointed in his place (1759). He was made a privy councillor (1760). Granby was a splendid soldier and was always careful of his men. He led a famous cavalry charge at **Warburg** (1760) in the course of which his wig fell off, giving the language the expression 'to go for something bald-headed', meaning to act very enthusiastically. He returned home to become **Master-General of the Ordnance** (*see* **Ordnance, Board of**) (1763) and Commander-in-Chief of the Army (1766), in which post he was attacked by political commentators. He resigned all public appointments, except his colonelcy of the Horse Guards (1770). *Also known as* **Manners, John**

Grand Alliance, War of the (1688–97)

The aggression of Louis XIV of France in Europe led to the defensive League of Augsburg being formed (1686). Its members included the Holy Roman Empire, Spain, Sweden, the Netherlands and various lesser German states. War began when France invaded the Palatinate (1688) and from 1689 more countries, including Britain and Savoy, joined the anti-French coalition, which became known as the Grand Alliance. When the fighting spread to North America it was known as **King William's War**. The war was ended by the treaty of Ryswick (1697).

Grant, James Hope (1808–75)

Grant was born in Perthshire and educated in Edinburgh and Switzerland. He was commissioned in the 9th Lancers as a **cornet** (1826) and was promoted to **captain** (1835). He was also an accomplished cellist. He served throughout the war in China and was promoted to **major** (1842). He rejoined his **regiment** in India (1844) and took part in the battle of **Sobraon**. With his regiment he played a major part in the campaign in the Punjab (1848–9, Second **Sikh War**) and Grant was promoted to **brevet lieutenant-colonel** in command of the regiment (1849). Grant was at Umballa at the start of the **Indian Mutiny** in which his regiment fought. It took part in the first and second reliefs of **Lucknow** and was at **Cawnpore** (now Kanpur) as well as fighting in several other engagements. For his services during the Mutiny, Grant was promoted to **major-general** and created **KCB** (1855). In 1860 Grant, with the local rank of **lieutenant-general**, took command in China, a command he conducted so successfully that he was created **GCB**. He returned to India as **commander-in-chief** at Madras (now Chennai) (1862–3). He returned home to be quartermaster-general at the Horse Guards (1865) and then commanded the camp at Aldershot (1870) where he brought about many reforms.
See also **Taku, battle of**

Grantham, battle of

(1643; *Civil War*) After the indecisive battle of **Edgehill**, **Cromwell** spent the winter raising a disciplined force of **cavalry** in the eastern counties. 400 of these troops routed 800 Royalists at Grantham. This was the beginning of the career of the **New Model Army**.

grape shot *See* shot

Graziani, Rodolfo (1882–1955)

Field Marshal Graziani was **commander-in-chief** of the Italian forces in Libya (1930–34), governor of Italian Somaliland (1935–36), viceroy of Ethiopia (1936–37) and honorary governor of Italian East Africa (1938). He commanded the Italian forces in Libya at the outbreak of **World War II** but his advance against Egypt (1940) was defeated by the British, commanded by Sir Archibald **Wavell**. Graziani resigned (February 1941). After the Italian armistice (1943) he became defence minister in the German-backed Italian government and took part in anti-partisan warfare. He was tried for war crimes after the war and sentenced to 19 years' imprisonment (1950). He was released during the same year and became leader of the Italian neo-fascist movement.
See also **Bardia, battle of**; **Beda Fomm, battle of**

Greathed, William Wilberforce Harris (1826–78)

Greathed was commissioned in the Bengal **Engineers** (1844) and went to join the Bengal Sappers and Miners (1846), working in the irrigation department. He was involved in the **Sikh War** (1848) and took part in the siege of Mooltan (1849) and the battle of **Gujarat**. During the **Indian Mutiny** he was directing engineer of the attack on **Lucknow**. For his services during the Mutiny he was promoted to **major** and created **CB**. He went to China as **aide-de-camp** to Sir Robert **Napier** and was present at the battles of Seuho, **Taku**, and the capture of Peking (now Beijing). He returned home (1860) and was promoted to **brevet colonel** (1861) and assistant military secretary at the Horse Guards (1861–65). He worked in England for a short time and then returned to India where he continued his irrigation work. Ill-health forced his return home (1876) when he was promoted to **major-general**.
See also **Agra, battle of**

Greece

(1940–41; *World War II*) The Italians occupied Albania (April 1939) and from there invaded Greece (28 October 1940) on four fronts and with six **divisions** commanded by General Visconti Prasca. The advance was halted by 8 November and the Greek **commander-in-chief**, General Alexandros Papagos, counter-attacked with a force of 16 divisions. The Italian Army was now increased to 26 divisions but the situation was a stalemate. In March 1941 British commanders sent troops to help Greece. Australian and New Zealand forces with the 1st Armoured Brigade took up positions west of Salonika. The German 12th Army of 15 divisions, commanded by Field Marshal Sigmund List, invaded Yugoslavia and Greece (6 April) and pushed down into the Salonika section where they met the British forces commanded by General Sir Henry Maitland-Wilson. This move separated the Allied forces which then fell back to a line in the Mount Olympus area (12–13 April). By 20 April intense air attack and pressure on the ground forced 300,000 Greek troops isolated near the Albanian border to surrender and 41,000 British troops were evacuated. Greece surrendered on 24 April. 5,000 British troops were killed and 8,000 taken prisoner. The Italians suffered 125,000 casualties and the Germans 5,500. The Germans claimed 270,000 Greek prisoners were taken.
See also **Crete, battle of**

Green Howards, The

The **regiment** was formed by the amalgamation (1688) of various companies of foot by Colonel Francis Luttrell to aid William III. In 1751 it became the 19th Regiment of Foot, in 1782 the 19th (1st Yorkshire North Riding) Regiment of Foot and in 1875 the 19th (1st Yorkshire North Riding) (The Princess of Wales's Own). In 1902 it was re-named Alexandra, Princess of Wales's Own Yorkshire Regiment. In 1921 the name was changed to The Green Howards (Alexandra, Princess of Wales's Own Yorkshire Regiment). This regularised the long-standing use of the nickname Green Howards which had originated from a commanding officer named 'Howard' who chose green facings for the regiment to distinguish it from the **Buffs** whose **colonel** of the time was also named 'Howard'. In 2006 it is expected to unite with The Prince of Wales's Own Regiment of Yorkshire and The Duke of Wellington's Regiment to form The Yorkshire Regiment (14th/15th, 19th, and 33rd/76th Foot).
See also **Alma, battle of the**

Green Jackets *See* **Royal Green Jackets**

Green Jackets, 1st

The re-designation (1958) of the **Oxfordshire and Buckinghamshire Light Infantry**

Green Jackets, 2nd

The re-designation (1958) of the **King's Royal Rifle Corps**

Green Jackets, 3rd

The re-designation (1958) of the **Rifle Brigade** (Prince Consort's Own)

grenade

Originally grenades were about the size of a cricket ball and were filled with **black powder**. A projecting fuse was lit by a slow match wound around the left wrist of the **grenadier**. Grenades were employed in assaults on trenches or forts but went out of use c. 1750. They came back into use during the Russo-Japanese War (1904–05) and have been standard equipment for the **infantry** ever since. The first grenades in modern British use were employed in the early part of **World War I** and were made from improvised materials. Purpose-built types soon followed. The most common form of grenade is the explosive grenade that consists of a core of TNT encased in a metal jacket. This explodes on contact or is fired by a time-delay, usually of about four seconds. This is long enough for the grenade to be thrown accurately but not long enough for the enemy to throw it back. Gas, smoke and incendiary grenades are also used. Other types of grenade are launched from rifles using blank cartridges to propel them while others are propelled from special launchers or by rockets.

[From French, shortening of *pome grenate* 'pomegranate', based on Spanish *granada*]

grenadier

A soldier who specialised in using **grenades**. Grenadiers were introduced into the British Army in 1678, and every **infantry regiment** had a **company** of grenadiers. The tallest and most efficient men were selected to be trained in handling and throwing **grenades**. The grenadiers were the showpiece of the regiment and usually marched in front and were stationed at the right of a **battalion** line in battle. They earned higher pay and were awarded special privileges. They wore the tall **grenadier cap** and carried hatchets for cutting through barricades and other obstacles. The formation of grenadier companies is one of the first examples of the formation of specialist units within a regiment. The use of grenades declined during the 18th century but the grenadiers were retained as elite troops. The term is now obsolete except in the titles of the **Grenadier Guards**. During **World War I** some men were given special training in the use of grenades, but they were then known as 'bombers'.

See also **flank company**

[From French, from *grenade* 'grenade']

grenadier cap

A smaller fur-edged cap which changed (1765) to being an all-fur cap. It was introduced to make it easier for a grenadier to sling his musket over his shoulder when throwing a grenade – the broad brim of the traditional hat would get in the way. The broad brim would also get in the way if the grenade was thrown over-arm. The introduction of the **shako** in the 19th century saw the grenadier cap's gradual disuse.

Grenadier Guards

The senior **regiment** of **Foot Guards**. The regiment was raised (1656) by the exiled King Charles II and styled the Royal Regiment of Guards. It was commanded by Colonel Lord Wentworth. At the Restoration (1660) another regiment, the King's Own Regiment of Foot Guards, was raised under Colonel John Russell. When Wentworth died the regiments were amalgamated as the Royal Regiment of Foot Guards and re-named (1685) the 1st Regiment of Foot Guards. After defeating the Grenadiers of the French Imperial Guard at **Waterloo** (1815) the regiment was re-named the 1st or Grenadier Regiment of Foot Guards; the name changed to the **Grenadier Guards** (1877) and the regiment continues in this form to the present day.

Grenville's Regiment *See* **Royal Lincolnshire Regiment**

Grey, Charles (1729–1807)

Grey was born at Howick. He was a **lieutenant** in the 6th Foot (**Royal Warwickshire Fusiliers**) (1752) and ultimately **captain** in the 20th Foot (**East Devonshire Regiment**) (1755) of which **Wolfe** was **lieutenant-colonel**. He served at Rochefort (1757) and was wounded at **Minden**. Grey was promoted to lieutenant-colonel of the 98th Foot (1761). The **regiment** was disbanded after the battle of **Havana** and Grey was put on half pay. He was promoted to **colonel** in the army and became an **aide-de-**

camp to the king (1772). In 1776 he went to America with the local rank of **major-general** and was appointed colonel of the 28th Foot (**North Gloucestershire Regiment**) (1778). He returned home (1782) when he was promoted to **lieutenant-general** and created **KB**. He was one of the board of land and sea officers nominated by the king to oversee the structure and administration of land and sea forces (1785), and by 1793 was colonel of the 7th Dragoons (**Queen's Own Hussars**). In 1793 Grey and Admiral Sir John Jervis (later Earl St. Vincent) went to subdue the French possessions in the West Indies. After a successful expedition he returned home (1794) and was promoted to **general** and became a privy councillor. He transferred to the colonelcy of the 20th (Jamaican) Light Dragoons (**Hussars, 20th**) and in 1799 to the 3rd Dragoons (**King's Own Hussars**). He was created Baron Grey de Howick (1801) and Viscount Howick and Earl Grey (1806). He was made governor of Guernsey.
See also **Paoli, battle of**

Guards
Historically these **regiments** were raised specifically to protect the monarch – they were the household troops. They have always consisted of the **Foot Guards** and the **Household Cavalry** (also known as the Horse Guards).

Gubat *See* **Abu Kru, battle of**

guided missile
A rocket or similar projectile guided to its target electronically from a remote control centre

guidon
A flag which is broad at the end near the staff and forked, sometimes pointed, at the other. Guidons were carried by sub-units of **cavalry regiments** but were abandoned by **hussar**, **lancer** and **light dragoon** regiments (1834). Their use was continued by heavy cavalry until they were disbanded.
[Via French from Italian *guidone*, from *guida* 'guide']

Guilford Courthouse, battle of
(1781; *American War of Independence*) Having failed to trap the Americans commanded by General Nathaniel Greene south of the Dan river, the British commander, General Lord Charles **Cornwallis**, turned back into North Carolina. Greene re-crossed the Dan with 4,400 men (25 February) and took up a defensive position at Guilford Courthouse. Cornwallis, with 1,400 men, attacked and forced Greene to withdraw. Cornwallis, having lost 78 killed and 183 wounded, was too weak to pursue and fell back to Wilmington to gather reinforcements and supplies. He then moved into Virginia.

Guinegate, battle of *See* **Spurs, battle of the**

guisarme
An early form of lance with a hook on the side of the blade. It developed into a heavy, broad pointed blade that could be used for cutting or thrusting.
Also called **glaive**

Gujurat, battle of
(1849; *Sikh Wars*) After his victories in the Punjab, General Sir Hugh **Gough** took his Anglo-Indian army north and reached Gujurat (22 February). He now commanded 20,000 men and opened a bombardment on a Sikh force of 40,000. The 84 guns carried out the bombardment for two hours and the Sikhs broke their lines. The Anglo-Indian **cavalry** and **infantry** then destroyed the rest of the army. This battle ended the Sikh War, leaving the Punjab under British control.

Gulf War (1990–91)
On 2 August 1990 the Iraqis, under their leader Saddam Hussein, invaded Kuwait to gain advantage of its oil reserves and command of the head of the Persian Gulf. Resistance ceased within 24 hours. Saudi Arabia was reinforced by forces from the USA, Europe (mainly Britain and France) and Arab nations. The United Nations

passed a resolution giving authority for the re-taking of Kuwait. The UN commander, the American General Norman Schwartzkopf, imposed a blockade. The UN air forces destroyed the Iraqi communications and electronic systems (from 17 January 1991). The Iraqi air force was destroyed on the ground. The UN land forces then attacked by land and overwhelmed the Iraqi ground forces in 100 hours forcing them to surrender. About 18 of the 24 Iraqi **divisions** were immobilised by loss of their logistic support along with 4,900 tanks and 2,300 guns. The UN lost 211 sailors, soldiers and airmen.

gun

An **artillery** weapon. Strictly speaking a gun is a member of the class of artillery weapon which normally fires on a relatively flat trajectory and whose barrel is elevated from the horizontal to gain increased range. This contrasts with **howitzers** and **mortars**, which fire on a high trajectory, often with shorter range; however, developments in artillery since World War II have blurred the distinction between guns and howitzers, with modern weapons being able to fire at both high and low trajectories.

[Probably from the Scandinavian name Gunnhildr, from *gunnr* 'battle' + *hildr* 'war', from the custom of giving women's names to weapons]

gunlock

The mechanism that caused the gunpowder charge to explode in early guns.
See also **flintlock**; **matchlock**; **wheellock**

gunner

The most junior rank in the **Royal Artillery**, equivalent to private in most other arms

gunnery

The art of firing and maintaining **artillery**

gunpowder *See* **black powder; nitrocellulose**

gunsight

Any device for aiming **small arms** or **artillery**. The earliest sights were made for **muskets** before 1450. They consisted of a small bead at the front of the barrel that was lined-up with a notched sight at its rear. Various methods of elevating the rear sight, to compensate for the distance of the target, were developed. By the mid-17th century, the telescope had been introduced instead of a rear sight to increase accuracy. Such sights have developed enormously since those times and are still used, e.g. by snipers. Specialised rifle sights now use infrared radiation to enable the target to be seen in the dark (see **thermal imager**), and infrared and other electronic sighting technologies are also used by modern artillery and tanks.

Gurkhas, Brigade of

Originally the troops of Prithvi Narayan Shar, who founded the state of Nepal, the Gurkhas were heavily recruited by the British from the middle of the 19th century. Some 50,000 Gurkhas served in the Indian Army after 1947, while some 10,000 still serve in British Gurkha units. The Brigade of Gurkhas was formed (1948) to control the four Gurkha **regiments** (of the original 10) which joined the British Army after India became independent and the former Indian Army, of which the Gurkhas had been part, ceased to exist. Other Gurkha regiments joined the new independent India's army. The brigade included **King Edward VII's Own Gurkha Rifles (2nd)** (The Sirmoor Rifles), the 6th Gurkha Rifles (later **Queen Elizabeth's Own Gurkha Rifles (6th)**), the 7th Gurkha Rifles (later the **Duke of Edinburgh's Own Gurkha Rifles (7th)**) and the 10th Gurkha Rifles (later **Princess Mary's Own 10th Gurkha Rifles**) as well as the Queen's Gurkha Engineers, the Queen's Gurkha Signals and the Gurkha Transport Regiment. In 1994 the four infantry regiments were amalgamated as the **Royal Gurkha Rifles**.

Gustav Line

(*World War II*) A belt of fortresses held by the Germans in Italy in 1943–44. It ran from the mouth of the Garigliano river in the west to just north of Ortona in the east. It was defended by nine German **divisions** with nine in reserve and commanded Highways 6 and 7 – the main roads into Rome. Breaking this line was one of the chief objectives of the Allied forces in Italy. This was finally achieved at **Cassino** and by the breakout of the allied forces from **Anzio**.

Gwalior, battle of

1. (1780; *Maratha Wars*) This strong fortress was captured from the Marathas by a surprise attack by 2,000 British-led troops (mostly sepoys) commanded by Captain Popham. The wall was scaled and the fort surrendered without resistance.

2. (1858; *Indian Mutiny*) The rebels had seized Gwalior and a British force led by Major-General Sir Hugh **Rose** moved against them (17 June). The rebel force of 12,500 was dispersed and the fortress of Gwalior was captured. The rebel leaders Tantia Topi and Rao Sahib fled, but were captured and hanged. This was the last major battle of the Mutiny.

H

Habbaniya, battle of
(1941; *World War II*) A pro-German government had been established in Iraq (March 1941) under Rashid Ali and the regent Emir Abdul-Ilah fled to a British warship at Basra. The British landed a **brigade** from India at Basra (18 April) and Rashid attacked the British air base at Habbaniya (2 May). The British were out-numbered and had no artillery, but the RAF finally silenced the assailants' 50 guns. Rashid Ali withdrew (6 May) and the British counter-attacked, and, having been reinforced by a motorised brigade from Haifa, captured Al Falluja (19 May) and Baghdad (30 May). Rashid Ali fled, and Abdul-Ilah resumed government.

hackbut *See* **arquebus**

hackle
A bunch of short-cut feathers worn on the headdress of Scottish troops since the 18th century
[Probably from assumed Old English *hacule* 'little hook']

Hague conventions
International agreements adopted at conferences held at The Hague in 1899 and 1907. These were convened by the Russians mainly to limit the size of armed forces and armaments. In this they failed, but they did produce agreements on various aspects of the conduct of war. These included a prohibition on the use of such weapons as dum-dum **bullets** (bullets with expanding heads) and **gas**, and a clarification of the position of neutral powers in times of war. The first convention also established the Permanent Court of Arbitration, an early attempt to resolve international disputes by arbitration rather than conflict.

Haidar Ali, Hayder Ali (1728–82)
Initially Haidar Ali was a soldier but ultimately replaced the maharajah of Mysore. He conquered Calicut, Bednor and Cannanore. He withheld tribute from the Marathas, and waged war against the British (1767–69). When Haidar was defeated by the Marathas (1772) he asked for support from the British, and when it was refused he became their bitter enemy. When war broke out between Britain and France, Haidar supported the French in India, attacking the Carnatic and routing the British around Madras (now Chennai). He was defeated finally by troops led by Eyre **Coote**.

Haig, Douglas (1861–1928)
Haig graduated from the Royal Military College at Sandhurst and served in the **Sudan** (1898) and the **Boer War** (1899–1902). He was Director of Military Training at the **War Office** (1906–09) and was instrumental in establishing the general staff and the **Territorial Army**. At the beginning of **World War I** he commanded I Corps in northern France and became commander of the 1st Army (1915). In December 1915 he succeeded Sir John **French** as **commander-in-chief** of the **British Expeditionary Force**. His commitment of large numbers of British troops, and the consequent heavy casualties, during the **Somme** offensive (1916) and at the Third Battle of **Ypres** (1917) shocked the British public. He was promoted to **field marshal** (1916) and during the first half of 1917, at Prime Minister Lloyd George's instigation, was made subordinate to the French General Robert **Nivelle** as supreme Allied commander. Haig did not work well with Nivelle but he agreed to serve under **Foch** as supreme allied commander when the Germans attacked in the spring of 1918. Haig played a prominent part in

stopping these last German offensives (March–July 1918) and in leading the final very successful Allied attacks (August–November 1918). After the war Haig formed the British Legion to provide for needy ex-servicemen. He was created an earl in 1919.
See also **Amiens, battle of; Arras, battle of; Loos, battle of**

halberd

A weapon resembling a spear with a head consisting of a sharp-edged pointed blade with a hatchet head at its base. It was mounted on a shaft 5–7 feet long. It was introduced during the 11th century to increase the fighting capabilities of the foot soldier. After the late 16th century it was a weapon only for **sergeants**, and was replaced by the **spontoon** in 1792.
See also **pike**
[Via French from Middle High German *helmbarde*, from *helm* 'handle' + *barde* 'hatchet']

Hales, Edward (d. 1695)

Hales succeeded to his father's baronetcy during the reign of Charles II and purchased estates near Canterbury. He was a Roman Catholic. He was admitted to the rank of **colonel** of a foot **regiment**, but could not hold active office of any kind because of his religious beliefs. He was granted a dispensation by James II and sworn to the privy council. He held several offices including Lieutenant of the Tower (of London) from which he was dismissed (1688). Hales was one of the three who accompanied James II on his attempted escape to France (1688). He was imprisoned in the Tower but was released (1690). He left England and joined James at St. Germain, where he died.
See also **West Yorkshire Regiment**

half pay

The pay of officers was reduced when they were not on active service. From the formation of a regular army until the late 19th century armies were recruited to fight in a particular campaign, after which **regiments** were reduced in number or disbanded. The **other ranks** were discharged without compensation and left to fend for themselves while commissioned officers had their pay cut by half, but were retained in their regiments or transferred to other regiments. This treatment of the troops greatly reduced the strain of the national budget imposed during any war.

Halidon Hill, battle of

(1333; *English-Scottish Wars*) During the civil war in Scotland between King David and the pretender Edward de Balliol, Edward III of England laid siege to Berwick-on-Tweed. Sir Archibald Douglas, King David's regent, marched to relieve Berwick and met the English at the nearby Halidon Hill (19 July). He attacked with **cavalry** but they were cut to pieces by flanking English archers. The rout was completed by a counter-attack by mounted men-at-arms. Douglas was killed, David fled to France and Berwick surrendered. Edward de Balliol did homage to Edward III.

Hamilton, Ian Standish Monteith (1853–1947)

Hamilton was born in Corfu. His father was a **captain** in the 92nd Highland Regiment of Foot (**Gordon Highlanders**). He was educated at Wellington College and the **Royal Military Academy** at Sandhurst. He was posted to the 12th Foot (**Suffolk Regiment**) and served in Ireland (1873). He was then posted to the Gordon Highlanders in India (1873). His first active service was in **Afghanistan** (1879) for which he was twice mentioned in dispatches. He was wounded at the battle of **Majuba Hill**, his left arm being permanently crippled. He was invalided home and studied for the **Staff College** examinations (1882), becoming **aide-de-camp** to General Sir Frederick Roberts, **commander-in-chief** at Madras (now Chennai). In 1884 he went to Cairo, was present at the battle of **Kirbekan** and was promoted to **brevet major**. Hamilton returned to India (1886), went to Burma (now Myanmar) with Roberts, and was promoted to brevet **lieutenant-colonel** (1887). In 1897 he was given command of the Tirah Expeditionary Force. He left India (1888) but was soon serving in Natal (1889) as **major-general** and was present at **Ladysmith** and **Bloemfontein**. He was promoted to **lieutenant-general** and soon afterwards was appointed **chief-of-staff** to **Kitchener** in charge of the great drive that ended the **Boer War**. In 1903 he was appointed Quartermaster-General at the **War Office** and in 1904 led a military mission to the Japanese during the Russo-Japanese War. In 1905 he was appointed Commander-in-Chief, Southern Command, and was made Adjutant-General (1909). In 1911 Hamilton was appointed to the Mediterranean Command at Malta but returned to England (1914) when he was in command of the forces responsible for the defence of the UK. On 12 March 1915 he was given command of the forces shortly to be sent to **Gallipoli**. After the failure of that campaign, in part because of Hamilton's weak leadership, he was given no further command. In 1918 he became Lieutenant of the Tower (of London). He retired in 1920 and was **colonel** of the Gordon Highlanders for many years.

Hampshire Regiment *See* Royal Hampshire Regiment

hand grenade *See* grenade

hanger *See* sword

Harfleur, battle of

(1415; *Hundred Years' War*) The civil war in France between the Burgundians and the Orleanists led Henry V of England to lead an invasion of France. He supported the Burgundians and landed an army of 10,000 men at the mouth of the Seine, moving to lay siege to Harfleur (19 August). The English troops suffered from dysentery and the defence was strong so that the town did not surrender until 22 September. Henry expelled the inhabitants and garrisoned the town as an English settlement, leaving him with only 5,000 men to march towards **Calais**.

harquebus *See* arquebus

Harris, George (1746–1829)

Harris was educated at Westminster School and the **Royal Military Academy** at Woolwich from which he passed out as a lieutenant-fireworker in the **artillery** (1760). He transferred to the 5th Foot (**Royal Northumberland Fusiliers**) (1762), was promoted to **lieutenant** (1765) and appointed **adjutant** (1767). He went to Ireland and purchased his **company** (1771). He went to America (1774) and served as **captain** of a **grenadier** company at **Lexington** and **Bunker Hill**, where he suffered a severe head wound. He was present at every major engagement in America in 1776–78 except **Germantown**. He was promoted to **major** and went to the West Indies where he took part in the fighting on St. Lucia. When returning home (1779) in a neutral ship he was captured by French privateers but was released on parole. He married (1780) and went to Ireland, being shipwrecked on the way there. His **regiment** went to America but Harris transferred to the **76th Foot** and went to India where he was present at the battle of **Seringapatam** (1792). He returned home as private secretary to General Medows but returned to India (1794) as a **major-general** and commandant of Fort William. He was promoted to the local rank of **lieutenant-general** (1796) and appointed to the staff at Fort St. George. Harris was commander of the troops in Madras (now Chennai) (1796–1800) and commanded 50,000 troops at the taking of Seringapatam (1799). He was appointed **colonel** of the 73rd Highlanders (**Perthshire Regiment of Foot**) (1800) when he returned home. He was promoted to lieutenant-general (1801) and **general** (1812).

Hartley, James (1745–99)

Hartley joined the army of the Bombay presidency (1764) and by 1774 was a **captain** in command of the 4th **Battalion** of **sepoys**. He took part in the First **Maratha War** and went to Gujurat. During the Second Maratha War he commanded six **companies** of **grenadiers** who saved a British-Indian force from annihilation during its retreat from Poona. He was promoted to **lieutenant-colonel** in command of the European **infantry** at Bombay (now Mumbai). He led the party that captured **Ahmadabad** (1779) and took part in the series of battles that secured Bombay. Hartley continued as military commandant in the Konkan only to be told that his promotion to lieutenant-colonel had been informal. He left the army and returned to England (1781). After discussion the king appointed him lieutenant-colonel of the 75th Foot (**Stirlingshire Regiment**). He returned to India with his **regiment** (1788) and was appointed quartermaster-general in Bombay. During the **Mysore Wars** he defeated the Mysoris at **Calicut** and was promoted to commander of the forces in the south-west provinces. Hartley commanded the forces that defeated the French in Malabar (1793). He was promoted to **colonel** (1794) and returned to England. In 1796 he was promoted to **major-general** on the staff in India. He returned to Bombay (1797) as supervisor and magistrate of Malabar. He was second-in-command to General Stuart at the taking of **Seringapatam** (1799). He returned to Malabar but died after a short illness.

Hashin, battle of

(1885; *Sudan War*) A British force of 8,000 men, commanded by Colonel Graham, defeated a section of Osman Digna's army, inflicting some 1,000 killed. The British lost 48 killed and wounded (20 March).

Hastenbeck, battle of

(1757; *Seven Years' War*) Frederick II (the Great) of Prussia was fighting the Austrians, France's allies, in Bohemia while an Anglo-Hanoverian army of 36,000 men commanded by the Duke of **Cumberland** defended Hanover against a French invasion. A French army of 74,000 men, commanded by the Marquis de Courtanvaux, moved towards Hanover and attacked Cumberland's forces at Hastenbeck, near Hamelin (26 July). After a confused battle, in which both commanders thought themselves defeated, Cumberland withdrew to the Elbe. In September Cumberland signed the Convention of Kloster-Zeven, dissolved his army and abandoned Hanover and Brunswick to the French. This exposed Frederick's flank to the French. The British parliament repudiated the Convention and George II dismissed Cumberland.

Hastings, battle of

(1066; *Norman Conquest of England*) While Harold II was defeating the Norsemen at **Stamford Bridge**, William of Normandy landed 7,000 men at Pevensey in Sussex (28 September). William established his base and Harold marched from York to London in seven days. Here he recruited reinforcements and deployed his 7,000 Saxons on Senlac Hill, eight miles north of Hastings, barring the road to London (13 October). William then attacked (14 October), the site of the engagement being that of the present town of Battle. The Saxon foot-soldiers withstood repeated attacks by the Norman **cavalry** and archers, but in the late afternoon William feigned a retreat by the cavalry which drew the Saxons down from their vantage point. The cavalry turned and slaughtered the Saxon **infantry**. Harold was killed, supposedly by an arrow in the eye. The way was now open for William to move to London. This he did slowly, to be crowned King in Westminster Abbey on Christmas Day 1066.

Havana, battle of

(1762; *Seven Years' War*) Early in 1762 Spain entered the war on the side of France. A British fleet of 19 warships, commanded by Admiral Sir George Pocock, with 10,000 troops, commanded by George Keppel, Earl of Albemarle, blockaded Havana (Cuba), trapping 12 Spanish ships. The troops forced the surrender of Morro Castle, protecting the harbour (30 July). Havana surrendered (14 August). The fall of Cuba cut Spain's communications with its American colonies. Of the original British force only 2,500 remained active. Most of the casualties were caused by disease.

Havelock, Henry (1795–1857)

Havelock was born near Durham and obtained a **commission** in the army (1815). After spending eight years studying military strategy he joined his brothers in India as a **lieutenant** in the 13th Foot (**Somerset Light Infantry**). He distinguished himself during the Burmese War (**Burma campaigns**) and the **Afghan Wars**. He was made a **CB**, but was still only a **captain** due to the system of purchasing commissions. He received further promotion (1843) when serving as an interpreter to Sir Hugh **Gough**. He returned home (1849) due to ill health. Havelock returned to India (1851) and was promoted to quartermaster-general (1854) and then to **adjutant-general**. He took part in Sir James **Outram's** campaign in Persia (1857) and on returning to India commanded a mobile column during the **Indian Mutiny**. He failed to save **Cawnpore** (now Kanpur) or **Lucknow** but achieved a series of victories during July and August 1857. At his fourth attempt (September 1857) Havelock relieved the residency at Lucknow. He was promoted to **major-general** but died of dysentery in the same year.

Haviland, William (1718–84)
Haviland was born in Ireland. He was appointed **ensign** in Spottiswood's Regiment (Gooch's Regiment – the old 43rd Foot – disbanded in 1742) (1739). He joined the 27th Foot (**Inniskilling Regiment of Foot**) and was **aide-de-camp** to **Colonel** William Blakeney at the defence of Stirling Castle against the Jacobites (1745–46). He served in Ireland and by 1752 he had been promoted to **lieutenant-colonel**. He took the **regiment** to America (1757) and commanded the troops at Fort Edward (1757–58). He was present at several operations under **Amherst**, including the attack on **Montreal**. Haviland then went to the West Indies and was second-in-command at the taking of Martinique. He commanded a **brigade** at the conquest of **Havana** (1762). Haviland was promoted to **major-general** and **colonel** of the 45th Foot (**Nottinghamshire (Sherwood Foresters) Regiment**) (1762). He was further promoted to **lieutenant-general** (1772) and **general** (1783). He was commander of the western **division**, based in Plymouth (1779).

headdress
Any form of cap or hat worn on the head as part of uniform

Heathfield, Lord *See* **Eliott, George Augustus**

heat-seeking missile
A missile, usually rocket-powered, that is guided to the target by the heat emitted from the target

heaume *See* **helmet**

heavy brigade
The name given to various military formations, most notably the **cavalry brigade** sent to the Crimea under the command of General **Scarlett** and consisting of the **Royal Scots Greys**, **Inniskilling Dragoons** and the 4th and 5th Dragoon Guards (**Princess Charlotte of Wales's Dragoon Guards**). At the battle of **Balaclava** the Heavy Brigade made a notable and successful charge shortly before the more famous but disastrous Charge of the **Light Brigade**.

Hedgeley Moor, battle of
(1464; *Wars of the Roses*) The Lancastrian Henry Beaufort, Duke of Somerset, raised a revolt against the Yorkist King Edward IV. Beaufort was joined in Northumberland by Sir Ralph Percy. The rebels met a royalist force commanded by Lord Montague at Hedgeley Moor near Alnwick (25 April). The Lancastrians were defeated and Percy was killed.
See also **Hexham, battle of**

heliograph
A two-mirrored signalling system that reflected sunlight. The light beam was interrupted by a hand-operated shutter so that messages could be sent by Morse code. It was invented by Sir Henry Mance (1840–1926) and first used during the Second **Afghan War** (1878).

helm *See* **helmet**

helmet
A defensive head-covering. Helmets have been worn since ancient times to protect the head against blows and missiles. The Persians and Assyrians wore helmets of leather and iron while the Greeks and Romans developed complex helmets made of bronze. The early helmet of northern and western Europe was a leather skullcap reinforced by bands of iron or bronze straps. By the early 13th century the helm (or heaume) had developed. This was a flat-topped helmet worn over a fabric skullcap. It was soon

realised that a conical helmet was more effective in warding off blows to the head and so the basinet developed from a reinforced skullcap. By the 16th century the basinet had been elaborated by the addition of hinged flaps which made the helmet fit the head and neck, giving more protection and assuring that it was not knocked off during combat. Lighter, more open brimmed helmets became popular during the later 16th and 17th centuries but by the 18th and 19th centuries helmets had disappeared from use, except in some heavy **cavalry regiments**, due to the increase in the use of firearms and the decrease in the use of sword and spear. The **steel helmet** was introduced to modern warfare by the French during 1915 mainly as a protection against shrapnel. It quickly became standard issue for British and other nationalities' troops also. Helmets remain a standard part of combat equipment at the start of the 21st century though their effectiveness has been increased and weight reduced by modern ceramics, plastics and other materials. The current standard helmet for the British Army is the **Mark 6 combat helmet**, which is made of **Kevlar**. Different helmets are also worn for particular tasks, e.g. by engineers who are clearing mines, or by special forces in hostage rescue situations.

[From Old French, diminutive of *helme* 'helmet']

Herefordshire Regiment of Foot

The **regiment** was raised (1701) as Viscount Charlemont's Regiment of Foot. The name changed with the **colonel** until 1751 when it was named the 36th Regiment of Foot. It was changed further (1782) to the 36th (or the Herefordshire) Regiment of Foot. In the 1881 reorganisation it amalgamated with the 29th to become the **Worcestershire Regiment**.

Hesilbridge's Regiment *See* Coldstream Guards

Hexham, battle of

(1464; *Wars of the Roses*) Henry Beaufort, Duke of Somerset, having escaped from the battle of **Hedgeley Moor**, took refuge in Hexham and re-organised his Lancastrian forces. The Yorkist commander, Lord Montague, attacked the Lancastrian camp (15 May) and annihilated them. Somerset and several other Lancastrian nobles were captured and executed.

Hicks, William (1830–83)

Hicks entered the Bombay Army as an **ensign** in 1849. He was in command of a **company** during the campaign in **Abyssinia** (now Ethiopia) (1867–68) and ultimately became an honorary **colonel** (1880). He left the British Army and took command of the Egyptian Army (1883) as a **general** and set out to suppress the **Madhi's** revolt. He personally took part in most of the campaign and was killed at the battle of Kashgal. During his command in the Sudan he was known as Hicks Pasha.

See also **El Obeid, battle of**

Highland dress

The first **regiment** to wear highland dress was the **Black Watch** (1739). Various other Highland regiments were raised and disbanded but in 1787 the 74th and 75th Foot were raised and in 1793–94 eight new Highland regiments were formed. These regiments continued to wear highland dress despite its wearing being forbidden by law.

Highlanders, 93rd *See* Argyll and Sutherland Highlanders

Highland Light Infantry

The **regiment** was raised (1777) by Lord Macleod as the 73rd (Highland) Regiment of Foot, called Macleod's Highlanders. It was re-numbered (1786) as the 71st (Highland Regiment of Foot) and in 1808 became the 71st (Glasgow Highland) Regiment of Foot. From 1855 it was called the 71st (Highland Light Infantry) Regiment of Foot. A new regiment, the Highland Light Infantry (City of Glasgow) Regiment, was formed (1881) by the amalgamation of the 71st (Highland Light Infantry) and the 74th (Highlanders) Regiment. A further amalgamation in 1959 saw the regiment become part of the **Royal Highland Fusiliers**.

Hill, Rowland (1772–1842)

Hill was born near Shrewsbury and educated privately. He entered the Strasbourg Military School having joined the 38th Foot (**Staffordshire (1st) Regiment of Foot**) as an **ensign** (1790). He distinguished himself at the siege of Toulon (1793). When Thomas **Graham** raised the 90th Foot (**Perthshire Volunteers**) he made Hill a **major** in it. He was promoted to **lieutenant-colonel** (1794). He served in Egypt (1801) where he was wounded. He was appointed **brigadier** (1803), served in Ireland, and was promoted to **major-general** (1805). He went to Portugal as a **brigade** commander (1808) and took part in the battles of **Vimiero** and **Corunna**. He was given command of the 2nd **Division** (1809–11) and distinguished himself at the battle of **Talavera** (1809). He commanded the troops in southern Portugal but brought them back by forced marches to take part in the battle of **Bussaco**. He left the division (January 1811) through illness, but then led small picked forces into Spain to make important surprise attacks at Arroyo dos Molinos and Almaraz. For the rest of the war he commanded **Wellington**'s right flank. An excellent and careful commander, he cared for his men who called him affectionately 'Daddy' Hill. He was promoted to **lieutenant-general** and made a **KCB** (1812) and elected MP for Shrewsbury in the same year. Hill was created Baron Hill of Almaraz and Hawkstone (1814). During the **Waterloo** campaign, Hill commanded the II Corps. When Wellington became Prime Minister (1828) and resigned as **commander-in-chief**, Hill was appointed **general** and commander-in-chief, a post that he filled until he resigned in 1842.

Hindenburg, Paul von (1847–1934)

Hindenburg was the son of a Prussian officer. He joined the Prussian Army as a cadet (1858) and served in the Austro-Prussian War (1866) and the Franco-Prussian War (1870–71). Ultimately he was promoted to **general** and retired (1911). He was recalled to service (1914) and in 1916 was given nominal command of all the German land forces with the rank of **field marshal**, though his principal assistant, **Ludendorff**, was the real brains of the team. When Germany finally surrendered Hindenburg collaborated with the new republican government while living in retirement in Hanover (1919). He was elected the second president of the Weimar Republic (1925–34) and, following the economic depression and political instability, appointed Hitler as chancellor (1933).

Hindenburg Line

(*World War I*) The heavily fortified defensive line taken up by the German forces on the **Western Front** in the early spring of 1917. The Germans planned on and succeeded in holding this line throughout 1917 and concentrated on attacking on the Eastern Front to win the war against Russia there. The Allies did not succeed in breaching the line in 1917 but did break though it in their attacks in August and September 1918, proving that Germany had finally lost the war.

[So named by allied troops because Field Marshall Paul von *Hindenburg* (1847–1934) directed retreat to it]

Hindoostan Regiment *See* Foot, 76th

Hislop, Thomas (1764–1843)

Hislop entered the **Royal Military Academy**, Woolwich, and was appointed **ensign** in the 39th Foot (**Dorsetshire Regiment of Foot**) (1778). He served in Gibraltar (1779–83) and was promoted to **lieutenant**. He was appointed **aide-de-camp** to Major-General David Dundas with whom he served in Ireland, Toulon and Corsica (1792). He was appointed aide-de-camp to the **commander-in-chief**, Lord **Amherst**, and was promoted to **lieutenant-colonel** of the 115th Foot. He transferred back to the 39th Foot and went to the West Indies where he was ultimately appointed lieutenant-governor of Trinidad, from which post he retired (1811). Hislop was appointed commander-in-chief at Bombay (now Mumbai) (1812) but was captured by an American frigate on the outward journey. He was paroled and returned home. He was then appointed

commander-in-chief of Fort St. George at Madras (now Chennai) (1814) and commanded the 'forces of Deccan' during the **Maratha Wars** (1815).
See also **Mahidpur, battle of**

Hodges's (Colonel Hodges's Regiment of Foot) *See* Bedfordshire and Hertfordshire Regiment

Holland Regiment *See* East Kent Regiment

holster
Originally part of a cavalryman's equipment fitted to the front of a saddle for carrying a firearm. It was covered with a piece of fur or embroidered cloth called a holster cap. It was later adapted for carrying a pistol or revolver on the person.
[Probably from Dutch]

Home Guard
A part-time volunteer force established in **World War II** to resist any German invasion of the UK. Raised as the Local Defence Volunteers in 1940 but quickly renamed, this organisation soon had over a million members, many of whom were veterans from **World War I**. It included men too young for **conscription**, men of military age who were not eligible for conscription because of their occupations, and older men not required for full military service. In the early stages it had few rifles, little ammunition and no heavier weapons, but was better equipped later. The Home Guard was placed in a state of 'instant readiness' (7 September 1940) in anticipation of a German invasion, but it was a false alarm. After this the Home Guard was built up to 1,800,000 men. It was disbanded at the end of the war.

Hong Kong
(1941; *World War II*) The Japanese 38th **Division** attacked three British **battalions** commanded by General C.M. Maltby on the mainland of the Hong Kong colony (8 December). On 12–13 December the British withdrew to the island, joining a further three battalions. The Japanese crossed to the island (19 December). The fighting continued for another week but the island surrendered on Christmas Day. The Japanese took 11,000 prisoners. Like all prisoners of the Japanese they were brutally treated and many were murdered, until the survivors were released at the end of the war.

Honourable Artillery Company
The oldest unit in the British Army, now a **Territorial Army** unit of the Royal **Artillery**. It is descended from the Guild of St. George, formed by Henry VIII (1537) 'to be overseers of the science of artillery, that is to wit, long bows, cross bows and hand guns'. The **regiment** has the privilege of marching through the City of London with fixed bayonets, beating drums, and with **colours** flying.

Horne, Henry Sinclair (1861–1929)
Horne was educated at Harrow and the **Royal Military Academy** at Woolwich. He was commissioned in the Royal **Artillery** (1880). In 1890 he was appointed staff **captain**, Royal Artillery in Meerut and then **adjutant** of the **Royal Horse Artillery** at Kirkee. He was promoted to **major** (1898). Horne took part in the **Boer War** and was present at the relief of **Kimberley** and the occupation of **Bloemfontein**. On his return home he was placed in charge of the artillery depot at Weedon. He was promoted to **lieutenant-colonel** (1905). By 1912 he was inspector of horse and field artillery with the rank of **brigadier-general**. In 1914 he went to France as Commander Royal Artillery in the I Army Corps. **Haig** put Horne in command of the rearguard during the retreat from **Mons** and he played a prominent part in the battles of the **Marne** and Aisne and the first battle of **Ypres**. He was promoted to **major-general** and made a CB (1914). He was given command of the 2nd **Division** of the I **Corps** and led it at Givenchy, Festubert and **Loos**. In November 1915 Horne was moved to take part in the evacuation from the **Dardanelles** and was given command of the XV Corps defending Suez. The corps moved to France (March 1916) and captured Fricourt and Flers during the battle of the **Somme**. Horne was given command of the 1st Army as temporary

general. He was in command at the taking of **Vimy Ridge** during the battle of **Arras** (April 1917) and its defence (May 1918). Horne was promoted to substantive general (1919). In 1918 he was made **colonel**-commandant of the Royal Artillery and in 1919 created Baron Horne of Stirkoke. In 1919 he was made **aide-de-camp** general to King George V and retired in 1926.

See also **Amiens, battle of**

Horse, 2nd *See* **Princess Charlotte of Wales's Dragoon Guards**

Horse, 6th *See* **Princess Charlotte of Wales's Dragoon Guards**

Horse, 7th *See* **Princess Charlotte of Wales's Dragoon Guards**

Horse Guards *See* **Household Cavalry**

Horse Regiments

When **regiments** in the modern sense were first formed in the 17th century the **cavalry** regiments were simply known as regiments of horse. The nomenclature was changed in the 18th century when these regiments became known as **dragoon guards**.

Hospital Corps

The corps was founded after the **Crimean War** had revealed serious deficiencies in the care of the wounded. It consisted of NCOs and orderlies previously employed in regimental or other hospitals. The Corps eventually came under the command of the Medical Staff Corps and ultimately became the **Royal Army Medical Corps**.

Household Cavalry

The **cavalry regiments** that act as a personal bodyguard to the monarch. Long used as a descriptive term, the regiments belonging to the Household Cavalry have changed over time. In the 18th and 19th centuries they came to be the **Life Guards** and the Royal Horse Guards (later the **Blues and Royals**). In 1991 these regiments amalgamated and now form two units: the **Household Cavalry Regiment**, which undertakes normal military operations, and the **Household Cavalry Mounted Regiment** for ceremonial duties. However, within this combined body the Life Guards and Blues and Royals maintain their separate identities and traditions.

Howe, George Augustus (1724–58)

Howe was the son of Emmanuel Scrope, 2nd Viscount Howe, who was governor of Barbados (1732–35). Howe succeeded to the title in 1735 when his father died. He entered the 1st Foot Guards (**Grenadier Guards**) as an **ensign** (1745) and was promoted to **lieutenant** (1746). He served as **aide-de-camp** to the Duke of **Cumberland** in the Netherlands (1746–47). He was elected MP for Nottingham, in his absence (1747), and held the seat for the rest of his life. In 1757 he went to America as **colonel** of the 60th Foot – the Royal Americans (later the **King's Royal Rifle Corps**). In September 1757 he commanded the 55th Foot (**Westmorland Regiment**) and was given the local rank of **brigadier**. He was second-in-command to **Abercromby** at **Ticonderoga**. During 1758 he reorganised the army in America on the ranger principle, where each man carried the minimum of equipment and was expected to use his initiative in combat rather than simply follow drill commands, making the army a more effective fighting force under the prevailing conditions of forests, where the traditional equipment and methods of fighting were inappropriate. Consequently he was much-loved by his men who showed great confidence in him as a leader. He was killed during a skirmish at Trout Brook. With his death the morale declined in the Army, which was left to the ineffectual leadership of Abercromby. The colony of Massachusetts subscribed to place a memorial to Howe in Westminster Abbey.

Howe, William, 5th Viscount Howe (1729–1814)

Howe was educated at Eton and by December 1759 was a **lieutenant-colonel** of the 58th Foot (**Rutlandshire Regiment**). He took his **regiment** from Ireland to North America where he commanded a light infantry battalion under **Wolfe** at the siege of **Quebec** (1759). He had a brilliant career during the occupation of Canada, commanded a **brigade** at the siege of Belle Isle, Brittany, (1761) and was **adjutant-general** at the conquest of **Havana** (1762). Howe was made governor of the Isle of Wight (1768) and was MP for Nottingham (1758–80). At the beginning of the **American War of Independence** Howe was sent with reinforcements to General **Gage**. He was in command at **Bunker Hill** and was made **colonel** of the 23rd **Royal Welch Fusiliers** and a **KB**. He succeeded Gage as commander in America (1775) and led the British and Loyalist forces throughout the early part of the war. Howe returned to Britain (1778) and was made a full **general** (1793). He was put in command of the Northern District based at Newcastle (1795) and later of the Eastern District based at Colchester. He resigned through ill-health (1803).

howitzer

A type of **artillery gun**. Howitzers usually have shorter barrels than standard guns, and fire their shells on higher trajectories. Strictly speaking, at minimum range a howitzer would have its barrel elevated more than 45 degrees and would then lower the barrel to increase the range. Howitzers have been used since the 18th century; however, developments in artillery since **World War II** have blurred the distinction between guns and howitzers, with modern weapons being able to fire at both high and low trajectories.

See also **artillery**

[Via Dutch *houwitser* from Czech *haufnice* 'catapult']

Hundred Years' War (1337–1453)

The war, which was not continuous for the whole period, being interspersed by several treaties, was a dispute between France and England over the English claims to Aquitaine and the French throne, and France's alliance with Scotland. England under Edward III began attacking north-east France (1338), and later made alliances with Portugal and Burgundy while France allied with Castile. The English were expelled from France, except from **Calais** (1453), without any formal peace treaty.

See also **Agincourt, battle of; Auray, battle of; Beaugé, battle of; Castillon, battle of; Chizai, battle of; Cravant, battle of; Crécy, battle of; Formigny, battle of; Najera, battle of; Harfleur, battle of; Jargeau, battle of; Orleans, battle of; Patay, battle of; Poitiers, battle of; Pont Valain, battle of; Rouen, battle of; Verneuil, battle of**

Huntingdonshire Regiment

The **regiment** was raised (1702) by Colonel George Villiers as Colonel George Villiers' Regiment of Marines. The name was changed (1713) to the 31st Regiment of Foot, in 1782 to 31st (or Huntingdonshire) Regiment of Foot, in 1855 to 31st (Huntingdonshire) Regiment. In the 1881 reorganisation it merged with the 70th to become the **East Surrey Regiment**.

Huntingdon's Regiment of Marines, Earl of *See* Duke of Wellington's Regiment

Husky, Operation *See* Sicily, battle of

hussar

A member of a type of light **cavalry regiment**. This name for light cavalry originated in Hungary during the 15th century, the original hussars specialising in a skirmishing style of fighting. Hussar regiments first appeared in the British Army in 1806 when several **light dragoon** regiments were renamed. These regiments adopted uniforms in a supposed Hungarian style which were more elaborate and fashionable than those previously worn by light dragoons, but fought and were equipped in exactly the same way as the other light cavalry units. Other regiments were retitled as Hussars later in the 19th century and two modern cavalry regiments retain this designation.

[Via Hungarian *huszár* 'light horseman' from Italian *corsaro* 'corsair']

Hussars, 3rd *See* **King's Own Hussars**

Hussars, 4th *See* **Light Brigade; Queen's Own Hussars**

Hussars, 7th *See* **Queen's Own Hussars**

Hussars, 8th *See* **King's Royal Irish Hussars; Light Brigade**

Hussars, 10th *See* **Royal Hussars (Prince of Wales's Own)**

Hussars, 11th
The name of the 11th **Light Dragoons** after 1840.
See also **Cardigan, 7th Earl of**; **Light Brigade**

Hussars, 13th
The **regiment** was raised (1715) by Brigadier-General Richard Munden as Munden's Dragoons. The name changed with its **colonels** until 1751 when the regiment was designated the 13th Regiment of Dragoons. In 1783 the name was changed to the 13th Regiment of (Light) Dragoons and in 1862 to the 13th Hussars. They amalgamated with the 18th Hussars (Queen Mary's Own) in 1922 and later became part of the **Light Dragoons**, formed in 1992.

Hussars, 14th *See* **Dormer, James; King's Hussars (14th)**

Hussars, 15th *See* **King's Hussars (15th)**

Hussars, 15th/19th *See* **King's Royal Hussars**

Hussars, 18th *See* **Royal Hussars (Queen Mary's Own)**

Hussars, 19th
A regiment bearing this number was first raised (1759) in Ireland as the 19th Light Horse or Drogheda's Light Horse. It was re-numbered the 18th Light Dragoons (1763) and is therefore more properly considered the predecessor of the **Royal Hussars (Queen Mary's Own)**. The 19th's second existence began in 1779 when it was raised as the 19th Light Dragoons but this unit was disbanded in 1783. In 1786 the 23rd Light Dragoons were re-numbered the 19th Light Dragoons. The name was changed to the 19th Lancers (1817) and the regiment disbanded (1821). The 1st Bengal European Light Cavalry was raised by the East India Company (1858) and taken into the British Army (1861) as the 19th Hussars. The name was changed to 19th (Princess of Wales's Own) Hussars (1881); 19th (Alexandra Princess of Wales's Own) Hussars (1902); 19th (Queen Alexandra's Own Royal) Hussars (1908); and the 19th Royal Hussars (Queen Alexandra's Own) (1921). It merged with the 15th Hussars (1922) to form the **15th/19th Hussars** (*see* **King's Royal Hussars**).

Hussars, 20th
The **regiment** had a chequered history, being formed as the 20th Light Inniskilling Dragoons when the 6th **Inniskilling Dragoons** was expanded to regimental size. This 20th regiment was disbanded (1763) but re-formed (1779) as the 20th Light Dragoons. It was disbanded (1783). Later (1791) it was raised as the 20th Jamaican Light Dragoons, becoming simply the 20th Light Dragoons (1802), only to be disbanded in 1819. In 1857 a regiment was formed as the 2nd Bengal European Light Cavalry in the army of the East India Company, which was then taken into the British Army as the 20th Light Dragoons, and within a year was re-named the 20th Hussars. It amalgamated with the **King's Hussars (14th)** (1922) to form the 14th/20th Hussars.

Hussars, 21st
The **regiment** was converted to **lancers** in 1897

Hyderabad, battle of
(1843; *British War in the Sind*) After his victory at **Meanee**, Sir Charles James **Napier** pushed down the Indus river and attacked Hyderabad (24 March) with 6,000 troops. The city, which was defended by Shir Mohammed with 20,000 troops, fell after a heavy artillery bombardment. Sind then came under British control.

I

IDSM *abbreviation of* **Indian Distinguished Service Medal**

image intensifier

Any device that magnifies small amounts of visible or near-infrared light into a useful visual image. Image intensifiers can thus be used to provide **night vision**. Originally developed in **World War II**, they convert the captured light into electrons, which are multiplied and then converted back into an enhanced visual image – usually in shades of green because the human eye is most sensitive to that colour. Image intensifiers do not illuminate the scene they are viewing and therefore cannot work in the complete absence of light; and sensitivity to near-infrared light is important because starlight is stronger in this than in visible light. Modern devices, which are small enough to be built into goggles and can be powered by a battery, have become standard military equipment.

See also **thermal imager**

Imphal, battle of

(1944; *Burma campaigns*) The Japanese isolated 60,000 British and Indian troops of the 14th Army at Imphal in north-east India (March). The town held out for 3 months, being supplied by air, before it was relieved, and thus prevented the Japanese penetration into India.

See also **Slim, William Joseph**

India

Systematic English involvement in India began with the formation of the East India Company (1600) to trade in the Far East. Trading stations were established, and in the 18th century the Company gradually became powerful and involved in politics, acting as an agent of British imperialism in India. The Company even had its own army, and the early wars in India were conducted by this force in alliance with friendly Indian rulers. In 1757 the Company gained control of Bengal, leading ultimately to Pitt's India Act (1784) which established the control of political policy in India by the British government. By 1834 the Company was merely a managing agent for the British government. It was deprived of this position after the **Indian Mutiny** (1857). Up to the time of the Mutiny the wars fought in India were largely to strengthen the British trading position and to curb the influence of other countries, especially France. Gradually during this period the British began to care about the welfare of the Indian people and they, through the individual Indian rulers, became *de facto* rulers of India. This is well illustrated by the take-over of Mysore (1831), which was considered by the British to be poorly governed, after which the British administered the territory on behalf of the rajah for the next 50 years. The Indian Mutiny led to the abolition of the East India Company, and the government of India was taken over by the British government. The Indian administration was revised and the Indian Army was created, coming under the control of the government rather than being controlled and in the pay of the East India Company.

Indian Distinguished Service Medal

An award instituted (1907) to reward distinguished service by all ranks of the Indian Army. It was discontinued on Indian independence in 1947.

Abbreviation **IDSM**

Indian Mutiny (1857–58)

The tightening control of India by the East India Company and the unfounded threat of forcible conversion to Christianity led to the revolt of the sepoy troops at Meerut (10 May 1857). The jail was stormed, and troops that were imprisoned there for refusing to bite the paper **cartridges** allegedly greased with pork or beef fat, forbidden to the Moslems and Hindus respectively, were released. The revolt spread down the Ganges Valley in north India where 80% of the troops were natives. The revolt was suppressed and the rule of India transferred to the Crown from the East India Company (1 September 1858), after which many reforms were instituted.

See also **Agra, battle of; Aong, battle of; Azimghur, battle of; Banda, battle of; Betwa, battle of; Delhi, battle of; Gaulauli, battle of; Gwalior, battle of; Jhansi, battle of; Kalpi, battle of; Cawnpore, battle of; Kotah, battle of; Lucknow, siege of; Maharajpur, battle of; Musa Bagh, battle of; Nujufghur, battle of; Onao, battle of; Pandu Naddi, battle of; Campbell, Colin; Havelock, Henry; Nicholson, John; Outram, James; Rose, Hugh Henry**

Indian Order of Merit

The order was created as the Order of Merit (1837) by the East India Company. It became an official British award when India was taken over by the Crown (1858) and was awarded for outstanding gallantry. In 1902 it was re-named the Indian Order of Merit (on the introduction of the British Order of Merit) and a civil division created. The military division originally had three classes, but the highest was abolished when Indian troops became eligible to receive the **Victoria Cross** (1911); the division was later reduced to one class (1944). The Order became obsolete on Indian independence (1947).

Abbreviation **IOM**

infantry

Soldiers who usually fight on foot and traditionally manoeuvred on the battlefield itself and from battle to battle on foot. With the advent of firearms the infantry became more important and were organised so that pikemen could protect the musketeers while the latter were re-loading. By the early 18th century pikemen had become obsolete because **muskets** could be loaded and fired faster and were fitted with **bayonets**, meaning that musketeers could defend themselves successfully against **cavalry**. At this period infantry almost always fought in close formation, moving and firing strictly according to drill commands. In the **Seven Years' War** the British Army began to field a new type of **light infantry**, men capable of operating as individuals or in loose formation and used for skirmishing, scouting and similar tasks. The two types of light and 'line' infantry remained in existence in broadly this style until the late Victorian period, when improved artillery weapons and faster-firing and more accurate small arms lead to the abandonment of **red coats** and the adoption of a light infantry style of fighting by all infantry units. In very general terms this prevails to the present day. However, the means of delivering the soldiers to the scene of battle was revolutionised in the 20th century by the adoption of various forms of mechanical transport. Infantry began to be transported in motor vehicles in the 1920s, and mechanised and armoured infantry formed distinct units in **World War II**. The development of aircraft allowed the creation of paratroops, which were again first widely used in World War II (see **Parachute Regiment**). Later, the USA pioneered the use of helicopters as fast and flexible infantry transports in the Vietnam War (1961–75).

The infantry have always formed the largest element in all armies since ancient times. They have generally been drawn from the poorer sections of society and therefore looked down on and discounted by other sections of the army, such as the mounted feudal lords of the Middle Ages or their successors, the cavalry. Sometimes their importance has been underestimated: a criticism made of the US army that led the invasion of Iraq in 2003 was that it did not contain enough infantry, emphasising high technology over manpower. However, infantry remain irreplaceable because of their unique ability to seize, occupy and hold ground, and their flexibility to do this in the widest variety of conditions.

[From French *infanterie*, from Italian *infante* 'youth, foot soldier' from Latin *infant-* 'infant']

infantryman
A **private** soldier in an **infantry regiment**

Ingogo, battle of
(1881; *Boer Wars*) A column of five companies of British **infantry** with four guns attacked the Boer position (8 February). The British were repulsed with the loss of 139 killed and wounded. The Boers lost 14 men.

Inkerman, battle of
(1854; *Crimean War*) The British and French had laid siege to **Sebastopol** (now Sevastopol). To break the siege the Russians, commanded by Prince Aleksandr **Menshikov**, moved out of the city (5 November) against the Allied line at the mouth of the Chernaya river. The British Guards Brigade and French forces, commanded by General Aimable Pélissier, met the Russians at Inkerman. After fierce hand-to-hand fighting the Allies repulsed the larger Russian force, compelling them to retire to Sebastopol. The Russians lost some 12,000 men and the Allies some 3,500.

Inniskilling Dragoons
Colonel Sir Albert Conyngham regularised the various **troops** of horse raised to defend Inniskilling against the ex-king James II. The **regiment** was known as Conyngham's Dragoons (6th Dragoons). The title of the regiment changed with the name of the **colonel** until 1751 when it became the 6th (Inniskilling) Dragoons. Its name was not changed until 1921, and it was amalgamated as part of the **Royal Inniskilling Dragoon Guards** in 1922. The regiment fought at the battle of **Warburg** and was part of the **Heavy Brigade** at the battle of **Balaclava**.
See also **Hussars, 20th**

Inniskilling Regiment of Foot
The **regiment** was raised (1689) as Colonel Zachariah Tiffin's Enniskillen Regiment of Foot. The name was changed with its **colonels** until 1751 when it became the 27th (or Inniskilling) Regiment of Foot. The regiment fought at Waterloo. In the 1881 reorganisation the regiment merged with the 108th to become the **Royal Irish Fusiliers**.

insignia
Badges showing identity, e.g. of a **regiment**, and the position held by an individual.
See also **rank badges**; **stripe**
[From Latin, from *insignis* 'marked', from *signum* 'sign']

Intelligence Corps
The section of the army responsible for gathering and processing military intelligence. It also handles counter-intelligence and security. The Corps was founded in 1914 but disbanded in 1929. Re-formed on an *ad hoc* basis at the beginning of **World War II** (1939), it was formally constituted in 1940. Its members provided such services as the interpretation of aerial reconnaissance photographs, the interrogation of **prisoners of war**, the interception and decoding of radio signals, and general intelligence gathering and analysis; some were sent to occupied Europe as Special Operations Executive agents. These activities have subsequently adapted to take in technological advances, such as satellite reconnaissance and computerised communications.

Inverlochy, battle of
(1645; *Civil War*) Having occupied Perth and Aberdeen (1644), the Marquis of **Montrose** turned west and led his 1,500 Royalist Highlanders against a force of 3,000 Campbells and Lowland Covenanters at Inverlochy. Montrose was victorious, destroying the power of the Campbells for many years.

invest

To surround or besiege a place or forces

[Directly or via French from Latin *investire* 'to clothe (in), surround', from *vestis* 'clothing']

IOM *abbreviation of* **Indian Order of Merit**

IRA *See* **Northern Ireland**

Iranian Embassy Siege *See* **Special Air Service Regiment**

Iraq War (2003)

As a result of the **Gulf War** (1990–91) Saddam Hussein was given an ultimatum to destroy all his **weapons of mass destruction**, which were thought to comprise chemical and biological weapons. A no-fly zone was established, and economic sanctions were imposed on the country. These sanctions brought great hardship to the people of the country. No evidence of the destruction of the weapons was forthcoming and Saddam Hussein denied having any such weapons. UN inspectors were sent into Iraq to look for weapons (2002) but none were found. The US government was convinced that the weapons existed and proposed that the UN send another force to find them and to remove the government of Saddam Hussein. A majority of the members of the Security Council of the UN opposed such action, and the US and UK invaded Iraq unilaterally (21 March 2003). After an intense air bombardment, particularly of Baghdad, the Americans advanced to capture Baghdad, while British forces attacked Basra in the south of the country. Neither force met much opposition, and the campaign ended with the capture of Tikrit on 14 April. Saddam Hussein was captured in December 2003 and put on trial in 2005. However, the **peacekeeping** operations following the war and the establishment of a democratic government proved much more difficult than anticipated. Iraqi politics quickly fractured along communal lines, into Kurd, Sunni and Shia factions. A terrorist insurgency broke out in Sunni areas, possibly with al-Qaeda backing; and armed Sunni and Shia militia fought with each other and with the peacekeeping forces. By 2006 over 2,400 US and over 100 UK soldiers had been killed in the war and its aftermath. These continuous casualties, allied with long-standing doubts about the war's legality and the coalition's post-war failure to find any weapons of mass destruction, undermined support in the coalition countries for continued involvement in Iraq and the popularity of the politicians who had ordered it.

Irish Guards

A **regiment** of **Foot Guards** raised (1900) at the instigation of Queen Victoria, who wished to show her appreciation of the part played by Irish troops during the **Boer War**. The regiment remains in existence in the 21st century.

Irish Republican Army *See* **Northern Ireland**

Irish resistance to William and Mary

The deposed King James II raised troops in Ireland in an attempt to re-establish his claim to the throne of the UK. The Irish, who were predominantly Roman Catholic, were prepared to support him against the Protestant William and Mary. The resistance was crushed finally at the **battle of the Boyne**.

iron ration

A small quantity of dried food carried by an individual for use in an emergency. Iron rations contain high-energy foods such as chocolate, dried fruits and biscuits.

Ironsides

The nickname given to members of **Cromwell's New Model Army**

Isandlwana, battle of

(1879; *Zulu War*) Although the British had acknowledged the sovereignty of Cetshwayo as king of the Zulus in south-east Africa (1872), by 1879 the Zulus had begun to build up their army. 1,500 British and colonial troops and a native force were sent to disarm them and were attacked by 20,000 Zulus at Isandlwana (22 January).

During the ensuing battle all but 55 of the British troops were killed. Cetshwayo then moved on to invade Natal.

See also **Rorke's Drift, battle of**

Italy, South

(1943; *World War II*) Having occupied **Sicily**, two **divisions** of the British 8th Army, commanded by General Sir Bernard **Montgomery** landed at Reggio Calabria (3 September). Meeting little opposition, the XIII **Corps** moved north, the British 5th Division moving up the west coast and the Canadian 1st Division up the east, occupying Calabria. Marshal Pietro Badoglio, who now headed the Italian government, surrendered to the Allies (8 September) but the Germans immediately took control of the country. The Allied 5th Army landed at **Salerno** (9 September) and the 5th Army and the XIII Corps joined together at Vallo (16 September). Meanwhile the British V Corps had landed at Taranto (9 September) and the 1st Airborne Division attacked the air-bases at Foggia. The British 78th Division landed at Bari (22 September) and Foggia fell (27 September). A **commando** strike (3 October) at Termoli ensured Allied control of the airfields at Foggia. The British 8th Army then joined the US 5th Army and moved towards the **Gustav Line**.

See also **Sangro, battle of**

IW *See* **SA80**

J

jack

A short, sleeveless coat, probably the precursor of the regular uniform, worn as a means of identification. Edward III ordered his archers to wear white jacks with the red cross of St. George.

[Via French *jaque* from Spanish or Portuguese *jaco*]

jack boots

Long boots worn by the cavalry. These had been treated with wax and tar to give them a hard surface – a process called 'jacking'.

Jacobite Rebellions (1689–91, 1715–16, 1745–46)

When James II, after his accession in 1685, made it apparent that he intended to restore Roman Catholicism and rule as an absolute monarch, William of Orange and his wife Mary, James's daughter by his first wife, were invited (1688) by eminent citizens to take the throne. This they did without bloodshed. James fled to France. James still had support (called Jacobites after the Latin Jacobus = James) and landed in Ireland. Meanwhile Viscount **Dundee** rallied the Highland supporters of James in Scotland and defeated the Royalists at **Killiecrankie**. Dundee was killed and the Scottish revolt petered out. William defeated James at the battle of the **Boyne** in Ireland. James fled to France and died (1701). During 1715 there were attempts to place James II's son, James Edward, the Old Pretender, on the throne instead of George I. This led to risings in Scotland and northern England but these were soon suppressed. In 1745 the Scots rallied to the Old Pretender's son Charles, the Young Pretender or Bonnie Prince Charlie, but were finally defeated at **Culloden** (1746).

See also **Carlisle, battle of; Falkirk, battle of; Limerick, battle of; Londonderry, battle of; Preston, battle of; Prestonpans, battle of; Sheriffmuir, battle of; Cope, John; Cumberland, Duke of (William Augustus); Sarsfield, Patrick**

Jamaica, battle of (1655)

The island of Jamaica had been a Spanish possession since its discovery by Columbus in 1494. A combined British naval and army expedition led by General Robert **Venables** and Admiral William Penn captured the island (11 May) which led to the declaration of war between Britain and Spain.

Jamaican Light Dragoons *See* **Hussars, 20th**

Jamaican Volunteers *See* **Princess Charlotte of Wales's (or Hertfordshire) Regiment**

Jameson Raid (1895)

Although not involving British troops, the Jameson Raid was a catalyst in polarising British and Boer attitudes in South Africa. Leander Star Jameson was a lieutenant to Cecil Rhodes, the Prime Minister of the Cape. Jameson led a small force from Bechuanaland (now Botswana) to support an uprising of the Uitlander (Outlander) immigrants in Johannesburg against the Boer government. The uprising was called off, but Jameson continued with the raid (December). It was a failure. Jameson's force was rounded up and Rhodes was forced to resign when his involvement was discovered, but Joseph Chamberlain, the British Colonial Secretary, succeeded in covering up the British involvement in the plan.

Jargeau, battle of
(1429; *Hundred Years' War*) After relieving **Orleans** (8 May) Joan of Arc moved to re-possess the north bank of the Loire. She attacked and took the fortress of Jargeau, 10 miles east of Orleans (12 June). The English Duke of Suffolk, William de la Pole, was captured. Meung and Beaugency soon fell (19 June), and the English commander John Talbot, Earl of Shrewsbury, fell back towards the Seine.

Jellalabad, battle of
(1842; *Afghan War I*) The fort of Jellalabad was held by the British (13th Foot **Somerset Light Infantry**) commanded by Brigadier-General Sir Robert **Sale** and was under siege by the Afghans following the retreat from **Kabul** and the defeat at **Gandamak**. An attempt to relieve Jellalabad (January 1843) by Brigadier-General Wild failed when he was defeated in the Khyber Pass. The British broke out of the fort and routed the assailants (April 1843). A strong relieving force under General George **Pollock** arrived (18 April 1843) and completed the rout of the Afghans.

Jhansi, battle of
(1858; *Indian Mutiny*) The rebels had seized Jhansi and it was placed under siege by General Sir Hugh **Rose**. A rebel relief force led by Tantia Topi was repulsed (13 April) largely by a **cavalry** charge and Jhansi capitulated (14 April). Tantia Topi fled but was captured a year later and hanged.

Joffre, Joseph-Jacques-Césaire (1852–1931)
Joffre was a subaltern serving at the siege of Paris (1870–71). He then served in Indochina, West Africa and Madagascar before being promoted to general of division (1905). He was appointed chief of the French general staff (1911). He led the French armies in their initial defeats in **World War I** but redeemed himself with the formation of the new 6th French Army and the stopping of the German advance on Paris at the first battle of the **Marne**. During the resulting stalemate and the failure of the French forces to gain a significant victory, in spite of heavy losses, Joffre lost popularity and was stripped of office and resigned (1916). On the day he resigned, he was created a marshal of France (December 26).

Johannesburg, battle of
(1900; *Boer Wars*) The Orange Free State having been annexed, General Lord Frederick **Roberts** sent a British army into the Transvaal. The Boers, commanded by General Louis **Botha**, fell back to the north. **Mafeking** (now Mafikeng) was relieved (17 May); Johannesburg was taken (31 May) and Pretoria fell (5 June). General Sir Redvers **Buller** then invaded the Transvaal from Natal (10 June) and the two armies met at Vlakfontein (4 July). The Transvaal was annexed (3 September).

Johnson, William (1715–74)
Johnson was born in Ireland and joined his uncle on his estates in the Mohawk Valley in America (1738). His fair and honest treatment of the Indians led to their being persuaded to fight for the British and was recognised when he was appointed superintendent of Indian affairs in North America (1755). In the same year he was created a baronet in recognition of the defeat of the French at Crown Point by the provincial force he commanded.
See also **Niagara, battle of**

Joint Service Command and Staff College *See* **Staff College**

Joubert, Petrus (Piet) Jacobus (1831–1900)
Joubert was the son of a farmer-missionary, born in Cape Colony. He was largely self-educated but became a property agent. By 1860 he was a member of the Volksraad (Transvaal parliament). When the British annexed the Transvaal, Joubert and **Kruger** negotiated with the British, but when negotiations failed, advocated rebellion (1880). Joubert became commandant-general, and commanded the Boer forces in their victories at **Laing's Nek**, **Ingogo** and **Majuba Hill**. He took part in the Pretoria Convention (1881) which restored independence to the Transvaal. His progressive

views led to his conflict with Kruger, who defeated him three times in the election for president (1888, 1893 and 1898). Before the Second **Boer War** Joubert advocated reconciliation, but at the beginning of the war commanded the Boer forces. He became ill and died before the end of the war.

See also **Colenso, battle of**

K

Kabul, battle of
(1842; *Afghan War I*) The British took Kabul (1839) and deposed Dost Mohammed Khan to prevent a feared Russian intrusion into Afghanistan. This was resented by the Afghans, and the British, commanded by Major-General William **Elphinstone**, withdrew (6 January). The retreating force was attacked by the Afghans, led by Akbar Khan, the son of Dost Mohammed, and some 4,500 Anglo-Indian troops and 12,000 civilians were massacred. Elphinstone was captured and died in captivity soon afterwards. A punitive expedition led by Sir George **Pollock** defeated Akbar Khan (14 September) and occupied Kabul. He withdrew for political reasons, and Dost Mohammed resumed his rule.
See also **Gandamak, battle of**

Kaffir Wars (1779–1879)
Aggression by the Cape Colonists in South Africa against the Xhosa people indigenous to the Eastern Cape region continued for a century. The Xhosa territories were annexed finally into the Eastern Cape (1879).

Kalpi, battle of
(1858; *Indian Mutiny*) The town was besieged by the British, commanded by Sir Hugh **Rose** (19 May). After two ineffectual sorties by the rebels, the town was occupied (23 May).

Kamarut, battle of
(1824; *Burma campaigns*) A small British force, commanded by Sir Archibald **Campbell**, stormed the stockades held by 10,000 Burmese. The stockades were taken leaving 800 Burmese dead, including their leader Tuamba Wangyee.
See also **Burma campaigns 1**

Kambula, battle of
(1879; *Zulu War*) The Zulus attacked the British camp at Kambula, near the Transvaal border (28–29 March). The British force of 2,086 men, better prepared than in the earlier defeat at **Isandlwana**, repulsed a 22,000-strong Zulu force, with a loss of 29 killed. The Zulus lost some 2,000. The defeat practically broke the power of the Zulu leader, Cetshwayo.

Kandahar, battle of
(1880; *Afghan War II*) The hostility of the Afghan leader Shere Ali towards the British precipitated the Second Afghan War which opened with the British, commanded by General Sir Frederick **Roberts**, occupying Kabul (7 October 1879). Earlier in the year Shere Ali had died and his nephew Abd-er-Rahman Khan became ruler. South of Kabul the son of Shere Ali, Ayub Khan, revolted and overran the British garrison at **Maiwand**, west of Kandahar (June 1880). Roberts promptly marched south and arrived at Kandahar (1 September) where he defeated Ayub. The British withdrew from Afghanistan; Abd-er-Rahman Khan increased his power and exiled Ayub.

Karee, battle of
(1900; *Boer Wars*) The Boers held a line of hills 18 miles north of Bloemfontein. They were driven from there (29 March) by a British force commanded by General Charles **Tucker**. The British casualties were 182.

KB *See* **Order of the Bath**

KBE *See* **Order of the British Empire**

KCB *See* **Order of the Bath**

KCIE *See* **Order of the Indian Empire**

KCMG *See* **Order of St Michael and St George**

KCSI *See* **Order of the Star of India**

KCVO *See* **Royal Victorian Order**

Keane, John (1781–1844)

Keane was born in Ireland and by 1799 was a **captain** in the 44th Foot (**East Essex Regiment**) with which he served in Gibraltar and Egypt. He returned home from Gibraltar (1804) as **lieutenant-colonel** in the 13th Foot (**Somerset Light Infantry**) and served in Ireland. He went to Bermuda and commanded his **regiment** at the reduction of Martinique (1809). He was promoted to **brevet colonel** of the 60th Foot (**King's Royal Rifle Corps**) (1812) and joined **Wellington** at **Vitoria**. He was with Wellington until 1814. Keane was promoted to **major-general** (1814) and created **KCB** (1815). He was sent to America and commanded part of the assault on **New Orleans** (1815). He returned home and commanded a **brigade** in the army of occupation in France (1815–17). Keane commanded the troops in Jamaica (1823–30) and was promoted to **lieutenant-general** (1830) and colonel of the 68th Foot (**Durham Light Infantry**) (1831). He was appointed **commander-in-chief** of Bombay (now Mumbai) (1831–39). He was created **GCB** (1839) and in the same year was raised to the peerage as Baron Keane of Ghazni and of Cappoquin, Co. Waterford.

See also **Ghazni, battle of**

Kemendine, battle of

(1824; *Burma campaigns*) 3,000 British troops commanded by Sir Archibald **Campbell**, drove a large force of Burmese from their stockades (10 June)

Kenilworth, battle of

(1265–66; *Barons' Wars*) Simon de Montfort (Earl of Leicester) had established his position by defeating Henry III at **Lewes**. While the barons disputed amongst themselves, Henry's son, Prince Edward (later Edward I) was building up Royalist forces in the Severn Valley, thus dividing de Montfort's forces from those of his son, also Simon, at Kenilworth. The Royalists attacked Kenilworth (31 July 1265) where the young Simon held out. His father was killed at **Evesham**, releasing more Royalist forces for the siege. Kenilworth surrendered (14 December 1266) but not before the young Simon had escaped to **Axholme**.

Kesselring, Albert (1885–1960)

Kesselring was born in Bavaria and joined the German army as a cadet (1904). He served in the army during **World War I** but transferred to the Luftwaffe (German Air Force) in 1935. He was promoted to **lieutenant-general** (1936) and commanded air fleets during the German conquest of Poland and France in 1939–40 and in the Battle of Britain. In 1941 he was appointed Commander-in-Chief, South, in overall charge of all German land and air forces in Italy and North Africa during which appointment he was **Rommel's** superior, and later fought the rear-guard action through Italy. He surrendered the German forces in Italy (May 1945). He was found guilty of war crimes and sentenced to death, but the sentence was commuted to life imprisonment and he was freed in 1952.

Kevlar

Trademark A synthetic fibre developed in the 1960s that is light, flexible, and five times as strong as steel. It is widely used in modern **helmets** and body **armour**.

KG *See* **Order of the Garter**

khaki

Khaki uniforms originated during the **Indian Mutiny** when some British units dyed their white uniforms with coffee, mulberry juice or curry powder to make them less conspicuous. The blotchy effect was not acceptable to the troops who refused to leave their barracks during their free time wearing these uniforms. Khaki was not worn again immediately after the Indian Mutiny but came into use during the Afghan War (1878) and soon entirely replaced the former **red coats** for combat and general use.

[From Urdu *kaki* 'dust-coloured', from Persian *kak* 'dust']

Khartoum, battle of

(1884–85; *Sudan War*) The British government sent General Charles **Gordon** to organise the Anglo-Egyptian evacuation of the Sudan. He arrived in the Sudan (18 February 1884) and decided not to abandon the country to the **Mahdi**. He sent to London asking for reinforcements that the government was reluctant to provide. Meanwhile Gordon evacuated some 2,500 women, children and wounded from Khartoum. By 12 March 1884 he found himself trapped in the north fort of the city. He held out there until 26 January 1885 when the Mahdi's forces stormed the fort killing every defender, including Gordon. A relief column, commanded by General Sir Garnet **Wolseley** had left Cairo (October 1844) and arrived at Khartoum two days after it had fallen.

Khelat, battle of

(1839; *Afghan War I*) Khelat was defended by the Baluchis under Mehrab Khan. It was captured by a British force of 1,000 commanded by General Thomas **Willshire**.

Khojah, battle of

(1842; *Afghan War I*) General Richard **England** with only 500 men attempted to relieve General William **Nott** at Kandahar without waiting for reinforcements (28 March). His force was defeated by the Afghans in the Khojah Pass with the loss of 100 killed or wounded. He returned to Quetta.

Killiecrankie, battle of

(1689; *Jacobite Rebellions*) Viscount **Dundee** raised a rebellion to support the deposed James II in Scotland. General Hugh **Mackay** took 4,000 Royalist troops to Scotland to suppress the rebellion. These were ambushed at Killiecrankie Pass by Dundee (27 July) and more than half the Royalist force was killed or captured. Dundee himself was killed. His death radically affected the cohesion of the clans whose forces soon dispersed and the rebellion collapsed.

See also **bayonet**

Kilsyth, battle of

(1645; *Civil War*) The Royalist leader the Marquis of **Montrose** moved south after his victory at **Alford**. He encountered the combined **Covenanter** forces of General William **Baillie** and the Marquis of Argyll (Archibald Campbell) at Kilsyth. Montrose won a decisive victory making him, although temporarily, supreme in Scotland.

Kimberley

(1899–1900; *Boer Wars*) The town was attacked by the Boers (14 October 1899). The attack was repelled and developed into a siege. The town held out until 15 February 1900, when it was relieved by cavalry led by General Sir John **French**. The garrison sustained casualties of 180 killed and wounded.

King Edward VII's Own Gurkha Rifles (2nd)

The **regiment** was originally the Sirmoor Battalion of the East India Company, formed in 1815. In 1858, after being taken into the newly-formed Indian Army when the East India Company's army was disbanded, it was named the Sirmoor Rifle Regiment. The name was changed, and by 1876 it was the 2nd (Prince of Wales's Own) Gurkha Regiment (The Sirmoor Rifles); in 1906 the 2nd King Edward's Own Gurkha Rifles (The Sirmoor Regiment) and the 2nd King Edward VII's Own Gurkha Rifles (The

Sirmoor Rifles) (1922). It was one of the Gurkha regiments which transferred to the British Army in 1948, keeping the same name until 1994 when it became part of the **Royal Gurkha Rifles**.

King George's War (1744–48)

This was the American component of the War of the **Austrian Succession**, named after King George II. The chief encounter was the capture of **Louisbourg** on Cape Breton Island by the British (1745). This was returned to the French at the Peace of Aix-la-Chapelle (1748).

King's African Rifles

The **regiment** was formed (1899) to replace the Sikh troops sent from India to check raids into Uganda across the border from Abyssinia (now Ethiopia)

King's Dragoon Guards, 1st *See* **Dragoon Guards, 1st**

King's Hussars (15th)

This was the first **regiment** of light **dragoons** and was raised in 1759 by Colonel George **Eliott** as the 15th Light Dragoons (known as Eliott's Light Horse), from London tailors who were on strike. In 1766 it became the 1st (or the King's Royal) Light Dragoons and then (1769) the 15th (or The King's) Light Dragoons. In 1806 the name was changed to the 15th (or The King's) Light Dragoons (Hussars); the 15th (King's) Hussars (1861); the 15th (The King's Hussars) (1901); and the 15th The King's Hussars (1921). In 1922 it became part of the **15th/19th Hussars** (*see* **King's Royal Hussars**).

King's Hussars (14th)

The **regiment** was formed (1922) by the amalgamation of the 14th King's Hussars and the **20th Hussars**. The original 14th was raised (1715) by Brigadier-General James **Dormer** as Dormer's Dragoons. The name changed with the **colonel** until 1751 when it was designated the 14th Regiment of Dragoons. The name changed further to the 14th Regiment of (Light) Dragoons (1776); the 14th (or the Duchess of York's Own) Regiment of Light Dragoons (1798); the 14th (The King's) Regiment of Light Dragoons (1830); 14th (King's) Hussars (1861); and the 14th King's Hussars (1921). It amalgamated with the **20th Hussars** (1922) to form the 14th/20th Hussars, which was renamed (1936) the **14th/20th King's Hussars**. In 1992 this regiment in turn amalgamated with the **Royal Hussars (Prince of Wales's Own)** to form the **King's Royal Hussars**.

King's Light Infantry

The **regiment** was raised (1793) as the 85th Regiment of Foot (or Buck's Volunteers). The name was changed (1805) to the 85th Regiment of Foot (Buck's Volunteers) (Light Infantry) and to the 85th King's Light Infantry (1815). It became part of the **King's Shropshire Light Infantry** in 1881.

King's Mountain, battle of

(1780; *American War of Independence*) After his victory at Camden (South Carolina) (August 1780), the British **general**, Lord Charles **Cornwallis**, moved into North Carolina. To protect his flank Cornwallis sent a force of 1,000 men, commanded by Major Patrick Ferguson, into the hills of west Carolina and eastern Tennessee. They took up a position on King's Mountain where they were surrounded by 900 frontiersmen (7 October). The long-range rifle fire of the frontiersmen killed or wounded 320 of the defenders and the rest surrendered. Ferguson was killed. Cornwallis then abandoned his move into North Carolina.

King's Own Hussars

The **regiment** was raised (1685) from three troops of royal dragoons and called the Queen Consort's Regiment of Dragoons. The name changed with the **colonels** until 1714 when it became the 3rd King's Own Regiment of Dragoons. The name was changed to the 3rd King's Own Hussars (1861) and the 3rd The King's Own Hussars

(1921). In 1958 it amalgamated with the Queen's Own Hussars (7th) to form the **Queen's Own Hussars**.

King's Own Light Dragoons *See* **King's Hussars (15th)**

King's Own Regiment of Dragoons *See* **King's Own Hussars**

King's Own Regiment of Horse *See* **Dragoon Guards, 1st**

King's Own Royal Border Regiment

The **regiment** formed (April 1958) by the amalgamation of the **King's Own Royal Regiment (Lancaster)** and the **Border Regiment**. It remains in existence in the 21st century, having most recently seen service in Basrah, Iraq. It is expected to unite with The King's Regiment and The Queen's Lancashire Regiment (2006) to form The Duke of Lancaster's Regiment (King's, Lancashire and Border).

King's Own Royal Regiment (Lancaster)

4th Foot. The **regiment** was raised (1680) as a Tangier garrison regiment by the Earl of Plymouth as the Earl of Plymouth's Regiment of Foot for Tangier. By 1715 it was called the King's Own Regiment of Foot. The association with the king continued, so that in 1881 it was the King's Own (Royal Lancaster Regiment) and the King's Own Regiment (Lancaster) (1921). By an amalgamation in 1958 it became part of the **King's Own Royal Border Regiment**. The regiment was known as 'The Lions' and 'Barrell's Blues'. It was one of the infantry regiments that fought at **Minden**.

King's Own Scottish Borderers

The **regiment** was raised (1689) as the Earl of Leven's Regiment of Foot to defend Edinburgh during the early stages of the **Jacobite Rebellion**. It was also known as the Edinburgh Regiment. The name changed with the **colonel** until 1751 when it was re-designated the 25th (Edinburgh) Regiment of Foot. In 1782 it became the 25th (or the Sussex) Regiment of Foot. In 1802 the Scottish connection was restored and the regiment was named the 25th (or King's Own Borderers) Regiment of Foot and in 1881 the King's Own Borderers. In 1887 it became the King's Own Scottish Borderers. The regiment has the privilege of marching through Edinburgh with fixed bayonets and **colours** flying. It was one of the infantry regiments which fought at **Minden**. In 2006 it united with The Royal Scots, The Royal Highland Fusiliers, The Black Watch, The Highlanders (Seaforth, Gordons and Camerons), and The Argyll and Sutherland Highlanders to form The Royal Regiment of Scotland.

King's Own Yorkshire Light Infantry

The **regiment** was formed (1881) by the amalgamation of the 51st (**Yorkshire West Riding (2nd) Light Infantry Regiment**) and the 105th (**Madras Light Infantry**) Regiment. It became part of The Light Infantry in 1968.

King's Regiment

This has been the name since 1968 of **The King's Regiment (Manchester and Liverpool)**, which was formed (1958) by the amalgamation of the **King's Regiment (Liverpool)** and the **Manchester Regiment**. It is expected to unite with The King's Own Border Regiment and The Queen's Lancashire Regiment (2006) to form The Duke of Lancaster's Regiment (King's, Lancashire and Border).

King's Regiment (Liverpool)

The **regiment** was raised (1685) by Earl Ferrers as the Princess Anne of Denmark's Regiment of Foot. The name was changed to the Queen's Regiment of Foot (1702); King's Regiment of Foot (1716); 8th (or the King's) Regiment of Foot (1751); the King's (Liverpool) Regiment (1881); and the King's Regiment (Liverpool) (1921). It amalgamated with the Manchester Regiment in 1958 to form **The King's Regiment (Manchester and Liverpool)**.

See also **Chippewa river, battle of**; **Delhi, battle of**; **King's Regiment**

King's Regiment of Foot *See* **West Suffolk Regiment of Foot**

King's Royal Hussars

1. The **regiment** was formed (1922) as the **15th/19th Hussars** by the amalgamation of the **15th King's Hussars** and the **19th Royal Hussars (Queen Alexandra's Own)**. It was renamed in 1932. In 1992 it became part of The **Light Dragoons**.

2. The regiment was formed (1992) by the amalgamation of the **Royal Hussars (Prince of Wales's Own)** and the **14th/20th King's Hussars** (*see* **King's Hussars (14th)**). It is part of the **Royal Armoured Corps**.

King's Royal Irish Hussars

The **regiment** was raised (1693) from Irish Protestants by Colonel Conyngham of the **Inniskilling Dragoons**. It was known initially as Conyngham's Regiment of Irish Dragoons. Its name changed with its **colonel** until 1751 when it became the 8th Regiment of Dragoons. The name was changed further to 8th Regiment of Light Dragoons (1775); 8th (or The King's Royal Irish) Regiment of Light Dragoons (1777); 8th (or King's Royal Irish) Regiment of Light Dragoons (Hussars) (1822); 8th (King's Royal Irish) Hussars (1861); and the 8th King's Royal Irish Hussars (1920). It became part of the **Queen's Royal Irish Hussars** in 1958.

King's Royal Light Dragoons *See* **King's Hussars (14th)**

King's Royal Rifle Corps

The **regiment** was raised (1755) by John **Campbell**, Earl of Loudoun, in the American colonies of Maryland, Pennsylvania, and Virginia. It was named the 62nd or Royal American Regiment of Foot, but was soon renumbered as the 60th Regiment. One of the regiment's **battalions** was the first British unit to be armed with **rifles** during the **French Wars** (1792–1815). The name was changed to the 60th or the Duke of York's Rifle Corps (1824); 60th or the King's Royal Rifle Corps Regiment of Foot (1830) and the King's Royal Rifle Corps (1881). The regiment was present at the battle of Peking (now Beijing) (1860). In 1958 it was re-designated the 1st **Green Jackets** and its modern identity is as part of the **Royal Green Jackets**.

See also **Delhi, battle of**

King's (Queen's) shilling

During the 18th and early 19th centuries it was customary for the recruiting officer to give a new recruit one shilling (5 pence) when he signed up for the army. The acceptance of the shilling sealed his obligation to the army and immediately put him under army discipline. This practice was discontinued in 1879.

King's Shropshire Light Infantry

The **regiment** was formed (1881) by the amalgamation of the 53rd (**Shropshire**) Regiment of Foot and the 85th **King's Light Infantry**. It became part of The Light Infantry in 1968.

King's Troop, Royal Artillery *See* **Artillery, Royal Regiment of**

King William's War (1689–97)

This was the American component of the War of the **Grand Alliance** between England and France. It was named after King William III. The only major conflict was the battle of **Port Royal** in Nova Scotia (1690).

Kirbekan, battle of

(1885; *Sudan War*) A British force of 1,000 men, commanded by General William **Earle**, routed a Madhist force holding the Kirbekan heights (10 February). The British lost 60 killed, including Earle.

Kirkee, battle of

(1817; *Maratha Wars*) After the Second Maratha War, Baji-Rao II was the only remaining Maratha ruler, retaining control in Poona. He came into conflict with the British and attacked four British **regiments** at Kirkee, a suburb of Poona (5 November).

Baji-Rao was defeated here and at Sholapur a year later. The British then took control of Poona.

Kitchener, Horatio Herbert (1850–1916)

Kitchener was born near Listowel, Co. Kerry, Ireland, and educated at the **Royal Military Academy**, Woolwich. He was commissioned in the **Royal Engineers** and served in the Middle East (1874–86). In 1892 he was appointed **commander-in-chief** in Egypt. He defeated the **Mahdi** at **Omdurman** and re-built Khartoum as the centre of government. He was created Baron Kitchener and governor-general of the Sudan (1898). Kitchener was then appointed **chief-of-staff** to Field Marshal Lord **Roberts** in South Africa (1899) and succeeded him as commander-in-chief (1900). His ruthless treatment of the Boer civilians has given rise to criticism during recent years but it was a major factor in their defeat. He was created Viscount Kitchener on his return to the UK (1902) and went to India as commander-in-chief (1902–09). He quarrelled with Lord Curzon, the viceroy, over the management of the army. Curzon resigned but Kitchener was disappointed at not being asked to replace him as viceroy. He went to Egypt as proconsul (1911–14). He returned home on leave (1914) and received a further viscountcy and a barony. He was promoted to **field marshal** and joined the cabinet as Secretary of State for War on the outbreak of **World War I**. He was one of the first British leaders to recognise that the war would be likely to last for several years and he accordingly began work to expand Britain's small professional army into a much larger force. His appeal for volunteer recruits was answered by hundreds of thousands of men, and Kitchener himself appeared in perhaps the most famous recruiting posters ever designed. He was less successful in mobilising industry to supply and equip his New Army and came to be disliked by his colleagues in the cabinet. He was killed when the cruiser HMS Hampshire, on which he was travelling on a mission to Russia, was sunk by a German mine.

Kohima, battle of

(1944; *World War II*) During the early part of 1944 the Japanese forces crossed the Chindwia River into Assam and surrounded Kohima. The Allied forces (14th Army) were now superior in aircraft and tanks and the defenders of Kohima were reinforced by Indian forces from Arakan, which was now secure. With these forces General **Slim** was able to defend both Imphal and Kohima and by May 1944 was able to mount an advance eastwards, thus averting the Japanese invasion of Assam.

Kokein, battle of

(1824; *Burma campaigns*) A British force of 1,800, commanded by Sir Archibald **Campbell**, stormed and captured two stockades held by 20,000 Burmese (12 December)

Korean War (1950–53)

Korea had been annexed by Japan after the Russo-Japanese War and had been promised its freedom at the Cairo Conference of British and US leaders (1943). After Japan surrendered to the Allies in 1945, the Allies agreed that the Russians would accept the surrender of the Japanese in Korea north of the line of 38 degrees latitude while the US would accept the surrender south of that line. This led to tension between the Communist north, which became the Democratic People's Republic of Korea, and the south, the Republic of Korea (1947). The North Korean forces invaded the South (25 June 1950). The Security Council of the United Nations demanded an end to hostilities and when this did not happen the Americans, commanded by General MacArthur, landed in support of the South (30 June 1950). By early 1951 14 UN member states besides the US were involved. Britain provided a **brigade** of troops, as well as an aircraft carrier, two cruisers and eight destroyers. The UN lost 118,515 soldiers killed, 264,591 wounded and 92,987 prisoners (many of whom died of maltreatment).

Korygaom, battle of

(1818; *Maratha Wars*) An Anglo-Indian force of less than 1,000, commanded by Captain Francis Staunton, was attacked by 25,000 Marathas (1 January). They held their ground until reinforcements led by General Smith forced the Marathas to withdraw.

Kosovo (1999)

A **NATO peacekeeping** force, spearheaded by British and French troops, entered the Serbian province of Kosovo in 1999 under a United Nations mandate. Various units of the British Army have served there since.

Kotah, battle of

(1858; *Indian Mutiny*) Kotah had been seized by 5,000 rebel troops led by the Rajah of Kotah. It was besieged by the British, commanded by General Henry **Roberts** (22 March). After a bombardment the town fell to a frontal assault (30 March).

KP *See* Order of St Patrick

Kruger, Stephanus Johannes Paulus (1825–1904)

Kruger was the son of a farmer and was born on the outskirts of Cape Colony. He was a member of the commission that drew up the constitution of the newly-formed Transvaal (1855–56). When the British annexed the Transvaal (1877) he was the champion of the people and went to London (1877 and 1888) to persuade the British government to rescind the annexation. When this failed he led a movement of passive resistance to the British administration. He then commanded Boer forces in the First **Boer War** and after the battle of **Majuba Hill**, negotiated a peace (1883). He was elected president of the Transvaal (1883–1902). The discovery of gold in the Transvaal precipitated an influx of newcomers and British interest, represented by Cecil Rhodes, in incorporating the territory into British South Africa. Kruger's resistance to this precipitated the Second Boer War (1899–1902). After the initial Boer victories had been overturned, Kruger was too old to keep up with the ensuing guerrilla struggle and retired to Holland where he stayed until 1902. He died in Switzerland (1904) and was buried in Pretoria in the same year.

KSI *See* Order of the Star of India

KT *See* Order of the Thistle

Kumasi, battle of

1. (1873; *Ashanti War*) The kingdom of Ashanti had warred intermittently with the British colony of the Gold Coast (now Ghana) throughout the 19th century. The second major conflict began in 1873 when General Sir Garnet **Wolseley** led an expedition against the Ashanti capital, Kumasi. The city was taken (4 February 1874) and the Ashanti chief, Koji Karikari, made peace.

2. (1896; *Ashanti War*) General Sir Francis **Scott** took Kumasi (28 January) and the area was made a British protectorate

Kut-al-Imara, battle of

(1915; *World War I*) The British forces, commanded by General Sir John **Nixon**, had occupied Basra in Mesopotamia (now Iraq) and pushed up the Tigris and Euphrates towards Baghdad. Moving up the Tigris, the Anglo-Indian force, commanded by General Sir Charles **Townshend**, met the Turks at Kut-al-Imara (28 September). The Turks were beaten but most of them escaped to **Ctesiphon**. Townshend followed but was defeated at Ctesiphon and fell back to Kut where he was besieged. A relief column, commanded by General Sir Fenton Aylmer was twice turned back (21 January and 8 March 1916). General Sir Percy **Lake**, who had succeeded Nixon as **commander-in-chief**, sent a third relief force, commanded by General Sir George Gorringe. This was repulsed (22 April 1916) and Townshend surrendered (29 April). Many of the prisoners died of starvation in Turkish captivity.

Kuwait, battle of (1991) *See also* Gulf War

L

L4 *See* **Bren gun**

L85 Individual Weapon *See* SA80

L86 Light Support Weapon *See* SA80

laager, lager

A defensive position, especially a circle of wagons protecting a camp, used by the Boers in the **Boer Wars**

La Coruña *See* **Corunna, battle of**

Ladysmith, siege of

(1899–1900; *Boer Wars*) At the outbreak of the war the Boer **commander-in-chief** General Petrus **Joubert** sent General Piet Cronjé to attack **Mafeking** (now Mafikeng) and **Kimberley** while he moved towards Durban. The British force of 10,000, commanded by General Sir George **White**, was forced back towards Ladysmith. Two battalions were taken prisoner during the action at Nicholson's Nek (3 October) and White retired into Ladysmith where he was besieged until 28 February 1900 when the town was relieved by General Sir Redvers **Buller**. The British lost 900 casualties with many more suffering from diseases.

See also **Botha, Louis**

Laffeldt *See* **Lauffeld, battle of**

Laing's Nek, battle of

(1881; *Boer Wars*) A force of 1,000 British troops, commanded by Sir George Colley, moved from Natal to suppress the Boers who were revolting in the Transvaal. The Boers, commanded by Petrus **Joubert**, blocked their passage at Laing's Nek, a pass in the Drakensberg Mountains (28 January). Colley attacked the Boers and was repulsed with the loss of 200 men.

Lake, Gerard (1744–1808)

Lake was appointed an **ensign** in the 1st Foot Guards (**Grenadier Guards**) in 1758. He served in Germany (1760–62) and then under **Cornwallis** in America. When Cornwallis surrendered (17 October 1781) Lake was a prisoner on parole. He was MP for Aylesbury (1790–1802). Lake commanded a **brigade** of Guards in France (1793) and was present at the battle of Valenciennes. He returned home (1794) and became **colonel** of the 73rd Foot (**Perthshire Regiment of Foot**). In 1794 he was appointed lieutenant-governor of Berwick-on-Tweed and governor of Limerick. In 1796 he was in command in Ulster and in 1798 **commander-in-chief** in Ireland on the resignation of **Abercromby**. He was largely responsible for suppressing the Irish rebellion. In 1800 Lake was appointed commander-in-chief in India. He paid great attention to training the Bengal **cavalry** and was in command during the **Maratha Wars**. When Cornwallis replaced Wellesley as governor, Cornwallis also became commander-in-chief with Lake as second-in-command. Cornwallis's policies were more pacific than Lake's. Cornwallis died (1805) and was replaced by the equally pacific Sir George Barlow. The territories annexed by Lake were restored and he returned to England (1807).

See also **Aligarh, battle of**; **Farrukhabad, battle of**

Lake, Percy Henry Noel (1855–1940)

Lake was **gazetted** to the 59th Regiment (**Nottinghamshire (2nd) Regiment of Foot**) (1873) and served in the **Afghan Wars**. He passed **Staff College** (1884) and served in the Sudan (1885), ultimately as quartermaster-general. In 1887 he was appointed **staff captain** in the Intelligence Department at the **War Office**. He was promoted to **major** (1891) and served in Dublin. In 1893 Lake sailed to Canada as quartermaster-general of the Canadian Militia. He was made **brevet colonel** (1899) and after a short time in India came back to the War Office (1899) in charge of mobilisation and as chief **staff officer** of the II Army Corps. Lake returned to Canada (1904) and was promoted to **major-general** (1905). By 1908 he was inspector-general of the Canadian Militia. In 1911 he was promoted to **lieutenant-general** and sent to India, becoming Chief of the Indian Army General Staff (1912). He commanded the Indian forces sent to Mesopotamia (1915). He returned to the UK (1916) and was given a post in the Ministry of Munitions (1917) and retired from the Army in 1919, when he settled in Canada.

Lake Champlain, battle of

(1814; *War of 1812*) The northern thrust of the British offensive against the USA in 1814 was from Canada down Lake Champlain. A force of 11,000 men commanded by Sir George **Prevost** moved down the west side of the lake (31 August) to Plattsburg which was occupied (6 September). Prevost waited for naval support from a fleet of 16 ships and 92 guns commanded by Captain George Downie. This fleet was met by the US fleet of 14 ships and 86 guns, commanded by Captain Thomas Macdonough, anchored across the narrow strait off Cumberland Head (11 September). The British fleet was defeated in a two-hour battle, and Prevost was forced to retreat back into Canada. This was the last battle of this offensive.

Lanarkshire Regiment *See* Duke of Edinburgh's Regiment of Foot

Lancashire Fusiliers

The name given to the **East Devonshire Regiment** in 1881. In 1968 the **regiment** became part of the **Royal Regiment of Fusiliers**.

Lancashire Regiment (The Prince of Wales's Volunteers)

The **regiment** was formed (1958) by the amalgamation of the **East Lancashire Regiment** and the **South Lancashire Regiment** (The Prince of Wales's Volunteers). By an amalgamation in 1970 it became part of the **Queen's Lancashire Regiment**.

Lancashire Regiment of Foot

The **regiment** was raised (1741) as Colonel Maudant's Regiment of Foot. The name was changed with its **colonels** until 1751 when it became the 47th Regiment of Foot; and the 47th (or the Lancashire) Regiment of Foot (1782). In the 1881 amalgamations it became part of the **Loyal Regiment**.

lance

A weapon with a long shaft and a relatively small metal head, used by horsemen charging at full speed
[Via French from Latin *lancea*]

lance bombardier

A **lance corporal** in the **Royal Artillery**

lance corporal

The lowest rank of **non-commissioned officer** in the British Army. It corresponds to lance bombardier in the **Royal Artillery**. The insignia is one **chevron** worn on the upper arm.

lancers

Strictly speaking lancers are troops armed with **lances** but the title 'lancers' survives into the modern army. Lances were common **cavalry** weapons of the medieval period but were no longer used in warfare by British forces by the 17th century. They remained popular in eastern Europe, however, through the horse and musket era. and a number of lancer **regiments** were formed by the French Army and fought against British troops during the **French Wars** (1792–1815). Napoleon's Polish lancers were judged to have been very effective at **Waterloo** and, as in the formation of **hussar** regiments from former **light dragoon** units, conversion of existing light dragoon regiments to lancers offered the officers the possibility of introducing more flamboyant and fashionable uniforms. Consequently (1816) some of the light dragoon regiments were converted to lancers, but kept their former numbering. Other regiments were designated as lancers during the 19th century. By later in the century lances were issued as weapons to most cavalry regiments, not just to those titled as lancers, and they were used in action in the early stages of **World War I**.

Lancers, 9th *See* **Delhi, battle of**

Lancers, 16th
The **regiment** was raised (1759) as the 16th Regiment of (Light) Dragoons. It changed from dragoons to lancers in 1816 and, after several name changes, became the 16th (or Queen's) Lancers (1861), the 16th (The Queen's) Lancers (1905) and 16th The Queen's Lancers (1921). It amalgamated (1922) with the **5th Royal Irish Lancers** to form the **16th/5th Lancers** (*see* **Queens' Royal Lancers, 16th/5th**).
See also **Aliwal, battle of**

Lancers, 16th/5th *See* **Queens' Royal Lancers, 16th/5th**

Lancers, 17th
Initially raised in 1759, the **regiment** became the 17th Regiment of (Light) Dragoons (1769). It converted to lancers (1823) and was renamed the 17th Regiment of Lancers (1861), 17th (The Duke of Cambridge's Own) Lancers (1876) and 17th Lancers (Duke of Cambridge's Own) (1921). It amalgamated (1922) with **21st Lancers (Empress of India's)** to form the **17th/21st Lancers**.
See also **Light Brigade**; **Wood, Henry Evelyn**; **Ulundi, battle of**

Lancers, 17th/21st
The regiment was formed (1922) by the amalgamation of the **17th Lancers (Duke of Cambridge's Own)** and the 21st Lancers (Empress of India's). It amalgamated (1993) with the **16th/5th Queens' Royal Lancers** to form the **Queen's Royal Lancers**.

Lancers, 21st
The regiment was raised (1858) by the East India Company as the 3rd Bengal European Light Cavalry, but was transferred to crown control the same year and incorporated into the British Army (1862) as the 21st Regiment of Hussars. It became the 21st Lancers (1897) and took part in the battle of **Omdurman** (1898). After being further renamed 21st (Empress of India's) Lancers (1898) and 21st Lancers (Empress of India's) (1921), it was temporarily disbanded (1921) before amalgamating (1922) with the **17th Lancers (Duke of Cambridge's Own)** to form the **17th/21st Lancers**.

Langport, battle of
(1645; *Civil War*) Having beaten the Royalists at **Naseby**, **Cromwell** and Sir Thomas **Fairfax** moved into the south-west. The Royalist General Lord George Goring attempted to hold Bridgwater but was defeated at Langport (10 July). The Parliamentarians moved into Gloucestershire and Prince **Rupert** surrendered Bristol (11 September).

Lanier, John (d. 1692)
Lanier served with the Duke of **Monmouth** in France where he lost an eye. Lanier was made **colonel** of the **1st Dragoon Guards** (1687) and **lieutenant-general** (1688). He supported William III and went to Scotland to take Edinburgh Castle (12 June 1689). He then went to Ireland and played a major part in reducing that country. His **regiment** was present at the battles of the **Boyne**, **Limerick** and **Aughrim**. William III then appointed him one of his generals of horse in Flanders. He was wounded at the battle of **Steenkerke** and died a few days later.

Lansdowne, battle of

(1643; *Civil War*) The Royalist forces, commanded by General Sir Ralph Hopton, moved towards Bath from Stratton. They were met by the Parliamentarians commanded by Sir William Waller at Lansdowne, to the east of Bath. The Royalists routed Waller's troops but were heavily mauled themselves and retired to Devizes.

Laswari, battle of

(1803; *Maratha Wars*) Having taken **Aligarh**, **Delhi**, and **Agra**, the British commander General Gerard **Lake** moved on Laswari which he took (1 November)

Lauffeld, battle of

(1747; *War of the Austrian Succession*) A new British force, commanded by the Duke of **Cumberland**, joined the Austrian-Dutch force, commanded by General Count Leopold von Daun. This force isolated 30,000 French troops at Lauffeld in the northeast of present-day Belgium. The French commander, Comte Maurice de **Saxe**, force-marched a relieving force and attacked the Allies (2 July). The Allies suffered some 6,000 casualties and withdrew. Saxe moved on to lay siege to **Bergen-op-Zoom**.

Lawrence, Henry Montgomery (1806–57)

Lawrence, the son of Colonel Alexander Lawrence, was born in Ceylon (now Sri Lanka) and educated in England. He was commissioned as **second lieutenant** in the Royal **Artillery** (1822). He went to India were he came under strong Christian influences. He went to Burma (now Myanmar) with Amherst and was promoted to **lieutenant** (1825). He suffered an attack of fever and dysentery and returned home. Lawrence returned to India (1829) where he led a quiet life with his brother and sister, and qualified as an interpreter. By January 1833 he was with the horse artillery at **Cawnpore** (now Kanpur) and by 1835 was revenue surveyor at Moradabad. He was promoted to **captain** (1837). He took part in the First **Afghan War** and was promoted to **brevet major** (1842). He was appointed governor of Nepal (1843). Lawrence then took part in the First **Sikh War**, was promoted to brevet **lieutenant-colonel** for his services at **Sobraon**, and after the war was appointed resident at Lahore (1847). He returned to England on sick leave (1847) but on the outbreak of the Second **Sikh War** hastened his return to India (1848) and resumed his duties as resident at Lahore (1849). At Lahore he was assisted by his brother, John, but they differed fundamentally on matters of policy so Henry resigned leaving John in full charge. Henry was appointed resident at Ajmeer (1853). He was appointed **aide-de-camp** to the queen and was promoted to **colonel**. In January 1857 he was appointed chief commissioner and agent based at **Lucknow**, where he was in command during the siege (**Indian Mutiny**) in which he was killed.

Lawrence, Stringer (1697–1775)

Lawrence was born in Hereford and was appointed **ensign** in Clayton's Regiment (later the 14th Foot (**West Yorkshire Regiment**)) at Gibraltar. He was promoted to **lieutenant** (1736). The **regiment** went to Flanders and then fought at **Culloden**. By 1748 Lawrence was a **major** in command of the troops of the East India Company based at Fort St. David. Here he formed the Madras European Regiment. He was in command in India of all the campaigns against the French during the **Seven Years' War**. He served at **Wandiwash** after which he was promoted to the local rank of **brigadier-general**. He took command at Fort St. George and was responsible for reorganising the independent **companies** of sepoys into an army based on the European pattern. His health declined and he returned to England with the rank of 'major-general in the East Indies only' (1759). In 1765 he was president of the board advising on the reorganisation of the Madras Army. He died in London. Lawrence was a personal friend of Robert **Clive** who was his subordinate and who owed his early recognition to Lawrence.

See also **Madras, battle of**

Lawrence, Thomas Edward (1888–1935)

Lawrence was born in North Wales and was educated at Jesus College, Oxford, where he graduated in history (1910). He assisted Leonard Woolley in his archaeological expeditions in Egypt. He served in Cairo in military intelligence concerned with Arab affairs (1914–16). He went to Arabia as adviser to Faisal, the Arab leader, in their war against the Turks. He organised and implemented the British aid to the Arabs. Lawrence retired and returned home (1918), traumatised by his wartime experiences and disappointed that Britain and France had broken promises given to the Arabs to support their independence after the war. He was elected a research fellow at All Souls', Oxford (1919), and was appointed political adviser to the Middle Eastern Department of the Colonial Office (1921). He resigned (1922) and joined the RAF as an aircraftsman (or private), using the name J.H. Ross. He also served briefly in the **Royal Tank Corps** (*see* **Royal Tank Regiment**) as T.E. Shaw before returning to the RAF. He was killed in a motor-cycle crash.

Also known as **Lawrence of Arabia**

LDV *abbreviation of* **Local Defence Volunteers**. *See* **Home Guard**

leaguer

1. An encampment, particularly of a besieging army
2. An encampment of armoured vehicles

Le Cateau, battle of

(1914; *World War I*) Following the defeat at **Mons** the **British Expeditionary Force**, commanded by Field Marshal Sir John **French**, together with the French armies, retreated into France, harried by the massive German advance. The German 1st Army, commanded by General Alexander von Kluck, caught up with French's left flank (II Corps) at Le Cateau. Being separated from General Sir Douglas **Haig's** I Corps by the Oise river, its commander, General Horace **Smith-Dorrien**, had no alternative but to fight (26 August). The Germans were repulsed but the British lost 8,077 men and 36 guns. The delay caused by the battle enabled the British Expeditionary Force to avoid the German sweep towards western France.

Lee-Enfield rifle *See* **rifle**

Lee-Metford Rifle

The first British military **rifle** with a bolt action. It was first issued in 1888.

Leese, Oliver William Hargreaves (1894–1978)

Leese was commissioned in the **Coldstream Guards** (1914) and served in France during **World War I**. He was wounded three times and was awarded the **DSO** (1916). He was **adjutant** of the 3rd Battalion, Coldstream Guards (1920–22), studied at the **Staff College**, Camberley (1927–28), held various posts at the **War Office** and became commander of the 1st Battalion, Coldstream Guards (1936). He went to India (1938) as chief instructor at the Staff College, Quetta. He returned home (1940) and helped in the planning of the evacuation from Dunquerque (**Dunkirk**). In September 1942 he was promoted to temporary **lieutenant-general** and joined General **Montgomery** to command the XXX Corps before the battle of **El Alamein**. Leese's **corps** led the advance to Tripoli and Mareth. In July 1943 Leese landed in Sicily with Canadian troops under his command and then returned to the UK with the XXX Corps. In December 1943 he was appointed to command the 8th Army in Italy. In October 1944 Leese was appointed **commander-in-chief** Land Forces South East Asia. He retired from the army in 1946.

See also **Burma campaigns 2**; **Cassino, battle of**; **Gothic Line**; **Gustav Line**

Leicestershire Regiment *See* **Royal Leicestershire Regiment**

levee dress

The most elaborate uniform, worn for presentations at royal palaces

Lewes, battle of

(1264; *Barons' Wars*) The forces of King Henry III and Simon de Montfort, Earl of Leicester, met outside Lewes. The royal forces were defeated and Henry was captured, leaving de Montfort effective ruler of England.

Lewis gun

A type of **machine gun**, first made in Belgium. It was introduced to British Army service in 1915. It was lighter than the existing **Vickers machine gun** but had a tendency to jam. The Lewis replaced the Vickers in ordinary **infantry** units, with the Vickers then being allocated to the newly-formed Machine Gun Corps. It was in turn replaced by the **Bren gun** for most infantry uses in **World War II** and was phased out completely after the war.

[After Colonel Isaac Newton *Lewis* (1858–1931), a US soldier who invented it]

Lexington and Concord, battles of

(1775; *American War of Independence*) As tensions between the British government and radical colonists grew, the Massachusetts Militia established an arms depot at Concord near Boston. The British **commander-in-chief**, General Thomas **Gage**, resolved to destroy the depot and capture the rebel leaders. He sent 700 troops, commanded by Lieutenant Francis Smith, which were waylaid at Lexington by 70 militia (18 April). The British opened fire and killed eight militiamen. This was the beginning of the American War of Independence. The British moved on towards Concord, but a **platoon** was attacked at North Bridge and there were 14 casualties. The British then re-formed to return to Boston but were harried by 4,000 militiamen resulting in 73 killed and 174 wounded. At Charleston Bay they were protected by a bombardment from British ships in the harbour. The militia then laid a siege to Boston that lasted almost a year.

See also **Bunker Hill, battle of**

LG *See* **Order of the Garter**

lieutenant

A commissioned officer ranked immediately below a **captain** and acting as his second-in-command. The insignia is two stars worn on both shoulders.

See also **first lieutenant**; **second lieutenant**

lieutenant-colonel

A commissioned officer ranked immediately below a **colonel** and acting as second-in-command. Originally, when colonel was still an honorary rank, a lieutenant-colonel took command in the field. The insignia is a crown with one star worn on each shoulder.

lieutenant-general

The grade of **general officer** senior to **major-general** and junior to **general** since the 18th century. In earlier times it simply meant the officer second in command to a general, who was often the commander of the **cavalry** in an army.

See also **sergeant-major general**

Life Guards

The senior regiment of the British Army and part of the **Household Cavalry**. Originating as a mounted troop formed by Charles II's companions in exile, three Troops of Horse Guards were established following the Restoration (1660) and first saw action at the battle of **Sedgemoor**. The number of troops varied thereafter, but in 1778 they were disbanded and reformed as the 1st and 2nd Life Guards. They gave up their horses early in 1918, becoming machine gun battalions and, subsequently, armoured regiments. The two regiments amalgamated (1922) as the Life Guards (1st and 2nd), which was renamed the Life Guards (1928). In 1991 the Life Guards amalgamated with the **Blues and Royals** but maintained its own identity and traditions.

Light Brigade

The name given to various military formations, notably various groups of **light infantry** serving in the **Peninsular War**, and perhaps more famously a light **cavalry brigade** formed to take part in the **Crimean War**. This brigade consisted of the 4th Hussars (**Queen's Own Hussars (4th)**), 8th Hussars (**King's Royal Irish Hussars**) and 11th Hussars, the 13th Light Dragoons (**13th Hussars**) and the 17th Lancers and made the disastrous Charge of the Light Brigade at the battle of **Balaclava**.

See also **Cardigan, 7th Earl of; Craufurd, Robert**

light dragoons

In the mid-18th century a tactical need developed for light **cavalry**; ideally smaller men mounted on nimble horses and capable of reconnaissance and skirmishing duties. The **regiments** chosen for conversion to light dragoon status were the **dragoon** regiments numbered from 7th upwards. They retained their old numbers but simply adopted the light dragoon title. From 1806 some light dragoon regiments were renamed as **hussars**, who wore different uniforms but had identical duties and equipment, and from 1816 others became **lancers**.

Light Dragoons

The **regiment** was formed (1992) by the amalgamation of the **King's Royal Hussars** and the **18th Royal Hussars** (Queen Mary's Own)

Light Dragoons, 3rd *See* **King's Own Hussars**

Light Dragoons, 5th

The **regiment** was converted to **lancers**

Light Dragoons, 7th *See* **Queen's Own Hussars**

Light Dragoons, 9th *See* **Queen's Royal Lancers, 9th**

Light Dragoons, 10th *See* **Royal Hussars (Prince of Wales's Own)**

Light Dragoons, 12th *See* **Royal Lancers, 12th (Prince of Wales's)**

Light Dragoons, 13th *See* **Hussars, 13th**

Light Dragoons, 14th *See* **King's Hussars (14th)**

Light Dragoons, 15th *See* **King's Hussars (15th)**

Light Dragoons, 16th

The **regiment** was converted to **lancers**

Light Dragoons, 17th

The **regiment** was converted to **lancers**

Light Dragoons, 20th *See* **Hussars, 20th**

light infantry

Light infantry units were first formed in the British Army by General **Wolfe** during the campaign against the French in America. Originally they were a small corps of selected men specially trained on the lines of the American rangers for fighting in forests and mountains. They were lightly equipped and highly mobile. The system was so successful that a light **company** was formed in every foot **regiment**, which, with the **grenadiers**, guarded the flanks of the regiment. Permanent light infantry regiments date from the early 19th century and Sir John **Moore's** training camp at Shorncliffe.

See also **infantry**

Light Infantry, The

The **regiment** was formed (1968) by the amalgamation of the **Somerset and Cornwall Light Infantry**, the **King's Own Yorkshire Light Infantry**, the **King's Shropshire Light Infantry** and the **Durham Light Infantry**. In 2007 it is expected to unite with The Devonshire and Dorset Light Infantry, and The Royal Gloucestershire, Berkshire and Wiltshire Light Infantry and The Royal Green Jackets, to form The Rifles.

Lille, battle of
(1708; *War of the Spanish Succession*) After his victory at **Oudenarde** the Duke of **Marlborough** sent Prince Eugene of Savoy to lay siege to the French at Lille (12 August) while he covered the siege. The French commanders, the Duc de Vendôme and the Duke of **Berwick**, failed to relieve Lille. When Marlborough opened up a line of communication to Ostend the siege could be maintained indefinitely and Lille surrendered (25 October). Having captured Lille, Marlborough moved on to re-capture Bruges and Ghent (January 1709).

Lillington's (Colonel Lillington's Regiment of Foot) *See* Staffordshire (1st) Regiment of Foot

Limerick, battle of
(1691; *Jacobite Rebellions*) After the battle of the **Boyne**, Limerick was the last Jacobite stronghold in Ireland. A siege by the Royalists in 1690 had been broken by the Earl of Lucan, Patrick **Sarsfield**, but it was renewed (summer 1691) by General Godbert de **Ginkel**, William III's lieutenant in Ireland. The position was hopeless, and the town surrendered (3 October).

Lincoln, battle of
1. (1141; *The Anarchy*) Some barons used the civil war of King Stephen's reign to further their own territorial ambitions. In 1140 Ranulf, Earl of Chester, and his brother seized Lincoln castle, but in January 1141 Stephen besieged it. Ranulf escaped and declared his support for Matilda to win the help of her half-brother and principal supporter, Robert, Earl of Gloucester. Their combined forces surprised Stephen who, although heavily outnumbered, decided to give battle (2 February). However, he was undermined by desertions among his noble supporters during the battle and his forces were comprehensively defeated. Stephen, fighting valiantly to the end, was captured.
2. (1217; *Barons' Wars*) Following King John's repudiation of Magna Carta (1215), his baronial opponents offered the throne to Prince Louis of France, who landed in England (1216). John died (October 1216) and was succeeded by the child Henry III, with William Marshal, Earl of Pembroke, as regent. In 1217 Louis split his forces, besieging both Dover and Lincoln castle. Marshal exploited this opportunity to the full: on 20 May his forces entered Lincoln and won a complete victory. Louis' position was greatly weakened and, after a crushing naval defeat off Sandwich (24 August), he resigned his claim to the throne and returned to France.

Lincolnshire Regiment *See* Royal Lincolnshire Regiment

line regiment
Any **regiment** that is not a Guards regiment, i.e. belonging to the **Household Cavalry** or **Foot Guards**

Local Defence Volunteers *abbreviation of* LDV

Londonderry, battle of
(1689; *Jacobite Rebellions*) The army of the deposed James II moved from Dublin and laid siege to the royalist Londonderry (17 April). The garrison, commanded by Major Henry Baker, held out until 30 July when a naval expedition broke the boom across the river Foyle and raised the siege. James II's forces retired.

longbow
The longbow probably originated in Wales and was used extensively and effectively by the English during the **Hundred Years' War**. The best bows were made from yew and were about 6ft long. Their pulling force was about 100lb and they fired an arrow about 1 yard long a distance of about 200 yards. The longbow had a much quicker rate of fire than the **crossbow**. With the increased efficiency of **muskets**, the longbow had disappeared from military use by 1627.

Long Island, battle of
(1776; *American War of Independence*) Having abandoned Boston (March 1776), the British commander, General Sir William **Howe**, prepared to attack New York,

defended by an army led by General George **Washington**. The British landed 20,000 troops on the south-west of the island (22–25 August). An encircling movement by the British forced the Americans back to Brooklyn Heights (26 August). Howe laid siege to **Brooklyn** but Washington managed to extricate his forces, commanded by General Isaac Putman, to Manhattan Island (29 August). Washington made a further retreat to Haarlem Heights to the north of the island (12 September) preventing his being outflanked when the British landed at Kip's Bay (15 September).

Long Range Desert Group *See* **Special Air Service Regiment**

Long's (Colonel James Long's Regiment of Foot) *See* **East Essex Regiment of Foot**

Loos, battle of

(1915; *World War I*) The British part in the battle of **Artois-Loos**. This was the first occasion on which British commanders used poison **gas** to support an offensive. Much of the gas drifted back on the British troops. Small gains were made at the cost of some 60,000 British and 30,000 German casualties. Recriminations followed the battle and the British **commander-in-chief**, Field Marshal Sir John **French** was replaced by General Sir Douglas **Haig**, who had commanded the British 1st Army at Loos.

Lord Castleton's Regiment of Foot *See* **Cambridgeshire (1st) Regiment of Foot**

Lord George Germain *See* **Sackville, George**

Lord George Sackville *See* **Sackville, George**

Lord Lucas Regiment of Foot *See* **Cumberland Regiment**

Lostwithiel, battle of

(1644; *Civil War*) In spite of his defeat at **Marston Moor**, Charles I led his troops in pursuit of the Parliamentarians, commanded by the 3rd Earl of Essex, Robert Devereux, who were attacking Cornwall. Charles caught up with Essex at Lostwithiel, 30 miles west of Plymouth (2 September). Essex and his **cavalry** escaped, but Charles killed or captured 8,000 **infantry** and all of Essex's **artillery**. Charles then turned to march on London.

Loudon Hill, battle of

(1307; *English-Scottish Wars*) The Scottish King Robert I the Bruce returned from exile during the winter of 1306–07 and renewed the war against England. He rallied an army at Loudon Hill in Ayrshire (May 1307). The English, commanded by the Earl of Pembroke, attacked the Scottish spearmen with a **cavalry** charge that was repulsed with heavy loss. After this defeat the English King Edward I took personal command of the Scottish campaign but died (7 July) at Burgh-by-Sands. His son, Edward II, withdrew from Scotland and abandoned the campaign.
See also **Bannockburn, battle of**

Louisbourg, battle of

1. (1745; *King George's War*) The French in Canada had fortified Louisbourg on Cape Breton Island at the mouth of the St. Lawrence river. A combined British naval and land force attacked the fort. The land force of New Englanders, commanded by Colonel William **Pepperell**, attacked the fort (30 April) which finally fell to the combined assault on 17 June. The fort was returned to the French by the Treaty of Aix-la-Chapelle (1748).

2. (1758; *French and Indian War*) A British expedition, commanded by General Jeffrey **Amherst** and supported by a fleet of 40 ships, landed (June 8) and invested the fort at Louisbourg, using artillery landed from the fleet (18 June). The French, who were holding the fort, surrendered (26 July).

Loyal Lincolnshire Volunteers

The **regiment** was raised (1793) by Major-General Albemarle Bertie as the 83rd (Loyal Lincolnshire Volunteer) Regiment of Foot. It was re-numbered (1794) the 81st

Regiment of Foot and re-named (1832) the 81st (Loyal Lincoln Volunteers) Regiment of Foot. In the 1881 reorganisation it became part of the **Loyal Regiment**.

Loyal Regiment

The Loyal Regiment (North Lancashire) was created (1881) by the amalgamation of the **Lancashire Regiment of Foot** and the **Loyal Lincolnshire Volunteers**. Originally called the Loyal North Lancashire Regiment, the name changed (1921) to the Loyal Regiment (North Lancashire). In 1970 it became part of the **Queen's Lancashire Regiment**.

LSW *See* SA80

LT *See* **Order of the Thistle**

Lucan, Lord[1] (1800–88)

George Bingham was educated at Westminster School and purchased a commission as an **ensign** (1816). He purchased other commissions to become **lieutenant-colonel** (1837) and commanded the 17th Lancers. He resigned his commission in 1837 and in 1839 succeeded to his father's title as 3rd earl of Lucan. He was an MP (1826–30). Although he had little military experience, he was promoted to **major-general** (1851) and was given command of a cavalry division that went to the **Crimea**. The division consisted of two **brigades**, the **Heavy Brigade**, commanded by James York **Scarlett** and the **Light Brigade** commanded by Lucan's brother-in-law Lord **Cardigan**. The brothers-in-law disliked each other intensely, and this dislike, together with the confused orders Lucan received from Lord **Raglan**, contributed to the famous Charge of the Light Brigade at the battle of **Balaclava**. Lucan was recalled to the UK (1855) and was refused a court martial to enable him to clear his name. He saw no further active service, but was promoted to **general** (1865) and to **field marshal** (1887).

Also known as **Bingham, George Charles**

Lucan, Lord[2] *See* **Sarsfield, Patrick**

Lucknow, siege of

(1857–58; *Indian Mutiny*) A garrison of 1,700 British and Indian troops, commanded by Sir Henry **Lawrence**, was trapped in the residency at Lucknow by some 60,000 rebels (1 July 1857). A British army of some 3,000, commanded by Generals Sir Henry **Havelock** and Sir James **Outram**, fought its way to Lucknow from Cawnpore (now Kanpur) with the loss of 500 men. The garrison had lost a similar number, and Lawrence had been killed. The mutineers tightened the siege on the reinforced garrison. Havelock died of exhaustion leaving Outram in command. A second relief force led by Sir Colin **Campbell** arrived bringing reinforcements, but Campbell had to leave to put down a rebellion in Cawnpore. Outram continued to hold out until Lucknow was relieved (21 March 1858) by Campbell.

Ludendorff, Erich (1865–1937)

Ludendorff was the most important German military commander of the second half of **World War I**. At the outbreak of the war (1914) he was appointed to the staff of the 2nd Army in the west. When the Russians threatened to overrun the German 8th Army Ludendorff was appointed its **chief-of-staff**, nominally serving under **Hindenburg**. The two commanded all German forces on the Eastern Front (1915–16) and in September 1916 took command of the whole German Army. They defeated Russia in 1917 but Ludendorff's ambitious attack plans failed to win the war in the west in a series of offensives in the spring of 1918. When the Allies attacked in the summer he lost his nerve and demanded that Germany surrender, then blamed the civilian politicians when they did just that. The truth was that the German Army had been badly defeated, in large part because of Ludendorff's unrealistic aims. In the 1920s Ludendorff supported the early activities of the Nazi party, taking part in the unsuccessful Beer Hall Putsch (1923) and serving as a Nazi member of the Reichstag (1924–28). However, he then quarrelled with the Nazis and later (1935) refused Hitler's offer to promote him to **field marshal**. He died in Munich.

Ludford Bridge, battle of

(1459; *Wars of the Roses*) After his victory at **Blore Heath**, the Earl of Salisbury combined his forces with those of Richard, Duke of York. The Yorkists advanced to Worcester, but the approach of a superior Lancastrian army commanded by King Henry VI forced them to retreat towards Ludlow, eventually establishing a fortified position at nearby Ludford Bridge. Heavily outnumbered, suffering desertions and reluctant to fight against the king in person – to whom they still professed loyalty – York, Warwick and other Yorkist leaders fled during the night of 12–13 October 1359. Their leaderless troops dispersed the next day.

Lundy's Lane, battle of

(1814; *War of 1812*) After the American victory at **Chippewa river** the British fell back towards the Niagara Falls. The British commander General Gordon **Drummond** deployed 3,000 troops across the roadway at Lundy's Lane to prevent any pursuit. The American General Winfield Scott attacked the position (25 July) with 2,700 troops. The attack was repulsed and the Americans withdrew to Fort Erie.

LVO *See* Royal Victorian Order

lyddite

A high explosive based on picric acid, used in the shells of **howitzers** and heavy guns [From *Lydd* in Kent, where it was developed during the late 19th century]

Lys river, battle of

(1918; *World War I*) Having won a substantial victory in his first 1918 offensive on the **Somme** front, the German commander, General Erich **Ludendorff**, launched an attack on the Lys river in Flanders (9 April). The German 6th Army moved west from Armentières and broke through a Portuguese division at the centre of General Henry **Horne's** British 1st Army. The German 4th Army attacked north of Armentières and, through lack of reserves, General Sir Herbert **Plumer's** 2nd Army pulled back. The two German armies linked up (11 April) and began to move towards the sea. Field Marshal Douglas **Haig** rushed reinforcements north and the British stemmed the German advance (29 April). The Germans had gained about 10 miles at the cost of 350,000 casualties. The Allies, mostly British, lost 305,000.

M

machine gun

Any gun which is self-actuated using the energy generated from a fired round to eject the spent **cartridge**, reload, and prepare the weapon for firing again. The energy can be generated directly from the recoil force created when a round is fired or, in the blowback system, by diverting some of the gas generated by the propellant explosion. In theory a machine gun will keep firing for as long as the trigger is pressed and ammunition is fed to the mechanism. Similar principles have also been used in the design of **submachine guns** and automatic **rifles**. The first successful automatic machine gun was invented (c. 1884) by Hiram Maxim, an American working in Europe. This, and similar weapons, played a major role in **World War I**, though not the dominant role that is often popularly believed – this was played by **artillery**. Since World War I machine guns have provided the principal firepower of the **infantry** and have been fitted in military vehicles and many other types of installations. The Maxim-type machine guns, the main example in British service being the **Vickers machine gun**, were heavy and rather immobile weapons. Also developed were lighter weapons, such as the **Lewis gun** and **Bren gun**, that were easier to use in mobile warfare. Since **World War II** the distinction between light and heavy machine guns has been lost with most designs now being 'general purpose' weapons. The machine guns currently used by the British Army are the **L1A1 12.7 mm Heavy Machine Gun**, the **7.62 mm General Purpose Machine Gun**, and the **5.56 mm Light Machine Gun**.

Mackay, Hugh (1640?–92)

In 1660 Mackay became an **ensign** in Douglas's Regiment (later the **Royal Scots**) and went to France with the **regiment**. He inherited the family estates (1668) but continued to live abroad and served in the Venetian army. He returned home and was made **captain** (1672) in Dumbarton's Regiment (also later the **Royal Scots**). He then served in the Netherlands, and by 1677 was a **colonel**. In 1685 he was called back to England to command a **brigade** in the quelling of the **Duke of Monmouth's** rebellion. Mackay supported William III and was appointed **major-general** (1689) and **commander-in-chief** in Scotland. In 1690 he went to Ireland as second-in-command to General **Ginkel**. He was largely responsible for the victory at **Aughrim**. After the fall of **Limerick** he returned to Holland as **lieutenant-general** in command of the British forces in Flanders. He was killed at the battle of **Steenkerke**.

See also **Killiecrankie, battle of**

MacLeod's Highlanders *See* Highland Light Infantry

Madagascar, battle of

(1942; *World War II*) The island of Madagascar was under the control of the Vichy French pro-German government commanded by Governor-General Armand Annet. To secure the harbour of Diego Suarez the British landed a force under Admiral Neville Syfret and General Sturges (5 May). Diego Suarez was taken (7 May). During negotiations with the French, the British battleship *Ramillies* was torpedoed in the harbour and General William **Platt**, commander in East Africa, was ordered to occupy the whole island. Annet surrendered (5 November) and the Free French took over the island (8 January 1943).

Madras, battle of

1. (1746; *War of the Austrian Succession*) The French, commanded by Marquis Joseph Dupleix, governor of Pondicherry, attacked the British settlement 80 miles north at Madras (now Chennai) (5 September). After a five-day attack by land, and a bombardment from the sea, the fort surrendered. Some of the defenders, including Robert **Clive** who was then a clerk, escaped to Fort St. David. The settlement was returned to the British under the treaty of Aix-la-Chapelle (1748).

2. (1758–59; *Seven Years' War*) The French, having captured Fort St. David from the British (June 1758), pressed north to attack Madras (now Chennai), which was under the command of Colonel Stringer **Lawrence** (16 December). The French raised the siege (16 February 1759) after being bombarded by a British fleet that had arrived in the harbour.

Madras Fusiliers *See* **Royal Dublin Fusiliers**

Madras Infantry

The **regiment** was raised (1854) as the 3rd Madras European Regiment in the army of the East India Company. It was taken into the British Army (1861) as the 108th (Madras Infantry) Regiment of Foot. In the 1881 re-organisation it amalgamated with the 51st to form the **King's Own Yorkshire Light Infantry**.

Madras Light Infantry

The **regiment** was raised (1839) as the 2nd Madras European Regiment (Light Infantry) in the army of the East India Company. The name changed (1858) to the 2nd (Madras) Light Infantry Regiment and it was taken into the British Army (1861) as the 105th (Madras Light Infantry) Regiment.

Mafeking, siege of

(1899–1900; *Boer Wars*) The Boer **commander-in-chief**, General Petrus **Joubert**, launched an offensive in west Transvaal under General Piet Cronjé, with 5,000 troops attacking Mafeking (now Mafikeng) (13 October) where Colonel Sir Robert **Baden-Powell** had only 700 troops and 600 armed civilians. The attack was repulsed and Cronjé instituted a siege. The town held out until it was relieved (17 May 1900) by a column of cavalry under Sir Bryan **Mahon**. The Boers suffered 1,000 casualties and the British 273.

Magdala, battle of (1868)

Ras Kassa had seized the throne of Abyssinia (now Ethiopia) (1855) under the name of Theodore. In 1864 he imprisoned the British consul, Charles Cameron, and in 1866 imprisoned the British envoy sent to negotiate Cameron's release at Magdala. In 1868 General Sir Robert **Napier** led a punitive expedition into Abyssinia and stormed Magdala (13 April). The prisoners were released and Napier withdrew.

See also **Abyssinian campaign**

Magersfontein, battle of

(1899; *Boer Wars*) After his victory at **Modder river** the British General Lord Paul **Methuen** moved towards the besieged **Kimberley**. He was opposed by 9,000 Boers, commanded by General Piet Cronjé, who had taken up a strong position at Magersfontein. The Highland Brigade attacked but suffered 700 casualties. The attack failed and Methuen withdrew.

Maginot line

A French defensive line constructed along the eastern border with Germany from 1923 through the 1930s. It was easily outflanked by Germany's **tank** forces in 1940 because it did not extend to cover France's border with Belgium.

[After André *Maginot* (1877–1932), the French war minister]

Maharajpur, battle of

1. (1843; *Sikh Wars*) A force of 18,000 Marathas with 100 guns occupied a strong defensive position at Maharajpur. They were attacked and charged by a 14,000 strong

British force, commanded by Sir Hugh **Gough** (29 December). The position was carried with a loss of 787 killed. The Marathas lost 3,000 men and 56 guns.

2. (1857; *Indian Mutiny*) A rebel force of 3,000 under Nana Sahib held a defensive line across the road to **Cawnpore** (now Kanpur). A British relieving force, commanded by General Sir Henry **Havelock**, was forced to attack (16 July) on the left flank. The rebels were defeated, but Havelock was left with only 800 able-bodied men. Cawnpore was re-occupied on the following day.

Mahdi, the (1844–85)

The son of a ship-builder from the Dongola district of Nubia, he studied religion and as a young man began to attract his own disciples at a hermitage on Aba Island in the White Nile, 175 miles south of Khartoum. The Sudan was a dependency of Egypt and the Turkish-speaking ruling classes contrasted sharply in all aspects of their life from the Sudanese people. The Mahdi was able to convert the diversified tribes of the Sudan into a co-ordinated religious movement and an efficient military machine which he used to create a vast Islamic state extending from the Red Sea to Central Africa.

Born **Muhammad Ahmad ibn As-Sayyid 'abd Allah**

Mahdists

Followers of the **Mahdi**

Mahidpur, battle of

(1817; *Maratha Wars*) A force of Marathas with 70 guns, under the Holkar of Indore, was in a defensive position behind the Sipra. A British force, commanded by Sir Thomas **Hislop**, was forced to cross in the face of their fire (21 December) but completely defeated the Marathas who lost some 3,000 men. The British lost 778 killed and wounded.

Mahon, Bryan Thomas (1862–1930)

Mahon was born in Ireland and joined the Connaught Rangers. He was **gazetted** as **lieutenant** in the 21st Hussars (January 1883) but after three weeks transferred to the 8th (**King's Royal Irish**) Hussars. He served in India for five years and was promoted to **captain** (1888). In 1893 he resigned and joined the Egyptian Army. He was awarded the DSO (1896) and was promoted to major (1897). Mahon was present at the battles of **Atbara** and **Omdurman**. He was promoted to **brevet colonel** (1899). In 1900 he went to South Africa and in May 1900 was promoted to **brigadier-general** in command of the force sent to relieve **Mafeking** (now Mafikeng). He then served in the Transvaal. He went back to Egypt (1901) as governor of Kordofan. In 1904 he was promoted to substantive colonel and went to India in command at Belgaum. He was promoted to **major-general** (1906) and was given command of the Lucknow **Division** (1909). He returned to the UK (1913) and was promoted to **lieutenant-general**. At the beginning of **World War I** he was given command of the 10th (Irish) Division, went to **Gallipoli** and was subsequently the British **commander-in-chief** at **Salonika**. In 1916 he was appointed commander-in-chief in Ireland and was responsible for defusing the Easter Rising. In 1918–19 he was military commander at Lille. Mahon retired in 1921. He became a senator of the newly formed Irish Free State.

Maida, battle of

(1806; *French Wars*) After his victory at Austerlitz, **Napoleon** installed his brother Joseph as King of Naples. The British landed a force of 5,000 men, commanded by General John **Stuart**, in Calabria (6 June). This was opposed by the French under General Jean Reynier. The British routed the French and established a bridgehead, but the French Marshal André Masséna began to concentrate a much larger French force and Stuart was forced to re-embark. Naples now came completely under Joseph's control.

Maiwand, battle of

(1880; *Afghan War II*) Ayub Khan, son of Shere Ali, the former emir, organised a revolt against the British in Afghanistan. He stormed the small British garrison at

Maiwand (27 July) killing 970 Anglo-Indian troops and wounding 160. The few survivors escaped to **Kandahar**.

major
A field officer ranked immediately below a **lieutenant-colonel**

major-general
A staff officer ranked immediately below a **lieutenant-general**.
See also **sergeant-major general**

Majuba Hill, battle of
(1881; *Boer Wars*) After his defeat at **Laing's Nek** the British General Sir George Colley occupied Majuba Hill which commanded the pass through the Drakensberg Mountains. The Boer General Petrus **Joubert** attacked and drove the British off the hill, killing half of the 550-man force, including Colley. The battle ended the First Boer War.

Malavilly, battle of
(1799; *British in India*) The camp of a British contingent marching to **Seringapatam** was attacked by a Mysore force led by **Tipu Sahib**. They were driven off by a **cavalry** charge with the loss of some 1,000 men.

Malaya
(1941–42; *World War II*) The Japanese began the invasion of the Malaya (Kra) Peninsula (8 December 1941) by landing forces at Singora and Patani (both in South Thailand), and at Alor Star and Kota Bharu in Malaya. They advanced rapidly against the 9th and 11th Indian **divisions** commanded by General A.E. **Percival**. The Japanese also occupied airfields in the north of the colony. Although the 8th Australian and 18th Indian Divisions joined the original force, by 31 January 1942 the Allied troops had been forced back across the causeway over the Jahore Strait into **Singapore**.

Malplaquet, battle of
(1709; *War of the Spanish Succession*) Having captured **Tournai**, the Duke of **Marlborough** with Prince Eugene of Savoy moved his 100,000 men to besiege Mons. He was opposed by a French Army of 90,000, commanded by Marshal Duc Claude de Villers, at Malplaquet. The Allied army of British, Dutch, Germans and Austrians attacked (11 September) and after seven hours' fighting the French withdrew. These were two of the largest armies ever to have met. The Allies lost 24,000 men killed and wounded and the French lost about 12,000. Mons surrendered (20 October). The Allied losses were so severe as to preclude any further major campaign during that year. This was Marlborough's last major battle. He was dismissed in 1711.

Manchester Regiment
The **regiment** was formed (1881) by the amalgamation of the 63rd (**West Suffolk**) Regiment of Foot and the **96th Foot**. It amalgamated with the King's Regiment (Liverpool) in 1958 to form **The King's Regiment (Manchester and Liverpool)**.

Mandalay, battle of
(1945; *World War II*) Having been victorious at **Imphal** and Kohima the British commander, General Sir William **Slim**, led the 14th Army on an offensive to destroy the Japanese Burma Area Army and reopen the road between Burma (now Myanmar) and China (14 January–21 March). The British established bridgeheads across the Irrawaddy on either side of Mandalay (January–February) and the Japanese communication centre at Meiktila was captured. The Japanese fronts collapsed and Mandalay fell (21 March).

Mangalore, battle of
(1783; *British in India*) The small British garrison at Mangalore, commanded by Colonel Campbell, was besieged by the forces of **Tipu Sahib** (20 June). In spite of the conclusion of a peace between Britain and France, the garrison received no supplies. Tipu renewed the siege. No attempt was made to relieve Mangalore and Campbell was forced to surrender.

Manila, battle of
(1762; *Seven Years' War*) Spain entered the war on the side of France (1762) making its possessions in the Far East vulnerable to British attack. A British expeditionary force under Admiral Samuel Cornish and General William **Draper** therefore sailed from India to Luzon. The British entered Manila harbour (4 October) and forced the surrender of the city. It was restored to Spain (1763) at the end of the war.

Maori War (1845–70)
Initially the conflict arose from disputes over land ownership between the British settling in New Zealand and the native Maoris, but this developed into a pseudo-religious war when the Maori leader, Te Kooti Rikirangi, developed his own form of Christianity and used it as a focus on which to rally dissident Maoris. By 1870 the Maoris were suppressed and the acquisition of their land by the British by punitive means followed.

Maratha Wars (1779–1818)
There were three periods of conflict between the British and the Marathas of the Deccan, in south India. In 1779–81 the conflict did not escalate, but in 1803–04 and 1817–18 there were pitched battles.
See also **Ahmadabad, battle of; Agra, battle of; Aligarh, battle of; Aras, battle of; Assaye, battle of; Bassein, battle of; Bhurtpore, battle of; Deeg, battle of; Delhi, battle of; Fort Sitabaldi, battle of; Gwalior, battle of; Kirkee, battle of; Korygaom, battle of; Laswari, battle of; Mahidpur, battle of**

Mareth Line, battle of
(1943; *World War II*) After his retreat across Libya, the German Field Marshal **Rommel** dug in behind the Mareth Line inside the Tunisian frontier. The British 8th Army commanded by General Sir Bernard **Montgomery** moved slowly from the east, hampered by increasingly long lines of communication, allowing Rommel time to attack the 1st Allied Army (14–22 February) which had landed in west Tunisia the previous November. Rommel then turned east to face the 8th Army. On 6 March the 21st Panzer Division tried to break Montgomery's line at **Medenine** but failed, losing 52 of its 104 tanks. The Germans pulled back and Rommel returned to Germany. Joined by the Free French forces and the New Zealand Division, Montgomery attacked the Mareth defences (20 March) with an **artillery** bombardment and a wide flanking movement by the New Zealanders. The Italian General Giovanni Messe withdrew the combined Italian-German forces northwards to Gabès. Montgomery attacked at Gabès (6 April) and the British met up with the US II Corps (7 April), which had been pushing east from Gafsa.

marines
Soldiers that specialise in ship-based operations. Detachments of infantry from existing **regiments** were sent with naval vessels during the First Dutch War (1652–54) but in 1664 the Duke of York and Albany's (or Lord High Admiral's) Maritime Regiment of Foot of 1,200 men was raised. The regiment was divided into six **companies**, but after the immediate conflicts three of these were disbanded. The regiment was disbanded following the Glorious Revolution (1688), but further marine regiments were raised and disbanded as necessary until 1748. A new force of marines raised in 1755, which endures today as the Royal Marines, was part of the Royal Navy.
[Via French from Latin *marinus* from *mare* 'sea']

Mark 6 combat helmet *See* **helmet**

Marlborough, 1st Duke of (1650–1722)
John Churchill was the son of Sir Winston Churchill, a poor Devonshire royalist. He became page to the Duke of York (later James II) and found favour with Barbara Villiers (Duchess of Cumberland), who secured him an ensigncy in the Guards. He served in **Tangier** and under the Duke of **Monmouth** in Holland. He was promoted partly due to the influence of his cousin, Arabella Churchill (mistress to James II). He

married Sarah Jennings, a close friend of Princess (later Queen) Anne. He quelled **Monmouth's Rebellion** (1685) and supported William of Orange (1688). He was created Earl of Marlborough and served in William III's campaign in Ireland. He nevertheless fell from favour in 1691 and came under suspicion of Jacobite sympathies. He was restored to favour on the accession of Queen Anne (1702), who immediately appointed him supreme commander of the British and Dutch forces during the War of the **Spanish Succession** and, later that year, created him Duke of Marlborough. His victory at the battle of **Blenheim** earned him what is now Blenheim Palace at Woodstock. Among his other notable victories were **Ramillies**, **Oudenarde** and **Malplaquet**. It was said of him that he never fought a battle which he did not win or besieged a town and failed to capture it. These successes were all the more remarkable because his campaigns were beset with difficulties in gaining the whole-hearted co-operation of his allies and the support of the government at home. Through political intrigue he was removed from office (1711). He is regarded as one of the most able **generals** of any age and perhaps as the finest ever British commander.

Also known as **Churchill, John**; *See also* **Donauwörth, battle of**

Marne river, battle of

1. (6–8 September 1914; *World War I*) The French 6th Army faced the German 1st Army in the west, the **British Expeditionary Force** (five **divisions** commanded by Field Marshal Sir John **French**) was in the centre and the French 9th Army faced the German 2nd and 3rd Armies, all straddling the Marne and Morin rivers and threatening Paris. The battle moved backwards and forwards over a 30-mile front involving some 900,000 Germans and 1,080,000 Allied troops. Each side lost about 5% of its men. The Allied, largely French, line held and the German commander, Bülow, ordered the retreat of his 2nd Army, thus initiating a general retreat. Paris was saved, but this indecisive result ensured that the war would be prolonged.

2. (15 July–6 August 1918; *World War I*) The Germans, commanded by General Erich **Ludendorff**, began an assault to reach the Marne river. The advance was stalled by an Allied force of 23 French, nine American, two British and two Italian **divisions**. The Allied **commander-in-chief**, General Ferdinand **Foch**, launched a counter-attack (18 July) by the French 5th, 9th, 6th and 10th Armies and eight American, four British and two Italian divisions. By 3 August the Germans had fallen back to a line along the Vesle and Aisne rivers, but by 6 August the Germans were firmly entrenched. Foch then switched the Allied attacks to other areas.

See also **Amiens, battle of**

Marquess of Worcester's Regiment of Foot *See* **Devonshire Regiment**

marshal

Originally the king's **farrier** and later an officer responsible for the arrangement of ceremonials at court. The post evolved to become the chief officer in command of a particular campaign but has been replaced by the rank of **field marshal**.

See also **constable**

Marston Moor, battle of

(1644; *Civil War*) The Royalist Prince **Rupert** successfully relieved York which had been held by the Parliamentarians. The latter retired to Marston Moor, seven miles from York. This force, commanded by Lord **Fairfax**, and the allied Scots, commanded by Alexander Leslie, was then reinforced by **Cromwell's Ironsides**. Prince Rupert, with a force from York commanded by the Earl of Newcastle and **cavalry** under General Lord George Goring, pursued the Parliamentarians and came upon them at Marston Moor (2 July). After initial skirmishing, the Royalists withdrew to re-form, only to be attacked by the entire Parliamentarian line early in the evening. Cromwell's cavalry and the Scottish horsemen routed the Royalists. There were 4,000 casualties; Newcastle fled into exile. The Royalist army, including Rupert's cavalry, was destroyed. York surrendered (16 July) and Newcastle (16 October). Charles I had lost control in the north.

martello towers
A series of stone towers built along the southern coasts of the UK in 1803–05. These were lookout posts to determine the presence of an invasion by the French. They also acted as platforms for warning beacons or had semaphore signalling arms mounted on them to enable messages to be sent rapidly along the coast.

Martini-Henry rifle *See* **rifle**

Martinique, battle of
(1762; *Seven Years' War*) A combined naval and army force, consisting of veterans from the war in Canada and commanded by Admiral George Rodney, attacked the French island of Martinique which surrendered (12 February). This gave the British control over the Windward Islands. The island was restored to France by the Treaty of Paris (1763).

mascot *See* **regimental mascots**

Massue, Henri de (1648–1720)
Massue was born in Paris and served as **aide-de-camp** to Marshal Turenne (1672–75). Massue was a prominent Huguenot who, on the revocation of the Edict of Nantes (1685), moved with his family to England. He served as a **major-general** of horse (1690) and fought in the Irish campaign. He was created Viscount Galway (1692). He was trusted absolutely by William III of England and appointed to command the Allied armies in Savoy (1694). He received an earldom (1697) and went to Ireland as lord justice. He retired (1701) but was called to command the Allied forces in Portugal (1704) during the War of the **Spanish Succession**. After his defeat at **Almanza** (1707) he again retired but was recalled as lord justice of Ireland (1715–16).

Masulipatam, battle of
(1759; *Seven Years' War*) This fortress, 200 miles north of Madras (now Chennai), was held by the French, commanded by Marshal de Conflans. During March, it was besieged by 2,500 British commanded by Colonel Forde. After a fortnight's bombardment the French surrendered to the smaller British force with little resistance.

match
A piece of twisted slow-burning material used to fire a **matchlock** or **artillery** piece. It was carried in the hat, wound around the waist or around the wrist when in action.
[From Old French *meiche*, ultimately from Greek *muxa* 'lampwick']

matchlock
A mechanism for firing small arms. It was invented during the 15th century and consisted of an S-shaped arm (serpentine) that held a glowing match. Pulling the trigger released the serpentine which lowered the **match** into the priming pan which was attached to the side of the barrel. This fired the priming powder that in turn fired the main charge through a small hole in the side of the gun. The whole firing mechanism was protected inside the lock. This was the first mechanical firing device and although it was difficult to use in wet or windy weather it was simpler than firing directly by hand and gave the user more freedom. By 1675, it had been superseded by the **flintlock**.
[From its having a gunlock in which a match was placed to ignite the powder]

Maude, Frederick Stanley (1864–1917)
Maude was educated at Eton and the **Royal Military Academy** at Sandhurst. He joined the **Coldstream Guards** (1884) and served in the Sudan. In 1895 he attended the **Staff College** at Camberley and was made a brigadier-major of the Guards. At the outbreak of the Second **Boer War** he joined his **brigade** at the **Modder river**. He took part in many of the battles of the campaign. In 1901 Maude was made military secretary to the Earl of Minto (Governor-General of Canada). In 1905 he rejoined his **regiment** and held various staff appointments until 1914 when he joined the staff of the III Corps and took part in the battles of the **Marne**, Aisne and Armentières. He was appointed **brigadier-general** of the 14th Brigade (1914). He was wounded at St. Eloi and

returned home. He was promoted to **major-general**, and given command of the 13th Division in the **Dardanelles**. He took his **division** to Mesopotamia (1916) and assumed command of the forces there, leading them in their successful campaign the next year. He was made a KCB and promoted to **lieutenant-general** (1917). Maude died of cholera in Baghdad.
See also **Baghdad, battle of**

Maudent's (Colonel Maudent's Regiment of Foot) *See* **Lancashire Regiment of Foot**

Maxim gun
This type of **machine gun** was invented by the American Hiram Maxim (1882). It was introduced into the British Army (1891) and was used in the **Sudan War**, on the **North-West Frontier** of India and in the **Boer War**. It was superseded by the similar **Vickers machine gun** before **World War I**.

MBE *See* **Order of the British Empire**

MC *abbreviation of* **Military Cross**

McCarthy, Charles (1770?–1824)
McCarthy was an **ensign** in the **regiment** of James Henry (later the 5th Regiment of the Irish Brigade) (1794). He went to the West Indies and was promoted to **lieutenant** (1796). He was **captain** in the 52nd Foot (**Oxfordshire Regiment of Foot**) (1800) and was promoted to **major** (1804) in the New Brunswick Fencibles (104th Foot). McCarthy was then promoted to **lieutenant-colonel** of the Royal African Corps (1811) and made governor of Sierra Leone (1812). When Cape Coast Castle was taken out of the hands of the Africa Company he was made governor there as well. He was knighted (1820) and promoted to **colonel** (1821). He was killed during the **Ashanti War**.
See also **Accra, battle of**

Meanee, battle of
(1843; *War in the Sind*) The hostility between the British in India and the rulers of Sind (in modern west Pakistan) erupted into war in 1843. General Charles James **Napier** with 2,800 Anglo-Indian troops encountered 20,000 Baluchistanis at Meanee (17 February). The Baluchistanis lost 5,000 casualties and the British 256. The victory allowed Napier to move south.
See also **Cheshire Regiment**

medals
Medals fall into five categories: gallantry, war service, commemorative, long service and good conduct. The medals for gallantry may also be considered as **decorations**. Medals had been worn in early times only by officers, and it was not until the 18th century that they were awarded to **other ranks**. Exceptionally medals were issued commemorating the battle of **Dunbar** (1650) and for the capture of **Seringapatam** (1799). **Waterloo** was the first battle for which all British troops who participated were awarded a medal (in 1816). The **Peninsular War** medal was awarded later by Queen Victoria (1848). After 1848 it was customary to award campaign medals to all officers and men who had taken part in a particular campaign.

Medenine, battle of
(1943; *World War II*) The German Field Marshal Erwin **Rommel** moved to check the British 8th Army, commanded by General Sir Bernard **Montgomery**, at Medenine, about 15 miles south-east of the **Mareth Line** in Tunisia. The attack was repulsed (6 March) and Rommel, who was ill, handed over command to General Jürgen von Arnim and returned to Germany.

Megiddo, battle of
(1918; *World War I*) British Empire forces, commanded by General Sir Edmund **Allenby**, had captured Jerusalem (December 1917) and the army had been built back up to 60,000 men by recruits from India after the original troops had been withdrawn to France. Minor raids east of the Jordan and the harassing of Turkish communications

by Colonel T.E. **Lawrence** led the commander of the Turkish forces, General Otto Liman von Sanders, to deploy one third of his 4th Army (30,000) men east of the Jordan. Meanwhile Allenby attacked along the coast (19 September). The Turkish line collapsed quickly and Allenby took Megiddo. He cut off most of the Turkish 4th Army, taking 25,000 prisoners. The Turks retreated to Damascus which fell on 2 October. Aleppo surrendered (28 October) and the Turkish government asked for an armistice (30 October).

Menshikov, Aleksandr Sergeyevich, Prince (1787–1867)
By 1816 Menshikov was a **major-general** in the Russian army. His insistence (1853) that the Russian government be recognised as the protectors of the Orthodox Christians in the Ottoman Empire led to a breakdown in the negotiations between Russia and Turkey and to the beginning of the **Crimean War**. He was appointed supreme commander of the Russian forces, but after the defeat at the **Alma**, the failure to relieve **Sebastopol** (now Sevastopol), and the losses at **Inkerman** he was relieved of his command (1855). Later he was appointed military governor-general of Kronstadt.

Mercian Regiment
The **regiment** is due to be formed in 2007 by the amalgamation of the Staffordshire Regiment (Prince of Wales's), The **Cheshire Regiment** and the Worcestershire and Sherwood Foresters Regiment

Mersa-Matruh, battle of
(1942; *World War II*) The British 8th Army had retreated eastward from **Tobruk** and finally halted at the Egyptian base of Mersa Matruh. The British commander-in-chief, General Sir Claude **Auchinleck**, placed the X Corps in the town on the coast and the XIII Corps 10 miles inland. The German Afrika Korps, commanded by Field Marshal Erwin **Rommel**, cut through between these two forces (26 June) capturing 6,000 men and 40 tanks. The British fell back to **El Alamein**.

mess dress
Originally a more comfortable dress than the regulation uniform, introduced for wear in the mess and at dinner. The fashion began in India at the beginning of the 19th century and spread gradually to home-based units. In the modern army mess dress is more formal (and may be less comfortable) than ordinary working uniforms and is only worn on celebratory occasions.

Messines, battle of
(1917; *World War I*) The main attacks planned for 1917 by the British **commander-in-chief** in France, Field Marshal Sir Douglas **Haig**, were to be from the **Ypres** salient. A preliminary stage was the taking of Messines Ridge in the south. Hundreds of tons of explosive were planted in mines dug under the German trenches and the assault began (7 June) when this explosive was detonated. The 2nd Army, commanded by General Sir Herbert **Plumer**, moved to take the Ridge followed by the 5th Army, commanded by General Hubert **Gough**, and the French 1st Army. The Germans fell back but they later counter-attacked. This limited the British advance which was called off (14 June).

Metford rifle *See* rifle

Methuen, Paul Sanford (1845–1932)
Methuen was born in Wiltshire, the son of the 2nd Baron Methuen. He was educated at Eton and by 1876 was **lieutenant-colonel** in the Scots Fusilier Guards (**Scots Guards**). He held several staff appointments, saw active service in the **Ashanti War** (1873–74) and was on the staff of Sir Garnet **Wolseley** in Egypt (1882) having been promoted to **brevet colonel** (1881). Methuen then commanded Methuen's Horse in Bechuanaland (now Botswana) (1884). He was made temporary **major-general** (1888) and substantive colonel in the same year. He inherited the title (1891) and commanded the home district, i.e. troops based in the UK, (1892–97). In 1897 he was promoted to **lieutenant-general** (1898) and given command of the 1st Division in South Africa. In

his attempt to relieve **Kimberley** his attack over the **Modder river** succeeded but his failure at **Magersfontein** was criticised at home. His **commander-in-chief**, Lord **Roberts**, supported Methuen and he remained in South Africa until 1902. Methuen was appointed colonel of the Scots Guards, promoted to **general** and made commander of the IV Army Corps (1904). He was appointed commander-in-chief in South Africa (1908) and made governor and commander-in-chief of Natal (1910). He was promoted to **field marshal** (1911) and made governor of Malta (1915–19) and Constable of the Tower of London (1919).

Methven, battle of
(1306; *English-Scottish Wars*) After the execution of William Wallace (1305), Robert the Bruce was crowned Robert I of Scotland. This angered Edward I of England who sent an army into Perthshire where it met the Scots at Methven. The Scots were routed (19 June) and Robert fled to Rathlin Island only to resume the war in the next year.

Miani, battle of *See* **Meanee, battle of**

Middlesex Regiment
The Middlesex Regiment (Duke of Cambridge's Own) was formed (1881) by the amalgamation of the 57th (**West Middlesex**) Regiment and the 77th (**East Middlesex**) Regiment (Duke of Cambridge's Own). A further amalgamation in 1966 saw the **regiment** merged into the **Queen's Regiment**.

Military Cross
An award instituted (1914) for officers below the rank of **major** and for **warrant officers** to mark gallant and distinguished services in action. (Officers of the rank of major and above were awarded the **Distinguished Service Order**.) It was extended to majors in 1931 and to all other ranks in 1993, replacing the **Military Medal**.
Abbreviation **MC**

Military Medal
An award instituted (1916) for **NCOs** and **privates** in the Army to mark acts of bravery in the field. Later in **World War I** members of all the armed forces, including women, became eligible to receive it. It was discontinued in 1993 when the **Military Cross** became available to all ranks.
Abbreviation **MM**

Military Provost Staff Corps
The **corps** that ran military prisons for most of the 20th century. It was formed (1901) as the **Military Prison Staff Corps** and was re-named in 1906. In 1992 it was absorbed into the Provost Branch of the **Adjutant General's Corps** as the **Military Provost Staff**.

militia
There had been an obligation since medieval times on men to take up arms to defend the realm. With the inauguration of the first **standing army** under Charles II, a series of statutes (1661–63) established a regular militia of part-time soldiers commanded by the Lord Lieutenant of each county, to serve within England during emergencies. Property owners were required to provide men and equipment, although an individual thus selected would be excused if he could produce a substitute to serve in his place. In 1757 the Militia Act reorganised this system, with a quota of men required to serve being fixed for each county; selection was by ballot, although substitutes were still allowed. Provision was also made for annual training. The Act was soon amended (1758) to allow volunteers to count towards the quota. In 1852 the element of compulsion was reduced and the militia became a mainly voluntary service. In 1881 the militia battalions became the 3rd and 4th battalions of the appropriate county regiment of the regular army; and in 1908 the militia as such disappeared and became the Territorial Force, later known as the **Territorial Army** (1921).
See also **Cardwell reforms; reforms after the Boer War; volunteers**
[From Latin, 'military service, body of soldiers', from *milit-*, stem of *miles* 'soldier']

Minden, battle of

(1759; *Seven Years' War*) After their victory at Bergen (April 1759), 60,000 French troops marched towards Hanover. To prevent this advance Ferdinand, Duke of Brunswick, decided to hold Minden on the Weser river with 45,000 troops including six British **infantry regiment** and a **cavalry** detachment under General Lord George **Sackville**. The French attacked (1 August) with cavalry, but due to a misunderstanding the British infantry advanced towards them. This surprised the French who retreated and Brunswick ordered a final cavalry charge. Sackville refused to obey (for which he was court-martialled later) allowing the French to withdraw. They had lost 7,000 men and 43 guns, and the last French threat to Hanover had been removed. The Allies lost 3,000 men, half of whom were British infantry.

See also **King's Own Royal Regiment (Lancaster)**; **King's Own Scottish Borderers**; **Yorkshire West Riding (2nd) Light Infantry Regiment**

mine

In siege warfare from the earliest times mines, broadly similar to the mines used for extracting underground minerals, were dug under enemy defences, and by the defenders in attempts to disrupt the attackers' mining operations. The purpose of offensive mining was to cause the defences to collapse which, once gunpowder was available, could readily be done by placing a charge in the mine and detonating it. Mines of this sort were commonly used in sieges in the 18th century and again in **World War I**, notably at **Messines**. Digging mines was obviously time-consuming and they were made obsolete by the more mobile forms of war that prevailed later in the 20th century. In **World War II** and since, a mine was a container of explosive buried just below the surface of the ground and detonated by the weight of a vehicle or person passing over it, or possibly by remote control. A primitive form of mine was used to a limited extent during World War I but they were not used extensively until World War II when large areas in the battlefields of Russia, North Africa and elsewhere were mined. There are two main types of mine, larger anti-tank mines and smaller anti-personnel mines. Originally mine casings were made of metal, but modern mines use other materials to make detection by electronic mine detectors more difficult.

[Directly or via Old French from assumed Vulgar Latin *mina*]

minefield

An area in which **mines** are buried

Minorca, battle of

(1781–82; *American War of Independence*) During the Spanish-French siege of Gibraltar a fleet sailed from Cadiz (22 July 1781) with 14,000 troops to capture the British-held island of Minorca. They overran the island quickly, apart from the naval base of Port Mahon. Here the British General James **Murray**, with fewer than 1,000 men, withstood a siege for six months before surrendering (5 February 1782).

missile

A rocket-propelled projectile with a high explosive or nuclear warhead.

See also **rocket**

[From Latin *missilis*, from *mittere* 'to send']

MM *abbreviation of* **Military Medal**

Modder river, battle of

(1899; *Boer Wars*) In an attempt to relieve **Kimberley**, General Lord **Methuen** moved the 1st British Division into the Orange Free State. He encountered a Boer force of over 9,000 under General Piet Cronjé at the Modder river (28 November). After a fierce battle the Boers withdrew towards **Magersfontein**. Methuen followed, having lost 24 officers and 460 men.

Moltke, Helmuth Johannes Ludwig von (1848–1916)

By 1882 Moltke was **adjutant** to his uncle, victor of the Franco-Prussian War, who was chief of the general staff of the German Army. Moltke was promoted to quartermaster-general (1903) and chief of the general staff (1906). In the early weeks of **World War I** his poor planning and lack of control of the German forces led to their offensive being halted at the battle of the **Marne** (1914). **Falkenhayn** replaced him as **chief-of-staff** and he died a broken man.

Also known as **Moltke the Younger**

Monck, George (1608–70)

Monck was born in Devon and served in the Netherlands against the Spaniards (1629–38). He suppressed a rebellion in Ireland (1642–43) and at first fought for the Royalists during the **Civil War**. He was captured at Nantwich in Cheshire and imprisoned in the Tower of London (1644) for two years. Monck was made a **major-general** in the Parliamentarian army after the defeat of the king and was sent to Ireland to suppress the rebellion. He fought under **Cromwell** at the battle of **Dunbar** and remained in Scotland as **commander-in-chief**. He was appointed one of the three **generals** at sea during the First Dutch War. Monck then conducted another campaign against the Royalist rebels in the Highlands and remained in Scotland as governor. When the Rump Parliament was overthrown by Major-General John Lambert (1659), Monck refused to recognise the new military regime and led an army from Scotland to restore the Rump. This was then dissolved and a new Convention Parliament elected. This invited Charles II back to England as king. Monck played a major role in the Restoration, for which service he was created Duke of Albemarle and a Knight of the Garter.

Monckton, Robert (1726–82)

Monckton was commissioned in the 3rd (Earl of Dunmore's) Regiment of Guards (now the **Scots Guards**) and served in Flanders. He was in the king's guard at **Dettingen**. In 1744 he was commissioned **captain** in the 34th Foot (**Cumberland Regiment**). He was promoted to **major** (1747) and in 1751 to **lieutenant-colonel** in the 47th Foot (**Lancashire Regiment**). Monckton was elected MP for Pontefract (1751) but was sent to Nova Scotia (1752) and appointed lieutenant-governor of Annapolis Royal (1754), subsequently waging war on the French. He was second-in-command to **Wolfe** during the assault on **Quebec** after which he was appointed **colonel** of the 17th Foot (**Royal Leicestershire Regiment**). He then went to New York as governor and was promoted to **major-general** (1761). Monckton then commanded the expedition to **Martinique**. He returned to New York (1762) and then to Britain (1763) where he was appointed governor of Berwick-on-Tweed and Holy Island. He was promoted to **lieutenant-general** (1770), received the freedom of the city of Edinburgh (1771) and made governor of Portsmouth (1778). He was MP for Portsmouth from 1778 until his death.

See also **Beauséjour, battle of**

Monmouth, battle of

(1778; *American War of Independence*) The French joined the Americans in the war against Britain (1778) and the British commander, General Sir Henry **Clinton**, fearing a French naval attack on Philadelphia, withdrew from there (18 June) and moved across New Jersey. The American General George **Washington** broke out from his camp at Valley Forge and began to pursue the British. His advance guard of 6,400 men, commanded by General Charles Lee, caught up with the British rearguard, commanded by Lord **Cornwallis**, at Monmouth (28 June). Lee's attack failed, but the Americans, reinforced by Washington's 7,000 men, repulsed further British attacks. Clinton marched away to Sandy Hook and embarked his army (30 June) for New York. Lee was court-martialled for his mishandling of the assault.

Monmouth, Duke of (1649–85)

Monmouth was the illegitimate son of Charles II and, as a Protestant, looked upon by some as his potential successor. He was **captain** of the king's guard (1668) and a privy councillor (1670). He commanded the British troops during the Dutch War (1672–74) and was captain-general of all the armed forces (1678). Having defeated the Scottish Presbyterian rebels at **Bothwell Bridge**, Monmouth was banished (1679) by Charles II for fear that he would form a nucleus for rebellion against the Roman Catholic James, Charles' brother and heir. He returned soon afterwards and became involved in the Rye House Plot against both Charles and James. Although pardoned, he was banished and lived in the Netherlands. When Charles II died (1685) Monmouth landed at Lyme Regis (Dorset) and raised an army of local people that was defeated at the battle of **Sedgemoor**. Monmouth was captured and executed.

Born **James Scott**

Monmouthshire Light Infantry

The **regiment** was raised as Colonel Fowke's Regiment of Foot and numbered the 54th Foot. It changed its name with its **colonels** until 1748 when it was re-numbered the 43rd Foot. The name was subsequently changed to the 43rd Regiment of Foot (1751); 43rd (or Monmouthshire) Regiment of Foot (Light Infantry) and later (1803) to the 43rd (Monmouthshire Light Infantry) Regiment of Foot. It became part of the **Oxfordshire and Buckinghamshire Light Infantry** in 1881.

Monmouth's Rebellion *See* **Monmouth, Duke of**

Mons, battle of

(1914; *World War I*) The British II Corps, commanded by General Sir Horace **Smith-Dorrien**, confronted the German IV, III and IX Corps along the line of the Mons-Condé canal in Belgium (23 August). The German advance was checked and the II Corps withdrew to conform with the movements of the French 5th Army on the right. This was the first significant encounter between British and German forces during **World War I**. In these and other early battles of the war a substantial proportion of Britain's small but well-trained pre-war professional army was wiped out but in the process their marksmanship made a strong impression on the Germans.

Mons Officer Cadet School

A training centre for officer cadets (1947–72). **Conscription** meant that the post-World War II Army had a large number of short-term troops, which required a proportionately large number of junior officers. Many of these were also two-year conscripts or short service soldiers (serving three years), for whom the eighteen-month officer training course provided by the **Royal Military Academy Sandhurst** (*see* **Royal Military Academy**) (RMAS) was too long. Two officer cadet schools were established in 1947, at Mons Barracks in Aldershot and at **Eaton Hall** in Cheshire, to provide six-month courses that trained junior officers, while the RMAS provided the longer training necessary for future field officers and generals. Originally Mons only trained cadets for the **Royal Armoured Corps** and **Royal Artillery**, with all others going to Eaton Hall; however, Eaton Hall was closed when conscription ended in 1960 and Mons became the sole officer cadet school. It moved to New College, Sandhurst, in 1972 and merged with the RMAS later that year. Its popular six-month training course was retained and is now standard for all officer cadets.

Montcalm, Louis Joseph, Marquis de (1712–59)

Montcalm joined the French army when he was 12 years old and later fought in the War of the **Austrian Succession** (1740–48). He was captured at Piacenza (1746) but was exchanged (1747) and raised to the rank of **brigadier** commanding a **cavalry regiment**. He was promoted to **major-general** (1756) and sent to Canada as the French **commander-in-chief**. Initially he strengthened the French position but was gradually forced to abandon a succession of French forts and fell back on **Quebec**. He was killed, with **Wolfe**, during the British assault on the Heights of Abraham.

Monte Cassino *See* **Cassino, battle of**

Montevideo, battle of

(1807; *French Wars*) The city was taken (3 February) by an assault by 3,000 British troops, commanded by Sir Samuel **Auchmuty**, with the loss of 300 men. The 95th Rifle Corps (later the **Rifle Brigade**) played a notable part in this action.

Montgomery, Bernard Law (1887–1976)

Montgomery was the son of Bishop Montgomery and was educated at St Paul's School, London, and at Sandhurst. He was commissioned in the Royal Warwickshire Regiment (**Royal Warwickshire Fusiliers**) and served in **World War I** during which he was wounded three times, awarded the **DSO** and the French Croix de Guerre. He was selected for training at the **Staff College** at Camberley (1920) and was posted to Cork as **brigade major** of the 17th Infantry Brigade in the final stages of the Irish War of Independence. In 1926 he returned to the Staff College as an instructor. He compiled the army's official 'Infantry Training' manual (1929). He then commanded his own **regiment** in Jerusalem, Alexandria and Poona before being appointed chief instructor at Quetta (1934–37). Montgomery was then given command of the 8th Infantry **Division** in Palestine (1938) and as **major-general** commanded the 3rd Division at the outbreak of **World War II**. He took part in the evacuation of Dunquerque (**Dunkirk**) and took over command of the V Corps (1940). By the end of 1941 he was in command of the South-Eastern Army. He took over command of the 8th Army in North Africa (August 1942) and led it at the battle of **El Alamein** and during the drive across North Africa. He commanded the 8th Army during the advance through **Sicily** and Southern Italy and returned home to command the Allied ground forces during the invasion of **Normandy** (D-Day). Later in the campaign he mainly commanded the British and Canadian forces. After World War II Montgomery was **commander-in-chief** of the British forces of occupation in Germany (1945–46), Chief of the Imperial General Staff (1946–48) and deputy commander of the **NATO** forces (1951–58). He retired and devoted himself to writing and lecturing. He was created Viscount Montgomery of Alamein (1946) and a **KG** in the same year.

Montreal, battle of

(1760; *French and Indian War*) The British commander in North America, General Jeffrey **Amherst**, organised an offensive against Montreal, the last French stronghold in Canada. Amherst moved from Oswego with 10,000 men, General William **Haviland** brought 3,400 men up the Richelieu river while General James **Murray** moved 2,500 men up the St. Lawrence river. The French governor-general of Montreal, the Marquis de Vaudreuil-Cavagnal, surrendered (8 September). Soon all the French outposts, including Detroit (29 November), came under British-American control. By the Treaty of Paris (1763) the French ceded Canada to Britain.

Montrose, Marquis of (James Graham) (1621–50)

Graham inherited the earldom of Montrose from his father (1626). He signed the covenant in support of the Scottish Presbyterians, but was still a Royalist and consequently became the enemy of Archibald Campbell (Earl of Argyll) who led the anti-Royalist party in Scotland. He served with the Covenanter army that invaded England (1640) but was imprisoned by Argyll at Edinburgh during 1641. When the **Covenanters** invaded England in support of Parliament (1644), Charles I appointed Montrose **lieutenant-general** in Scotland and created him Marquess of Montrose and Earl of Kincardine. He raised an army in the Highlands (1644). His army won victories at Tippermuir, Aberdeen, Inverlochy, **Auldearn**, **Alford** and Kilsyth. Charles made him lieutenant-governor and captain-general of Scotland. With the defeat of Charles at **Naseby**, Montrose's force dissolved and he was defeated at **Philiphaugh** (September 1645). Montrose fled to France but returned to Scotland with a force of 1,200 men (March 1650). He was defeated at **Carbiesdale** (27 April 1650) and was hanged in Edinburgh (May 1650).

Moore, John (1761–1809)

Moore was born in Glasgow and was the stepson of the Duke of Argyll. He was elected to parliament (1784–90) and in 1793 obtained a commission in the army. He served in Corsica, the West Indies, Ireland, the Netherlands and Egypt. He commanded (1803) the training camp at Shorncliffe (Kent) and was **colonel** of the 52nd Foot (**Oxfordshire Regiment of Foot**). At Shorncliffe he pioneered the development of **light infantry** tactics, laying the groundwork for the conversion of various **infantry regiments** to light infantry status and preparing the way for the creation of the highly successful light brigades and later Light Division of the **Peninsular War**. As well as developing light infantry tactics Moore also insisted that his officers be properly trained, knowledgeable in their profession and interested in the welfare of their men; simple but important and far-reaching ideas. He also taught his men to act independently and not become over-reliant on merely responding to commands and drill movements. After Shorncliffe Moore then served in the Mediterranean command and in Sweden. In 1808 he took command of the British Army in Portugal and died of wounds received at the battle of **Corunna**.

See also **Craufurd, Robert**

Mordaunt, Charles *See* **Peterborough, Earl of**

Morshedabad, battle of
(1763; *British in India*) The Indian troops of the deposed Nawab of Bengal were entrenched near Morshedabad. They were attacked by an Anglo-Indian force commanded by Major Adams. The Nawab's forces were defeated and Morshedabad was occupied.

mortar
A short-ranged **artillery** piece with a short barrel and low muzzle velocity. Mortars fire projectiles in a high-arched trajectory. Very large mortars were used as siege weapons in the 17th and 18th centuries but with the development of more powerful **howitzers** in the 19th century these fell out of use. In **World War I** mortars were brought back into widespread service. These were of two categories: heavier weapons broadly similar to the earlier designs, and lighter **infantry** weapons capable of being carried and operated by a crew of two or three men. These lighter types were also used extensively in **World War II** and continue in service with modern armies. The mortars currently used by the British Army are the **L16A2 81 mm Mortar** and the **51 mm Light Mortar**.

[From French *mortier* 'bowl for mixing']

Mortimer's Cross, battle of
(1461; *Wars of the Roses*) After the Lancastrians had defeated the Yorkists at **Wakefield** they began to move on London to release the captive Henry VI. The Yorkists rallied to Edward (later Edward IV) in the west. The two forces met at Mortimer's Cross in Herefordshire (2 February). The Lancastrians were defeated and Owen Tudor, grandfather of the future Henry VII, was executed. Edward moved east to join the Earl of Warwick in preventing the Lancastrian advance on London.

Mudki, battle of
(1845; *Sikh Wars*) The British commander, General Sir Hugh **Gough**, was moving through the Punjab to contain the Sikh army. His force of 12,000 Anglo-Indian troops was attacked by some 30,000 Sikhs at Mudki (18 December). The Sikhs were defeated and lost some 20 guns. Gough's casualties were 870, including Sir Robert **Sale**, who was wounded and later died.

Multan, battle of
(1848; *Sikh Wars*) The city, which was defended by the Sikh leader Dewan Mulraj, was besieged by 1,500 British troops (July). The siege was raised (22 September) but was renewed (17 December) by General **Whish** with a force of 33,000 and 64 guns. The city surrendered (2 January 1849) and the Mulraj surrendered the citadel (22 January). The British lost 210 killed and 910 wounded. Prizes worth £5 million were taken.

Multiple Launch Rocket System *See* **rocket artillery**

Munden's Dragoons *See* **Hussars, 13th**

Munro, Hector (1726–1805)
Munro was appointed **ensign** in Lord Loudoun's Highlanders (1747) and probably fought at **Bergen-op-Zoom**. The **regiment** was disbanded; Munro was re-appointed

ensign in the 48th Foot (**Northamptonshire Regiment of Foot**) and was ultimately appointed junior **major** in the newly-formed 89th Foot (1759). The regiment went to India (1761). Most of the regiment came home (1765) and was disbanded but Munro stayed on in the service of the East India Company. He took men who had stayed on from the 89th and 96th Foot to Patna (13 August 1764) and stamped out a mutiny. He routed the Hindustanis at the battle of **Buxar**, saving Bengal. He was made **lieutenant-colonel** (1765) and returned home. He became a **brevet colonel** (1777) and returned to India where he took command of the army (1778). He captured Pondicherry from the French (1778) and was made a KB (1779). During a disastrous campaign in 1780, Munro was forced to fall back to Chingleput and then to St. Thomas Mount where Sir Eyre **Coote** took over command, with Munro as his second-in-command. Munro commanded the right **division** at the battle of **Porto Novo**. He returned home (1781) and was appointed **major-general** (1782) with the sinecure of barrack-master-general in north Britain. He was appointed colonel of the **Black Watch** (1787), **lieutenant-general** (1793) and **general** (1798).

Murray, Archibald James (1860–1945)

Murray attended the Royal Military College at Sandhurst and was **gazetted** (1879) to the 27th Regiment of Foot. He remained in the newly formed (1881) **Royal Inniskilling Fusiliers**. He served in Hong Kong, Singapore and the Cape where he was promoted (1888) to **captain**. He entered the **Staff College** (1897). In the Second **Boer War** he was staff intelligence officer in Natal and on the death of the **commander-in-chief** (Sir William Penn Symons) became **chief-of-staff**. He succeeded in extracting the British forces from Natal and brought them back to **Ladysmith**. Murray was made **brevet lieutenant-colonel** (1900). He commanded the 2nd **battalion** of his **regiment** in India (1901) but returned to South Africa (1902) and commanded an attack at Pilskop, where he was wounded and for which he was awarded the **DSO**. He was promoted to **major-general** (1910). On his return home he held several staff appointments until the beginning of **World War I**. He was appointed chief of the general staff to the **British Expeditionary Force** in France (1914) but returned home after a nervous breakdown. There were various staff changes and Murray was appointed to a command in Egypt (1916). He was in command during the advance into Palestine, laying a railway and water pipes (1917), but his failure to take **Gaza** led to his replacement by **Allenby**. He returned home and was appointed to the Aldershot command, which he held until 1919, when he was appointed **general**. He retired in 1922.

Murray, James (1719?–94)

Murray served with the 15th Foot (**East Yorkshire Regiment**) in the West Indies, Flanders and Brittany. He purchased a lieutenant-colonelcy in the 15th Foot in Ireland (1751) and commanded the **regiment** at Rockfort (1757). He took the regiment to America (1751) and was a **brigadier** under **Wolfe** at the capture of **Quebec**, where he was left in command. After repelling a French attack on Quebec with the aid of a naval bombardment, Murray embarked his much-depleted force for **Montreal**. He was appointed governor of Quebec (1760); promoted to **major-general** (1762) and made governor of Canada (1763). He returned home (1766) to face charges of maladministration, of which he was acquitted. He was promoted to **lieutenant-general** (1772) and governor of Minorca (1774). The French besieged **Minorca** (1781), the garrison of which consisted of a small number of old men, many of whom were suffering from diseases, especially scurvy. After the fall of Minorca, Murray was again accused of various illegalities (by his second-in-command, William Draper). He was acquitted. He was then accused by a Mr Sutherland of unreasonably suspending his appointment as judge in Minorca. Sutherland won the case but Murray's fine of £5,000 was paid out of public funds authorised by an act of Parliament. Murray was promoted to **general** (1783), **colonel** of the 21st Foot (**Royal Scots Fusiliers**) (1789) and was governor of Hull.

Musa Bagh, battle of

(1858; *Indian Mutiny*) A force of 7,000 mutineers was holding Musa Bagh, a fortress outside **Lucknow**. They were routed by a British force commanded by General Sir James **Outram**.

Musgrave, Thomas (1737–1812)

By 1776 Musgrave had been promoted to **lieutenant-colonel** in command of the 40th Foot (**Somersetshire (2nd) Regiment of Foot**) which he took to Philadelphia. The **regiment** played a prominent part in the battle of **Germantown** which they held until reinforcements arrived. In 1778 Musgrave went to St. Lucia but returned to be the last British commandant of New York. He was made a **brevet colonel** (1781) and returned home as **aide-de-camp** to the king. In 1787 Musgrave was appointed colonel of the newly formed **76th Foot** raised for service in India. He served on the staff in Madras (now Chennai) for several years and was promoted to **major-general** (1790). On his return home he became **lieutenant-general** of Tilbury Fort (1792) and was promoted to **general** (1802).

musket

A type of muzzle-loading firearm, the standard **infantry** weapon from the late 17th to the early–mid 19th century. It was developed in Spain from the **harquebus** during the 16th century. Early muskets were about 5.5 feet long and weighed about 20 pounds, firing a 2 ounce ball about 175 yards. They were mounted on a portable rest, handled by two people and were very inaccurate. They originally had **matchlock** firing mechanisms but were later **flintlock** and, by the early 19th century, percussion lock designs. The later flintlock muskets were lighter and were capable of being aimed accurately up to 80–100 yards. They had a calibre of 0.69–0.75 inch and could fire two or three rounds a minute under battle conditions. They were superseded by various types of **rifle** in the 19th century.

See also **Brown Bess; cartridge; harquebus; percussion cap**

[Via French *mousquet* from Italian *moschetto* 'crossbow bolt', from *mosca* 'fly (the insect)', from Latin *musca*]

mustard gas *See* gas

Mutiny Act (1689)

From medieval times parliament had control over taxation to finance the armed forces. With the establishment of a **standing army** after the restoration of Charles II and fears that such an army might be a tool of royal despotism, parliament was keen to assert similar control over military discipline. The Declaration of Rights of 1689 (see **Bill of Rights**) asserted that it was illegal for the king to maintain a peacetime standing army without the consent of parliament. The Mutiny Act followed (April) when a Scots **regiment** raised by William III for service in Holland mutinied at Ipswich. The act established a statutory basis for military law and military courts in time of peace. Initially it was passed for six months only, but was then passed annually (under slightly varying titles later) until 1955 when it was replaced by the Armed Forces Act, which must be passed every five years. The Mutiny Act did not initially cover military discipline or command in time of war; these were subject to the Articles of War which were established by royal prerogative until 1803, when they were also given a statutory basis.

See also **War Office Act**

muzzle

The front open end of the **barrel** of a gun.

See also **breech**

muzzle-loading

A gun that is loaded by ramming an explosive charge and a projectile down the muzzle

See also **breech-loading**

MVO *See* **Royal Victorian Order**

Mysore Wars (1767–69, 1780–84, 1790–92, 1799)

About 1761, **Haidar Ali** made himself ruler of Mysore. In 1766 the East India Company allied itself with the Nizam of Hyderabad against Haidar Ali. The Nizam abandoned the war and in 1769 Haidar Ali made peace with the British. In 1780 Haidar Ali joined with the Marathas and devastated the Carnatic. With the aid of help from Calcutta (now Kolkata) and with the death of Haidar Ali, the British gained dominance and peace was made with **Tipu Sahib**, Haidar Ali's son. The third war began when the Governor-General Lord **Cornwallis** refused to recognise Tipu as one of the Company's allies. Tipu was defeated at **Seringapatam** (1792) and forced to cede half his territory. The fourth war broke out when Tipu was believed to be receiving help from the French. The British captured Seringapatam (1799). Tipu was killed during the battle.

Myton, battle of

(1319; *English-Scottish Wars*) The English King Edward II laid siege to the Scottish-held Berwick-upon-Tweed. The Scottish King Robert I, the Bruce, sent a diversionary force under James Douglas to raid into Yorkshire. This force met the English at Myton (20 September) and defeated them, thus establishing a threat to Edward's rear. He abandoned the siege of Berwick.

N

Najera, battle of

(1367; *Hundred Years' War*) Edward the Black Prince was created Prince of Aquitaine by his father, King Edward III, in 1362 and took up his rule there the following year. In 1366 King Pedro I ('the Cruel') of Castile was ousted with French assistance by his half-brother, Henry of Trastamara, and appealed to Prince Edward for help. The Prince, accompanied by his brother John of Gaunt, led an Anglo-Gascon army of some 6,000 men across the Pyrenees in 1367 and confronted the Franco-Spanish army at Najera, where Henry had created a strong defensive position. Against the advice of his French allies, Henry elected to fight a pitched battle. With the river Najerilla at his rear, his forces were disrupted by the English **longbows** and outflanked by the cavalry; they broke and fled, many being drowned in the river. Although the battle was a crushing victory for Pedro over his rival and for the English over the French, the long-term consequences were less favourable. Pedro and Edward immediately argued over Pedro's failure to pay the money he had promised Edward for his aid. Faced with financial troubles and rebellion and, sick from a disease (probably dropsy) that he had contracted in Spain, Edward's rule in Aquitaine collapsed and he returned to England in 1370. Meanwhile, further French aid allowed Henry to defeat and kill Pedro in 1369, becoming King Henry II of Castile. Najera was the last important English victory over the French until **Agincourt**.

Namur, battle of

1. (1692; *War of the Grand Alliance*) The town of Namur at the junction of the Sambre and Meuse rivers was the key to the control of the Spanish Netherlands (now Belgium). The town was held by the Dutch, but after a 36-day siege it fell to the French (5 June 1692).

2. (1695; *War of the Grand Alliance*) William III, who was in command of the Alliance forces, laid siege to Namur, which the French commander, the Duc de Villeroi, finally surrendered (1 September)

Napier, Charles James (1782–1853)

Napier was commissioned in the 4th Foot (**King's Own Royal Regiment (Lancaster)**) and served with it in Ireland during the rebellion (1803). By 1806 he was a **major** in the Cape Colonial Corps and then served with Sir John **Moore** in Spain. He was wounded at La Coruña (**Corunna**) and taken prisoner, but was exchanged (1810) and returned to the 50th Foot (**Queen's Own Regiment**). He was wounded again and returned home (1811) when he was promoted to **lieutenant-colonel**. Napier then served in Bermuda and Nova Scotia, and on returning home attended the military college at Farnham until 1817. In 1821 he served in Greece as resident in Cephalonia where he carried out many public works such as road-building. He retired from Greece (1830) largely due to political intrigues. His wife died (1833) and he devoted himself to writing. In 1839 he was in command of the troops in the north where there was Chartist rioting, which he dealt with humanely. In August 1841 he was given command in Sind, India, and won the battle of **Meanee**. Following his victory in this campaign he is reputed to have reported home using the single Latin word *peccavi* ('I have sinned'). As administrator in Sind he was involved in acrimonious correspondence with the home government, and having taken part in the First **Sikh War**, resigned as governor of Sind and returned home. He returned to India (1849) to find the Sikh problem solved but then took some allegedly irregular actions in quelling a mutiny in the army. Napier resigned and returned home (1850).

Napier, Robert (1810–90)

Napier was the son of a British artillery officer stationed in Ceylon (now Sri Lanka). He joined the Bengal Engineers (1826). He was stationed in Calcutta (now Kolkata) (1828) and carried out various engineering works until the beginning of the First **Sikh War**, when he was commanding officer of the engineers at **Mudki**, **Sobraon** and **Ferozeshah**, where he was wounded (1846). He was then consultant engineer to the resident at Lahore. He played a prominent part in the Second Sikh War and then worked as a civil engineer in the Punjab (1849–51). He was recalled to military service (1852–53). Napier went on leave (1856) and returned to India as **lieutenant-colonel** at the beginning of the Mutiny (1857). He was chief engineer of the force that relieved **Lucknow**, and was promoted to **brigadier-general** (1858) and put in command of the final operations in the area. He then took part in the expedition to China (1860) and on his return to India (1861) was promoted to **major-general**. He served on the governor-general's council (1861–65). He commanded the Bombay Army (1865), was promoted to **lieutenant-general** (1867) and commanded the expedition to **Abyssinia** (now Ethiopia) where he was victorious at the battle of **Magdala**. He was created Baron Napier of Magdala (1868) and served as **commander-in-chief** in India (1870–76). Napier was appointed governor of Gibraltar (1876–82), promoted to **field marshal** (1883) and was appointed constable of the Tower (of London) (1887).

Napier's Regiment of Foot *See* Yorkshire West Riding (2nd) Light Infantry Regiment

Napoleon Bonaparte (1769–1821)

Napoleon was born at Ajaccio in Corsica and trained at the military schools in Brienne (1779) and Paris (1784). He commanded the **artillery** of the Revolutionary army at the siege of Toulon (1793) and was promoted to **brigadier-general**. He then fought and defeated the Piedmontese and Austrians in Italy (1796–9). Napoleon captured Malta (1798) and defeated the Turks in Egypt, but when the French fleet was defeated by Nelson at the battle of the Nile he returned to France. He assumed power as First Consul, forming a military dictatorship. He defeated the Austrians at Marengo and consolidated French power by the Concordat with Rome and the Peace of Amiens with Britain (1802), which lasted only until 1803. He assumed the title of emperor (1804) and renewed the war with Austria and Russia (1805). His defeat at sea at Trafalgar (1805) caused Napoleon to abandon plans to invade Britain but his armies were victorious against Austria and Russia at Ulm and Austerlitz (1805). After Prussia and Russia were defeated (1806–07) he controlled all continental Europe except Spain and Portugal which he invaded, beginning the **Peninsular War** (1808–14). Believing Russia to be forming an alliance with Britain, he invaded Russia (1812). His stretched lines of communication and the severe Russian winter forced Napoleon into a disastrous retreat and he was heavily defeated at the battle of Leipzig (1813) and, when France was invaded (1814), forced to abdicate. He was exiled to Elba. He returned to France to replace the unpopular Bourbon monarchy (1815). His so-called Hundred Days of rule ended with his defeat at **Waterloo**. He abdicated and surrendered to the British. He was exiled to St. Helena where he died.

Napoleonic Wars *See* French Wars

Naseby, battle of

(1645; *Civil War*) In the spring of 1645 Charles I moved from Oxford and sacked Leicester. The Parliamentarian **New Model Army** of 14,000 men led by **Fairfax** and **Cromwell** moved to intercept the Royalists and met them at Naseby, Northants (14 June). The Royalist **cavalry**, commanded by Prince **Rupert**, broke the Parliamentarian left but pursued too far, exposing the rest of the Royalist army, which was defeated. Some 3,500 Royalist **infantry** were killed or captured and the baggage and **artillery** lost. Charles escaped with Rupert's cavalry. This was the last major battle of the first phase of the Civil War.

national service *See* conscription

NATO
A political, military and financial alliance established by the North Atlantic Treaty (4 April 1949) between the USA, Canada and several European countries, including the UK; although no specific enemy was named, its purpose was to counter any potential aggression by the then USSR. In this it succeeded without the need to go to war, ensuring that the Cold War in Europe remained a military standoff and did not develop into conflict. Although the original perceived threat to its members passed with the dissolution of the USSR (1991), NATO's fundamental role – to safeguard the freedom and security of its member countries by political and military means – is unchanged. Indeed, the alliance expanded in the 1990s and the 2000s to incorporate many former satellite states of the USSR. It performs an increasing **peacekeeping** and crisis management role, under which remit it engaged in its first military conflicts in the 1990s, in particular wresting control of **Kosovo** from Serbia on behalf of the United Nations (1999). In 2003 it took over control of international forces in **Afghanistan**.
Full form **North Atlantic Treaty Organisation**

NCO *abbreviation of* **non-commissioned officer**

Negapatam, battle of (1781)
A British force of 4,000, commanded by Colonel Braithwaite, besieged a garrison of 8,000 Dutch and Mysore troops at Negapatam (21 October). The garrison surrendered (3 November), after offering little resistance.

Neuve-Chapelle, battle of
(1915; *World War I*) The British commander, Sir John **French**, launched an **artillery** bombardment on German-held Neuve-Chapelle (10 March) followed by an assault by the British 1st Army commanded by General Sir Douglas **Haig**. The initial assault succeeded but was held (13 March) by 16,000 German reserves who were rushed to the front before the key ridge east of Neuve-Chapelle could be taken. The 1st Army suffered some 13,000 casualties.

Neville's Cross, battle of
(1346; *English-Scottish Wars*) King David II of Scotland returned from exile and invaded England, penetrating as far as County Durham. He was challenged at Neville's Cross by an English force led by Henry Percy and Ralph Neville. The Scots were defeated (17 October) and David was taken prisoner.

Newburn, battle of
(1640; *Bishops' Wars*) The Scots rejected the Anglican episcopacy imposed by Charles I. After a year of temporising the Scots sent an army, commanded by Alexander Leslie, later Lord Leven, across the Tweed into Northumberland. They were met by an English force commanded by William Seymour, Duke of Somerset, at Newburn (28 August). The Royalist army was routed by an opening cannonade and Charles, to avoid further trouble, agreed to subsidise the Scottish troops until a final settlement could be agreed.

Newbury, battle of
1. (1643; *Civil War*) During August–September Charles I laid siege to Gloucester which was relieved by the Parliamentarian Robert Devereux, 3rd Earl of Essex. Charles withdrew and advanced on London. Essex followed rapidly and the two forces converged at Newbury (20 September). The battle was indecisive but Charles withdrew to Oxford.
2. (1644; *Civil War*) Following victories over the Earl of Essex in Cornwall, Charles turned to march on London. He met a combined Parliamentarian force at Newbury (27 October) but failed to break through. Although the battle was indecisive Charles again withdrew to Oxford. The lack of a positive result to the battle led Parliament to replace

Essex and Manchester as leaders of the army. The **New Model Army** led by Sir Thomas **Fairfax** and Oliver **Cromwell** would now come to the fore.

Newcastle, Earl of (1592–1676)
The nephew of the 1st Earl of Devonshire, William Cavendish was educated at St. John's College, Cambridge. He was created Earl of Newcastle by Charles I and appointed governor to the future Charles II. During the **Civil War** he commanded all the Royalist forces north of the Trent, which gave him great power. After the battle of **Marston Moor** he lived on the Continent until the Restoration. He was created Duke of Newcastle in 1655. He also wrote poems and plays.
Also known as **Cavendish, William**; *See also* **Adwalton Moor, battle of**

New Model Army
The first English **standing army** formed (1645) by Oliver **Cromwell** during the **Civil War**. It was a properly disciplined and trained force, and could be kept as such because it was regularly paid. As well as its formidable military prowess it became an important political force throughout the remainder of the Civil War. The New Model Army was disbanded (1660) by Charles II, except for a few **regiments**.
See also **Coldstream Guards**

New Orleans, battle of
(1815; *War of 1812*) A British force of 7,500 troops, commanded by General Sir Edward Pakenham, landed from some 50 ships in Lake Borgne, east of New Orleans (13 December 1814). This force was met by some 5,000 American troops, whom their commander, General Andrew Jackson, had rushed from Baton Rouge. The Americans built a barricade along the dry Rodriguez canal which was flanked by cypress swamps and the Mississippi river thus forcing the British to make a frontal assault (8 January). During the assault the British lost 2,036 men; Pakenham was killed and the British retreated. The Americans lost only eight killed and 13 wounded. The war itself had been concluded before the battle (this news was still en route to America) by the Peace of Ghent (24 December 1814), but the battle did much to enhance Jackson's reputation.

Ney, Michel (1769–1815)
Ney was born at Saarlouis in France. He became a **general** of **division** (1799) and a marshal of the empire. He was created Duke of Elchingen (1805) and fought at Jena, Eylau and Friedland. He served in the **Peninsular War** from 1808, including at **Talavera**, but left Spain in 1811 following a quarrel with Marshal Masséna. He was the hero of the French retreat from Russia in 1812–13. When Napoleon abdicated Ney served briefly under the Bourbons, but when Napoleon returned Ney rejoined him and was Napoleon's principal subordinate at **Waterloo**. When Napoleon was defeated he was condemned for high treason and shot in Paris.

Niagara, battle of
(1759; *French and Indian War*) The French-held fort was besieged (June) by a force of 2,500 British and 900 Indians commanded by General John **Prideaux**. Prideaux was killed by the premature explosion of a shell and Sir William **Johnson** took command. An attempt to relieve the fort (24 July) was repulsed and the fort surrendered.

Nicholson, John (1821–57)
Nicholson was born in Dublin and became a cadet in the Bengal Army (1839). He held political appointments in Kashmir and the Punjab and took part in the Second **Sikh War**. He was promoted to **brigadier-general** (1857) and led the force that relieved **Delhi** during the **Indian Mutiny**. He was wounded during the assault on the Kashmir Gate and died shortly afterwards.

night vision
Until recently the operations of an army were limited when darkness fell. Nighttime operations that involved the use of torches and searchlights would make an attacking force visible for any counter-attack. This led to the development, mainly after **World War II**, of optical instruments that were sensitive to infrared light. Later developments

include instruments that are sensitive to the heat generated by individual bodies or machinery (see **thermal imager**), that detect ultraviolet light, or use **image intensifiers** to create useful images out of tiny amounts of visible light or near-infrared light. Such systems have been fitted to military vehicles and are used by individuals in the form of **night vision goggles**, binoculars or rifle sights.

nitrocellulose

An explosive manufactured by treating cellulose with concentrated nitric acid. It was discovered (1838) by T.J. Pelouse who discovered that cotton (cellulose) dipped into concentrated nitric acid was explosive (guncotton). It was unsuccessfully used as an ingredient of gunpowder (1860s) but the manufacturing process was modified and it was used as a propellant for ammunition by the 1870s, replacing the traditional **black powder** because it was more powerful and 'smokeless' (i.e. it generated far less smoke which could obscure vision and give a firing unit's location away to the enemy). Wood pulp is now used as the source of cellulose for its manufacture.
See also **cordite**

Nive, battle of

(1813; *Peninsular War*) A British and Portuguese force of 14,000, commanded by **Wellington**, crossed the Nive river (10 December) and took up a defensive position near the village of St. Pierre. They were attacked (13 December) by 35,000 French commanded by Marshal **Soult**. The attack was repulsed, the French losing 10,000 men and the British 5,019 killed and wounded.

Nivelle, battle of

(1813; *Peninsular War*) A French force, commanded by Marshal **Soult**, was driven from a strong position and forced to retreat behind the Nivelle river by the British, led by **Wellington** (10 November). The French lost 4,265, including 1,200 prisoners, and 51 guns. The British lost 2,694 killed and wounded.

Nivelle, Robert Georges (1856–1924)

Nivelle was born in Tulle (France) and graduated from the Ecole Polytechnique (1878). He served as an **artillery** officer in Indochina, Algeria and China and was made **general** of **brigade** at the beginning of **World War I**. He commanded the III Corps (1915) and succeeded **Pétain** as commander of the 2nd Army at **Verdun** (1916) where his use of creeping **artillery** barrages regained the ground occupied by the Germans over the previous six months. He succeeded **Joffre** as **commander-in-chief** of the French armies (December 1916) and was given nominal command of the British armies in France in 1917 when Prime Minister Lloyd George wished to limit **Haig's** powers. The failure of his methods on the Aisne front (April 1917) and the consequent large number of French casualties (120,000) led to mutinies in the French armies. Nivelle was replaced by **Pétain** as commander-in-chief and was transferred to North Africa (1917).
See also **Arras, battle of**

Nixon, John Eccles (1857–1921)

Nixon was commissioned in the 75th Foot (**Stirlingshire Regiment**) (1875) and then served with the 18th Bengal Cavalry in India, finally leaving the **regiment** (1901) as **brigadier-general**. During this time he served in South Africa (1901), commanding a **cavalry** column in the Transvaal. He then returned to India, finally being promoted to **general** (1914) and commander of the Northern Army (1915). In 1915 (April) he was given command of the Indian forces at Basra (Mesopotamia, now Iraq), gaining control of the area by 3 October 1915. He then began to advance on Baghdad, but his force, directly commanded by **Townshend**, was defeated at **Ctesiphon** and **Kut-al-Imara**. Nixon was summoned home to explain the shortcomings of the Mesopotamian campaign (which were due largely to the failure of the government to supply water transport) and was finally (1918) acquitted of any misconduct.

Noailles, Adrien Maurice, 3rd Duke of (1678–1766)

He served in most of the important wars during the early part of the reign of Louis XV in Italy and Germany. He was made a **marshal** (1734). His last command was when he was beaten by the British at **Dettingen**.

no-man's land

The area of ground between two opposing forces. The term was applied particularly to the area between the German and Allied trenches on the **Western Front** during **World War I**.

noncombatant

A person who is present at the scene of fighting but who takes no part in it, e.g. **Red Cross** members or stretcher bearers. In former times **buglers** and **drummers** were also considered to be noncombatants.

non-commissioned officer

An officer who has not received a **commission** from the sovereign and is below the rank of a commissioned officer. A soldier will probably have been promoted to this rank through merit and experience from the most junior rank, which is **private** in most cases, to become one of the various grades of **corporal** or **sergeant**, or the equivalent in arms or **corps** which use other terms for these grades. NCOs are normally appointed within the **regiment** or equivalent body to which they belong by the authority of the commander of that unit, and traditionally they can also lose their rank by the same officer's authority, although in the modern army examinations and other procedures have made the process more formalised. This contrasts with officers and **warrant officers**, who are more senior than NCOs and whose status is established by a **commission** or a warrant from the monarch or another central body.
Abbreviation **NCO**

Norfolk Regiment *See* Royal Norfolk Regiment

Norman conquest of England

After the **battle of Hastings**, William moved to secure the lands around London, rather than attack the city directly. The major Anglo-Saxon nobles surrendered to him at Berkhamstead, and William entered London to be crowned at Westminster Abbey on Christmas Day 1066. After his coronation there were several unsuccessful revolts, the chief being in Northumbria (1069–70). These were savagely repressed and William established his control of the countryside by building many castles controlled by his countrymen.

Normandy

(1944; *World War II*) By May 1944 a combined US-British force of 800,000 combat troops (47 **divisions**) was stationed in Britain ready to invade Europe. It was commanded by the US General Dwight **Eisenhower** with the British General Sir Bernard **Montgomery** in command of the ground forces for the channel crossing. The invasion, known as Operation Overlord, took place (6 June, D-Day) on the Normandy coast between Caen and the Cherbourg peninsula. From east to west there were five **infantry** assaults – Sword (British 3rd Division), Juno (Canadian 3rd Division), Gold (British 5th), Omaha (US 1st and part of the 29th) and Utah (US 4th). The assault was supported by previous airborne landings (5 June) by the 6th Airborne (British) to the east and the 82nd and 101st Airborne (US) in the west. There was a massive assault on the German coastal defences by 5,800 bombers and 4,900 fighters. The German force consisted of the 7th Army (commanded by General Friedrich Dollmann, and part of Army Group B, commanded by Field Marshal **Rommel**, with the overall commander being Field Marshal Gerd von **Rundstedt**) with 36 infantry and 6 **tank** divisions. By 12 June the beachheads had linked up forming a front some 80 miles long and 10 miles deep, enabling reinforcements to be landed. By 18 June the Americans from Utah had crossed the base of the Cherbourg peninsula and they had occupied Cherbourg by 27 June. By 18 July Saint Lô had fallen to the Americans. Meanwhile the British were held near **Caen**, finally taking the town and breaking out by 20 July. By 24 July the Allied forces were poised for a major breakthrough. So far the invasion had cost the Allies 122,000 casualties and the Germans 117,000. During the assault the 7th Army commander, Dollmann, was killed (28 June), and SS-General Paul Hausser took his place. Rundstedt was relieved of command (3 July) and replaced by Field Marshal Günther von Kluge.

See also **Falaise Gap, battle of**

Northampton, battle of

1. (1264; *Barons' Wars*) Northampton castle was held for the barons by Simon, the son of the rebel leader Simon de Montfort. Henry III and Prince Edward (later Edward I) led a royalist force from Oxford and attacked the castle (6 April). The castle surrendered (7 April) before Simon's father could bring a relief force from London. Simon was taken prisoner and Simon de Montfort turned to lay siege to Rochester castle.

2. (1460; *Wars of the Roses*) Richard Neville (Earl of Warwick and leader of the Yorkists) landed at Sandwich (June) and the Lancastrians (Henry VI) prepared to face the Yorkists at Northampton. Before the Lancastrians had completed their defences, Warwick attacked (10 July). The Lancastrian Lord Grey of Ruthin, later Earl of Kent, changed sides and assisted the Yorkists. The Lancastrians were defeated; the Duke of Buckingham was killed, along with many Lancastrian nobles, and Henry VI was captured and came under Yorkist control.

Northamptonshire Regiment

The **regiment** was formed by the amalgamation of the 48th **Northamptonshire Regiment of Foot** and the 58th **Rutlandshire Regiment**. The 1st Battalion of the regiment was transported by air from Ismailia in Egypt to Iraq (1932). This was one of the earliest times that a significant number of troops had been transported by air. In 1960 it amalgamated with The Royal Lincolnshire Regiment to form the 2nd East Anglian Regiment (Duchess of Gloucester's Own Royal Lincolnshire and Northamptonshire).

Northamptonshire Regiment of Foot

The **regiment** was raised (1741) as the 59th Regiment of Foot, also called Colonel Cholmondeley's Regiment of Foot. The name changed with the **colonel** until 1751, but the number was changed in 1748 to the 48th Regiment of Foot. In 1782 it was styled the 48th (or the Northamptonshire) Regiment of Foot.

See also **Northamptonshire Regiment**

North Atlantic Treaty Organisation *full form of* NATO

North British Fusiliers

The term 'North British' was used instead of 'Scots' in the official titles of various **regiments** in the late 18th and early 19th centuries, including the Royal North British Fusiliers and the Royal North British Dragoons (**Royal Scots Greys**).

See also **Royal Scots Fusiliers**

Northern Ireland

Since the partition of Ireland (1922) into the Irish Free State (now the Republic of Ireland) and Northern Ireland, there has been constant agitation to re-unite the predominantly Protestant North with the predominantly Roman Catholic South to form a united Ireland. The main agitation for this reunion has come from the paramilitary **Irish Republican Army** (IRA) and its political wing, Sinn Fein. Originating in the early 20th century in the struggle for Irish independence, the IRA maintained a continuous existence thereafter, but its levels of activity varied and by the 1960s it was widely regarded as moribund. However, a campaign for Catholic civil rights in Northern Ireland (1968), the consequent inter-communal violence, and the deployment of the British Army in a **peacekeeping** role (1969) caused a revival. In 1969 a faction known as the **Provisional IRA** broke away and over the next 25 years waged a terrorist campaign aimed at driving the British out of Northern Ireland. In response, dormant Protestant 'Loyalist' paramilitary groups again became active. The British military presence was a natural IRA target, and a primary strand of the so-called period of **The Troubles** was therefore a terrorist–counter-terrorist conflict between the IRA and the British Army. Over 3,500 people were killed in the The Troubles, including almost 500 British soldiers. Violence declined in the 1990s as the IRA began to seek a political solution, and the Good Friday Agreement (1998) established a framework for peaceful power-sharing. Although this agreement's implementation has been fraught with difficulties, violence has not resumed and the British military presence has been considerably reduced. In 2005 the IRA declared that its 'war' was over and decommissioned its remaining weapons.

See also **Special Air Service Regiment; peacekeeping**

North Gloucestershire Regiment

The **regiment** was raised (1694) as Colonel Gibson's Regiment of Foot. It changed its name with its **colonels** until 1742 when it became the 28th Regiment of Foot. The title changed (1782) to the 28th (or North Gloucestershire) Regiment of Foot. Its members wore a number '28' badge at the back of the headdress to commemorate its back-to-back stand at the battle of **Alexandria** (1801). This was later replaced by a small sphinx. In 1881 it merged with the 61st to become the **Gloucestershire Regiment**.

North Hampshire Regiment of Foot

The **regiment** was raised (1702) as Colonel Meredith's Regiment of Foot. The name changed with the **colonels** until 1751 when it became the 37th Regiment of Foot. The name was further changed (1782) to the 37th (or North Hampshire) Regiment of Foot. In 1881 it merged with the 67th to become the Hampshire Regiment (later the **Royal Hampshire Regiment**).

North Lancashire Regiment *See* **Loyal Regiment**

North Staffordshire Regiment

The **regiment** was formed (1881) by the amalgamation of the 64th (**2nd Staffordshire**) Regiment of Foot with the 98th (**Prince of Wales's**) Regiment of Foot. It was originally called the Prince of Wales's (North Staffordshire Regiment), but this was changed (1921) to the North Staffordshire Regiment (Prince of Wales's). In a reorganisation in 1959 it became part of the **Staffordshire Regiment (Prince of Wales's)**.

Northumberland Fusiliers *See* **Royal Northumberland Fusiliers**

North-West Africa

(1942; *World War II*) Concurrent with the British advance from **El Alamein** an Anglo-American force of 107,000 men, under the command of the US General Dwight **Eisenhower**, landed (8 November) in north-west Africa (Operation Torch). The landings took place at Casablanca, Oran and Algiers and were initially opposed by the local French forces. Algiers fell (8 November) followed by Oran (9 November), while Casablanca surrendered on 10 November. Admiral Darlan, the senior French officer in north Africa, ordered a general ceasefire (10 November) and was appointed by the Allies as the chief French official in Africa (13 November). He was assassinated (24 December) and replaced by General Henri Giraud. The Allied forces pressed on to **Tunisia** but their advance was held for several months by rapidly assembled German reinforcements.

North-West Frontier

This area of South Asia, bounded by Afghanistan, Jammu and Kashmir, Punjab and Baluchistan, is now the most northern province of Pakistan. It was strategically important as it controlled the eastern end of the Khyber Pass. It was invaded by various rulers during its history and from 1818 gradually came under the control of the Sikhs invading from the Punjab. In 1849 the British annexed the territory to India after the Second **Sikh War** when it became part of the Punjab. The North-West Frontier

Province was created (1901) and this became a province of Pakistan when Pakistan achieved independence (1947).

Norway

(1940; *World War II*) German troops occupied Denmark (9 April) and on the same day groups of German troops invaded the six major ports of Norway. These were airborne troops and assault troops smuggled into the harbours in merchant ships. By 11 April the ports were under German control and Oslo had fallen to 1,500 airborne troops. The remnants of the disorganised Norwegian Army, accompanied by King Haakon VII, withdrew inland and attempted to organise resistance. The British and French launched a counter-attack with 30,000 men (14–19 April) near Trondheim, but because they occupied no large port or airfield, were forced to withdraw (3 May). Another landing of 20,000 troops at Narvik, commanded by General Sir Claude **Auchinleck**, was more successful. Narvik fell to the Allies (28 May) but the ever-worsening situation in France forced a total Allied withdrawal from Norway by June. Norway remained in German hands until the end of the war, though various coastal installations were subjected to **commando** attacks.

Norwegian invasion of England (1066)

The Norwegians recognised the instability in the English government and took the opportunity to invade with a view to territorial expansion

Nott, William (1782–1845)

Nott, the son of a farmer and innkeeper, was born near Neath, South Wales. He enrolled as a volunteer at Carmarthen and was subsequently appointed **ensign** (1800) in the Royal European Regiment at Barhampur. He transferred to the 20th Native Infantry and was promoted to **lieutenant** (1801). He served in Sumatra (1804). He married (1805) and was promoted to **captain** (1814) at Barrackpur. By 1825 he had been promoted to **lieutenant-colonel** of the 20th Native Infantry. By 1829 he was **colonel** of the 38th Native Infantry at Benares (now Varanasi). During 1838 he was promoted to **brigadier-general** in command of the 42nd Native Infantry. By 1839 Nott was in command of a large force at Quetta and later at Kandahar where he took a prominent part in the First **Afghan War**. He was appointed resident at Lucknow (1842) and created **GCB**. He contracted a heart disease and returned home (1844). He died in Carmarthen.

See also **Ghoaine, battle of**

Nottinghamshire and Derbyshire Regiment *See* **Sherwood Foresters**

Nottinghamshire (Sherwood Foresters) Regiment

The **regiment** was raised (1741) as Colonel Houghton's Regiment of Foot. The name changed with its **colonels** until 1751 when the regiment was named the 45th Regiment of Foot. The name was further changed to 45th (or Nottinghamshire) Regiment of Foot (1779) and to the 45th Nottinghamshire (Sherwood Foresters) Regiment of Foot (1866). In 1881 it merged with the 95th, eventually being titled the **Sherwood Foresters**.

Nottinghamshire (2nd) Regiment of Foot

The **regiment** was raised (1755) by Colonel Sir Charles Montagu as the 61st Regiment of Foot. It was re-numbered (1757) the 59th Regiment of Foot and re-named (1881) the 59th (2nd Nottinghamshire) Regiment of Foot. Later in the same year it became part of the **East Lancashire Regiment**.

Nujufghur, battle of

(1857; *Indian Mutiny*) A rebel force of 6,000 was defeated by a small British force, commanded by John **Nicholson**

O

OBE *See* **Order of the British Empire**

OBI *abbreviation of* **Order of British India**

O'Brien, Daniel (1577?–1663)

O'Brien supported Elizabeth I in Ireland during the Irish rebellion, for which service he was knighted (1600). He became an ardent Roman Catholic and was a supporter of Charles I during the **Civil War**. When **Cromwell** finally suppressed Ireland, O'Brien joined Charles II in France (1651). For his services Charles created him Viscount Clare. *See also* **Royal Northumberland Fusiliers**

O'Connor, Richard Nugent (1889–1981)

O'Connor was born in India, the son of a **major** in the **Royal Irish Fusiliers**. He was educated at Wellington College and Sandhurst and commissioned in the Scottish Rifles (**Cameronians**) (1909). He fought at **Ypres**, **Neuve-Chapelle** and **Loos** (1915), where he was awarded the **MC**, and on the **Somme** (1916). He was promoted (1917) to **lieutenant-colonel** of the 2nd Battalion of the **Honourable Artillery Company** and took part in the third battle of **Ypres**. O'Connor attended the **Staff College** at Camberley (1920) and was then an instructor there. He held various staff appointments and commanded the Peshawar **brigade** in India (1935). He was promoted to **major-general** (1938) and was appointed military governor of Jerusalem. In 1940 O'Connor was promoted to temporary **lieutenant-general** in command of the Western Desert Force in Egypt and forced the Italian surrender at **Beda Fomm**. He then returned to Cairo to command the British troops in Egypt. He was sent to Benghazi just before the British troops abandoned it in the face of **Rommel's** first offensive. Here he was captured and sent to Italy. He got away after the Italian surrender (1943). He took over command of the VIII Corps (1944) and took part in the **Normandy** landings. He then went to Calcutta (now Kolkata) in command of the Indian Eastern Command but soon took over command of the North-West Army in India. He was promoted to **general** (1945). He returned home (1946) as one of **Montgomery's** colleagues on the Army Council but resigned over a dispute concerning demobilisation (1947) and retired (1948). He was **colonel** of the Cameronians (1951–54).

Officers' Training Corps *abbreviation* OTC

OM *abbreviation of* **Order of Merit**

Omdurman, battle of

(1898; *Sudan War*) During the previous two-and-a-half years General Horatio Herbert **Kitchener** had pushed up the Nile, finally arriving at Omdurman (2 September) with 26,000 troops. The opposing Mahdists commanded by the Khalifa, Abdullah el Taaisha, were attacked and routed with the loss of some 15,000 men, about one third of the force. Kitchener's army lost 500 men. The Khalifa escaped but was killed in the next year. This battle completed the conquest of the Sudan which was then ruled as a condominium by Britain and Egypt.

Onao, battle of

(1857; *Indian Mutiny*) The town of Onao was besieged by the rebels and relieved in a frontal attack on the rebel forces (18 July) by a British force commanded by General Henry **Havelock**

Oondwa Nullah, battle of
(1763; *British in India*) A force of 3,000 British and Indian troops commanded by Major Adams stormed the fortress which was held by 60,000 troops of Mir Kasim's Bengal army (September). The Bengal army fled with the loss of 100 guns.

Operation Avalanche *See* Salerno, battle of

Operation Crusader *See* Sidi-Rezegh, battle of

Operation Overlord *See* Normandy

Operation Torch *See* North-West Africa

Opium Wars
1. (1839–42; *First Opium War*) The First Opium War between Britain and China began when the Chinese tried to suppress the illegal British exportation of opium to China. It was sparked off when the British refused to turn over two drunken sailors, who had killed a villager, to the Chinese authorities. The small British force was victorious, resulting in the Treaty of Nanking (1842) and the Treaty of Bogue (1843). Five Chinese ports were ceded to the British and an indemnity paid by the Chinese.

2. (1856–60; *Second Opium War*) The French joined the British in the Second Opium War when a French missionary was killed by the Chinese. The Allies were victorious. The resulting Treaties of Tientsin (1858) and, after the capture of Peking (now Beijing) (1860), the Peking Convention legalised the opium trade and opened several more Chinese ports to European trade.

Oporto, battle of
(1809; *Peninsular War*) After the British evacuation of **Corunna** (now La Coruña) (January), only a British **garrison** and the small Portuguese army, commanded by General William Carr **Beresford**, remained in the area. The French **marshals** Nicolas **Soult** and Claude Victor soon overwhelmed the Portuguese and Oporto itself. But before the French could move on, Sir Arthur Wellesley (**Wellington**) attacked Oporto (12 May) with 30,000 men, having crossed the Douro river at night. The town was taken with few casualties and Wellesley was poised to conduct a second invasion of Spain.

Order of British India
The order was established (1837) by the East India Company as an award to Indian officers for long and faithful service. It became obsolete on Indian independence (1947).
Abbreviation **OBI**

Order of Merit
The order was instituted (1902) and consists of the Sovereign and a maximum of 24 members. It is awarded for exceptional military service and for services to art, literature or science.
Abbreviation **OM**

Order of St Michael and St George
The Most Distinguished Order of St Michael and St George was established by the Prince Regent (later George IV) in 1818 to reward service in Malta and the Ionian Islands. Later in the 19th century the purpose was altered to reward foreign and colonial service; it is not generally used to reward military service. Women have been admitted since 1965. The Order has three classes: Knight or Dame Grand Cross (GCMG), Knight or Dame Commander (KCMG or DCMG) and Companion (CMG). Excluding members of the royal family and foreign honorary members, they are respectively limited to 125, 375 and 1750 members.

Order of St Patrick
The Most Illustrious Order of St Patrick was instituted by George III (1783) to reward his Irish peers and holders of office in Ireland. Originally it consisted of the sovereign and 15 knights (KP), but was extended (1833) to 22 knights. Although it still exists, the

Order effectively ceased on the partition of Ireland (1922), although two members of the royal family were subsequently appointed members. Its last member (Henry, Duke of Gloucester) died in 1974.

Order of the Bath

References to 'Knights of the Bath' exist from medieval times, and ritual bathing was an important part of the preparation for receiving knighthood. The modern order, The Most Honourable Order of the Bath, was founded (1725) by George I as a source of political patronage. It was divided (1815) into military and civil divisions, with the former being greatly enlarged to reward the military taking part in the Napoleonic Wars; most awards today are to military personnel. Women have been admitted since 1971. The Order has three classes: Knight Grand Cross (GCB), Knight or Dame Commander (KCB or DCB) and Companion (CB). They are respectively limited to 120, 295 and 1,455 members.

Order of the British Empire

The Most Excellent Order of the British Empire was founded (1917) by George V to reward civilian and military service during **World War I**. It was divided into military and civilian divisions in 1918 and has developed into a general-purpose national order. Women have been eligible for the Order since its formation. It has five classes: Knight or Dame Grand Cross (GBE), Knight or Dame Commander (KBE or DBE), Commander (CBE), Officer (OBE) and Member (MBE).

Order of the Garter

The Most Noble Order of the Garter is the premier Order of knighthood in the UK. It was founded in 1348 and is probably the oldest such order in Europe. It consists of the sovereign, the Prince of Wales and 24 Knights (KG) or Ladies (LG); members of the royal family and foreign reigning monarchs may be admitted in addition. Women have been admitted since 1987.

Order of the Indian Empire

The Most Eminent Order of the Indian Empire was instituted (1877) to commemorate Queen Victoria's assumption of the title of Empress of India. It was awarded for meritorious service in India and was seen as the junior alternative to the **Order of the Star of India**. Originally there was one class with the Sovereign, Grand Master and Members of the Council of the Governor-General of India as ex-officio companions. By 1887 there were three classes: Knight Grand Commander (GCIE), Knight Commander (KCIE) and Companion (CIE). The order became obsolete on Indian independence (1947).

Order of the Star of India

The Most Excellent Order of the Star of India was established (1861) by Queen Victoria to reward military and civilian officers for services exclusively to the Queen in India. Originally it consisted of the Sovereign, a Grand Master and 25 Knights (KSI). It was restructured (1866) into three grades: Knight Grand Commander (GCSI), Knight Commander (KCSI) and Companion (CSI). The order became obsolete on Indian independence (1947).

Order of the Thistle

The Most Ancient and Most Noble Order of the Thistle is the premier Order of knighthood in Scotland, ranking second in the UK after the **Order of the Garter**. Legends of its origin date from the Middle Ages, but the modern order was established by James VII (James II of England) in 1687. It fell into disuse on his deposition (1688) but was later revived (1703). Originally consisting of the sovereign and 12 Knights, since 1827 its membership has been extended to 16 knights (KT) or (since 1987) Ladies (LT).

Ordnance, Board of

The original specialist agency responsible for procuring, developing, storing and issuing military ordnance and ammunition was the Privy Wardrobe, an offshoot of the royal household, which established itself in the Tower of London in the 14th century. This developed into the Office of Ordnance (1414), which became the Board of Ordnance (1683). From 1544 it was headed by the **Master-General of the Ordnance**. Between the 17th and the 19th centuries it was particularly responsible for raising and maintaining **artillery** and **engineers**. Trains (self-contained units) of artillery were raised for each campaign, with the commissions for artillery officers and engineers being signed by the Master-General. The commissions were not purchased but awarded on merit or on personal recommendation from the Board of Ordnance. These trains were disbanded after the campaign. This system was unsatisfactory as the commanders of the regular army had no control over the quantity of artillery that would be available for a particular campaign. The situation was resolved in 1855 when the Board of Ordnance was abolished and its responsibilities transferred to the War Office. The Master-General survived this abolition and the title still exists.

In 1763 a William Roy was commissioned by the Master-General to carry out the first **Ordnance Survey**, with the first one-inch map being produced in 1801. The Ordnance Survey was under the control the Board of Ordnance and its successors until 1899, when it became a separate entity.

See also **Royal Army Ordnance Corps**; **Woolwich**; **Royal Military Academy**
[Contraction of Old French *ordenance*, ultimately from Latin *ordinare* 'to set in order']

Ordnance, Master-General of the *See* Ordnance, Board of

Orleans, battle of
(1428–29; *Hundred Years' War*) After their victory at **Verneuil** the English and Burgundians held most of France north of the Loire and began an assault on Orleans. The English commander, the Duke of Bedford, sent Thomas Montague, 4th Earl of Salisbury, with 5,000 men to lay siege to Orleans (23 October 1428). Although Salisbury was killed by a cannon ball (3 November) and replaced by William de la Pole, Earl, later Duke, of Suffolk, the besiegers met with no attempt to relieve the city. The French dauphin, Charles, now gave Joan of Arc command of the relief of Orleans. She marched from Blois (25 April 1429) and persuaded the French commander, Comte de Dunois, to attack the English bridgehead on the south bank of the Loire (7 May). The English were driven from their position with the loss of 300 dead and 200 taken prisoner. The next day the English abandoned the siege. This was the turning point in the Hundred Years' War.

Orthez, battle of
(1814; *Peninsular War*) A British force, commanded by **Wellington**, drove a French force, commanded by Marshal **Soult**, out of Orthez across the Luy de Béarn. The French lost 4,000 killed and wounded.

Oswego, battle of
(1756; *French and Indian War*) During this third year of the war in North America John **Campbell**, Earl of Loudoun, had taken command of the British forces and General Marquis Louis de **Montcalm** had taken command of the French forces. There was little combat during the year except when Montcalm led an expedition from Fort Frontenac across the eastern end of Lake Ontario to attack the British at Oswego (New York). The French landed (11 August) and attacked the garrison which surrendered after three days, their commander having been killed. The French destroyed the fort at Oswego and then returned to their base.

other ranks
All ranks below that of **second lieutenant**, i.e. those that do not hold a **commission**

Otterburn, battle of
(1388; *English-Scottish Wars*) After several minor skirmishes the Scots, aided by a French contingent and commanded by James Douglas, 2nd Earl of Douglas, invaded northern England. A large force of 4,000 English commanded by Sir Henry Percy (Hotspur) attempted a night attack on the Scottish camp at Otterburn. Douglas was killed but the Scottish spearmen inflicted some 2,000 casualties on the English. Percy

was taken prisoner but was later ransomed. This victory gave the Scots dominance over the Border counties for some years.

Oudenarde, battle of

(1708; *War of the Spanish Succession*) King Louis XIV of France sent the Duc de Vendôme to occupy Bruges and Ghent. From Ghent Vendôme moved up the river Scheldt towards Oudenarde. The Duke of **Marlborough** moved westwards rapidly with 80,000 British, Dutch and German troops and surprised the 100,000-man French force at Oudenarde (11 July). Before the French could organise Marlborough began attacks on both flanks as well as in the centre, crushing the French in a pincer movement. By sundown 6,000 French had been killed or wounded and 7,000 taken prisoner. The Allies suffered 3,000 casualties. The battle restored the Allied initiative in Flanders.

Outram, James (1803–63)

Outram joined the Bombay Native Infantry (1819). In 1825 he was entrusted with raising a **light infantry regiment** from amongst the Bhils and during the next ten years used this force to quell local uprisings. He was made political agent at Gujurat (1835–38). He was promoted to **brevet major** (1839) and played an outstanding part in the First **Afghan War**. Outram was appointed political agent in Sind (1840). He opposed Charles **Napier's** aggressive policy towards the Sind amir. In May 1845 Outram was appointed resident at Satara and then at Baroda. He was promoted to **lieutenant-colonel** (July 1853) and **major-general** (November 1854). After his service in Baroda he had been on leave in England and had held various political appointments. During 1857 he commanded a brief but successful campaign in Persia (now Iran). He returned to India (July 1857) where the **Indian Mutiny** was beginning. He was given command of two **divisions** of the Bengal Army. Arriving in **Cawnpore** (now Kanpur) (15 September 1857) he met up with Henry **Havelock**, whom he accompanied as a volunteer and chief commissioner of Oudh, to the relief of **Lucknow**, thus giving Havelock credit for the successful action rather than taking it himself as the senior officer. Outram took command at Lucknow but was himself besieged until Lucknow was relieved by Colin **Campbell**. He was promoted to **lieutenant-general** (1858). Suffering from ill health Outram left India (1858) and died at Pau in France.

Overlord, Operation *See* Normandy

Oxfordshire and Buckinghamshire Light Infantry

The **regiment** was formed (1881) by the amalgamation of the 43rd (**Monmouthshire Light Infantry**) Regiment and the 52nd (**Oxfordshire Light Infantry**) Regiment. It was originally called the Oxfordshire Light Infantry, with the name being changed in 1908 to the Oxfordshire and Buckinghamshire Light Infantry and to the 1st **Green Jackets** (1958).

Oxfordshire Light Infantry *See* Oxfordshire and Buckinghamshire Light Infantry

Oxfordshire Regiment of Foot

The **regiment** was raised (1755) by Colonel Hedworth Lambton as the 54th Regiment of Foot. In 1757 it was re-numbered the 52nd Regiment of Foot and re-named (1782) the 52nd (or the Oxfordshire) Regiment of Foot. In 1809 it was named the 52nd (or the Oxfordshire) Regiment of Foot (Light Infantry). This was one of the first regiments to be changed to **light infantry**. The regiment played outstanding parts at **Badajoz** and **Waterloo** and in the assault on the Kashmir gate during the siege of **Delhi** when Bugler Hawthorn won the **Victoria Cross**.

P

Paardeberg, battle of

(1900; *Boer Wars*) After General Sir John **French** had relieved **Kimberley** (15 February) his rear was threatened by the Boer commander Cronjé who moved to Paardeberg to the south-east of the Modder river. Here he was attacked by the British, commanded by General Lord **Kitchener** (18 February). 1,000 men having been lost trying to dislodge the Boers from the dry river bed, the **commander-in-chief**, Lord **Roberts**, called off the attack, reverting to an **artillery** bombardment which caused the Boers to surrender (27 February). The following day General Sir Redvers **Buller** relieved **Ladysmith** and the initiative in South Africa passed to the British.

See also **Botha, Louis**

Paget, Henry William (1768–1854)

Paget was the eldest son of the Earl of Uxbridge and was educated at Westminster and Christ Church, Oxford. He was MP for Caernarvon Boroughs (1790–96) and MP for Milborne Port (1796, 1802–04 and 1807–10). He raised the **Staffordshire Volunteers** (1793) with himself as temporary **lieutenant-colonel**. The **regiment** came on to the regular establishment (1793) as the 80th Foot and joined the Duke of **York** in Flanders (1794). Through his influence and money, Paget was appointed permanent lieutenant-colonel in the 7th Light Dragoons (**Queen's Own Hussars**) in 1797. He took part in the Anglo-Russian expedition to Holland (1799), but did not see active service again until 1808 when he was promoted to **lieutenant-general** and went to Portugal. During the intervening period he had made his regiment one of the best in the army. He joined Sir John **Moore** at Salamanca and led Moore's **cavalry** in a brilliant rearguard action during the retreat to **Corunna** (now La Coruña). Paget was given command of an **infantry division** on the Walcheren expedition (1809). He became Earl of Uxbridge (1812) on the death of his father. He saw no further military service in the Peninsula because he had eloped with **Wellington's** brother's wife but in 1815 he was ordered to Flanders where he was given command of Wellington's entire cavalry and horse **artillery** at **Waterloo**. During the final stages of the battle he was shot in the knee and had to have his leg amputated. He was created Marquis of Anglesey (1815); full **general** (1819); **Master-General of the Ordnance** (*see* **Ordnance, Board of**) with a seat in the Cabinet (1827–28; 1846–52); **colonel** of the Royal Horse Guards (**Blues and Royals**) (1842) and **field marshal** (1846).

Pandu Naddi, battle of

1. (15 July 1857; *Indian Mutiny*) An Anglo-Indian force, commanded by General Henry **Havelock**, seized a bridge over the Pandu Naddi, leaving the road open for the relief of **Cawnpore** (now Kanpur)

2. (26 November 1857; *Indian Mutiny*) A British force of 1,400, commanded by General Sir Charles **Windham**, met the advance guard of the rebels. The British crossed the dry bed of the river and drove the rebels from their trenches. Windham found himself facing the main rebel army and retired to Cawnpore.

Paoli, battle of

(1777; *American War of Independence*) After the battle of the **Brandywine** the British and Americans manoeuvred around Philadelphia, the American capital. The American commander, George **Washington**, had his main force east of the Schuylkill river, with a force of 1,500 commanded by General Anthony Wayne west of the river at Paoli, threatening the British flank and rear. General Charles **Grey** led a night attack on the Americans (21 September) killing some 300 in a bayonet assault. The British suffered about eight casualties. This cleared General Sir William **Howe's** lines of communication, allowing him to enter Philadelphia.

Parachute Regiment
The first parachute battalion was formed in 1940 but it was not until 1942 that the **regiment** was formed. Until 1949 it was administered by the **Army Air Corps** and up to 1953 consisted of personnel seconded from other regiments. It remains in existence with three regular battalions in the 21st century. As well as its **World War II** exploits in **Normandy** and at **Arnhem**, the regiment has also played an important part in the **Falklands War**, in the Bloody Sunday events (1972) in Londonderry, **Northern Ireland**, and in the **Iraq War** at Basra.

parade
A formalised, often public, display of troops assembled for inspection by officers and to demonstrate their efficiency at **drill**

parade ground
An area on which **drill** or a **parade** takes place

Passchendaele, battle of
(6 November 1917; *World War I*) Military historians restrict this name to the final action of the 3rd Battle of **Ypres** (6 November) when Canadian troops captured the village of Passchendaele, but it is also commonly used to denote the whole of the 1917 Ypres fighting

passing-out parade
A **parade** of newly qualified officers held at the college at which they have been trained

Patay, battle of
(1429; *Hundred Years' War*) After their defeat at **Orleans** the English commanded by John Talbot (Earl of Shrewsbury) began a withdrawal along the Seine. The pursuing French, commanded by Estienne de Vignolles la Hire, caught up with the British at Patay. In a surprise attack (18 June) the French routed the English columns, killing about 2,000 of the 5,000-strong force and dispersing the rest.

Patton, George Smith (1885–1945)
Patton graduated from the US Military Academy at West Point (1909) and served in the US Tank Corps during **World War I**. He took part in the **North-West Africa** campaign (1942–43) and commanded the US 7th Army in **Sicily**. His chief claim to fame is the rapid and decisive movement made by his 3rd Army during the battle of the **Ardennes** and his advance into Germany. His reputation as a tough soldier and disciplinarian earned him the nickname of 'Old Blood and Guts'. He publicly criticised the Allies' post-war programme for denazifying Germany and was removed from command of the 3rd Army in Germany (October 1945). He died in Heidelberg after a car accident.

Paulus Hook, battle of
(1779; *American War of Independence*) After his success at **Stony Point**, the American **commander-in-chief**, George **Washington**, decided to attack the British at Paulus Point, further down the Hudson river, opposite New York. This was the last major British outpost in New Jersey. 300 Americans crossed the salt marshes in a night assault and attacked the 250-man British garrison commanded by Major William Sutherland (August 18). Only 40 of the garrison, including Sutherland, escaped being captured or killed. However, the Americans had to evacuate Paulus Point immediately before General Sir Henry **Clinton** could counter-attack.

pay in the 17th and 18th centuries
At the end of the 17th century officers, having purchased their **commissions**, had various deductions made from their pay. An officer's pay was divided into subsistence

money from which no deductions were made and arrears which were paid annually and from which the following deductions were made: one shilling (now 5p) in the pound to the Paymaster-General, one day's pay to the **Chelsea Hospital**, one day's pay to the Commissary-General of Musters (reduced to one third in 1680). As well as these, the officer paid fees to the Auditors, the **commissary of musters**, and to the Exchequer and Treasury for the issue of pay warrants. As officers were paid in arrears they frequently had to advance money from their own pockets. The private was paid eight pence a day (£12 3s 4d per year, equivalent to £12.16 in decimal currency). Of this £9 10s (£9.50) was deducted for subsistence and of the remaining amount (the gross off reckoning) 5% was paid to the Paymaster-General and one day's pay to the Chelsea Hospital. The remainder (the net off reckoning) was retained by the **colonel** for clothing and equipment. The whole system was open to corruption, especially by the Paymaster-General, who was responsible to nobody, and the Secretary of War. The Duke of **Marlborough** did much to remove these irregularities by setting up the Office of Controller of Army Pay Accounts (1703). All stoppages, except for clothing and to the Chelsea Hospital, were suppressed and NCOs and men were paid their subsistence every week. The Controllers took over the overall supply of food and clothing, making contracts with the suppliers. In 1707 the Board of General Officers (made up of regimental **colonels**) was set up to supervise the supplies to each individual colonel. Its function relaxed after the death of Marlborough, more attention being paid to the soldiers' uniforms than to their welfare.

See also **Pitt's Reforms**

paymaster
The officer in charge of the allocation and distribution of soldiers' pay

paymaster general *See* **pay in the 17th and 18th centuries**

pay warrant *See* **pay in the 17th and 18th centuries**

peacekeepers
Armed forces assigned to maintain law and order and maintain stable government in conflict areas

peacekeeping
The maintenance of law and order by military forces acting as armed police, keeping warring factions apart and helping to maintain a stable government in the territory concerned. In recent times, peacekeeping has been a major role for the British Army, e.g. in **Northern Ireland**, Bosnia, **Kosovo**, **Afghanistan** and Iraq (see **Iraq War**). Units of the British Army have frequently functioned as part of a United Nations peacekeeping force.

Pearce's Dragoons *See* **Somerset Light Infantry**

Peiwar Pass, battle of
(1878; *Afghan War II*) Increasingly friendly relations between the Afghan leader Shere Ali and Russia caused General Sir Frederick **Roberts** to lead an Anglo-Indian force of 3,200 from India against the Afghans. This force was met (2 December) by 18,000 Afghans in the Peiwar Pass. The Afghans were routed with heavy casualties and the loss of 11 pieces of artillery. Roberts pushed on to Kabul in the next year.

Peking, battle of
(1900; *Boxer Rebellion*) The incursion of European powers into China gave rise to anti-foreign feelings in the north of the country and to the formation of the Society of Harmonious Fists (Boxers). Outbreaks of violence prompted the British Admiral Sir Edward Seymour to lead an international expedition to Tientsin (now Tianjin). The Boxers in Peking (now Beijing) rose, killed the German ambassador and laid siege to the foreign legations (20 July). A six-nation expeditionary force landed at Tientsin (14 July) and marched north to Peking where they relieved the legations (14 August).

pelisse
A fur-lined coat worn over one shoulder. It originated from the wolf-skins worn by Hungarian light **cavalry** and became popular after the **light dragoons** took to wearing their jackets over one shoulder during the **American War of Independence**. By the beginning of the 19th century the pelisse was worn by the light dragoons and **hussars**.
[Via French from late Latin *pellicia*, from Latin *pellis* 'skin']

Pembrokeshire Yeomanry
This **regiment** had the unique distinction of being the only one to receive a battle honour for an action in Britain. In 1794 a small French contingent landed at Fishguard and surrendered to the Yeomanry when they mistook a crowd of Welsh women in their red capes for approaching infantry.

Peninsular War (1808–14)
During the height of **Napoleon's** power the French occupied Portugal and Spain. The Spanish patriots resisted, especially at Saragossa (now Zaragoza) and Bailén. A British army under Sir Arthur Wellesley, later the Duke of **Wellington**, was sent to support the patriots. The war continued for five years until the French were defeated finally at **Toulouse**. For service during the whole six years of the war a private received £3.50 in prize money while a general received £1,360.
See also **Albuera, battle of; Badajoz, battle of; Barossa, battle of; Bussaco, battle of; Castella, battle of; Ciudad Rodrigo; Corunna, battle of; Fuentes de Oñoro, battle of; Nive, battle of; Nivelle, battle of; Oporto, battle of; Orthez, battle of; Roliça, battle of; Sabugal, battle of; Salamanca, battle of; Sorauren, battle of; Talavera, battle of; Toulouse, battle of; Vimiero, battle of; Vitoria, battle of; Beresford, William Carr; Craufurd, Robert; Hill, Rowland; Moore, John; Paget, Henry William; Picton, Thomas**

Pepperell, William (1696–1759)
Pepperell's family emigrated from Devon to Massachusetts where his father became a prominent ship-owner and merchant. He and his brother continued and improved the business so that Pepperell soon became the foremost person in the colony of Maine where he was a **colonel** in the Militia (1722). The New England colonists had been consistently attacked by the French and so decided to attack the French at Louisburg (29 April 1745). Pepperell was in command of the force of 100 small ships that forced the French to surrender (16 June). He was made a colonel in the regular army, but saw no active service. In 1746 he was made a baron. He visited London and was cordially received. When war with the French was resumed (1754) he was given command of 1,000 men, but again saw no active service. In 1759 he was promoted to **lieutenant-general**.

Percival, Arthur Ernest (1887–1966)
Until 1914 Percival was in business in London. He served in France (1915–19) where he was wounded (1916) and awarded the **DSO** and **MC**. In 1916 he was promoted to **captain** in the **Essex Regiment** and made a **brevet major** (1919). In 1924 he joined the **Cheshire Regiment** as a major being promoted to **lieutenant-colonel** in 1936 and **major-general** in 1940. In 1941–42 Percival commanded land forces in **Malaya**. His weak leadership contributed to the disastrous defeat, culminating in the surrender at **Singapore**. He was captured and held in Manchuria until 1945, when he was released. He retired in 1946.

percussion cap
The percussion cap was invented (1805) by a Scottish minister, Alexander Forsyth, and was a small container that held mercury fulminate, an explosive material. This could be placed by the touch-hole of a **musket** and detonated on being hit by the hammer. Previously muskets had to be primed with a small quantity of powder and that then had to be ignited by sparks generated by a flint. This system was prone to misfire – not fire at all or fire incompletely – perhaps as often as once in every four shots, and might be impossible to use in wet weather; the percussion cap reduced misfires to negligible

proportions. The percussion cap was introduced into the British Army in 1838 when it was applied, unsuccessfully, to the Brunswick **rifle** and then to the smooth-bore **Brown Bess**.

See also **rifle**

Perembacum, battle of

(1780; *British in India*) An 11,000 strong Mysore force massacred 3,700 British soldiers (10 September)

Perthshire Regiment of Foot

The **regiment** was raised (1779) as the 2nd Battalion of the 42nd Foot (**Black Watch**), but became the 73rd (Highland) Regiment of Foot (1786). The name was changed to 73rd Regiment of Foot (1806) and to 73rd (Perthshire) Regiment of Foot (1862). The 73rd later merged with the Black Watch.

See also **Black Watch, The**

Perthshire Volunteers

The **regiment** was raised (1794) by Colonel Thomas **Graham** as the 90th Regiment of Foot (or Perthshire Volunteers). The title was changed in 1815 to 90th Light Infantry Regiment, Perthshire Volunteers.

Pétain, Henri-Philippe (1856–1951)

Pétain was the son of a farmer and entered the French military academy at Saint-Cyr. He was appointed a professor at the War College, but did not become a **general** until 1902 because his theories on tactics were at variance with those of the high command. In **World War I** he was given command of a **brigade**, a **corps** and then an **army** and was successful in defeating the Germans at **Verdun**. He was popular with the troops and successfully restored discipline to the French Army after the mutinies caused (1917) by the ill-considered tactics of his **commander-in-chief** Robert-George **Nivelle** whom he replaced. He led the French forces during the victorious advance of 1918 and was made a **marshal** of France (November 1918). When France was overrun in 1940 Pétain, who was vice-premier, asked for an armistice, and became head of the Vichy government in southern France. For his collaborationist conduct he was tried (1945) and imprisoned on the Île d'Yeu, where he died.

Peterborough, Earl of (1658–1735)

Born Charles Mordaunt, he spent a short time at university and then served in the navy, largely in the Mediterranean under his uncle, Henry, who was a vice-admiral. He inherited the title of Viscount Mordaunt (1675). Mordaunt returned home (1680) and supported William of Orange, from whom he received many preferments when William became king (1689). He was involved in various intrigues, quarrelling with **Marlborough** and Godolphin. He became Earl of Peterborough (1697) on the death of his uncle. In 1705 he was given command of the army sent to Spain and undertook the siege of **Barcelona**, for which he claimed all the credit. Mordaunt was then given full powers of civil administration by the recently crowned King Charles of Spain and moved to Valencia where he stayed despite various other upheavals throughout Spain. He was ordered by Queen Anne to leave Spain for Italy. The rest of his command in Spain was glad to see him go. He sailed for Genoa. He returned to Valencia (1706) but was recalled to England (1707) where he was indicted for his dilatory conduct in Spain and Italy. The case became a power struggle between Mordaunt and Marlborough, and as Marlborough was out of favour Mordaunt was acquitted. He was made ambassador-extraordinary to Vienna (1711), where he incurred further displeasure. He returned to England (1712) and was made **colonel** of the **Royal Horse Guards** (*see* **Blues and Royals**) of which post he was deprived (1715) on the accession of George I. He held no further military appointments of importance and spent the rest of his life in intrigue at home and on the Continent.

Also known as **Mordaunt, Charles**

petronel

A modified form of **harquebus** designed to be used on horseback. It was introduced c.1530 and was shorter than the harquebus and with a larger bore.

[From French *petrinal*, variant of *poitrinal* 'of the chest', from *poitrine* 'chest', because the butt rested against the chest when the gun was fired]

Philiphaugh, battle of

(1645; *Civil War*) The Royalist forces in Scotland, commanded by the Marquis of **Montrose**, were secure, but Parliamentarian victories in England released the Scottish component of the army for service at home. A force (4,000) of Parliamentarian **cavalry**, led by General David Leslie, rode north and met Montrose at Philiphaugh. The Royalists were taken by surprise and suffered a disastrous defeat. Montrose escaped and fled to France.

picket, picquet

A small party of soldiers sent on some form of guard or look-out duty. It originally meant a small party of men armed with **pikes**.

[From French *piquet* 'pointed stake', from *piquer* 'to prick, pierce']

Picton, Thomas (1758–1815)

Picton was born in Pembrokeshire and was **gazetted** as **ensign** in the 12th Foot (**Suffolk Regiment**) (1771). He served at Gibraltar (1773) and was promoted to **captain** in the 75th Foot (1778). His **regiment** was disbanded (1783) after the Treaty of Versailles. Picton was then promoted to **lieutenant-colonel** (1794) and joined the staff of the **commander-in-chief** of the West Indies. He took part in the capture of St. Lucia and St. Vincent (1796) and of Trinidad (1797). He was promoted to **colonel** and made Governor of Trinidad (1797). He did much to restore order and trade to the island, but he was accused of brutality and was forced to resign (1803). He returned home to defend himself in an inconclusive lawsuit. He was promoted to **major-general** (1808) and joined **Wellington** in the Peninsula as commander of the 3rd **Division** (1810–12, 1813, 1814). He wore eccentric civilian clothes and was noted for his foul language and for leading his men from the front in the thickest part of the fighting. He fought with distinction at **Bussaco**, **Fuentes de Oñoro** and **Ciudad Rodrigo**, but his most famous exploit was the capture of **Badajoz**. Picton was invalided home (1812) and promoted to **lieutenant-general** and knighted (1813). He returned to Spain and distinguished himself at **Vitoria**. He had command of the 5th Division in the 1815 campaign and was wounded at **Quatre Bras**. He was constantly in the saddle over the following two days despite his wound and led an important charge of the British infantry in the early stages at **Waterloo**. During this charge he was killed by a shot to the head.

Pieter's Hill, battle of

(1900; *Boer Wars*) The final and successful attempt by Sir Redvers **Buller** to relieve **Ladysmith**. The British captured Hlangwane (19 February), giving them command of the Tulega river which was crossed (21 February). They advanced up Pieter's Hill, where the Boer trenches were attacked unsuccessfully by the Irish Brigade (23 February). It was not until 27 February that Buller succeeded in capturing the position. The British lost 1,896 men during the assault.

pigtail *See* queue

pike

A spear with a shaft of some 8–10 feet carried by **infantry** pikemen. This was a very effective defensive weapon, especially against charging **cavalry**. The troops would form into a square with the pikemen on the outer perimeter enclosing archers or musketeers. When the pikes were grounded (with the butts pushed into the earth) they formed a barrier from behind which the other troops could fire in relative safety. By the end of the 17th century musketry had improved, the **bayonet** introduced, and the long pike was abandoned. They survived only as the shorter half-pikes (espontoons or spontoons) carried by officers, and as the **halberds** carried by non-commissioned officers.

[From French *pique*, from *piquer* 'to prick, irritate']

pillbox

Originally, an informal term for a small rounded concrete structure which housed **machine guns**. The term was first used in 1918 (the Germans had built many such structures in their defensive positions on the **Western Front**) and is often used for any of a variety of similar defensive fortifications.

Pinkie, battle of

(1547; *English-Scottish Wars*) The pro-French party in Scotland objected to the proposed marriage between the five-year-old Mary, Queen of Scots, and the ten-year-old Edward VI of England. The Duke of Somerset, Edward Seymour, and the Earl of Warwick, John Dudley, took an army towards Edinburgh. They were met by a Scottish army, commanded by George Gordon, Earl of Huntley, at Pinkie (10 September) east of the city. The Scots were defeated and Seymour entered Edinburgh only to abandon it three years later.

pioneers

Each **company** of **infantry** had at least one pioneer. During **World War I battalions** of pioneers were formed.

See also **engineers**

[From French *pionnier* 'foot soldier', ultimately from Latin *ped-* 'foot']

pistol

A small firearm that can be aimed and fired using one hand. Pistols have been carried as supplementary weapons since the 16th century when various forms were introduced as **cavalry** weapons. As they have to be light even the modern ones are accurate only to about 10 yards (though lethal to a great deal further) unless the user has been specially trained. Consequently they have never been a primary military weapon. By **World War II** they were issued to officers only as a badge of rank and carried by various personnel as a defensive weapon in the last resort.

[Via French *pistole* from Czech *pišt'ala* 'pipe', from *pišteti* 'to whistle', an imitation of the sound]

pith helmet

A sun helmet made from the pith of the spongewood tree. Also called a cork helmet (1861).

Pitt's Reforms

When William Pitt the Younger became prime minister (1783) he inherited a **standing army** of 52,000. The system whereby the **colonel** had complete control of his **regiment** was ended. The War Department became responsible for paying, recruiting and equipping the regiments, although pay and a grant for equipment still passed through the hands of the colonel or his agent. Pay for the ordinary soldier was increased to a shilling (now 5p) a day. Pitt started building barracks (1793), avoiding billeting troops in local taverns as had previously been the usual practice. This had the beneficial effect of reducing drunkenness somewhat though it was actually intended to distance the troops from contact with agitators who might spread revolutionary ideas, as in contemporary France. The first military manuals were issued. The **Royal Horse Artillery** was raised (1793) with the drivers being members of the regiment rather than civilians, as had previously been the case. The Corps of Artillery Drivers was formed (1794) to perform a similar role for the foot artillery.

Plassey, battle of

(1757; *Seven Years' War*) While Britain and France were fighting in Europe and North America, the Nawab of Bengal, Surajah Dowlah, took the side of France in India. With 50,000 men he dominated the province, but his cruelty incited Mir Jafa to rebel. The British commander, Robert **Clive** took advantage of this situation and supported Mir Jafa. With an army of 3,000 (about 1,000 British) he marched on Plassey, about 80 miles north of Calcutta (now Kolkata). Here the two armies met (23 June). There was a four-hour artillery bombardment by Clive's forces and Surajah Dowlah, troubled by treachery in his own ranks, withdrew. Clive attacked and the forces of the Surajah fled with 500 casualties. Clive lost 65 men killed, wounded or missing. This left Clive in control of Bengal which became the nucleus of the British Indian Empire. Surajah Dowlah was assassinated a few days later.

platoon

In the 17th century, a small group of musketeers which fired alternately with another platoon, giving the other group time to re-load their **muskets**. By the 18th century platoons were more organised, with a **battalion** when formed up for battle being divided into 16 platoons plus 2–4 platoons of **grenadiers**. In theory the platoons would fire in a prescribed sequence while others reloaded so that the battalion would sustain a nearly continuous fire. In practice such a system was impossible to achieve in a prolonged battle. By the end of the century firing by battalion volleys or by ranks was more common. In the modern army the platoon is the principal sub-division of a **company**, usually commanded by a **lieutenant** and consisting of 25 to 50 men, and in turn is divided into two or more sections or squads, each commanded by a **non-commissioned officer**.
[From French *peloton* 'small ball, platoon']

Platt, William (1885–1975)

Platt was educated at Marlborough College and the **Royal Military Academy** at Sandhurst. He was commissioned in the **Royal Northumberland Fusiliers** (1905) and served on the **North-West Frontier** in India. He returned from India (1913) and went to France (1914) where he was wounded. He was in France as a **staff officer** for the rest of the war, finally being promoted to **brevet lieutenant-colonel**. He attended **Staff College** (1919) and served in India and Egypt (1920–26). Platt held a **War Office** appointment (1927–30) and then commanded the 2nd Battalion of the **Wiltshire Regiment of Foot** (1930–33) and the experimental 7th Infantry Brigade (1933–37). In 1938 he was promoted to **major-general** in command of the Sudanese Defence Force and held the Sudan frontier against the vastly superior Italian force in Abyssinia (now Ethiopia) (1940–41), later to be supported by General **Wavell**. Wavell's combined force then defeated the Italians in Abyssinia. Platt was promoted to **lieutenant-general** in 1941 and in 1942 was appointed **commander-in-chief** in East Africa where he took control of the occupation of **Madagascar** (1942). He was promoted to **general** and put in charge of training African troops for service in **Burma** (now Myanmar). He retired in 1945 and joined the family engineering firm.

Plattsburg, battle of

(1814; *War of 1812*) The British occupied Plattsburg (6 September) as part of the offensive in Upper New York State, but were forced to abandon it a few days later after the American victory at Lake Champlain.
See also **Prevost, George**

Plumer, Herbert Charles Onslow (1857–1932)

Plumer was educated at Eton and joined the 65th Foot (**Yorkshire North Riding Regiment of Foot (2nd)**) at Lucknow (India) (1876). He was promoted to **captain** (1882). On the way home (1884) the **regiment** was diverted to take part in the war in the **Sudan**. Plumer was mentioned in dispatches. In 1885 he entered **Staff College** and in 1890 was appointed deputy assistant **adjutant-general** in Jersey. In 1893 he rejoined his regiment, now the **York and Lancaster Regiment**, in Natal, as a **major**. He was in command of the force that put down the Matabele rising (1896). He returned to a staff appointment at Aldershot (1897–99). In 1899 he returned to South Africa to raise a force to combat the Boers. After the relief of **Mafeking** (now Mafikeng) he commanded the northern column of the force that advanced on Pretoria. Plumer was promoted to **brevet colonel** and then **brigadier-general**. He returned home (1902) to a **brigade** command at Aldershot and was then promoted to **major-general**. In 1903 he was appointed Quartermaster-General in the **Army Council**. When R.B. Haldane (Secretary of State for War) reconstituted the Army Council (1905) he did not include Plumer due to a misunderstanding. In 1906 Plumer was placed in command of the Northumberland Fusiliers (**Royal Northumberland Fusiliers**) in Ireland. He was promoted to **lieutenant-general** (1908) and then **commander-in-chief** in York (1911). He was commander of the II Corps in France (1914) and then commanded the 2nd Army (1915). In 1917, following his success at **Messines**, his army was allocated an increased role in the main battle of **Ypres** after early progress had been poor. His methodical approach helped his troops play a major part in the taking of the Wytschaete plateau, though casualties were high because of the strong German defences and the vile weather and ground conditions. Plumer then took the 2nd Army to Italy (1917) to hold the Montello section. His success meant that he could return to France a few months later. With a depleted force, Plumer was unable to hold Messines and Wytschaete when the Germans attacked in early 1918 but held Ypres, giving the Allies time to prepare their final assault of the war. He was appointed commander in Germany and was raised to the peerage as Baron Plumer (1919). In 1919 Plumer was appointed governor of Malta, where there had been rioting. He handled the situation with understanding and left (1924) greatly respected. In 1925 he was appointed high commissioner in Palestine and Transjordan doing a great deal to stabilise the relationship between the Arabs and Jews. He resigned (1928) and was made a viscount (1929).

poison gas *See* gas

Poitiers, battle of

(1356; *Hundred Years' War*) The English Prince Edward (the Black Prince) led an attack deeper into France from the English territories of Gascony and Aquitaine. He moved towards Orleans, but as he turned west towards Tours his 7,000-man force was overtaken by a 16,000-man French force, commanded by King John II. Edward made a stand at Poitiers (17 September) amongst vineyards and hedges. The French knights were forced to dismount to attack and were routed by a flanking attack by 2,000 archers and a frontal attack by the more mobile English foot soldiers. Hampered by their armour, 2,000 French knights were killed and a further 2,000, including King John, were taken prisoner.

Pollicore, battle of

(1781; *British in India*) A British force of 11,000 commanded by Sir Eyre **Coote** seized the village of Pollicore from 80,000 Mysoris (27 August). The British lost 421 killed and wounded while the Mysoris lost some 2,000.

Pollock, George (1786–1872)

Pollock trained for the **Royal Engineers** at Woolwich but joined the **artillery** and sailed for India where he was promoted to **lieutenant** (1804) and served under Gerard **Lake**. He was promoted to captain-lieutenant (1805). By 1820 he was assistant **adjutant-general** of artillery at Dum-Dum. In 1824 he was promoted to **lieutenant-colonel** and served in Burma (now Myanmar) where his artillery played a major part in the British victory. Pollock received the CB and went home on sick leave (1827). He returned to India (1830) to be promoted to **colonel** in command of the Bengal Artillery (1835), and to **major-general** (1838). He was then commissioned to relieve **Jellalabad** (1842) in which he succeeded (16 April) after consistently defeating the Afghans on his march from Peshawar. He was met by **Sale** who had broken out of Jellalabad on 7 April. Pollock stayed at Jellalabad trying to negotiate the release of the British captives in **Kabul**. In this he failed. Together with a force from Kandahar, commanded by **Nott**, both under the overall command of **Sale**, he moved towards Kabul, having to fight through every pass on the way. Kabul was eventually taken. Pollock was created **CBE** (1843) and given command of the Danapur **Division**. He was appointed resident in Lucknow (1844), a post which Nott had resigned through ill-health, and in the same year was made a member of the supreme council of India. Pollock received many honours including being **gazetted** as **field marshal** (1870).

Pondicherry, battle of

(1761; *Seven Years' War*) After their victory at **Wandiwash**, the British forces in India commanded by Lieutenant-Colonel Eyre **Coote** pushed the French back to the east, finally investing them at Pondicherry (August 1760). The 8,000 Anglo-Indian troops were well-provisioned from the sea, while the 3,000 French, commanded by the Comte de Lally, were isolated. Coote's **artillery** opened their bombardment in December 1760, but it was not until 15 January 1761 that the French capitulated. Pondicherry was returned to the French by the Treaty of Paris (1763).

pontoon bridge

A temporary bridge laid on a series of flat-bottomed boats
[Via French *ponton* from Latin *ponton-* 'floating bridge']

Pont Valain, battle of

(1370; *Hundred Years' War*) A French force under Bertrand du Guesclin attacked an English force under Sir Thomas Granson encamped at Pont Valain. The English were defeated, with some 10,000 men killed, wounded or taken prisoner. Granson was taken prisoner.

Porto Novo, battle of

(1781; *British in India*) A Mysore force of 65,000 under **Haidar Ali** blocked the British advance on Cuddalore. They were attacked and routed by 8,500 British troops commanded by Sir Eyre **Coote** (1 July).

Port Royal, battle of

1. (1690; *King William's War*) A British force, commanded by Sir William Phipps, attacked the French-held Port Royal on the west coast of Nova Scotia. The fort capitulated (11 May) and Phipps moved on to attack Quebec but was repulsed. The French re-took Port Royal (1691).

2. (1710; *Queen Anne's War*) The British, commanded by Colonel Francis Nicholson and Sir Charles Hobby, attacked the fort at Port Royal. It surrendered (16 October) and was re-named Annapolis Royal in honour of Queen Anne.

Port Stanley, battle of

(1982; *Falklands War*) The Argentine forces commanded by Major-General Mario Benjamín Menéndez held defensive positions in the west of Port Stanley. These were attacked by the British force commanded by Major-General Jeremy Moore (11–14 June). Each hill and ridge was fought for fiercely but the Argentine troops were finally routed and fled into Port Stanley, opening negotiations for surrender. Sergeant Ian Mckay of the 3rd Battalion, **Parachute Regiment**, won a posthumous **Victoria Cross** during the action.

Po Valley, battle of

(1945; *World War II*) The Allied plan for the spring offensive in Italy was to break through the German **Gothic Line** situated in the mountains to attack the plains south of the river Po. Beginning on 4 April the V Corps of the British 8th Army fought its way up Highway 16 through the Argenta gap while the Polish II Corps captured Imola on the left. The II Corps of the US 5th Army moved north towards Bologna while the VI Corps struck to the west of the city. Bologna fell to the Poles (21 April). The US 10th Mountain Division crossed the Po south-east of Mantua (23 April). The German resistance collapsed and the Italian partisans revolted, taking control of Genoa, Milan and Venice. The 5th Army entered Verona (26 April) and Milan (29 April) while the 8th Army linked up with Tito's Yugoslavian partisans (1 May). On 29 April the German commander General Heinrich Vietinghoff-Scheel formally surrendered the German forces in Italy to Field Marshal Sir Harold **Alexander**.

Prendergast, Harry North Dalrymple (1834–1913)

Prendergast was born in India and educated in England. He obtained a commission in the Madras Engineers (1854) and after training at Chatham, returned to India (1856). He was wounded twice during the **Indian Mutiny**, once when saving the life of another officer. For this he was awarded the **Victoria Cross**. He was invalided home (1858) and became **brevet major** (1863). Prendergast commanded the Madras Sappers during the **Abyssinian** campaign and was present at the capture of **Magdala**. Now a brevet **colonel** he was in command of the Madras and Bombay Sappers and Military Secretary to the government of Madras (now Chennai). He was appointed to command the British Burma Division (1883) in Burma (now Myanmar) and in 1885 led the expeditionary force against Mandalay. He left Burma (1886) and became acting resident in various places in India. He was promoted to **general** (1887).

See also **Burma campaigns 1**

Preston, battle of

1. (1648; *Civil War*) After the Royalist collapse and the imprisonment of Charles I on the Isle of Wight there were many uprisings throughout the country against Parliament's government. James Hamilton, 1st Duke of Hamilton, commanded a force of 20,000 Scots led by General David Leslie which attacked Preston (17–20 August). This disorganised force was destroyed by 8,500 of **Cromwell's** disciplined troops. Hamilton was captured and executed. This battle ended active opposition to Parliament.

See also **Baillie, William**

2. (1715; *Jacobite Rebellions*) The Earl of Derwentwater, James Redcliffe, led a rebellion in the north of England in favour of the Stewart claimant to the throne, James Edward, the Old Pretender, against the Hanoverian George I. Reinforced by 4,000 Scots, he marched on Preston which he occupied. A royal army, commanded by General Charles **Wills**, re-took the town (14 November). Derwentwater was captured and executed, and the rebellion in England collapsed.

Prestonpans, battle of

(1745; *Jacobite Rebellions*) When Prince Charles Edward, the Young Pretender, landed in the Western Isles of Scotland from France (25 July) the clans rallied to his support and Lord George Murray raised an army of 2,500 at Glen Finnan in north-west Scotland. The Jacobites moved south to Prestonpans where they encountered a royal army of 3,000 commanded by General Sir John **Cope** (21 September). The Scottish charge routed the royal army, killing or wounding hundreds and capturing over a thousand. Charles then moved into England as far as Derby, but a lack of new recruits and his stretched lines of communication caused him to withdraw.

See also **Falkirk, battle of**; **Culloden Moor, battle of**

Pretorius, Andries Wilhelmus Jacobus (1798–1853)

Pretorius was born in Cape Colony, South Africa, and led the Great Trek from the British-dominated Cape Colony into Natal where, after conflict with the Zulus, he stabilised the position of the settlers by helping Mpande gain the Zulu throne. He then succeeded in forming a federal union between the settlers in Natal and those in the Transvaal. The British occupied Durban, Natal (1842) and Pretorius resigned as commandant-general. The governor of the Cape, Sir Henry Pottinger, ignored the Boers' grievances, so Pretorius led the Boers into the Transvaal (1847). This territory, Orange River Sovereignty, was annexed by the British (1848) which led the Boers to armed protest. Pretorius took Bloemfontein but was defeated at **Boomplaats** (August 1848). Pretorius fled deeper into the Transvaal and then took part in the negotiations which led to the independence of the Transvaal (1852) and to the independence of the Boers in the Orange River Sovereignty (1854) (concluded after Pretorius' death).

Prevost, George (1767–1816)

Prevost was born in New York and became a **major** in the British Army (1790). He served in the West Indies and was military governor of St. Lucia (1798). His conciliatory policy towards the French inhabitants gave some stability in the area and he was created a baronet (1805). He went to Nova Scotia as lieutenant-governor (1808) but moved to Quebec (1812) and become governor of both Upper and Lower Canada, doing much to placate the hostile French. During the **American War of 1812** he commanded the British forces in Canada, but his military reputation was marred particularly by his defeat at **Plattsburg** (1814). He was recalled to London to face a court-martial but died before it could take place.

Price's (Colonel John Price's Regiment of Foot) *See* **South Devonshire Regiment of Foot**

Prideaux, John (1718–59)
Prideaux was born at Honiton, Devon, and was appointed an **ensign** in the 3rd Foot Guards (**Scots Guards**) (1739). He served at **Dettingen** and was promoted to **lieutenant-colonel** (1748) and to **colonel** of the 58th Foot (**Rutlandshire Regiment**) (1758). He took his **regiment** to America (1759) and was killed at the battle of Fort Niagara.

Prince Albert's Light Infantry *See* **Somerset Light Infantry**

Prince Consort's Own *See* **Rifle Brigade, The**

Prince George of Denmark's Regiment of Foot *See* **East Kent Regiment**

Prince of Wales's *See* **North Staffordshire Regiment; Staffordshire Regiment (Prince of Wales's)**

Prince of Wales's Irish Regiment *See* **Royal Irish Fusiliers**

Prince of Wales's Own *See* **West Yorkshire Regiment**

Prince of Wales's Own Regiment *See* **Green Howards, The**

Prince of Wales's Own Regiment of Yorkshire
The **regiment** was formed (1958) by the amalgamation of the **West Yorkshire Regiment** (The Prince of Wales's Own) and the **East Yorkshire Regiment** (The Duke of York's Own). In 2006 it is due to unite with The Green Howards and The Duke of Wellington's Regiment to form The Yorkshire Regiment (14th/15th, 19th, and 33rd/76th Foot).

Prince of Wales's Own Royal Regiment of Welch Fusiliers *See* **Royal Welch Fusiliers**

Prince of Wales's Regiment of Foot
The **regiment** was raised (1824) as the 98th Regiment of Foot. The name was changed (1876) to the 98th (Prince of Wales's) Regiment of Foot. Following amalgamation in 1881 it became part of the **North Staffordshire Regiment**.

Prince of Wales's Volunteers *See* **Lancashire Regiment (The Prince of Wales's Volunteers); South Lancashire Regiment**

Princess Anne of Denmark's Regiment of Dragoons *See* **Queen's Own Hussars (4th)**

Princess Anne of Denmark's Regiment of Foot *See* **King's Regiment (Liverpool)**

Princess Charlotte of Wales's Dragoon Guards
The **regiment** was raised (1685) as the Earl of Shrewsbury's Horse (7th Horse) and re-ranked as the 6th Horse (1689). It then took its name from its **colonels** but joined the Irish establishment (1746) as the 2nd Horse. It became the 5th Dragoon Guards (1798) and was taken into royal patronage as the 5th (Princess Charlotte of Wales's) Dragoon Guards (1804). The regiment was part of the **Heavy Brigade** at the battle of **Balaclava**. It amalgamated (1922) with the **Inniskilling Dragoons**, eventually becoming the **Royal Inniskilling Dragoon Guards**.

Princess Charlotte of Wales's Regiment *See* Royal Berkshire Regiment (Princess Charlotte of Wales's)

Princess Charlotte of Wales's (or Hertfordshire) Regiment

The **regiment** was raised (1743) in Jamaica by the governor, Colonel Edward Trelawny, from several independent garrisons to aid the campaign in the West Indies. It was known as Colonel Trelawny's Regiment of Foot or the Jamaican Volunteers. The regiment was initially the 63rd Foot but became the 49th Regiment of Foot (1748). In 1782 it was called the 49th (or Hertfordshire) Regiment of Foot and in 1816 the 49th (Princess Charlotte of Wales's or Hertfordshire) Regiment. In the 1881 reorganisation it merged with the 66th to become the Berkshire Regiment.

See also **Royal Berkshire Regiment (Princess Charlotte of Wales's)**

Princess Louise's Argyllshire Highlanders

The **regiment** was raised (1794) by Colonel Douglas Campbell of Lochnell as the 98th (Argyllshire) Regiment of Foot (Highlanders). It was re-numbered (1798) as the 91st (Argyllshire) Regiment of Foot (Highlanders). The title was further changed to 91st Regiment of Foot (1809); 91st (Argyllshire) Regiment of Foot (1820); the 91st (Argyll Highlanders) Regiment of Foot (1864); and to the 91st (Princess Louise's Argyllshire Highlanders) Regiment of Foot (1872). It merged (1881) with the 93rd to form the **Argyll and Sutherland Highlanders**.

Princess Margaret's Own Glasgow and Ayrshire Regiment *See* Royal Highland Fusiliers (Princess Margaret's Own Glasgow and Ayrshire Regiment)

Princess Mary's Own 10th Gurkha Rifles

The original unit was raised (1887) as the Kubo Valley Police Battalion of military police. The name was changed to the 10th (Burma) Regiment Madras Infantry (1890); 10th Regiment (1st Burma Rifles) Madras Infantry (1892); 10th Regiment (1st Burma Gurkha Rifles) Madras Infantry (1896); 10th Gurkha Rifles (1901); and after transfer from the Indian Army to the British Army on Indian independence became the 10th Princess Mary's Own Gurkha Rifles (1949). In 1994, along with the three other remaining Gurkha infantry regiments, it became part of the **Royal Gurkha Rifles**.

Princess of Wales's Own Regiment *See* Green Howards, The; Queen's Bays, The

Princess of Wales's Own Royal Regiment of Dragoons *See* Queen's Own Hussars

Princess of Wales's Royal Regiment (Queen's and Royal Hampshires)

The regiment was formed (1992) by the amalgamation of the **Queen's Regiment** and the **Royal Hampshire Regiment**. It has seen service in conflicts in **Kosovo**, Bosnia and most recently in the **Iraq War**.

Princess Victoria's Regiment

The **regiment** was raised (1793) by Colonel William Crosbie as the 89th Regiment of Foot. (There had previously been an 89th Foot raised during the **Seven Years' War** and disbanded soon after; see **Munro, Hector**) The name was changed (1866) to the 89th (Princess Victoria's) Regiment of Foot and in 1881, following amalgamation with the 87th the regiment, became part of the **Royal Irish Fusiliers**.

prisoner of war

A member of the armed forces captured by the enemy. The treatment of prisoners of war is governed by the third **Geneva convention** (1929).

private

The lowest rank in the British Army. Privates are known by other names, e.g. gunner in the **Royal Artillery** and sapper in the **Royal Engineers**.

Provisional IRA *See* **Northern Ireland**

proximity fuse
Any sensory device that explodes a missile when it is near to its target, rather than on contact

purchase system
Though the sale of **commissions** was forbidden in the early 18th century the practice was widespread and a royal warrant (1720) fixed the price of a first commission at £450, with each commission paid for on a sliding scale (unless the vacancy was by death, then the promotion was by seniority). By 1856 a captaincy could cost £2,400. Prices officially varied between **cavalry** (dearer) and **infantry**, and unofficially (and illegally) between **regiments** depending how fashionable and socially desirable they were. Rules set down minimum periods of service in a rank before a more senior one could be bought and after 1711 no commission was supposed to be given to anyone under 16. Despite these safeguards the system led to experienced, but impecunious, officers being passed over for promotion in favour of young and inexperienced individuals. About two-thirds of commissions in the period 1700–1871 were obtained through purchase, but this proportion was much lower in wartime. The system was abolished (1871) by the **Cardwell reforms**, costing £7 million in compensation payments to the officers who thereby lost an asset they had paid for. In favour of the purchase system was the fact that it could allow ambitious officers to advance quickly to senior positions. In the **Royal Engineers** and Royal **Artillery** (not part of the Army but controlled for most of the period by the Board of **Ordnance**), however, promotion was strictly by seniority and painfully slow, whatever the merits of the individual.

puttees, putties
Long strips of cloth wound around the legs and the top of the boots to prevent mud getting in. They were introduced from India in the late 19th century and were standard during **World War I**. They were discontinued on the introduction of **battle dress** clothing and equipment in **World War II**.

Q

QGM *abbreviation of* **Queen's Gallantry Medal**

QRF *See* **rapid reaction force**

quarrel
The **bolt** of a crossbow

quartermaster
An officer with the responsibility of arranging supplies and accommodation for the troops

quarto-cannon *See* **cannon**

Quatre Bras, battle of
(1815; *French Wars*) **Napoleon** drove into present-day Belgium to force a wedge between the Prussian Army commanded by Field Marshal Gebhard von **Blücher** and the Anglo-Dutch army commanded by the Duke of **Wellington**. Napoleon attacked Blücher in the east, winning the battle of Ligny (16 June), while Marshal Michel **Ney** attacked Wellington in the west. Wellington had been taken by surprise by the speed and direction of the French advance and therefore his advance guard at Quatre Bras was initially greatly outnumbered by Ney's force (16 June). However, sufficient Anglo-Dutch troops, including the division commanded by General Thomas **Picton**, arrived in the course of the day to hold off the French advance. The battle was indecisive. Ney failed to use his I Corps due to a misunderstanding with Napoleon. Wellington withdrew towards **Waterloo**.

Quebec, battle of
1. (1759; *French and Indian War*) General James **Wolfe** took a force of 9,000 troops in boats up the St. Lawrence river and landed on the Ile d'Orléans opposite Quebec (27 June); some troops landed at Pointe Levi (Lévis) opposite Quebec and others moved up river to cut the French General **Montcalm's** communications. Wolfe landed a detachment commanded by General George **Townshend** on the north bank of the river (31 July) but the attack was repulsed and the position abandoned. On 12 September, Wolfe landed 4,500 men from boats and climbed up on to the Plains of Abraham on the landward side of the city. In the pitched battle that followed 1,400 French were killed, including **Montcalm**; 660 British were killed and Wolfe also died from his wounds. The French retired into the city, but surrendered (18 September).
2. (1760; *French and Indian War*) The French, having retreated up the St. Lawrence river to Montreal, moved to re-take Quebec. The French General Duc François de Lévis attacked the city with 8,500 men. The city was defended by General James **Murray** with 4,000 men. The armies met (27 April) outside the town and Murray was defeated, falling back into Quebec. The city held out until the British fleet arrived (May). The French withdrew to Montreal.
3. (1775; *American War of Independence*) Having occupied Montreal (13 November), the American General Richard Montgomery took 300 men to attack the British in Quebec. He was joined on the Plains of Abraham by 600 colonists led by Colonel Benedict Arnold. The Americans attacked, only to be repulsed by the 1,800-man garrison commanded by General Sir Guy **Carleton**. At the end of the winter the colonists fell back to Lake Champlain.

Queen Alexandra's Imperial Military Nursing Service *See* Queen Alexandra's Royal Army Nursing Corps

Queen Alexandra's Own Hussars *See* Hussars, 19th

Queen Alexandra's Royal Army Nursing Corps

By 1866 it was decided that civilian nurses could serve in army hospitals and they came under the control of the Army Nursing Service (1881). These nurses became part of the Army as Queen Alexandra's Imperial Nursing Service (1902). They were supplemented by the Territorial Nursing Service (1907). These two branches were combined (1949) as Queen Alexandra's Royal Army Nursing Corps, which still exists as part of the **Army Medical Services**.

Queen Anne's War (1702–13)

The fighting in America which was part of the War of the **Spanish Succession**. The only major battle was at **Port Royal** (1710).

[After *Queen Anne of England* (1665–1714), who reigned during this time]

Queen Consort's Regiment of Dragoons *See* King's Own Hussars

Queen Elizabeth's Own Gurkha Rifles (6th)

The **regiment** was formed (1817) as the Cuttack Legion. It underwent several changes of name: Rangpur Light Infantry Battalion (1823); 8th Rangpur Local Light Infantry (1826); 8th Assam Light Infantry (1827); and 1st Assam Light Infantry (1850). It became part of the Indian Army after the demise of the East India Company's Army and was known as: the 46th Bengal Native Infantry (1861); 42nd (Assam) Regiment of Bengal Native (Light Infantry) (1865); 42nd Goorkha Light Infantry (1886); 42nd (Goorkha) Regiment of Bengal (Light) Infantry (1889); 42nd Gurkha (Rifle) Regiment Bengal Infantry (1891); 42nd Gurkha Rifles (1901); 6th Gurkha Rifles (1903); and, after transfer to the British Army in 1948, the 6th Queen Elizabeth's Own Gurkha Rifles (1959). It is now part of the **Royal Gurkha Rifles** (1994).

Queen's Bays, The

The **regiment** was raised (1685) as the Earl of Peterborough's Regiment of Horse. The name changed with its **colonels** until 1715 when it became the Princess of Wales's Own Regiment. It became the Queen's Own Regiment (1727) and the 2nd or Queen's Own Regiment of Dragoon Guards (1747). It adopted the exclusive use of bay horses (1766) and was renamed the 2nd Dragoon Guards (Queen's Bays) (1870) and the Queen's Bays (2nd Dragoon Guards) (1921). The regiment fought at the battle of **Warburg**. It merged (1959) with the **1st King's Dragoon Guards** (*see* **Dragoons, 1st**) to form the 1st Queen's Dragoon Guards.

Also called **The Bays**

Queen's (King's) commission *See* commission

Queen's Dragoon Guards, 1st (The Welsh Cavalry)

The **regiment** was formed (1959) by the amalgamation of the 1st†King's Dragoon Guards and the The Queen's Bays and became part of the **Royal Armoured Corps**

Queen's Gallantry Medal

The award was instituted (1974) for exemplary acts of bravery. Primarily intended for civilians, it can also be awarded to military personnel. It replaced the **British Empire Medal**.

Queen's Lancashire Regiment

The **regiment** was created (1970) by the amalgamation of the **Lancashire Regiment (The Prince of Wales's Volunteers)** and the **Loyal Regiment** (North Lancashire). It is due to unite with The King's Own Royal Border Regiment and The King's Regiment in 2006 to form The Duke of Lancaster's Regiment (King's, Lancashire and Border).

Queen's Own Buffs, The Kent Regiment

The **regiment** was formed (1961) by the amalgamation of The Buffs (**East Kent Regiment**) and the **Queen's Own Royal West Kent Regiment**. In 1966 it became part of the **Queen's Regiment**.

Queen's Own Cameron Highlanders

The **regiment** was raised (1793) by Major Alan **Cameron** of Erracht and named the 79th Regiment of Foot (or Cameronian Volunteers). The name has been changed to 79th Regiment of Foot (or Cameronian Highlanders) (1804); 79th Regiment of Foot (or Cameron Highlanders) (1806); 79th Queen's Own Cameron Highlanders (1873); and The Queen's Own Cameron Highlanders (1881).

Queen's Own Highlanders

The **regiment** was formed (1961) by the amalgamation of the **Seaforth Highlanders** and the **Queen's Own Cameron Highlanders**. In 1994 it united with **Gordon Highlanders** (Seaforth and Camerons) to form The Highlanders (Seaforth, Gordons and Camerons).

Queen's Own Hussars

The **regiment** was formed (1958) by the amalgamation of the 3rd **King's Own Hussars** and the **Queen's Own Hussars (7th)**. In 1993 it became part of The Queen's Royal Hussars (The Queen's Own and Royal Irish).

Queen's Own Hussars (4th)

The **regiment** was raised (1685) by Colonel John Berkeley from several independent regiments of dragoons, and named the Princess Anne of Denmark's Regiment of Dragoons. The name was changed to the 4th Dragoons (1751); 4th (or Queen's Own) Regiment of Dragoons (1788); 4th Light Dragoons (1818); 4th (or Queen's Own) Light Dragoons (1819); 4th (Queen's Own) Hussars (1861); and 4th Queen's Own Hussars (1921). It became part of the **Queen's Royal Irish Hussars** in 1958.

Queen's Own Hussars (7th)

The **regiment** was raised (1690) by Colonel Richard Cunningham from several independent troops of Scottish dragoons. They were known originally as Cunningham's Dragoons and the name was then changed with the **colonel** until 1715 when the regiment was designated the Princess of Wales's Own Royal Regiment of Dragoons. The name was changed frequently: The Queen's Own Royal Regiment of Dragoons (1727); the 7th (or Queen's Own) Regiment of Dragoons (1751); the 7th (or Queen's Own) Light Dragoons (1783); the 7th (or The Queen's Own) Regiment of (Light) Dragoons (Hussars) (1807); the 7th (The Queen's Own) Regiment of Hussars (1861); the 7th (Queen's Own) Hussars (1880); and the 7th Queen's Own Hussars (1921). It became part of the **Queen's Own Hussars** in 1958.

Queen's Own Regiment

1. The **regiment** was raised (1756) by Colonel James Abercromby as the 52nd Regiment of Foot. It was re-designated (1756) the 50th Regiment of Foot; 50th or West Kent Regiment of Foot (1782); the 50th (or Duke of Clarence's) Regiment of Foot (1827); the 50th or the Queen's Own Regiment of Foot (1831) and the 50th (Queen's Own) Regiment (1856). It amalgamated with the 97th to form the **Queen's Own Royal West Kent Regiment** in 1881.

2.

See **Queen's Bays, The**

Queen's Own Regiment of Foot *See* **Foot, 96th**

Queen's Own Regiment of Hussars *See* **Queen's Own Hussars (4th)**

Queen's Own Royal Regiment of Dragoons *See* **Queen's Own Hussars (7th)**

Queen's Own Royal West Kent Regiment

The **regiment** was formed (1881) by the amalgamation of the 50th Regiment of Foot (**Queen's Own Regiment**) and the **Earl of Ulster's Regiment of Foot**. It amalgamated in turn with the **East Kent Regiment** in 1961 to form the **Queen's Own Buffs, The Kent Regiment**.

Queen's Regiment
The **regiment** was formed (1966) by the amalgamation of the **Queen's Royal Surrey Regiment**, the **Queen's Own Buffs, The Kent Regiment**, the **Royal Sussex Regiment** and the **Middlesex Regiment** (Duke of Cambridgeshire's Own). In 1992 it amalgamated with The Royal Hampshire Regiment to form The Princess of Wales's Royal Regiment (Queen's and Royal Hampshires).

Queen's Royal Hussars (The Queen's Own and Royal Irish)
The **regiment** was formed in 1993 by the amalgamation of The Queen's Royal Irish Hussars and the Queens' Own Hussars

Queen's Royal Irish Hussars
The **regiment** was formed (1958) by the amalgamation of the **Queen's Own Hussars (4th)** and the 8th **King's Royal Irish Hussars**. In 1993 it amalgamated with The Queen's Own Hussars, to form The Queen's Royal Hussars (The Queen's Own and Royal Irish).

Queen's Royal Lancers
The regiment was formed (1993) by the amalgamation of the **16th/5th Queens' Royal Lancers** and the **17th/21st Lancers**. It is part of the **Royal Armoured Corps**.

Queen's Royal Lancers, 9th
The **regiment** was raised (1715) as Owen Wynne's Regiment of Dragoons and changed name with its <IXREF[colonel]s until 1751, when it became the 9th Regiment of Dragoons. It subsequently became the 9th Light Dragoons (1783), converted to **lancers** (1816) and was renamed the 9th (or Queen's Royal) Lancers (1830), the 9th (Queen's Royal) Lancers (1861) and the 9th Queen's Royal Lancers (1921). It joined the **Royal Armoured Corps** (1939) and amalgamated (1960) with the **12th Royal Lancers** to form the **9th/12th Royal Lancers**.

Queens' Royal Lancers, 16th/5th
The regiment was formed (1922) as the **16th/5th Lancers** by the amalgamation of the **16th The Queen's Lancers** and the 5th Royal Irish Lancers and renamed 16th/5th The Queen's Royal Lancers (1954). It amalgamated (1993) with the **17th/21st Lancers** to form the **Queen's Royal Lancers**.

Queen's Royal Regiment (West Surrey)
The **regiment** was raised (1661) by the Earl of Peterborough as the Tangier Regiment of Foot. It became (1684) the Queen's Regiment of Foot; the Queen Dowager's Regiment of Foot (1686); the Queen's Royal Regiment (1703); HRH The Princess of Wales's Own Regiment of Foot (1714); the Queen's Own Royal Regiment of Foot (1727); 2nd Foot (Queen's Royal Regiment) (1751); the 2nd (Queen's Royal) Regiment (1855); the Queen's (Royal West Surrey) Regiment (1881); and in 1921 the Queen's Royal Regiment (West Surrey). It became part of the **Queen's Royal Surrey Regiment** in 1959. The badge of the lamb was given to the regiment by Charles II's queen, Catherine of Braganza.

Queen's Royal Surrey Regiment
The **regiment** was formed (1959) by the amalgamation of the **Queen's Royal Regiment (West Surrey)** and the **East Surrey Regiment**. It became part of the **Queen's Regiment** in 1966.

Queenston Heights, battle of
(1812; *War of 1812*) The Americans had surrendered at **Detroit** (16 August) but the centre prong of their three-pronged attack into Canada was more successful. General Stephen van Rensselaer crossed the Niagara river and attacked Queenston Heights. The British commander General Sir Isaac **Brock** was killed. The British rallied 1,000 men, and the expected reinforcements did not arrive to support the 600 Americans. The Americans were defeated and fell back.

queue

During the 18th and early 19th centuries soldiers were required to wear their hair long and tied back in a queue, or pigtail. This custom was abandoned officially in 1808.
[Via French from Latin *cauda* 'tail']

R

rabinet *See* **esmeril**

Raglan, Lord (1788–1855)
During the **Peninsular War**, Fitzroy Somerset was the Duke of **Wellington's** military secretary. He lost an arm at **Waterloo** when riding a few feet away from Wellington. He was Military Secretary at the Horse Guards from 1827 and was made **Master-General of the Ordnance** (*see* **Ordnance, Board of**) (1852) and created Baron Raglan. He was promoted **field marshal** and appointed the British **commander-in-chief** at the beginning of the **Crimean War**. The combined French and British forces won the battle of the **Alma** (20 September 1854). An ambiguous order he issued was largely responsible for the disastrous charge of the **Light Brigade** at the battle of **Balaclava**. Raglan was blamed for the lack of supplies arriving for the troops during the winter of 1854–55 and for the general tardiness of the campaign. By now he was ill and died soon after the resumption of the siege of **Sebastopol** (now Sevastopol).
Also known as **Somerset, Fitzroy James Henry**

Ramadi, battle of
(1917; *World War I*) Having captured Baghdad, the British commander in Mesopotamia (now Iraq), General Sir Frederick **Maude** consolidated his position and later in the year (September 28–29) attacked the Turks at Ramadi. The Turkish garrison was overwhelmed, many being taken prisoner. Maude returned to Baghdad where he died of cholera (18 November).

RAMC *abbreviation of* **Royal Army Medical Corps**

Ramillies, battle of
(1706; *War of the Spanish Succession*) In the Spanish Netherlands (now Belgium) the French marshal Duc de Villeroi moved eastwards to attack from the Dyle river to the Meuse between Namur and Liège. The French were intercepted at Ramillies by a 50,000-strong Anglo-Dutch-German force commanded by the Duke of **Marlborough** (23 May). The 25,000-strong Allied **cavalry** defeated a similar force of French cavalry on the southern flank while the **infantry** made a frontal attack on Ramillies. Villeroi's army of 50,000 was defeated, losing some 15,000 killed, wounded or captured. The Allies lost about 5,000. This victory led to the surrender of Brussels and Antwerp.

Ramnagar, battle of
(1848; *Sikh Wars*) The Sikhs wished to overthrow the government of Sir Henry **Lawrence** imposed after the First **Sikh War** and an insurrection took place in the Punjab. General Sir Hugh **Gough** moved an Anglo-Indian army up the Chenab river which he attempted to cross (22 November) at Ramnagar. He was opposed by 35,000 Sikhs and was repelled.

Rangpur Light Infantry *See* **Queen Elizabeth's Own Gurkha Rifles (6th)**

rank badges
In the early days of uniforms there were no badges of rank, the rank of an officer being indicated by the richness of his clothing. Badges of rank for officers were introduced in the East India Company Army during the 18th century but it was not until February 1810 that they were authorised in the British Army, when combinations of stars and crowns indicated the rank of regimental officers and the sword and baton were worn by **general officers**. Originally they were worn on the **epaulettes** but when epaulettes

became obsolete (1855) they were worn on the collar. In 1880 the badges were still worn on the collar but now on twisted cords.

ranker
A junior soldier, so-called because men of this status paraded in the rank and file (ranks going from left to right and files from front to rear). Officers did not parade in the rank and file but stood separately from the main body of troops.

rapid reaction force
A body of troops, usually small, trained and supplied ready to move quickly to a destination in response to an emergency.
Abbreviation **RRF**; *Also called* **quick reaction force**

rapier *See* sword

Rapier Field Standard C *See* anti-aircraft weapons

rattan
An Indian palm-tree, the leaves of which were plaited to make the insides of sun helmets.
[From Malay *rotan*]

Ravenspur
1. (1399) The government of Richard II was ineffectual and corrupt. This led to rebellion. Henry Bolingbroke of Lancaster landed at Ravenspur from France (4 July). He was opposed by King Richard II whom he captured (August) and imprisoned in the Tower of London.
2. (1471; *Wars of the Roses*) The Lancastrian Earl of Warwick, Richard Neville, had landed in Devon (September 1470) and marched on London, releasing King Henry VI from the Tower. The Yorkist Edward landed at Ravenspur (14 March) and marched into London, having outmanoeuvred a superior force commanded by the Earl of Northumberland, John Neville. Henry VI was again a captive in the Tower.

Rawlinson, Henry Seymour (1864–1925)
Rawlinson was educated at Eton and Sandhurst and was **gazetted** to the **King's Royal Rifle Corps** (1884) with which he served in India and Burma (now Myanmar) as **aide-de-camp** to Sir Frederick **Roberts**. He resigned this post and returned home on the death of his mother. He was gazetted as **captain** in the **Coldstream Guards** (1892) and attended the **Staff College** at Camberley. He was appointed brigadier-major at Aldershot (1895) having succeeded to the baronetcy on the death of his father. He served on **Kitchener's** staff at **Omdurman** and was promoted to **brevet lieutenant-colonel** (1899). Rawlinson then went to South Africa (1899) and served on the staffs of Sir George **White** and Lord **Roberts**. Having returned home he again went to South Africa to command a mobile column. For his service in South Africa he was promoted to brevet **colonel** (1902). He held an appointment in the **War Office**, was promoted to **brigadier-general** and became commandant of the Staff College (1903). In 1904 he was promoted to **major-general** and given command of the 3rd Division. In 1914 he served in Flanders, ultimately becoming **lieutenant-general** in command of the 4th Army. In this role he was the principal army commander during the battle of the **Somme** (1916) and was largely responsible for the tactical decisions that turned the first day of that battle into the worst in the British Army's history. After leading the 4th Army in the final successful advances of the war Rawlinson returned home (1919) and was appointed to carry out the evacuation of the Allied intervention force in northern Russia. In 1920 he was appointed **commander-in-chief** in India where he carried out radical reforms in the army. He died in India.
See also **Amiens, battle of**

rearguard
A body of troops positioned at the back of a moving column to protect it from attack.
See also **vanguard**

reconnaissance

A survey of the enemy position, usually by a small body of men, to ascertain their strength before attacking with the main force

Redan, battle of the

(1855; *Crimean War*) A defensive position south of **Sebastopol** (now Sevastopol) that was attacked unsuccessfully in June. It was attacked again on 8 September by the British, but did not fall until the French captured a nearby fortress. Its capture led to the fall of Sebastopol (11 September).

red coats

The typical uniform of the British **infantry** from the mid-1700s, last worn in action during the **Khartoum** expedition (1884)

Red Crescent *See* **Red Cross**

Red Cross

The International Committee for the Relief of the Wounded was founded in 1863, originating from the work of the Swiss philanthropist Henri Dunant, who campaigned to alleviate suffering in wartime after witnessing the battle of Solferino (1859). It was internationally recognised in 1864 at the meeting that agreed the first **Geneva convention**, when it adopted as its symbol the Swiss national flag (a white cross on a red background) with the colours reversed. It was renamed the International Committee of the Red Cross (ICRC) in 1875. Although its work has expanded to care for the needs of suffering civilians in peace time, in war time the society acts as guardian of the Geneva Conventions: a neutral intermediary providing for the wounded and **prisoners of war** on either side. National Red Cross societies have been founded in most countries, with those in Moslem states known as the Red Crescent since 1906. They are grouped with the ICRC in an umbrella organisation, the International Movement of the Red Cross and Red Crescent (known as the International Red Cross until 1986).

Reddersberg, battle of

(1900; *Boer Wars*) Five companies of British infantry were surrounded by a Boer force (3 April). The British were forced to surrender after a day through lack of water.

reforms after the Boer War

The wars in South Africa had revealed serious deficiencies in the forward planning of the Army. As a result the General Staff was formed (1904), at last giving the Army a central planning body responsible both for day-to-day operations and long-term strategy. The appointment of **commander-in-chief** was abolished and control was vested in the Army Council that consisted of the Secretary of State for War, four military members (with the most senior of them being the Chief of the General Staff), and two senior civil servants. The Defence Committee, which had existed on and off since the War of the **Austrian Succession** was re-instituted as the Committee for Imperial Defence which advised the Cabinet and in particular co-ordinated the functions of the Army and Navy, and later the Royal Air Force. The reforms continued until, under the Liberal Secretary of State for War, Richard Haldane, an expeditionary force was formed. This consisted of six **infantry divisions** and one **cavalry** division, each self-contained with staff and reserves. It was specifically designed for employment in a future European war. This was the first time that the peacetime British Army had established such an organisation, and marked a total change from the old style of Army organisation with small units scattered across the Empire that were neither trained nor equipped for operations in divisions or other higher-level formations. To support this new organisation some members of the former **militia** were transferred to the new Special Reserve and earmarked as reinforcements for the Regulars. The former **yeomanry** and **volunteer** units became the new **Territorial Army** and were formed into 14 Territorial divisions but these were allocated to home defence and not required to serve abroad. **Staff Colleges** were enlarged and Officers Training Corps were formed in universities and schools. The Dominions were now consulted on matters of defence, the first Imperial Defence Conference being held in 1907. The Chief of the General Staff became the Chief of the Imperial General Staff.

reforms after the Crimean War

The disorganisation that became evident during the **Crimean War** led to greater co-ordination and centralised control. The **Royal Engineers** and **Artillery**, which had been controlled by the Board of **Ordnance**, were transferred to the **War Office** and finally became fully integrated with the rest of the Army. An Army Clothing Factory was opened and **colonels** were no longer responsible for supplying uniforms to their **regiments**. The Small Arms Factory was opened at **Enfield**. The **Staff College** was built. Staff appointments were limited to three years tenure so that officers did not lose contact with the troops. Instruction camps were opened at Aldershot and then at the Curragh and Colchester. A School of Gunnery was established at Sheerness and a School of Musketry at Hyde. The Army's medical services were revised (see **Royal Army Medical Corps**) and military hospitals built. Parliament voted (1862) for a gradual withdrawal of British garrisons from the self-governing colonies.
See also **Cardwell reforms**

reforms of the Duke of York

After his return from the Netherlands (1794), Frederick, Duke of **York**, the **commander-in-chief** of the Army, undertook a programme of reform. He forced officers to apply for leave through the proper channels, and established a system of annual confidential reports. Officers were required to serve for six years before they could become **majors**. The **Royal Military College** (*see* **Royal Military Academy**) was established (1800) so that impecunious officers could qualify for promotion on merit. Frederick established the Duke of York's **Royal Military School** at Chelsea for soldiers' sons. It later moved to Dover. He established the Corps of Waggoners, the first regularly organised system of military transport (the Army previously relied on civilian contractors and personnel who were not subject to military discipline), and improved the medical services, making the government responsible for medical stores and hospitals. **Cavalry regiments** now had a uniform system of drill and their own veterinary officers, saddlers and armourers. He established the Chaplain-General's Department and a proper staff at the Horse Guards. The latter had Adjutant-General's and Military Secretary's departments while Operations and Intelligence sections were initiated. The duke took the administration of discipline at home away from the Secretary of State for War and assumed this responsibility himself.

regiment

When regiments were first formalised in the 17th century, a regiment was a body of troops, either **infantry** or **cavalry**, that were raised, equipped and trained by a nobleman or other prominent personality, and commanded by him as its **colonel**. In the infantry a regiment may have one or more **battalions** and in the cavalry usually has several **squadrons**. Since the early 18th century cavalry regiments have usually deployed with all of their squadrons serving together so that the regiment is both the administrative body (concerned with raising, training and equipping the troops), and the tactical body (which controls them in battle). In the British Army (though not in most other armies), infantry regiments have always been principally administrative bodies. Up to the **Cardwell reforms** of 1881, infantry regiments could have one or up to four or more battalions. Where a regiment had more than one battalion these might serve in different **brigades**, or in a two-battalion regiment one might be on home service, raising recruits and training them, while the other battalion was abroad defending the Empire. After 1881 regiments had two regular battalions, with others being available from the **Militia**, **Volunteers** or **Territorial Army** at various times. During the two World Wars regiments in the greatly expanded army might have had 20 or more battalions. Members of the Royal **Artillery** or the **Royal Corps of Signals** regard these bodies as regiments in the same way as the infantry or cavalry units, though in the case of the Royal Artillery and others their tactical subdivisions might themselves be titled the xxth Field Regiment. The regimental system has been both a source of strength and weakness to the British Army. Each regiment has always had its own distinctive uniform, badges, customs and **colours**; its members have always owed loyalty to the particular regiment, usually spending their whole military careers with the same regiment and often being recruited from a particular area of the country. This meant that the British Army infantry battalions and cavalry regiments have tended to be tight-knit troops who fought hard for their comrades, but co-operation between regiments was poor. Before the 20th century, brigades and **divisions** were assembled on an *ad hoc* basis in time of war with the constituent battalions having no experience of working with the others. Even in **World War II**, British **tank** and infantry units struggled to co-operate as effectively as those of the German Army, which had a different organisational system.

See also **colonel**

[Via French from late Latin *regimentum* 'rule', from Latin *regere* 'to rule']

regimental anniversaries

Most **regiments** celebrate the anniversaries of their most outstanding engagements. These are not necessarily victories. The first anniversary to be celebrated was **Blenheim** (2 August 1704), and this by the **King's Regiment** and the Royal Anglian Regiment, which fought as the 8th Foot and the 16th Foot (see **Bedfordshire and Hertfordshire Regiment**) respectively.

regimental bands *See* **bands**

regimental marches

Military bands have been used since the earliest times, but quick marches were not officially authorised for **infantry regiments** until 1882 and the slow marches for **cavalry** until 1903. From these dates regiments adopted their own particular quick march and slow march. The reasons for individual choices of marches by regiments are far from clear.

See also **bands**

regimental mascots

The adoption of regimental mascots goes back a long time: for instance, the **Royal Welch Fusiliers** have had a goat as their mascot since the 18th century. There are now nine regiments which have mascots officially recognised by the Ministry of Defence.

regiments, naming and numbering of

Up to 1751 **regiments** were named after their **colonels** who had virtually complete control over them. After 1751 regiments of both **infantry** and **cavalry** were numbered although they may still have been known by the **colonel's** name, by a royal connection, by a nickname like **Green Howards**, or by a territorial affiliation. The numbering of the regiments denoted an order of precedence; in earliest times the most senior regiment was entitled to take position on the right of the line of battle. For most of the 18th and 19th century territorial names, though used, did not have any real significance. After 1881 numbers were largely abolished and territorial titles were given – these denoted the area from which the regiment normally drew its recruits.

See also **Cardwell reforms**

regular army

The regular army came into existence on the accession of Charles II (1660). Before the **Civil War** the only **standing army** was a small force of Yeomen of the Guard. Previously, in time of war forces were recruited by local lords or land-owners, a tradition which extended into the 18th century and was reflected in the **regiments'** names such as 'Colonel X's Regiment of Foot'. These regiments wore their **colonel's** insignia. Since medieval times Parliament had kept the right to control taxation to finance expenditure on the armed forces but these were still commanded by the monarch. After the Glorious Revolution (1688) Parliament increased its control, establishing in the **Bill of Rights** (1689) that it was illegal for there to be a standing army in peacetime without parliamentary consent and taking control of its discipline by the **Mutiny Act**. Charles II's original army consisted of four regiments, the Life Guards, the Royal Horse Guards (**Blues and Royals**), the Royal Regiment of Guards (**Grenadier Guards**) and Monck's Regiment (**Coldstream Guards**). These regiments were added to (1685–89) and again in 1701 with more being formed during the major wars up to 1800 (regiments were also often disbanded at the end of wars). A few more were added after this date, but by the end of the 19th century amalgamations had begun. This has continued to the present day, particularly amongst **infantry** regiments, but new specialist regiments, like the **Army Air Corps** or the **Royal Electrical and Mechanical Engineers** have been added to the army in response to technological changes.

See also **Cardwell reforms; New Model Army; reforms after the Boer War; regiment**

REME *abbreviation of* **Royal Electrical and Mechanical Engineers**

reservist
A member of the armed forces who can be called upon for active service in time of war. A reservist is often a person who has served in the armed forces and is then on a reserve list for a specific number of years.

reveille
The playing of a **bugle** or the beating of a drum to awaken troops at the beginning of the day
[Alteration of French *réveillez* 'to wake up']

review
An inspection of a **parade** by a senior officer or the sovereign

revolver
A multi-shot **pistol** in which the bullets are contained in a revolving cylinder. Early versions, known as 'pepperpots' had several revolving barrels but during the 17th century pistols with a revolving chamber firing through a single barrel were invented. The first large scale production was of the revolver patented by Samuel Colt (1835–36). In Colt's early versions the cylinder revolved as the hammer was cocked manually, but by the mid-1800's the double-action revolver was perfected where the hammer was cocked and the cylinder revolved as the trigger was pulled.

Richard I (the Lionheart) (1157–99; reigned 1189–99)
The son of Henry II of England and Eleanor of Aquitaine. Devoted more than most medieval kings to the practice of warfare, at which he was exceptionally skilled, most of his adult life was taken up with battles in France to retain his possessions there and in his major role as a leader of the Third Crusade.

Richard's (Colonel Solomon Richard's Regiment of Foot) *See* **Royal Leicestershire Regiment**

Riding Troop, Royal Horse Artillery *See* **Artillery, Royal Regiment of**

Rietfontein, battle of
(1899; *Boer Wars*) A British force of 4,000, commanded by Sir George **White**, were moving to cover the retreat of Colonel Yule from Dundee. After an indecisive action against the Boers, White retired to Ladysmith, having prevented the Boers from interfering with Yule's retreat (24 October).

rifle
Any firearm that has grooves inside the barrel which spin the projectile is said to be rifled. Although **pistols**, **machine guns**, **field guns** and **howitzers** have rifled barrels, the term 'rifle' is confined to weapons that are fired from the shoulder by an individual soldier. It was recognised early that grooves inside the barrel of a gun increased its range and accuracy, and rifled firearms were in use by the 15th century. However, they did not become standard military firearms until the 19th century. This was because the bullet of a rifle must fit tightly inside the barrel if it is to be spun effectively by the

rifling. Because of the limitations of **flintlock** firing mechanisms and ammunition **cartridges**, a smoothbore **musket** could be fired and reloaded a great deal more quickly than a rifle and hence weapons of this type were preferred despite their poor accuracy. After experiencing losses at the hands of rifle-armed marksmen during the **American War of Independence**, the British Army began taking more interest in **light infantry** tactics and special weapons to accompany them. The first rifle used in quantity was the Baker rifle made by a Whitechapel (London) gun-maker and issued to the Experimental Corps of Riflemen (**Rifle Brigade, The**) (1800). The development soon after this of the **percussion cap** made different designs possible and also made it possible for these to be used by the whole army. The Brunswick percussion rifle, developed from the Baker **rifle**, was introduced around 1850. The barrel had two grooves in it, into which fitted the two sides of a raised band that went around the diameter of the shot. Although this increased the range to about 700 yards and improved the accuracy of the weapon, it made it difficult to load, the shot having to be rammed into it along the grooving. The Minié rifle, used in the **Crimea**, had a special design of bullet which helped with the speed of loading. The major development was the move to a breech-loading design, the Snider rifle, which was issued in 1866 and used in the campaign in Abyssinia (now Ethiopia). In 1871 the Army converted to the Martini-Henry rifle and in 1892 this was replaced by the bolt-action .303-inch Lee-Metford – the first magazine rifle – which was made possible by the development of metallic cartridge cases. The standard British rifle in both World Wars was the .303-inch Short Magazine Lee-Enfield (SMLE). Since then this has been replaced by self-loading automatic or **assault rifle** designs. These use the explosive power of the round just fired to reload the weapon and prepare it for firing again; they can fire either single shots or bursts of several rounds. The first designs were similar in calibre to the SMLE but more modern weapons are smaller calibre so that the soldier can carry more ammunition and the weapon can be reduced in size and made lighter. The design currently in service with the British Army is the 5.56mm **SA80** family of weapons. This was much criticised for the unreliability it showed in the 1991 **Gulf War** and other combats, but these problems have been resolved in the latest version, the SA80A2, which was introduced in 2002. Specialised snipers use either the **L96 Sniper rifle** or the **L115A1 Long Range Rifle**, conventional rifles designed to fire individual rounds accurately over 900 metres and 1100 metres respectively.

[From the verb to rifle, from French *rifler* 'to scratch']

Rifle Brigade, The

This **regiment** was initially established as the Experimental Corps of Riflemen (1800) by Colonel Coote Manningham with the intention of training selected men to use this specialist weapon and then return them to their former regiments to enhance the capabilities of the regiments' light **companies** (see **light infantry**). However, this policy was soon changed and a new regiment, the 95th Foot or Rifle Corps, was set up. From the start the regiment wore distinctive dark green uniforms. The regiment was so successful in the **Peninsular War** that it was quickly expanded to three battalions and in 1816 was taken out of the numbered sequence of infantry regiments and given an independent status as the Rifle Brigade; becoming the Prince Consort's Own Rifle Brigade (1862); the Rifle Brigade (Prince Consort's Own) (1868); the Prince Consort's Own (Rifle Brigade) (1881); the Rifle Brigade (the Prince Consort's Own) (1882); and the Rifle Brigade (Prince Consort's Own) (1920). Its modern identity is as part of the **Royal Green Jackets**.

Rifles, The

The **regiment** is due to be formed in 2007 by the amalgamation of the **Devonshire and Dorset Regiment**, the **Royal Gloucestershire, Berkshire and Wiltshire Light Infantry**, the **Light Infantry** and the **Royal Green Jackets**

Roberts, Frederick Sleigh (1832–1914)
Roberts was born in India where he joined the Army and took part in the suppression of the **Indian Mutiny**. During the Second **Afghan War** he defeated the Afghans at **Kandahar** (1880). He was created a baron (1892) and made **commander-in-chief** in India (1885–93). He was appointed **field marshal** (1895) and went to South Africa as the commander-in-chief when **Buller** was relieved. During the **Boer War** he captured **Bloemfontein** (13 March 1900), annexed the Orange River Colony (24 May 1900), occupied Johannesburg (31 May 1900) and Pretoria (5 June 1900). In November 1900 **Kitchener** took over as commander-in-chief in South Africa.

Roberts, Henry Gee (1800–60)
Roberts was born in Gloucestershire and was commissioned as a **lieutenant** in the 13th Bombay Native Infantry (1818). He was promoted to **captain** (1824) and commanded the resident's escort at Cutch. He was then put in command of the Cutch irregular horse and was influential politically in achieving peace in the area. He then raised a **regiment** of irregular **cavalry** in Gujarat. Roberts was promoted to **major** in the 13th Native Infantry (1835) and to **lieutenant-colonel** in command of the 11th Native Infantry (1841) but transferred to the 20th Native Infantry in the same year. He then took part as second-in-command in Charles **Napier's** campaign in Sind (1843). He returned to Cutch as resident and commander of the troops. He was promoted to **colonel** of the 21st Native Infantry (1852) and to **major-general** (1854). He went home on leave, returning to India at the beginning of the **Indian Mutiny** (1857), when he commanded the Rajputana field forces. He captured **Kotah** and defeated the mutineers at Sanganir. Roberts was then appointed commissioner and commander of the troops at Gujurat. He was created KCB (1859) and left India in the same year.

Rochester, battle of
1. (1215; *Barons' Wars*) The barons rebelling against King John occupied Rochester castle (30 September). John relieved the castle (30 November).
2. (1264; *Barons' Wars*) The rebel barons, commanded by Simon de Montfort and Gilbert de Clare, laid siege to Rochester but were forced to abandon it and withdrew to London when the forces of Henry III arrived (18 April)

rocket
Rockets were first used in warfare c. 1300 in Asia, using **black powder** as a propellant. They were developed for British military service by William **Congreve** and used on a small scale during the Napoleonic Wars. Congreve's rockets were essentially larger versions of the modern fireworks of the same name but fitted with an explosive or incendiary head. They were highly inaccurate, but when fired in large numbers were an effective weapon in destroying a town. They went out of use during the 19th century as standard **artillery** weapons became more powerful. Rockets again came to prominence as a military weapon with the development of liquid propellants, notably in the German V2 of **World War II**. This development resulted in the modern intercontinental ballistic missiles. On a smaller scale, advances in solid fuels and development of precision guidance systems have resulted in the development of anti-tank and anti-aircraft rockets, bombardment rockets and air-launched rockets, and have again made the rocket an effective battlefield weapon.
See also **rocket artillery**
[From Italian *rocchetta* 'small distaff', from its shape]

rocket artillery
A modern form of **artillery** that fires **rockets** rather than **shot** or **shells**. Dating from **World War II**, rocket artillery is usually in the form of an armoured vehicle equipped with a battery of rockets. Examples include the **Multiple Launch Rocket System** currently in service with the British Army. This is a tracked vehicle carrying two pods of six rockets; each rocket is 227mm in diameter and can deliver either 644 bomblets or 28 anti-tank mines over a range of more than 30km.

Roliça, battle of

(1808; *Peninsular War*) The first British engagement of the Peninsular War (17 August) when an Anglo-Portuguese force of 4,000, commanded by Sir Arthur Wellesley (**Wellington**), drove 3,000 French from Roliça, a village in Portugal

Rommel, Erwin (1891–1944)

The son of a teacher, Rommel joined the 124th Württemberg Infantry Regiment as an officer cadet. During **World War I** he fought in France, Romania and Italy. He had a great empathy with his troops and chose to remain an **infantry** front-line officer rather than take a post on the general staff. He then taught in various military academies. Having been in command of Hitler's bodyguard in 1939, he was given command of the 7th Panzer Division and took a prominent part in the drive to the French channel coast during 1940. In February 1941 he was appointed commander of the German forces in North Africa where his skills gained him the name of 'The Desert Fox' and the rank of **field marshal**. He had difficulties with his Italian allies, and with the High Command, who were reluctant to send supplies and fresh troops. He was defeated at the second battle of **El Alamein**. He was ordered home (March 1943) and entrusted with the defence of the French coast against potential Allied invasion. Shortly after the **Normandy** invasion he was wounded in an Allied air attack and while he was convalescing his peripheral involvement in a plot to assassinate Hitler became known to the Nazi authorities. He was forced to commit suicide to protect his family. The Nazis announced that he had died a hero's death.

Rorke's Drift, battle of

(1879; *Zulu War*) After defeating the British at **Isandlwana** (22 January) the Zulus immediately pressed into northern Natal. Some 4,000 Zulus were confronted by 140 British troops at the outpost of Rorke's Drift. The garrison, under the command of Lieutenant John Chard of the **Royal Engineers**, drove off a day and night of attacks (22–23 January) with the loss of 25 casualties. The Zulus lost at least 400 dead. Eleven **Victoria Crosses** were won during this action.

Rose, Hugh Henry (1801–85)

Rose was born in Berlin and by 1821 was a **lieutenant** in the 19th Foot (**Green Howards**) serving in Ireland. He was **gazetted major** in the 92nd **Gordon Highlanders** (1829) and was appointed equerry to the Duke of Cambridge (1830). In 1839 he purchased an unattached lieutenant-colonelcy and in 1840 went to Syria as deputy **adjutant-general** to the Turkish commander Omar Pasha. He was appointed consul-general in Syria (1841) where he did much to terminate the civil war and acted as a powerful supporter of the persecuted Christians. Rose left Syria (1848) and was promoted to **brevet colonel** (1851) while he was secretary to the embassy in Constantinople (now Istanbul). Following the Russian invasion of Turkey (1853), Britain and France declared war on Russia and Rose was appointed as liaison officer between the British and French **commanders-in-chief**. He was present at the battle of the **Alma** with the French forces and at the battle of **Inkerman**. He was wounded during the campaign and was promoted to **major-general** (1854). Rose then volunteered for service in India (1857) and was given command of the Méu column of the Central India Field Force. With this force he freed the roads from the west and north of rebels and pressed on to **Jhansi** and to the capture of Kalpi and **Gwalior**. Rose was gazetted as colonel of the 45th Foot (**Nottinghamshire (Sherwood Foresters) Regiment**) (1858). In 1860 he was promoted to **lieutenant-general** and commander-in-chief of the Bombay Army. In 1861 he was made commander-in-chief of India with the local rank of **general**. He improved the conditions of the army and negotiated the transition of the East India Company's Army to the Indian Army. He left India (1865) and was given command of the forces in Ireland. In 1866 he was raised to the peerage and promoted to general (1867). In 1869 Rose became colonel of the Royal Horse Guards (**Blues and Royals**). He retired from Ireland (1870) and was promoted to **field marshal** (1877).

Roses, Wars of the *See* **Wars of the Roses**

Ross, Robert (1766–1814)
Ross was born in Ireland and was commissioned as an **ensign** in the 25th Foot (**King's Own Scottish Borderers**) (1789), **lieutenant** in the 7th Fusiliers (**Royal Fusiliers (City of London Regiment)**) (1791), and **major** in the 19th Foot (**Green Howards**) (1795). He was put on half pay, then made major in the 20th Foot (**East Devonshire Regiment**) (1799). He served in Holland, Minorca and then in Egypt at the battle of **Alexandria** (1801). The **regiment** then went to Malta and then to Naples (1805) and took a prominent part in the battle of **Maida**. Ross was promoted to **lieutenant-colonel** and went to Portugal where he took part in the battle of **Corunna**. The much-reduced regiment returned to England. Ross was made **brevet colonel** (1810) and **aide-de-camp** to the king. The regiment returned to Portugal (1810) where Ross commanded a **brigade** as **major-general** (1813). He took part in the battles of **Vitoria**, Pampeluna (now Pamplona), **Sorauren** and **Nivelle**. From the Peninsula Ross went to North America where he took part in the battle of **Bladensburg** and the capture of Washington. He was killed during the attack on **Baltimore**.
See also **Fort McHenry, battle of**

Ross-shire Buffs
The **regiment** was raised (1793) by Lieutenant-Colonel Francis Mackenzie as the 78th (Highland) Regiment of Foot which was joined (1794) by the 2nd Battalion, 78th (Highland) Regiment of Foot, The Ross-shire Buffs. The combined battalions were called (1796) the 78th (Highland) Regiment of Foot (or the Ross-shire Buffs). In 1881 the 78th merged with the 72nd Highlanders to become the **Seaforth Highlanders**.

Rouen, battle of
1. (1418–19; *Hundred Years' War*) Having occupied Caen (1417) the English king Henry V took Falaise and Cherbourg and moved to lay siege to Rouen (summer 1418). The town surrendered (19 January 1419) and Henry moved on to Paris.
2. (1449; *Hundred Years' War*) Rouen had served as the English base in northern France since 1419, but after their victory at **Orleans** the French continued their advance to drive the English out of France. The **garrison** at Rouen held on stubbornly but due to a revolt within the town, the English commander Edmund Beaufort, Duke of Somerset, was forced to surrender (29 October).

roundelade *See* **artillery**

Roundway Down, battle of
(1643; *Civil War*) The Royalist commander, Sir Ralph Hopton, was besieged in Devizes by the Parliamentarians commanded by Sir William Waller. Prince Maurice of Germany, nephew of Charles I, brought a force of **cavalry** from Oxford to relieve Devizes. He met and defeated Waller's force at Roundway Down just outside Devizes (13 July). The Parliamentarians lost over 1,000 men killed or captured. The Royalists moved on to take Bristol (25 July).

Royal American Regiment *See* **King's Royal Rifle Corps**

Royal Anglian Regiment
The **regiment** was formed in 1964 by the amalgamation of the 1st East Anglian Regiment (Royal Norfolk and Suffolk), the 2nd East Anglian Regiment (Duchess of Gloucester's Own Royal Lincolnshire and Northamptonshire), the 3rd East Anglian Regiment (16th/44th Foot) and the **Royal Leicestershire Regiment**. It has seen service in the conflicts in **Northern Ireland**, Bosnia and most recently in Afghanistan.

Royal Armoured Corps
The **corps** was formed (1939) in recognition of the growing importance of mechanised warfare. It grouped together all mechanised former cavalry **regiments** as well as the **Royal Tank Corps** (*see* **Royal Tank Regiment**). It is currently composed of the **Queen's Dragoon Guards**, the 1st and 2nd **Royal Tank Regiments**, the **9th/12th Royal Lancers**, the **King's Royal Hussars**, the **Royal Dragoon Guards**, the **Light**

Dragoons, the **Queen's Royal Hussars**, the **Royal Scots Dragoon Guards** and the **Queen's Royal Lancers**.

Royal Army Chaplains' Department

An Army Chaplains' Department of Church of England ministers was formed (1796). Other denominations were later admitted – Presbyterians (1827), Roman Catholics (1836), Wesleyans (1881) and Jews (1892). It was re-named the Royal Army Chaplains' Department in 1919 and still exists under this name.

Royal Army Dental Corps

The Army Dental Corps was formed as a separate unit from the **Royal Army Medical Corps** in 1921, and re-named the Royal Army Dental Corps in 1946 and still exists under this name as part of the **Army Medical Services**

Royal Army Educational Corps

The Corps of Army School Masters was formed (1845) with a staff of warrant and **non-commissioned officers**. When it was staffed with commissioned and non-commissioned personnel (1920) it became the Army Educational Corps and the Royal Army Educational Corps in 1946. Staffed exclusively with commissioned officers from 1962, it has been part of the Educational and Training Services Branch of the **Adjutant General's Corps** since 1992.

Royal Army Medical Corps

Until 1850, when the Medical Staff Corps was formed, the regimental surgeons were responsible for the health of the troops. The Medical Staff Corps, staffed by non-commissioned medical orderlies, became the Army Hospital Corps (1857). This was supplemented (1873) by the medical officers of the Army Medical Staff. These distinct units were amalgamated (1884) as the Medical Staff Corps, which was re-named the Royal Army Medical Corps (1898) and still exists under this name as part of the **Army Medical Services**.
Abbreviation **RAMC**

Royal Army Ordnance Corps

After the abolition of the Board of **Ordnance** (1855), a variety of bodies filled the ordnance supply function for the next 40 years. From 1896 the officers assigned to such duties came under the Army Ordnance Department and the non-commissioned personnel under the Army Ordnance Corps. These two were amalgamated (1918) as the Royal Army Ordnance Corps. The Royal Army Ordnance Corps took on the supply function of the Royal Army Service Corps when the latter became the **Royal Corps of Transport** (1965), but in turn lost its staff clerks to the **Adjutant General's Corps** in 1992 and was then absorbed into the **Royal Logistics Corps** in 1993.
Abbreviation **RAOC**

Royal Army Pay Corps

It was not until 1792 that commissioned paymasters were introduced. Before this each **regiment** had its own civilian paymaster. A centralised paymaster service was created (1878) as the Army Pay Department. The non-commissioned personnel of this department were then taken into a separate Army Pay Corps (1893). A Corps of Military Accountants was formed (1919) but disbanded (1925). In 1920 the Army Pay Department and the Army Pay Corps were amalgamated as the Royal Army Pay Corps. This in turn amalgamated (1992) with the **Women's Royal Army Corps** (*see* **women soldiers in the British Army**) to form the Staff and Personnel Branch of the **Adjutant General's Corps**.

Royal Army Service Corps *See* **Royal Corps of Transport**

Royal Army Veterinary Corps

The Corps began its existence (1858) as the Veterinary Medical Department consisting only of officers. The name was changed (1881) to the Army Veterinary Department and to the Army Veterinary Corps (1881) when other ranks were admitted. The name was further changed (1918) to the Royal Army Veterinary Corps and still exists under this name as part of the **Army Medical Services**.

Royal Arsenal *See* Woolwich

Royal Artillery *See* Artillery, Royal Regiment of

Royal Berkshire Regiment (Princess Charlotte of Wales's)

The **regiment** was formed (1881) by the amalgamation of the 49th **Princess Charlotte of Wales's (or Hertfordshire) Regiment** and the 66th **Berkshire Regiment of Foot**. It was first called Princess Charlotte of Wales's (Berkshire Regiment), then (1885) Princess Charlotte of Wales's (Royal Berkshire Regiment) and finally (1921) the Royal Berkshire Regiment (Princess Charlotte of Wales's). In 1959 it was amalgamated with the **Wiltshire Regiment of Foot** to become the Duke of **Edinburgh's** Royal Regiment.

royal blue

Scarlet and blue were the colours of the king's livery during the 17th century. The blue, as ordered by James I (1622), was originally very light. This was altered by the Hanoverian kings to a dark blue shade to distinguish it from the light blue still worn by Stuart supporters in the French Army. In the 18th and 19th centuries **regiments** designated as 'royal' wore **facings** in this dark blue colour.

Royal Corps of Signals

Up to and including **World War I** communications were under the control of the Royal Engineers Signal Service. With the increasing importance of, and technical expertise needed in, communicating during modern warfare, the Corps of Signals was formed (1920), becoming the Royal Corps of Signals in the same year. This body still exists.

Royal Corps of Transport

Up to 1794 the provision and transport of all army supplies (excluding ordnance) were controlled by the Commissionary General in the Treasury. In 1794 the Army formed its own transport organisation for service on the continent of Europe. This was known as the Corps of Waggoners (1794); the Royal Waggon Corps (1799); and the Royal Waggon Train (1802). It was disbanded (1833) and replaced by the Land Transport Corps (1855) which was re-named the Military Train (1856) and designated the Army Service Corps (ASC) (1869). The Corps contained only non-commissioned ranks, the officers being provided from the Control Department, but in 1888 its own officers were appointed. The name was changed (1918) to the **Royal Army Service Corps** (RASC). In 1965 the RASC lost its supply functions to the **Royal Army Ordnance Corps** and merged with the transport functions of the Royal Engineers to form the Royal Corps of Transport. This body was absorbed into the **Royal Logistics Corps** in 1993.

Royal County Down Regiment

The **regiment** was raised (1793) by Major-General Sir Cornelius Cuyler as the 86th Regiment of Foot, but known as the Shropshire Volunteers from the county in which it was raised. It became known as the 86th (or Leinster) Regiment of Foot (1809) and the 86th (or Royal County of Down) Regiment of Foot (1812). In the 1881 reorganisation it merged with the 83rd **County of Dublin Regiment** to form the **Royal Irish Rifles**.

Royal Dragoon Guards

The regiment was formed (1992) by the amalgamation of the **4th/7th Royal Dragoon Guards** and the **Royal Inniskilling Dragoon Guards**. It is part of the **Royal Armoured Corps**.

Royal Dragoon Guards, 4th/7th

The regiment was formed (1922) by the amalgamation of the **4th Royal Irish Dragoon Guards** and the **7th Dragoon Guards (Princess Royal's)**. Mechanised from 1938, it became part of the **Royal Armoured Corps** in 1939. It amalgamated (1992) with the **Royal Inniskilling Dragoon Guards** to form the **Royal Dragoon Guards**.

Royal Dragoons

The **regiment** was raised as the Tangier Horse (1661) within the garrison at Tangier. It returned to England (1684) and was expanded to form the King's Own Royal Regiment of Dragoons, becoming (1690) the Royal Regiment of Dragoons. The name was further changed to 1st (Royal) Dragoons (1751); 1st The Royal Dragoons (1920) and the Royal Dragoons (1961). In 1969 it merged with the Royal Horse Guards to form the **Blues and Royals**.

Royal Dublin Fusiliers

The **regiment** was originally the Madras Fusiliers employed by the East India Company. It was absorbed into the regular army (1860), when the name was changed. The Royal Dublin Fusiliers were disbanded (1922) following Irish Independence.

Royal Electrical and Mechanical Engineers, Corps of

As the need for more complex electrical and mechanical expertise increased, the Royal Electrical and Mechanical Engineers was created (1942) largely from men of the **Royal Army Ordnance Corps**, the **Royal Engineers** and the **Royal Army Service Corps** (*see* **Royal Corps of Transport**). It became the Corps of Royal Electrical and Mechanical Engineers in 1949 and still exists under this name.
Abbreviation **REME**

Royal Engineers, Corps of

Before 1715 the Board of **Ordnance** and its predecessors recruited civilian engineers to build fortifications, supervise siege operations and other similar tasks, usually for the duration of a campaign. The inadequacies of the system were revealed during the first **Jacobite Rebellion** (1715) and the Board of Ordnance then recruited permanent engineers to serve in the Corps of Engineers (1717), which became the Corps of Royal Engineers in 1787. These engineers were all officers and the engineer rank and file were drawn from a body named the Royal Military Artificers and Labourers (1722) and the Corps of Royal Military Artificers (1797). In 1812 the Corps of Military Artificers became the Corps of Royal Sappers and Miners. In 1856 the Corps of Royal Sappers and Miners was amalgamated into the Corps of Royal Engineers, which still exists. It lost its transport functions to the **Royal Corps of Transport** in 1965 and its Postal and Courier Service to the **Royal Logistics Corps** in 1993.

Royal Field Artillery *See* **Artillery, Royal Regiment of**

Royal Fusiliers (City of London Regiment)

This was the earliest formed **fusilier regiment** (1685). It claims the privilege of marching through the City of London with bayonets fixed. The regiment took part in the battles of **Albuera** and the **Alma**. It ranked as the 7th Foot.

Royal Garrison Artillery *See* **Artillery, Royal Regiment of**

Royal Gloucestershire, Berkshire and Wiltshire Light Infantry

The **regiment** was formed in 1994 by the union of The Duke of Edinburgh's Royal Regiment (Berkshire and Wiltshire) and the **Gloucestershire Regiment**. It has seen service most recently as the main force deployed at Mazar-e-Sharif, Afghanistan. In 2007 it is due to amalgamate with the Devonshire and Dorset Light Infantry, the Light Infantry and the Royal Green Jackets to form The Rifles.

Royal Green Jackets

The **regiment** was formed (1966) by the amalgamation of the **1st Green Jackets**, the **2nd Green Jackets** and the **3rd Green Jackets**. In 2007 it is expected to unite with The Devonshire and Dorset Light Infantry, The Royal Gloucestershire, Berkshire and Wiltshire Light Infantry and The Light Infantry to form The Rifles.

Royal Gurkha Rifles

The **regiment** was formed in 1994 by the amalgamation of **Duke of Edinburgh's Own Gurkha Rifles (7th)**, **King Edward VII's Own Gurkha Rifles (2nd)**, **Princess Mary's Own 10th Gurkha Rifles** and **Queen Elizabeth's Own Gurkha Rifles (6th)**. It is part of the Brigade of **Gurkhas**.

Royal Hampshire Regiment

The **regiment** was formed (1881) by the amalgamation of the 37th **North Hampshire Regiment of Foot** and the 67th **South Hampshire Regiment of Foot** as the Hampshire Regiment, becoming the Royal Hampshire Regiment (1946). Rather than be amalgamated with the **Gloucestershire Regiment** (1969), the regiment opted to reduce to a one-company cadre, keeping its separate existence. It later grew back to battalion strength. In 1992 it amalgamated with The Queen's Regiment to form The Princess of Wales's Royal Regiment (Queen's and Royal Hampshires).

Royal Highland Fusiliers (Princess Margaret's Own Glasgow and Ayrshire Regiment)

The **regiment** was formed (1959) by the amalgamation of the **Royal Scots Fusiliers** and the **Highland Light Infantry**. In 2006 it united with The Royal Scots, The King's Own Scottish Borderers, The Black Watch, The Highlanders (Seaforth, Gordons and Camerons), and The Argyll and Sutherland Highlanders to form The Royal Regiment of Scotland.

Royal Highland Regiment *See* **Black Watch, The**

Royal Horse Artillery

Field artillery was initially moved by heavy farm horses with civilian drivers, while the gun crews walked. In 1793 'A' and 'B' Troops of the Royal Horse Artillery were formed. They had lighter guns that were pulled by six horses. The three nearside horses carried postillion riders while the other gunners rode, or were carried on limbers. These troops could keep up with the **cavalry** over short distances.

See also **Artillery, Royal Regiment of**; **Pitt's Reforms**

Royal Horse Guards *See* **Blues and Royals**

Royal Hussars (Prince of Wales's Own)

The **regiment** was formed (1969) by the amalgamation of the 10th **Royal Hussars (Prince of Wales's Own)** and the 11th Hussars (Prince Albert's Own). The original 10th was raised by Brigadier Humphrey Gore (1715) as Gore's Regiment of Dragoons. The name changed with the **colonel** until 1751 when the regiment was re-named the 10th Dragoons. The name was subsequently changed to 10th (Prince of Wales's Own) Regiment of (Light) Dragoons (1783); 10th (Prince of Wales's Own) Regiment of Light Dragoons (Hussars) (1811); the 10th (Prince of Wales's Own) Hussars (1860); and the 10th Royal Hussars (Prince of Wales's Own) (1921). In 1992 it amalgamated with the **14th/20th King's Hussars** (*see* **King's Hussars (14th)**) to form the **King's Royal Hussars**.

Royal Hussars (Queen Mary's Own)

The **regiment** was formed (1922) by the amalgamation of the 13th Hussars (**Hussars, 13th**) and the 18th Royal Hussars (Queen Mary's Own). The 18th was raised in 1858, but its origins are earlier. In 1759 Charles Moore, Marquess of Drogheda, raised the 19th Light Dragoons, known as Drogheda's Light Horse. It became the 18th Light Dragoons (1766) and the 18th Light Dragoons (Hussars) (1801). The regiment was disbanded in 1821, but re-formed (1858) in Yorkshire as the 18th Hussars. The title was changed (1903) to the 18th (Queen Mary's Own) Hussars and then to the 18th Royal Hussars (Queen Mary's Own) (1919). In 1992 it became part of The Light Dragoons.

Royal Inniskilling Dragoon Guards

The **regiment** was formed (1922) by the amalgamation of **Princess Charlotte of Wales's Dragoon Guards** and the **Inniskilling Dragoons** and called the 5th/6th Dragoons. The name was changed (1927) to the 5th Inniskilling Dragoon Guards and (1935) to the 5th Royal Inniskilling Dragoon Guards in celebration of the silver jubilee of George V. In 1992 it amalgamated with the **4th/7th Royal Dragoon Guards** to form the **Royal Dragoon Guards**.

Royal Inniskilling Fusiliers

The **regiment** was formed (1881) by the amalgamation of the **Inniskilling Regiment of Foot** and the 108th (Madras Infantry) Regiment of Foot. In an amalgamation in 1968 it became part of the **Royal Irish Rangers**.

Royal Invalids' Regiment of Foot *See* Welsh Regiment

Royal Irish Artillery *See* Artillery, Royal Regiment of

Royal Irish Dragoon Guards, 4th

The **regiment** was raised (1685) as the Earl of Arran's Regiment of Cuirassiers and changed name with its colonels until 1751, when it became the 1st Regiment of Horse. It was subsequently renamed the 4th (Royal Irish) Dragoon Guards (1788) and the 4th Royal Irish Dragoon Guards (1921) and amalgamated (1922) with the **7th Dragoon Guards (Princess Royal's)** to form the 4th/7th Dragoon Guards.

Royal Irish Fusiliers

The **regiment** was raised (1793) by Colonel John **Doyle** as the 87th (or Prince of Wales's Irish) Regiment of Foot. The name changed (1811) to the 87th (or Prince of Wales's Own Irish) Regiment of Foot and in 1827 to the 87th (or Royal Irish Fusiliers) Regiment of Foot. It became Princess Victoria's (Royal Irish) Fusiliers by the amalgamation of the 87th and the 89th **Princess Victoria's Regiment**. The name was changed (1921) to the Royal Irish Fusiliers (Princess Victoria's). In an amalgamation in 1968 it became part of the **Royal Irish Rangers**.

Royal Irish Lancers, 5th

The regiment was raised (1689) as James Wynne's Regiment of Dragoons and changed name with its colonels until 1751, when it became the 5th Regiment of Dragoons. Renamed (1756) the 5th (or Royal Irish) Regiment of Dragoons, it was disbanded in 1799 and reformed in 1858 as lancers. It was subsequently renamed the 5th (Royal Irish) Lancers (1861) and 5th Royal Irish Lancers (1921), then was temporarily disbanded in 1921 before amalgamating with 16th The Queen's Lancers (see **Lancers, 16th**) to form the 16th/5th Lancers (see **Queens' Royal Lancers, 16th/5th**).

Royal Irish Rangers

The **regiment** was formed (1968) by the amalgamation of the **Royal Inniskilling Fusiliers**, the **Royal Ulster Rifles** and the **Royal Irish Fusiliers** (Princess Victoria's)

Royal Irish Rifles *See* Royal Ulster Rifles

Royal Lancers, 9th/12th (Prince of Wales's)

The **regiment** was formed (1960) by the amalgamation of the **9th Queen's Royal Lancers** and the **12th Royal Lancers** and became part of the **Royal Armoured Corps**

Royal Lancers, 12th (Prince of Wales's)

The **regiment** was raised (1715) as Phineas Bowles's Regiment of Dragoons and changed name with its colonels until 1751, when it became the 12th Regiment of Dragoons. It subsequently became the 12th Light Dragoons (1768), converted to lancers (1816) and, after further name changes, became the 12th (Prince of Wales's Royal) Lancers (1861) and the 12th Royal Lancers (Prince of Wales's) (1921). Mechanised from 1928, it joined the **Royal Armoured Corps** (1939) and amalgamated (1960) with the **9th Queen's Royal Lancers** to form the **9th/12th Royal Lancers**.

Royal Leicestershire Regiment

The **regiment** was raised (1688) as Colonel Solomon Richard's Regiment of Foot. The name changed with the **colonel** until 1751 when it was designated the 17th Regiment of Foot. It became the 17th (or the Leicestershire) Regiment of Foot (1782); the Leicestershire Regiment (1881); and the Royal Leicestershire Regiment (1946). In 1964 it became part of the **Royal Anglian Regiment**.

Royal Lincolnshire Regiment

The **regiment** was raised (1685) by Colonel John Grenville, Earl of Bath. It was known as the Earl of Bath's Regiment or Grenville's Regiment. The name changed with the **colonel** until 1751 when it was designated the 10th Regiment of Foot. The name changed further to the 10th (or North Lincolnshire) Regiment of Foot (1782), to the Lincolnshire Regiment (1881) and the Royal Lincolnshire Regiment (1946). In 1960 it amalgamated with The Northamptonshire Regiment to form the 2nd East Anglian Regiment (Duchess of Gloucester's Own Royal Lincolnshire and Northamptonshire).

Royal Logistics Corps

The **corps** was formed (1993) by the amalgamation of the **Royal Corps of Transport**, the **Royal Army Ordnance Corps**, the **Royal Pioneer Corps**, the **Army Catering Corps** and the Postal and Courier Service of the Corps of **Royal Engineers**

Royal Military Academy

The Army's training centre for officer cadets. The original Royal Military Academy (RMA) was founded (1741) at Woolwich, London, under the auspices of the Board of **Ordnance** to train potential officers for the 'scientific arms' controlled by the Board (the **artillery** and **engineers**, and later the signals). All Ordnance officers were appointed by the Board and had to pass through the Woolwich Academy; purchase was not available in the Ordnance services. All engineer and artillery officers were trained at Woolwich until 1939.

For most of the 18th and 19th centuries those who wished to become officers in the **infantry** or **cavalry** did not have to undertake any form of training before they joined their **regiments**, nor for much of the period was there an institution for training established officers in staff duties. The senior department of the **Royal Military College** (RMC) was founded for the latter purpose in 1800 at High Wycombe. It later (1858) became the **Staff College**. A junior department of the RMC was founded (1802) at Great Marlow to train potential officers and transferred to Sandhurst (1812), where it was joined by the senior department in 1821. Some places at Sandhurst were free and some Sandhurst graduates gained commissions without purchase, but it was often easier for officer candidates simply to purchase their commissions in the traditional way. Purchase of commissions was abolished in 1870 and from 1877 attendance at the RMC became the normal route for obtaining a commission.

The present organisation, the **Royal Military Academy Sandhurst** (RMAS), was formed (1947) by the amalgamation of the RMA and the RMC. It absorbed the **Mons Officer Cadet School** (1972) to become the sole institution that trains officers for the British Army.

Royal Military Police, Corps of

In 1661 the enforcement of military law was formalised by the formation of a Provost Service. A military police unit was formed (1855), which became the Corps of Military Mounted Police (1877). This was complemented (1885) by the Corps of Military Foot Police and the two Corps were amalgamated (1926) as the Corps of Military Police and the Corps of Royal Military Police (1946). In 1992 it lost its **corps** status when it was absorbed into the Provost Branch of the **Adjutant General's Corps**.

Royal Military School *See* **reforms of the Duke of York**

Royal Norfolk Regiment

The **regiment** was raised (1685) as Colonel Henry Cornwall's Regiment of Foot. The title changed with the **colonel** until 1751 when it became the 9th Regiment of Foot. The name changed further to the 9th (or the East Norfolk) Regiment of Foot (1782); the Norfolk Regiment (1881); and the Royal Norfolk Regiment (1935). It amalgamated with the Suffolk Regiment in 1959 to form the 1st East Anglian Regiment (Royal Norfolk and Suffolk).

Royal Northumberland Fusiliers

The **regiment** was raised (1674) by Colonel Daniel **O'Brien**, Viscount Clare, to serve in Holland with William of Orange and came on to the permanent establishment with the accession of William of Orange as William III (1689). It was originally called Lord O'Brien's Regiment (or the Irish Regiment). On its entry into the British Army it was Colonel Tollemache's Regiment of Foot. The name changed with the **colonel** until 1751 when it became the 5th (or the Northumberland) Regiment of Foot. In 1836 the name changed to the 5th Regiment of Foot (Northumberland Fusiliers); in 1881 to the Northumberland Fusiliers; and in 1935 to the Royal Northumberland Fusiliers. The regiment became part of the **Royal Regiment of Fusiliers** in 1968.

Royal Pioneer Corps

The **corps** was raised (1939) from combatant soldiers as the Auxiliary Military Pioneer Corps. The name was changed (1940) to the Pioneer Corps and to the Royal Pioneer Corps (1946). It was absorbed into the **Royal Logistics Corps** in 1993.

Royal Regiment of Artillery *See* **Artillery, Royal Regiment of**

Royal Regiment of Foot *See* **Royal Scots**

Royal Regiment of Foot Guards *See* **Grenadier Guards**

Royal Regiment of Fusiliers

The **regiment** was formed (1968) by the amalgamation of the **Royal Northumberland Fusiliers**, the **Royal Warwickshire Fusiliers** and the **Lancashire Fusiliers**. The regiment played an important part in the **Gulf War** at Wadi al Batin and in the **Iraq War** at Basra.

Royal Regiment of Guards *See* **Grenadier Guards**

Royal Regiment of Horse (Guards) *See* **Blues and Royals**

Royal Regiment of Scotland

The **regiment** was formed in 2006 by the union of The Royal Scots, The Royal Highland Fusiliers, The King's Own Scottish Borderers, The Black Watch, The Highlanders (Seaforth, Gordons and Camerons), and The Argyll and Sutherland Highlanders

Royal Regiment of Wales

The **regiment** was formed (1969) by the amalgamation of the **South Wales Borderers** and the **Welsh Regiment**. In 2006 it united with The Royal Welch Fusiliers to form The Royal Welsh.

Royal Sappers and Miners, Corps of *See* **Royal Engineers, Corps of**

Royal Scots

The **regiment** was formed by Sir John Hepburn for service in France under Louis XIII (reigned 1610–43). It was augmented by a Scots force under Earl Grey that had been raised to aid Bavaria during the Thirty Years' War. This force itself had been augmented by Mackay's Scots who had been in service in Denmark. The new force of some 13 regiments was called the Green brigade. The regiment of 1633, called Le Régiment d'Hebron (Hepburn) in France, was officered by descendants of the Garde Ecossaise raised by Charles VII (reigned 1422–61). The Garde Ecossaise became the Scottish Archer Corps of Henri IV of France (reigned 1589–1610). The regiment became Le Régiment de Douglas (1637) and became part of the British establishment (1661). It did not return to England until 1678 when it was named the Earl of Dumbarton's Regiment (1st Foot). The regiment then served in Tangier and was re-named the Royal Regiment of Foot (1684). The name changed (1751) to the 1st (or the Royal) Regiment of Foot. Further changes in the name were 1st (or the Royal Scots) Regiment of Foot (1821); the 1st (or the Royal) Regiment of Foot (1821); the 1st (the Royal Scots) Regiment (1871); the Lothian (the Royal Scots) (1881); the Royal Scots (the Lothian Regiment) (1882); and the Royal Scots (the Royal Regiment) (1920). In 2006 it united with The Royal Highland Fusiliers, The King's Own Scottish Borderers,

The Black Watch, The Highlanders (Seaforth, Gordons and Camerons), and The Argyll and Sutherland Highlanders, to form The Royal Regiment of Scotland.

Royal Scots Dragoon Guards

The **regiment** was formed (1971) by the union of 3rd Carabiniers (Prince of Wales's Dragoon Guards) and the **Royal Scots Greys**. It has seen service in **Northern Ireland**, the **Gulf War**, **Kosovo** and most recently in Afghanistan.

Royal Scots Fusiliers

The **regiment** was raised (1678) as the Earl of Mar's Regiment of Foot. The name changed with the **colonel** and in 1691 it became a **fusilier** regiment (Colonel O'Farrell's Fusiliers). It became (1707) the North British Fusiliers; the Royal Regiment of North British Fusiliers (1713); and the 21st Regiment of Foot (or Royal North British Fusiliers) (1751). In 1871 the regiment became the 21st (Royal Scots Fusiliers) Regiment of Foot and in 1881 the Royal Scots Fusiliers. It became part of the **Royal Highland Fusiliers** in 1959.

Royal Scots Greys

The **regiment** was formed (1681) by Lieutenant-General Thomas **Dalyell** of the **carabiniers** when he amalgamated several independent troops of Scottish **dragoons** as the Royal Regiment of Scottish Dragoons (2nd Dragoons) in 1688. In 1700 the regiment decided to use only grey horses. In 1707 it was re-named The Royal Regiment of North British Dragoons (also called The Scots Regiment of White Horses). The nickname is of long standing but it was not until 1866 that Royal Scots Greys appeared in the title. In 1971 it became part of the **Royal Scots Dragoon Guards**.

See also **Warburg, battle of; heavy brigade**

Royal Sussex Regiment

The **regiment** was formed (1881) by the amalgamation of the 35th (Royal Sussex) Regiment and the 107th (Bengal Infantry) Regiment. The original Royal Sussex regiment was raised (1701) in Belfast by the Earl of Donegal as the Earl of Donegal's Regiment of Foot, known as the Belfast Regiment. The name changed with the **colonel** until 1751 when it became the 35th Regiment of Foot. The name was changed to the 35th (or the Dorsetshire) Regiment of Foot (1782), the 35th (or the Sussex) Regiment of Foot (1805) and to the 35th (Royal Sussex) Regiment (1832). It became part of the **Queen's Regiment** in 1966.

Royal Tank Corps *See* **Royal Tank Regiment**

Royal Tank Regiment

The Tank Detachment of the Machine Gun Corps was formed (1916) soon after the invention of the **tank** and became independent (1918) as the **Tank Corps**. It was subsequently renamed the **Royal Tank Corps** (1923) and the Royal Tank Regiment on its absorption (1939) into the **Royal Armoured Corps**. It is currently composed of the **1st Royal Tank Regiment** and the **2nd Royal Tank Regiment**.

Royal Ulster Rifles

The **regiment** was formed (1881) by the amalgamation of the 83rd **County of Dublin Regiment** and the 86th **Royal County Down Regiment** as the Royal Irish Rifles. The name was changed to the Royal Ulster Rifles in 1921. In an amalgamation in 1968 it became part of the **Royal Irish Rangers**.

Royal Victorian Order

The Order was established by Queen Victoria (1896) as a personal gift from the Sovereign. There are five classes: Knight or Dame Grand Cross (GCVO), Knight or Dame Commander (KCVO or DCVO), Commander (CVO), Lieutenant (LVO), and Member (MVO). Women have been admitted since 1936. Until 1984 the lowest two classes were known as Member (fourth class) and Member (fifth class).

Abbreviation **RVO**

Royal Warwickshire Fusiliers

The **regiment** was formed by the amalgamation of several independent companies fighting in Holland under the command of Sir William Vane. It was commanded by Colonel Luke Illinston after whom it was named. It came onto the regular establishment on the accession of William of Orange (1689) as Colonel Babbington's Regiment of Foot. The name changed with the **colonel** until 1751 when it was named the 6th Regiment of Foot. In 1782 it was called the 6th (or the 1st Warwickshire) Regiment of Foot and in 1832 6th (the Royal 1st Warwickshire) Regiment of Foot. In 1881 it was the Royal Warwickshire Regiment and the Royal Warwickshire Fusiliers in 1963. It became part of the **Royal Regiment of Fusiliers** in 1968.

Royal Welch Fusiliers

The **regiment** was raised (1689) as Lord Herbert of Chirbury's Regiment of Foot. The name was changed with its **colonel** until 1702 when it became the Welsh Regiment of Fusiliers. Further changes to the name were The Royal Welch Fusiliers (1727); 23rd (Royal Welch Fusiliers) Regiment of Foot (1751); the Royal Welch Fusiliers (1881); and the Royal Welch Fusiliers (1920). In 2006 it united with The Royal Regiment of Wales to form The Royal Welsh.

See also **Ashanti War**

Royal Welsh

The **regiment** was formed (2006) by the amalgamation of the **Royal Regiment of Wales** and the **Royal Welch Fusiliers**

Royal West African Frontier Force *See* **West African Frontier Force**

RRF *See* **rapid reaction force**

rubber bullet

A **bullet** made of hardened rubber or plastic used to disable rather than kill. Rubber bullets are used largely in riot control.

Rundle, Henry Macleod Leslie (1856–1934)

Sir Leslie Rundle was born at Newton Abbot (Devonshire) and was **gazetted** in the Royal **Artillery** (1876). He took part in the battle of **Ulundi** and the First **Boer War** (1881). He joined the Egyptian Army (1883) and served under **Kitchener** on the Nile expedition. He was promoted to **brevet major** (1885). He commanded the artillery at Toski and was promoted to brevet **lieutenant-colonel** (1889). By 1892 he was **adjutant-general** in Cairo where he served for nearly five years. Rundle served as Kitchener's **chief-of-staff** on the Dongola expeditionary force. He was promoted to **major-general** (1896) and fought at **Omdurman** (1898). When he returned home he held various staff appointments and then went to South Africa in command of the 8th Division of the South African Field Force (1900–02). He returned home and was appointed major-general in command of the North-Eastern Division (1903–05) after which he commanded the Northern Division as **lieutenant-general** (1905–07). He was made governor and **commander-in-chief** of Malta (1909) and promoted to **general**. He did not see active service in **World War I** and retired from the army (1919).

See also **Senekal, battle of**

Rundstedt, Karl Rudolf Gerd von (1875–1953)

Gerd von Rundstedt was an army officer from 1893, and during **World War I** was **chief-of-staff** of an army **corps** with the Turkish Army. He was involved in the German rearmament programme between the two wars and retired in 1938. He returned to active service at the outbreak of **World War II** and took command of an army group in Poland. He played a major part in the defeat of France (1940) but was blamed for allowing the British to escape from Dunquerque (**Dunkirk**). He then commanded the southern wing of the German Army in Russia (1941) which overran the Ukraine, but was dismissed by Hitler after the Russian winter offensive at the end of the year. He came back into active service (July 1942) as **commander-in-chief** of western Europe and had charge of the defence against the Anglo-American invasion (1944), particularly in directing the offensive in the **Ardennes**. He was relieved of command (March 1945) and captured by American forces (May 1945). He was released due to ill-health. He was greatly respected as a military leader by the commanders on both sides.

runner
A messenger, sometimes using a horse, bicycle, motor-bicycle or other vehicle

Rupert, Prince (1619–82)
Rupert was the son of Frederick V, elector Palatine and king of Bohemia, and nephew of Charles I of England. He fought on the continent during the Thirty Years' War when he was held captive in Austria. After his release he joined Charles in England just before the outbreak of the Civil War. He commanded the Royalist cavalry and was appointed **commander-in-chief** of the king's armies in 1644. This made him unpopular with some of the king's counsellors and prevented him from co-ordinating the Royalist campaign. When he surrendered Bristol to the Parliamentarians (1645) Charles dismissed him, and when Charles surrendered to the Scots (1646), Parliament banished him from England. Rupert took charge of the small Royalist fleet (1648) and, having defeated the Parliamentarian admiral Robert Blake in the Mediterranean, continued his activities in the Azores and West Indies (1651–52). He returned to the exiled Charles II in France, but quarrelled with him. Rupert retired to Germany. When Charles was restored to the English throne (1660) Rupert was made a privy councillor and was given naval commands during the 2nd and 3rd Dutch Wars (1665–67 and 1672–74). He became the first governor of the Hudson Bay Company (1670).
Also known as **Rupert of the Rhine**; *See also* **Brentford, battle of**; **Chalgrove Field, battle of**; **Edgehill, battle of**; **Langport, battle of**; **Marston Moor, battle of**; **Naseby, battle of**

Rutlandshire Regiment
The **regiment** was raised (1755) as the 60th Regiment of Foot and was renumbered the 58th Regiment of Foot in 1757. The name was changed (1782) to the 58th (or Rutlandshire) Regiment of Foot. Following an amalgamation with the 48th it became part of the **Northamptonshire Regiment**.

RVO *abbreviation of* **Royal Victorian Order**

S

SA80
The assault **rifle** that is currently the standard infantry weapon in the British Army. Introduced in 1985, it is used by the infantry in two variants: the **L85 Individual Weapon** (IW) and the **L86 Light Support Weapon** (LSW). The two are very similar, with several interchangeable parts; the main difference is that the LSW is heavier and has a longer barrel, which allows an increased muzzle velocity and a longer effective range (1000 metres rather than 400 metres). Although very accurate, the first version of the SA80 gained a reputation for poor design and unreliability; in particular, soldiers reported that heat and sand caused it to jam in Iraq during the **Gulf War** (1991). These problems have been resolved in the latest version, the SA80A2, which was introduced in 2002.

sabretache
A leather wallet suspended from a sword belt. It was introduced in about 1811 and worn by all ranks of **cavalry** until 1834 after which date it was no longer worn by heavy cavalry and lancers. It was retained by other cavalry until horse-mounted cavalry **regiments** were no longer active on the battlefield.
[From French, translation of German *Säbeltasche* 'sabre pocket']

Sabugal, battle of
(1811; *Peninsular War*) Three British **divisions** under **Wellington** drove the French from a salient on the Coa river (16 April) with the loss of only 200 men. The French lost 1,500.

Sackets Harbour, battle of
(1813; *War of 1812*) The British and Canadians were fighting the Americans for control of Lake Ontario. Sir George **Prevost**, Governor-General of Canada, led an attack on Sackets Harbour (28–29 May) held by the Americans. The attack was repulsed.

Sackville, George (1716–85)
The son of the 7th Earl and 1st Duke of Dorset, he was educated at Trinity College, Dublin, and by 1740 was **lieutenant-colonel** of the 28th Foot (**North Gloucestershire Regiment**). He was appointed **brevet colonel** and king's **aide-de-camp** a few days after the battle of **Dettingen**. He was seriously wounded at **Fontenoy**. His **regiment** went to Ireland but he was appointed colonel of the 20th Foot (**South Hampshire Regiment of Foot**) and went to Scotland (1746) but later returned to Flanders (1747). He held several political appointments, and was also an MP. By 1757 he was **lieutenant-general** of ordnance and colonel of the 2nd Dragoon Guards (**Queen's Bays**). He went to Hanover as second-in-command to Charles Spencer, Duke of Marlborough, and when Marlborough died at Münster (1758), Sackville took over command of the British troops on the Lower Rhine. He was now a member of the Privy Council. At the battle of **Minden** Prince Frederick of Brunswick ordered the British **cavalry** to attack but Sackville failed to carry this order out, possibly because of a misunderstanding, or allegedly through cowardice. He was dismissed from the army by a **court martial** (1760) and removed from the Privy Council but was later restored (1763). The rest of his life was devoted to politics. He was appointed Colonial Secretary (1775) and was largely responsible for the administration of the war in America. He was responsible for the mismanagement of the troop movements in

Canada and New York and hence for the British surrender at **Saratoga** (1777). When **Cornwallis** surrendered at **Yorktown** (1781), Sackville was in favour of continuing the war, but was dismissed. He changed his name to Germain (1770) and was created Viscount Sackville in 1782.

Also known as **Lord George Sackville (1716–70); Lord George Germain (1770–82)**

St Albans, battle of

1. (1455; *Wars of the Roses*) The opening battle of the Wars of the Roses. Richard of York with the Earls of Salisbury and Warwick (both Richard Neville, father and son) led an army of 3,000 from the north towards London. They were met at St. Albans (22 May) by the Lancastrian King Henry VI with Queen Margaret and the Dukes of Somerset (Edward Beaufort) and Buckingham (Humphrey Stafford). The Yorkists enveloped the town and the Lancastrians were routed. Beaufort was killed; Margaret and her son Edward fled to France and the king was taken to London under Yorkist control.

2. (1461; *Wars of the Roses*) Queen Margaret's Lancastrian army moved from **Wakefield** to free King Henry VI held by the Yorkists in London. They were met by the Earl of Warwick (Richard Neville) at St. Albans. While he was waiting for reinforcements from Edward of York, moving from **Mortimer's Cross**, the Lancastrians mounted a surprise attack (17 February). The Yorkists were routed and Henry VI freed. The Lancastrians made the tactical mistake of moving north, leaving the Yorkists free to return to London where Edward of York was crowned King Edward IV (4 March).

Sainte Foy, battle of

(1760; *French and Indian War*) A French force of 8,000 moved from Montreal with the object of recapturing **Quebec**. General James **Murray** led a force of 3,000 British out of Quebec (27 April) to attack the French. He was forced to return with the loss of 1,000 men.

saker

A type of **culverin**

Salamanca, battle of

(1812; *Peninsular War*) Having taken the forts of **Ciudad Rodrigo** and **Badajoz**, **Wellington** moved his 40,000 troops into northern Spain. After weeks of manoeuvring he finally met the French force commanded by Marshal Auguste Marmont at Salamanca (22 July). The French were defeated and suffered 12,000 casualties; the British lost 5,000. Wellington occupied Madrid but, because he could have been isolated there by the French Marshal **Soult** moving from Andalusia, he fell back to the Portuguese border.

Sale, Robert Henry (1782–1845)

Sale was born in Huntingdonshire and was commissioned in the 56th Foot (**West Essex Regiment of Foot**) (1795) and promoted to **lieutenant** (1797). He joined the 12th Foot (**Suffolk Regiment**) in Madras (now Chennai) (1798) and fought at **Seringapatam** where he stayed after its fall. He was promoted to **captain** (1806) and fought at Travancore after which battle he served in Mauritius (1809–13). He was promoted to **major** and moved between Bourbon and Mauritius until the **regiment** returned home (1815). The regiment moved to Ireland and was partially disbanded. Sale was put on **half pay** (1818) and brought back on full pay as major in the 13th Foot (**Somerset Light Infantry**) (1821). He returned to India (1823) where (1824–26) he took a prominent part in the campaign in Burma (now Myanmar). The regiment was then posted to Danapur (1826–31) and to Agra (1831–35). Sale moved to Karnal (1835) and was promoted to **colonel** commanding the 1st Bengal Brigade which formed the advanced **brigade** during the First **Afghan War**. He was given the local rank of **major-general** (1839). Sale was knighted for his defence of **Jellalabad** (1842) and made colonel of the 13th Foot (1843). He returned home, but was back in India (1844) as quartermaster-general of the army. He was wounded at the battle of **Mudki** and died soon afterwards.

See also **Kabul, battle of**

Salerno, battle of

(1943; *World War II*) The main Allied thrust in Italy began at Salerno, with the object of occupying the port of Naples. The Italian Army had surrendered (9 September) but the Germans, commanded by Field Marshal Albert **Kesselring**, pushed south. The Allied 5th Army, commanded by US General Mark Clark, made an amphibious assault on Salerno (9 September) (Operation Avalanche). On the right the American 36th and 45th Infantry Divisions took Paestum while the British X Corps under General Richard McCreedy captured Battipaglia and Salerno. A German counter-attack (12 September) re-captured Battipaglia. A combined bombardment from sea and air and reinforcements by the US 82nd Airborne and the British 7th Armoured Divisions stopped the counter-attack, and Kesselring withdrew. The British 8th Army, commanded by General Sir Bernard **Montgomery**, moved up from southern Italy and the Salerno beachhead was secured. Naples fell to the 5th Army (1 October).

salient

1. A projection built on a defensive line or fortress

2. A vulnerable part of an army's front line, sticking out at an angle towards the enemy. A salient may occur when only a small part of an advance has been successful in gaining ground, or when a small part of a defending force has held its position. A famous example is the **Ypres** salient on the **Western Front** in **World War I**.

[From Latin *salient-*, present participle of *salire* 'to jump']

Salonika, battle of

(1915–18; *World War I*) In 1915 Bulgaria mobilised with Austria-Hungary and Germany against Serbia. The Allies sent a French and a British division to Salonika (30 October) to support Serbia. The commander, the French General Maurice Sarrail, moved north to support the Serbs, but was too late. Serbia was overrun by the Bulgarians but the Allies decided to hold on to Salonika where they now had an army of 250,000. In the summer of 1916 Sarrail began an advance to aid Romania, which had now entered the war on the side of the Allies. Bitolj in Serbia was taken (19 November) but the Allied advance was checked and Romania was knocked out of the war. The German-Bulgars had suffered 60,000 casualties and the Allies 50,000. Another Allied offensive (March 1917) proved inconclusive. Greece entered the war on the side of the Allies (26 June 1917). Sarrail was relieved (22 December 1917) and General Louis Franchet d'Esperey ultimately took over command. By late summer 1918 the Germans had virtually abandoned the Salonika front to the Bulgarians who quickly collapsed in response to a new Allied advance. Bulgaria signed an armistice (30 September). The Allied casualties due to malaria and other diseases far outweighed those killed or wounded.

saluting

Saluting with the hand may have originated from the practice of knights in armour raising the visors of their helmets to be recognised. Alternatively, it may have been introduced during the 18th century as a substitute for doffing the hat, which made the hat dirty.

saluting base

A raised platform from which the inspecting officer or sovereign acknowledges the salutes given by the officers in a **parade**

salvo

The simultaneous firing of several pieces of **artillery**

[Via French *salve* or Italian *salva* 'greeting' from Latin *salvus* 'safe']

SAM *abbreviation of* **surface-to-air missile**. *See* **anti-aircraft weapons**

Sam Browne belt

A sword-belt with the scabbard suspended on short straps from the waist-belt to which was attached a strap over the right shoulder. A pistol holster was also attached to the waist belt. The design became universally popular and variations are still used in formal dress in many armies, usually in part as a distinguishing mark for officers.

[After General Sir Samuel Browne (1824–1901), an Indian Army officer who lost his left arm in battle and so could not draw his sword in the traditional way]

Sandhurst *See* Royal Military Academy

Sandwich, battle of

(1460; *Wars of the Roses*) The rebel Yorkists, led by Richard Neville, Earl of Warwick, held Calais against frequent Lancastrian attacks. He sailed from Calais with a body of troops and landed at Sandwich (20 June). He routed the Lancastrian opposition and thus established a bridgehead from which he was able to move north.

Sangro, battle of

(1943; *World War II*) General Bernard **Montgomery** with three **divisions** of **infantry** and an armoured **brigade** of the 8th Army forced a crossing of the Sangro river, 80 miles east of Rome, under heavy gun fire (19 November–3 December)

Sanna's Post, battle of

(1900; *Boer Wars*) A British force of **cavalry** and **artillery** were ambushed (31 March) by the Boers commanded by De Wet. The commander, Colonel Broadwood, succeeded in extricating his force, but with the loss of 19 officers and 136 men killed and wounded, as well as seven guns and all his convoy. Another column, commanded by Colonel Colville, was a few miles away but did not come to the rescue, in spite of hearing the gunfire.

San Sebastian, battle of

(1813; *Peninsular War*) The town was besieged (10 July) by a 10,000-strong Allied force commanded by General Thomas **Graham**. An assault (25 July) was repulsed. When heavy guns arrived from Britain the attack was resumed and the town fell to a final assault (31 July). The French, commanded by General Rey, held out in the citadel until 9 September. The French lost some 3,700 killed and wounded.

sapper

The rank of **private** in the Royal Engineers. Originally it referred to a labourer who was attached to the army to carry out various engineering tasks ('sap' was another word for trench and 'to sap' was to dig such a trench towards the wall of a besieged town or an enemy position). **Sappers** is now a nickname for the **Royal Engineers** and was included in the official name of one of the corps' predecessors, the Royal Sappers and Miners.

[From the verb *sap* 'to dig a covered trench' from French *saper*, from Italian *zappa* 'spade, spadework']

Saratoga, battle of

(1777; *American War of Independence*) In spite of his defeat at **Bennington** and the failure of the other two prongs of the British attack from the north, General John **Burgoyne**, with 6,000 men, pushed south, crossing the Hudson river 10 miles south of Saratoga. The American force of 7,000 men, commanded by General Horatio **Gates**, held the **Bemis Heights**. Burgoyne tried to outflank the Americans but was checked at **Freeman's Farm** (19 September) losing 600 men to the American loss of 319. General Sir Henry **Clinton** moved up the Hudson river to take the pressure off Burgoyne, but turned back when he heard of the British surrender of New York (17 October). Meanwhile, Burgoyne tried again to break out towards Albany (7 October). He sent a reconnaissance party of 1,600, but this was repulsed by a force increased to 11,000 Americans (the battle of Bemis Heights). Burgoyne was forced to retreat to the heights

of Saratoga where he became surrounded and finally surrendered to Gates (17 October). This battle was the turning point in the American War of Independence.
See also **Howe, William, 5th Viscount Howe**

Sarsfield, Patrick (d. 1693)
Sarsfield was born in Lucan, Co. Dublin, Ireland. He served in the army of King Louis XIV of France (1671–78) and then in Ireland in the army of James II. When James was deposed he went with him to France. He returned to Ireland to take part in the **Jacobite Rebellion** there. He was a **cavalry** commander and was promoted to **major-general** (1690). James made him Earl of Lucan (1691) and he negotiated the Jacobite surrender at **Limerick** in the same year. He joined Louis XIV's army in the Netherlands and was mortally wounded fighting the British at Neerwinden.
Also known as **Lord Lucan**

SAS *See* **Special Air Service Regiment**

sash
Before the advent of regular uniforms sashes were worn in national colours as a form of identification. **Infantry** usually wore them over the shoulder, and **cavalry** around the waist. The colour for British troops was red. The design later became formalised, and a few **regiments** such as the Royal Corps of Signals wore regimental colours, in this case blue.
[From Arabic *šaš* 'muslin']

Saunderson's (Colonel Saunderson's Regiment of Foot) *See* **Cambridge-shire (1st) Regiment of Foot**

Savandroog, battle of
(1791; *British in India*) A siege was laid (10 December) to the town by 4,000 British, commanded by Lord **Cornwallis**. Once a breach had been made the town fell with little resistance.

Savannah, battle of
1. (1778; *American War of Independence*) Having been frustrated in the north, the British commander General **Clinton** moved his attentions to the southern colonies of America. 3,500 British troops, commanded by Colonel Archibald Campbell, landed at the mouth of the Savannah river (27 December). 850 Americans, commanded by General Robert Howe, moved out of the town of Savannah. Clinton's force, by moving through the swamps, surrounded the Americans and routed them (29 December). The British occupied Savannah and the Americans retreated into South Carolina.
2. (1779; *American War of Independence*) The Americans enlisted the help of the French fleet in an attempt to recapture Savannah. The French landed 3,500 men on the Savannah river, some eight miles from the town (12 September). They were joined by an American force of 1,550 and the combined force attacked Savannah, held by 3,200 troops commanded by General Augustus Prevost. A five-day bombardment (4–8 October) had little effect and the final assault (9 October) by the Americans was repulsed. The French troops withdrew (23 October) and sailed for France. The siege was raised and the Americans withdrew to Charleston.

Saxe, Hermann-Maurice (1696–1750)
The illegitimate son of elector Frederick Augustus of Saxony. He was a distinguished military commander and developed new methods of training, especially of musketeers. King Louis XV of France made him commander of a force that was to invade England in support of Charles Edward, the Young Pretender, but the plan was thwarted by bad weather. In the War of the **Austrian Succession** Louis made Saxe a **marshal**, and he commanded an invasion of the Austrian Netherlands. Saxe defeated the Allies at **Fontenoy** (1745) and moved through the Austrian Netherlands, completing its conquest by defeating the Allies at Raucoux (1746). Saxe was promoted to marshal of France (1747) and invaded Holland, defeating the Allies at **Lauffeld** and at Bergen-op-Zoom (1747). Saxe then retired.

Scarlett, James York (1799–1871)
Scarlett was educated at Eton and Trinity College, Cambridge, and having joined the 18th Hussars (**Royal Hussars (Queen Mary's Own)**), went to Sandhurst. He was **gazetted** as **major** in the 5th Dragoon Guards (1830) and took command of the **regiment** (1840). Scarlett was about to retire (1853) but was appointed commander of the **Heavy Brigade**. He took the **brigade** to Turkey and then to the **Crimea**. He commanded the Heavy Brigade at the battle of **Balaclava** for which service he was promoted to **major-general** (1855). Scarlett then replaced Lord **Lucan** as commander of the British **cavalry** in the Crimea with the local rank of **lieutenant-general**. His time was spent re-organising his depleted forces. He returned home and took command of the cavalry at Aldershot and became **Adjutant-General** (1860).

schiltron
A dense circle of spearmen, a formation much favoured by Scots armies of the 13th and 14th centuries. This was an effective defence against charging **cavalry** but because the soldiers were so closely packed the schiltron was easily destroyed by assault from massed **longbows**.

School of Gunnery *See* **reforms of the Duke of York; reforms after the Crimean War**

School of Musketry *See* **reforms of the Duke of York; reforms after the Crimean War**

Scots Greys *See* **Royal Scots Greys**

Scots Guards
The third regiment of **Foot Guards** from the 17th century to the present day. The **regiment** was raised (1662) at the instruction of Charles II as the New Regiment of Foot Guards under the command of the Earl of Linlithgow. It was formed from four new companies and two others that had been raised in Scotland by Charles I (1642). It had various names (1662–86) and was finally called the Scotch Guards (or Scots Guards) (1686). The subsequent name changes were: 3rd Regiment of Foot Guards (1712); the Scots Fusilier Guards (1831); and the Scots Guards (1877).

Scott, Francis Cunningham (1834–1902)
Scott joined the **Black Watch** (1852) and became their **colonel** in 1881. He served in the **Crimean War**, the **Indian Mutiny** and the **Ashanti War** (1874). In 1891 he was appointed Inspector-General of the Gold Coast Constabulary in 1892. He commanded the Ashanti expedition (1895–96). He left West Africa to command the local forces in Trinidad.
See also **Kumasi, battle of**

Scottish Covenanters' Revolt
At the restoration of Charles II (1660) the **Covenanters** were deprived of all their rights and the Episcopal Church was restored in Scotland. The cruelty of this suppression led to three rebellions (1666, 1679 and 1685), all of which were unsuccessful. After the abdication of James II and the ascension of William and Mary (1688) the Presbyterian Church was re-established in Scotland.

scout
An individual sent out to carry out **reconnaissance**

Seaforth Highlanders, The
The **regiment** formed by the amalgamation (1881) of the 72nd Duke of **Albany's Own Highlanders** and the 78th (Highland) Regiment of Foot (the **Ross-shire Buffs**). In 1961 it amalgamated with the Queen's Own Cameron Highlanders to form the **Queen's Own Highlanders** (Seaforth and Cameron).

Sebastopol, battle of
(1854–55; *Crimean War*) Having defeated the Russians at the **Alma**, the Anglo-French force moved on to Sebastopol (now Sevastopol) (17 October 1854). The force was too

small to take the town so a siege was laid, the harbour being closed off by the British fleet. To relieve the city the Russians attacked the Allies at **Balaclava** (25 October). The Russian commander in Sebastopol, **Menshikov**, then ordered a sortie at **Inkerman** (5 November 1854) and (16 August 1855) on the **Chernaya river**. Both these assaults were repulsed. During this time both the besieged and the attackers suffered terrible hardships. Allied assaults during the spring of 1855 were repulsed. Finally (September 1855) the French took the Malakov fort at the south-east of the city and the British, now commanded by General James **Simpson** (Lord **Raglan** had died), took the **Redan** to the south. Prince Mikhail Gorchakov, who had succeeded Menshikov, abandoned Sebastopol (11 September). The Russians signed a peace at the Congress of Paris (30 March 1856) which preserved Turkey's independence.

second lieutenant
The most junior rank of commissioned officer. The insignia is one star worn on both shoulders.
See also **ensign**

Second World War *See* **World War II**

Sedgemoor, battle of
(1685; *Monmouth's Rebellion*) The accession of the Roman Catholic James II instigated a Protestant revolt in England. The Duke of **Monmouth** landed at Lyme Regis and began to raise a rebel force. This was met at Sedgemoor by a **regiment** of **dragoons** commanded by John Churchill (later Duke of **Marlborough**) (6 July). The rebels were defeated; Monmouth was captured a few days later and beheaded. Many of the rebels who were captured were tried by Judge George Jeffreys at the so-called Bloody Assizes. This was the last formal battle fought on English soil.

self-loading rifle *See* **rifle**

semi-automatic
Used to describe **small arms** that can fire a single shot or a series of shots in quick succession

Senekal, battle of
(1900; *Boer Wars*) A British force, commanded by General Henry **Rundle**, attacked a Boer force on the Biddulphsberg (29 May). The attack, which was confused by vast bush fires, was repulsed with the loss to the British of 184 killed and wounded.

sepoy
An Indian soldier under British command. From the early 18th century Indian troops were recruited locally by the British and formed into regiments. The officers were British, but as the new regiments became more experienced, sepoy **NCOs** were appointed.
[From Persian and Urdu *sipahi* 'horseman, soldier']

sergeant
A **non-commissioned officer** with a rank immediately above that of **corporal**. Originally a sergeant was a servant, and then a tenant who served a knight on the battle-field. Later a sergeant commanded a small body of men. The insignia is three **chevrons** worn on the upper arm.
[Via Old French *sergent* 'servant' from Latin *servient-*, present participle of *servire* 'to be a servant or slave']

sergeant-major
The highest rank of **non-commissioned officer**. Originally, a sergeant-major was a commissioned officer with any rank from **major** to **major-general**.

sergeant-major general
A professional soldier, not necessarily a nobleman, who had command of the **infantry** under a **general**. A sergeant-major general was also responsible for forming the army up for battle and for administrative duties. At the end of the campaign he lost his rank

and command and reverted to being **colonel** of his own **regiment**. The rank was comparable with that of the modern **lieutenant-general**.

Seringapatam, battle of

1. (1792; *British in India*) The Sultan of Mysore, **Tipu Sahib**, invaded the British protectorate of Travancore. The British governor-general of India, Lord **Cornwallis**, came to the aid of Travancore and laid siege to Seringapatam, the capital of Mysore. Tipu surrendered (19 March). He ceded half his territory and paid a large indemnity.

2. (1799; *British in India*) Tipu Sahib again began a war against the British in India. The British governor-general Richard Wellesley, brother of the Duke of **Wellington**, ordered an attack on Seringapatam, Tipu's capital. General George Horn led an Anglo-Indian attack that overpowered the fort. Tipu was killed and British supremacy in southern India established.

Sevastopol *See* Sebastopol, battle of

Seven Years' War (1756–63)

The increasing conflict (from c. 1754) between Britain and France in North America (the **French and Indian War**) joined with unresolved issues in Europe to provoke a general war between the European powers. France, Austria, Russia, Sweden and Poland joined in war against Britain, Hanover, Prussia and Portugal. The Prussians, under Frederick II (the Great), bore the brunt of the war in Europe, while the British fought the French in India and the West Indies. Spain joined the war (1762) on the side of France, but dropped out in the same year having been defeated in Cuba and the Philippines. Russia and Sweden dropped out (1762) and the Treaty of Paris was signed (1763). Great Britain gained Canada, Florida and Minorca; France ceded Louisiana to Spain and Prussia retained Silesia.

See also **Bahur, battle of**; **Calcutta, battle of**; **Hastenbeck, battle of**; **Havana, battle of**; **Madras, battle of**; **Manila, battle of**; **Martinique, battle of**; **Masulipatam, battle of**; **Minden, battle of**; **Plassey, battle of**; **Pondicherry, battle of**; **Wandiwash, battle of**; **Warburg, battle of**; **Abercromby, Ralph**; **Granby, Marquis of**; **Lawrence, Stringer**; **Sackville, George**

shako

A peaked military cap shaped like a truncated cone, made of felt. By 1800 shakos were worn by infantrymen below the rank of **field officer**. They were more comfortable and were less likely to be blown off than the **tricorn** hats they replaced. Shakos were variously decorated with cords and **hackles** indicating **regiments**. In 1812 a new design, later known as the Waterloo shako, was introduced which had a leather plate on the front. The shako became obsolete in 1879.

[Via French *schako* from Hungarian *csákós (süveg)* 'peaked (cap)']

Sharqat, battle of

(1918; *World War I*) The British resumed their offensive in Mesopotamia (now Iraq) with a view to securing the oil-fields at Mosul. An Anglo-Indian mounted force, commanded by General Sir Alexander **Cobbe**, moved north, covering 77 miles in 39 hours, reaching the Little Zab river. The Turkish 6th Army was forced to fall back on Sharqat, 60 miles from Mosul. The Allies attacked (29 October) taking 11,300 prisoners and 51 guns, with the loss of 1,886 men. The Turkish commander, General Ismail Hakki, surrendered (30 October) and an Indian **cavalry division** occupied Sharqat (14 November). This battle ended the fighting in Mesopotamia.

shell

An explosive device fired from **artillery** or **small arms**, containing an explosive charge that is detonated by various types of fuse rather than directly penetrating the target

[From Old English *scell*]

Sheriffmuir, battle of

(1715; *Jacobite Rebellions*) The unpopularity of the Hanoverian King George I led to the **Jacobite Rebellion** in Scotland. John Erskine, Earl of Mar, raised an army of 10,000 Scots at Perth (6 September). They were met at Sheriffmuir (13 November) by a Royalist army commanded by Archibald Campbell, Duke of Argyll. After an indecisive battle the rebel forces disintegrated. Mar abandoned the rebellion and fled to France with the Old Pretender, James Edward, in February 1716.

Sherpur, battle of

(1879; *Afghan War II*) 10,000 Afghans attacked the British fort at Sherpur, north of Kabul. The 6,500-strong British force repulsed the attack with a loss of three killed. The Afghans lost some 3,000 killed and wounded and their force dispersed.

Sherwood Foresters

The Sherwood Foresters (Nottinghamshire and Derbyshire Regiment) was formed (1881) by the amalgamation of the 45th **Nottinghamshire (Sherwood Foresters) Regiment** and the 95th (**Derbyshire Regiment of Foot**). The new **regiment** was called the Derbyshire Regiment (Sherwood Foresters) but was re-named the Sherwood Foresters (Derbyshire Regiment) later in 1881. The name was changed (1902) to the Sherwood Foresters (Nottingham and Derbyshire Regiment). It was amalgamated in 1970 becoming part of the **Worcestershire and Sherwood Foresters Regiment**.
See also **Abyssinian campaign**

Shingle, Operation *See* Anzio, battle of

shorts

Shorts were first worn (1873) by askaris (African troops) at **Kumasi** and by 1904 khaki shorts were being worn in India. They were worn extensively in combat in North Africa during **World War II**.

shot

Projectiles fired from a soldier's personal weapon or a larger artillery piece which are designed to have their effect by the kinetic energy dissipated in their impact. Shot does not explode, unlike shell which does. When applied to artillery ammunition of the 18th and 19th centuries, shot could mean both the single full-calibre cannonballs and the multiple anti-personnel weapons like **canisters**. Two cannonballs were sometimes linked together as chain or bar shot, but these were mainly naval weapons. The principal type of ammunition used by **tanks** in combat with other tanks has always been a solid non-explosive type and this is also sometimes referred to as shot.
Also called **solid shot**
[From Old English *sceot*]

shoulder cords

Gold or silver cords worn since 1880 by officers to carry their rank badges

shrapnel

A type of antipersonnel **shell**. Originally the shell was filled with small shot and fitted with a time fuse so that it exploded near the enemy troops, scattering the shot and the broken shell case. Shrapnel was used up to the beginning of **World War II** when it was discovered that the exploding shell case alone was sufficient to cause damage and the addition of small shot to the shell was discontinued.
[After General Henry *Shrapnel* (1761–1842), a British artillery officer who invented it]

Shrewsbury, battle of

(1403; *Baronial War*) A rebel force, led by Sir Henry Percy (Hotspur) and the Earl of Worcester, met the forces of King Henry IV and Prince Henry just outside Shrewsbury. The rebels attacked (21 July) before reinforcements led by the Earl of Northumberland and Owen Glendower arrived. They were defeated; Hotspur was killed and the rebellion collapsed.

Shropshire Light Infantry *See* **King's Shropshire Light Infantry**

Shropshire Regiment of Foot

The **regiment** was raised (1755) as the 55th Regiment of Foot but was re-numbered the 53rd Regiment of Foot (1757). In 1782 it became the 53rd (or Shropshire) Regiment of Foot. In 1881 it amalgamated with the 85th to become the **King's Shropshire Light Infantry**.

Shropshire Volunteers *See* **Royal County Down Regiment**

Sicily, battle of

(1943; *World War II*) The Allies, now victorious in North Africa, began an assault on the European mainland. An Anglo-American force, commanded by the US General Dwight **Eisenhower**, made an amphibious assault (Operation Husky) on southern Sicily (July 9–10). This was preceded by heavy bombing and a parachute assault by the British 1st Airborne and the US 8th Airborne Divisions. The British 8th Army, commanded by General Sir Bernard **Montgomery**, landed in the south-east; the XIII Corps, commanded by General Miles Dempsey, was on the right; General Oliver **Leese** with the XXX Corps was in the centre. The US 7th Army commanded by General George **Patton** was on the left. The 8th Army captured Syracuse (12 July), Palermo (22 July) and Catania (5 August). The Americans took Messina (17 August) to be joined by the 8th Army. This ended the battle for Sicily, which resulted in 31,158 Allied and 167,000 Axis casualties.

Sidassir, battle of

(1799; *British in India*) The advance guard of a British force was attacked by 12,000 Mysoris under **Tipu Sahib**. The small contingent withstood the attack until the arrival of the main force which drove off the enemy with the loss of 2,000 men. The British lost 143.

Sidi Barrani, battle of

(1940; *World War II*) The North African campaign of **World War II** began when the Italian 10th Army, commanded by Marshal Rudolfo Graziani, invaded Egypt. He set up his camp at Sidi Barrani, 60 miles into Egypt from Libya. The British Western Desert Force, later the 8th Army, commanded by General Sir Richard **O'Connor**, made a surprise attack from Mersa Matruh, surrounding the Italians. During the three days of fighting (9–11 December) the 36,000 British (4th Indian and 7th Armoured Divisions) routed the 75,000 Italians, taking 38,000 prisoners. There were about 600 British casualties.

Sidi-Rezegh, battle of

(1941; *World War II*) The second British offensive in Libya was ordered by General Sir Claude **Auchinleck**, commander in the Middle East. General Alan **Cunningham** led the newly-formed 8th Army in an attack called Operation Crusader (18 November). The XIII Corps moved along the coast while the XXX (Armoured) Corps moved into the desert and reached Sidi Rezegh, the key to **Tobruk** (19 November). The attempt to relieve Tobruk failed. Cunningham was replaced by General Neil Ritchie and the 8th Army opened a corridor to Tobruk (29 November). The German commander, **Rommel**, being short of supplies, fell back (7–8 December). The British occupied Gazala (15 December), Benghazi (25 December) and El Agheila (6 January). They were unable to follow up this victory as essential supplies had been diverted to the Far East and most of the gains were lost again when Rommel counter-attacked early in 1942.

siege

The surrounding of a fortress or town with a view to cutting off its supplies and communications, either forcing its surrender without the need for a direct assault, or weakening its capacity to resist so that such an assault becomes viable. Maintaining a

siege can be a very protracted affair, and may result in the besieging army suffering hardship that causes its withdrawal before the fortress or town falls.
[Via Old French *sege* 'seat' from Latin *sedere* 'to sit']

Siegfried Line
Built by the Germans along their western frontier during the 1930s, this system of concrete **pillboxes** and other emplacements was effective in delaying the American advance into Germany during **World War II** until early in 1945. Siegfried Line was an Allied nickname; the Germans called it the **West Wall**.

Sikh Wars (1845–46, 1848–49)
The first conflict developed over a dispute between the Sikhs in the Punjab and the British over the possession of the Sutlej river area. After three months' fighting, the Sikhs ceded their claim and recognised British supremacy in Kashmir. In 1848 the Sikhs rebelled again but were defeated, allowing the British to annex the Punjab. After the war the Sikhs became allies of the British.
See also **Aliwal, battle of; Chilianwala, battle of; Ferozeshah, battle of; Gujurat, battle of; Mudki, battle of; Multan, battle of; Ramnagar, battle of; Sobraon, battle of; Campbell, Colin; Gough, Hugh; North-West Frontier**

Simpson, James (1792–1868)
Simpson was born at Teviotbank, Roxburghshire, and educated at Edinburgh University. He was commissioned in the 1st Guards (**Grenadier Guards**) (1811) and went to Spain (1812) where he served at **Salamanca**. He was wounded at **Quatre Bras**. By 1826 he had been promoted to **lieutenant-colonel** of the 29th Foot (**Worcestershire Regiment**). He went to Mauritius (1826–37) and returned to England and was made **colonel** in the army (1838). He went on half pay (1839) and then took the 29th to Bengal (1842). He was second-in-command to Sir Charles **Napier** in Sind (1845). Simpson was made commandant at Chatham (1846) and promoted to **major-general** (1851). He went to the **Crimea** (1855) as **chief-of-staff**. On the death of Lord **Raglan** he was given command of the British troops with the local rank of **general**. Simpson was made colonel of the 87th Foot (**Royal Irish Fusiliers**). After differences of opinion with the French commanders he resigned his post (1855) and retired.
See also **Sebastopol, battle of**

Sind *See* **War in the Sind**

Singapore, battle of
(1942; *World War II*) The Japanese, commanded by Lieutenant-General Yamashita, had conquered **Malaya** and then moved to occupy the island fortress of Singapore where the British garrison was commanded by Lieutenant-General Arthur **Percival** (8–15 February). By 15 February the Japanese controlled the water supply of the island. Percival believed that if the Japanese stormed the island they would massacre the civilian population as they had in Nanking (now Nanjing) some years before. Percival surrendered his 70,000 men on the promise that the lives of civilians and troops would be safeguarded (though in fact the Japanese treated their captives brutally and murdered many). This was the worst military disaster in the history of the British Empire. In the whole of the campaign in Malaysia the British and Empire forces lost over 138,000 men; the Japanese fewer than 10,000.

Sir Edward Dering's Regiment of Foot *See* **South Wales Borderers**
Sirmoor Rifles, The *See* **King Edward VII's Own Gurkha Rifles (2nd)**
Sir William Clifton's Regiment of Foot *See* **East Yorkshire Regiment**
Slim, William Joseph (1891–1970)
Slim joined the army as a **private** at the beginning of **World War I**. He soon became an officer and served in the **Dardanelles**, France and Mesopotamia (now Iraq). He received a regular **commission** and joined the Indian Army. In **World War II** he took part in the conquest of Italian **East Africa** (1940) and in the Allied occupation of Iraq (1941). In 1942 he was given command of the 1st Burma Corps and was responsible

for organising the 900-mile retreat from **Burma** (now Myanmar) to the Indian frontier. He was given command of the 14th Army (1943) which successfully repelled the Japanese attack on north-east India at the battles of **Imphal** and Kohima. He developed methods of jungle warfare and was consequently successful in driving the Japanese out of most of Burma. Slim led the 14th Army in a series of substantial victories in late 1944 and early 1945, capturing Mandalay and advancing to Rangoon. These battles were the worst defeats Japan suffered on land during **World War II**. Slim was appointed Commander of Allied Land Forces in Southeast Asia (June 1945). After the war he returned to the UK as commandant of the Imperial Defence College (1946), was promoted to **field marshal** and appointed Chief of the Imperial General Staff (1948). He was governor-general of Australia (1953–60) and was created a viscount.

See also **Burma campaigns 2**; **Wingate, Orde Charles**

SLR *abbreviation of* **self-loading rifle**

small arms

Any form of weaponry that can be carried by individuals, in contrast to weapons such as **artillery** that have to be transported. Small arms include rifles, pistols of various types and machine guns.

Small Arms Factory *See* **Enfield Small Arms Factory; reforms after the Crimean War; reforms of the Duke of York**

Small Arms School Corps

The **corps** originated (1854) as the **School of Musketry** which was re-named the Small Arms School (1919). In the same year a Machine Gun School was formed. In 1923 the names were changed to the Corps of Small Arms and Machine Gun Schools. These two were combined (1929) as the Small Arms School Corps.

Smith, Harry George Wakelyn (1787–1860)

Smith entered the army (1805) as an **ensign** and served in South America (1807), in Spain (1808–14), in America (1814) and then at **Waterloo**. He served in England, was then sent to Jamaica and then to Cape Colony (1828) where he took part in the war of 1834–35. On being transferred to India, now as a **general** (1840), he fought against the Sikhs (1845–46), personally leading the final charge at the battle of **Aliwal**. He returned to the Cape (December 1847) as governor and high commissioner, having been created a baronet and promoted to **major-general**. He annexed the Orange River State, causing the Boers, led by Andries **Pretorius**, to rebel. Smith attacked and defeated them at **Boomplaats**. His unsympathetic handling of the non-British colonists and the cost of the Cape Frontier War (1850–53) led to his being recalled (1852) to Britain where he then held several further military posts.

Smith-Dorrien, Horace (1858–1930)

Smith-Dorrien was born in Hertfordshire and educated at Harrow School and the Royal Military College, Sandhurst. He was **gazetted** as **lieutenant** in the 95th Foot **(Derbyshire Regiment of Foot)** (1877). He fought in the **Zulu War** (1879) at **Isandlwana** and **Ulundi** and then went to Egypt (1882) and Lucknow. Smith-Dorrien then joined the Egyptian Army (1884). He attended the **Staff College** and served in India (1889–98). He returned to Egypt and commanded the 13th Sudanese Battalion at **Omdurman**. He then served in the **Boer War** (1899) and distinguished himself at **Paardeberg**. He was promoted to **major-general** and was sent to India as **adjutant-general** but soon commanded the 4th Division at Quetta (1902–07). He returned home to take command at Aldershot (1907) and then of Southern Command (1912). In 1914 he took command of the II Corps and later the 2nd Army in France. He led II Corps skilfully at **Mons** and **Le Cateau** but his leadership of the 2nd Army at the second battle of **Ypres** (1915) was criticised and he was ordered home to command the 1st Army for home defence. He was selected to command the troops attacking German East Africa but an attack of pneumonia and three operations precluded his taking up the appointment. He was appointed governor of Gibraltar (1918–23). He retired (1923) and was killed in a car accident.

SMLE *See* rifle

Smuts, Jan Christiaan (1870–1950)

Smuts was the son of a farmer, born in Cape Colony, South Africa. He studied science at Victoria College and then law at Christ's College, Cambridge, UK (1891). He returned to South Africa and ultimately became state attorney to President Kruger when he was 28 years old. When the British occupied Pretoria during the **Boer War** he became a full-time soldier and a master of guerrilla warfare. He invaded Cape Colony (1902) but the campaign failed, and when the Boers surrendered, Smuts was recalled and took part in the peace negotiations. He then devoted himself to public life. During **World War I** he and Botha suppressed a rebellion in South Africa, conquered German South West Africa and began the campaign in **East Africa**. He attended a conference in London (1917) and the Prime Minister, Lloyd George, made him minister for air. He took part in the peace negotiations. When Botha died he became Prime Minister of South Africa (1919–24) and again from 1939–48. He played only a minor role during **World War II**. He was made Chancellor of Cambridge University (1948).

Snider Rifle *See* rifle

Sobraon, battle of

(1846; *Sikh Wars*) The last battle of the First Sikh War. All the Sikhs still in the east Punjab had been forced back to the Sutlej river opposite Sobraon. The 25,000 Sikhs were attacked by 15,000 Anglo-Indian troops commanded by General Sir Hugh **Gough**. The Sikhs were driven from their trenches and forced into the river. They lost some 8,000 men, while Gough lost 2,300.

solid shot *See* shot

Sollum-Halfaya Pass, battle of

(1941; *World War II*) The Germans, commanded by General Erwin **Rommel**, had swept across North Africa and the British **commander-in-chief** General Sir Archibald **Wavell** launched a premature counter-attack to relieve **Tobruk**. The operation (Battleaxe) was commanded by General Noel Beresford-Peirse and consisted of one **division** attacking along the coast from Sollum and another attacking from inland through the Halfaya pass (15–17 June). The attack was repulsed with the loss of 1,000 casualties and 100 tanks, about half the British armour. Wavell was replaced and went to India.

Solway Moss, battle of

(1542; *English-Scottish Wars*) Henry VIII of England tried to force James V of Scotland to abandon his pro-Roman Catholic, pro-French policies. This failed, and border warfare broke out again. Some 10,000 Scottish invaders met a smaller English force at Solway Moss (24 November). The Scots were decisively defeated. The defeat contributed to the death of James V who was succeeded by his infant daughter Mary, Queen of Scots. A peace treaty was agreed (1543).

Somerset, Fitzroy James Henry *See* Raglan, Lord

Somerset and Cornwall Light Infantry

The **regiment** was formed (1959) by the amalgamation of the **Somerset Light Infantry** (Prince Albert's) and the **Duke of Cornwall's Light Infantry**. In 1968 it became part of The **Light Infantry** after a further amalgamation.

Somerset Light Infantry

The **regiment** was raised (1685) by Theophilus Hastings, Earl of Huntingdon, as the **Earl** of Huntingdon's Regiment of Foot. The name changed with the **colonel** until 1751 when it became the 13th Regiment of Foot. It was re-named the 13th (1st Somersetshire) Regiment of Foot (1782); the 13th (or 1st Somersetshire) Regiment of Foot (Light Infantry); the 13th or Prince Albert's Regiment of Light Infantry (1842); Prince Albert's Light Infantry (Somerset Regiment) (1881); Prince Albert's (Somerset

Light Infantry) (1912); and the Somerset Light Infantry (Prince Albert's) (1921). It amalgamated (1959) with the **Duke of Cornwall's Light Infantry** to form the **Somerset and Cornwall Light Infantry**.

See also **Jellalabad, battle of**

Somersetshire (2nd) Regiment of Foot

The **regiment** was raised in Nova Scotia (1717) from independent companies and was known as Colonel Phillip's Regiment of Foot. The name was changed with the **colonels** until 1751 when it was designated the 40th Regiment of Foot, becoming the 40th (2nd Somersetshire) Regiment of Foot (1782). In 1881 it amalgamated with the 82nd **Prince of Wales's Volunteers** to form what later became known as the **South Lancashire Regiment**.

Somme, battle of

1. (1916; *World War I*) This was planned as the main Anglo-French offensive of 1916. It was the first battle in which substantial numbers of the British New Army troops raised by Lord **Kitchener** participated, and, because the French Army was also heavily involved at Verdun, it turned out to be the first major battle of the war in which the British Army was the main force on the Allied side. The **infantry** attack began on 1 July after a week-long **artillery** bombardment. The French 2nd Army, commanded by General Marie Emile Fayolle, attacked in the south while the British 4th Army commanded by General Sir Henry **Rawlinson** attacked in the north; the 5th Army commanded by General Sir Hubert **Gough** was in reserve. The first day was disastrous, the worst in the history of the British Army. The British suffered 57,450 casualties and gained very little ground. The battle lasted until November with repeated attacks and counter-attacks by both sides. **Tanks** were used for the first time ever in warfare (15 September) but on a small scale and with limited success. Although the battle is popularly remembered in Britain for the great losses it caused to the British forces, the German Army probably suffered about as badly, with some 650,000 killed and wounded on both the Allied and German sides.

2. (1918; *World War I*) The German commander General Erich **Ludendorff** determined to achieve a major victory before the arrival of the American troops. To this end he launched (21 March) the first of five successive offensives against the Allies on a 50-mile front south of Arras. This was held by British troops commanded by Field Marshal Sir Douglas **Haig**. 71 German **divisions** were involved. The 15 British divisions in the south, commanded by General Sir Hubert **Gough**, withdrew behind the Somme (22 March) exposing the right flank of 14 divisions of General Sir Julian **Byng's** 3rd Army, which was forced to retire. The Germans advanced 14 miles during the first four days. Their southern flank continued to advance, but the attack petered out (4 April) as the troops were exhausted and supplies were low. Ludendorff's attempt to force a wedge between the British and French had nearly succeeded. The Allies lost some 160,000 casualties, 70,000 prisoners and 1,100 guns. The German losses were similar. The Allies recalled **Foch** as **commander-in-chief** (appointed in effect from 26 March, but officially from 14 April). Ludendorff now planned new attacks on the **Lys river** sector.

Sorauren, battle of

(1813; *Peninsular War*) A French force of 25,000 commanded by Marshal **Soult** attacked a 12,000-man force commanded by **Wellington** (28 July). The French made two attempts to dislodge the British but were repulsed on both occasions with the loss of 5,000 killed and wounded and 3,000 prisoners. The British lost some 4,900.

Soult, Nicolas-Jean de Dieu (1769–1851)

Soult enlisted in the French **infantry** (1775) and advanced rapidly until **Napoleon** made him a **Marshal** of France (1804). He went to Spain in 1808 and fought against British forces at La Coruña (**Corunna**) and in other battles. Later he was the French

commander-in-chief and was ultimately defeated by **Wellington** at **Toulouse** (1814). He was Napoleon's **chief-of-staff** at **Waterloo**.
See also **Albuera, battle of**; **Nive, battle of**; **Nivelle, battle of**; **Oporto, battle of**; **Orthez, battle of**

South Devonshire Regiment of Foot
The **regiment** was raised (1741) as Colonel John Price's Regiment of Foot. The name changed with the **colonel** until 1751 when it was re-named the 46th Regiment of Foot. The regiment became the 46th (or South Devonshire) Regiment of Foot in 1782. In the 1881 reorganisation it amalgamated with the 32nd to form the Duke of **Cornwall's** Light Infantry.

South Gloucestershire Regiment
The **regiment** was raised (1756) as the 2nd Battalion of the 3rd (or **East Kent**) **Regiment** of Foot (The Buffs). It became independent (1758) as the 61st Regiment of Foot. The name changed (1782) to the 61st (or South Gloucestershire) Regiment of Foot. It took part in the battle of **Toulouse** (1814) after which the regiment wore silver acorns on its coat-tails. In 1881 it amalgamated with the 20th **North Gloucestershire Regiment** to form the **Gloucestershire Regiment**.

South Hampshire Regiment of Foot
The **regiment** was raised (1756) as the 2nd Battalion of the 20th Regiment of Foot and became the 67th Regiment of Foot (1758). It was re-named (1782) the 67th (or South Hampshire) Regiment of Foot. It merged with the **North Hampshire Regiment of Foot** in 1881 to become the Hampshire Regiment, later the **Royal Hampshire Regiment**.

South Lancashire Regiment
The **regiment** was formed (1881) by the amalgamation of the 40th **Somersetshire (2nd) Regiment of Foot** and the 82nd Regiment of Foot (**Prince of Wales's Volunteers**). It was first known as the Prince of Wales's Volunteers (South Lancashire) and the name was changed (1938) to the South Lancashire Regiment (Prince of Wales's Volunteers). In 1958 it was amalgamated as part of the **Lancashire Regiment (The Prince of Wales's Volunteers)**.

South Lincolnshire Regiment
The **regiment** was raised (1756) as the 2nd Battalion of the 24th Foot (**South Wales Borderers**) but became a separate regiment (1758) as the 69th Regiment of Foot. The name was changed (1782) to the 69th (or South Lincolnshire) Regiment of Foot. It merged with the 41st in 1881 to become the **Welsh Regiment**.

South Staffordshire Regiment
The **regiment** was formed (1881) by the amalgamation of the 38th (1st **Staffordshire**) Regiment of Foot with the 80th Regiment of Foot (**Staffordshire Volunteers**). In 1959 it merged with the **North Staffordshire Regiment** to become the **Staffordshire Regiment (Prince of Wales's)**.

South Wales Borderers
The **regiment** was raised (1689) as Sir Edward Dering's Regiment of Foot. The name changed with the **colonel** until 1747 when it became the 24th Foot and in 1751 the 24th Regiment of Foot. The name was changed (1782) to the 24th (or 2nd Warwickshire) Regiment of Foot and to the South Wales Borderers (1881). In 1969 it amalgamated with the **Welsh Regiment** to become the **Royal Regiment of Wales**.
See also **Chilianwala, battle of**

Spanish Succession, War of the (1702–14)
King Charles II of Spain died childless (1700) and Louis XIV of France, following Charles' will but in defiance of an existing treaty, declared his grandson Philip, Duke of Anjou, the new king of Spain as Philip V. Britain, the Netherlands and Austria formed a new Grand Alliance and declared war on France (4 May 1702). Prussia (1702) and Portugal and Savoy (1703) joined the Alliance. The war was concluded by a series

of treaties (1713–14) whereby Philip was recognised as the king of Spain, but the Spanish Netherlands (now Belgium) were transferred to Austria. This war in North America was called **Queen Anne's War**.

See also **Almanza, battle of; Barcelona, battle of; Blenheim, battle of; Brihuega, battle of; Donauwörth, battle of; Gibraltar, battle of; Lille, battle of; Malplaquet, battle of; Oudenarde, battle of; Ramillies, battle of; Tournai, battle of; Cutts, John**

Special Air Service Regiment

The original name for the SAS was L Detachment, SAS Brigade, which was established some 60-strong in Egypt in the summer of 1941. Its mission was to raid airfields well behind the German lines and destroy aircraft on the ground. Its first operation, when the men were dropped by parachute, was a disaster but in December a second raid was a great success. Over the next year or so the gradually expanded but still tiny unit destroyed more enemy aircraft than the whole Desert Air Force. The 1st Special Air Services Regiment was formed in the autumn of 1942 and a 2nd Regiment was established later in the year. The SAS, like various other special forces units set up during the desert war, found the going harder when it moved on to operations in the more congested territory of Italy and France in 1943–45. Both SAS regiments were disbanded in 1945 but in 1947 a Territorial Army SAS unit was formed as the 21st SAS (Artists) Regiment. This unit was formed into the Malayan Scouts at the start of the 1950s emergency in Malaya and was taken on to the regular establishment (1952) as the 22nd Special Air Service Regiment. The 23rd Special Air Service Regiment was formed (1959) as a Territorial Unit. After **World War II** the SAS served in Malaya (1950–60), Borneo (1963–66), Aden (1964–67) and Oman (1970–76). Members of the Regiment went to Northern Ireland in 1969 and it was deployed in full strength in Ulster in 1976 where it took part in covert intelligence gathering for the regular forces. By the 1970s international terrorism had become a world-wide threat and the SAS then became involved in counter-terrorism, helping the Israelis, e.g., in the capture of a hijacked airliner at Mogadishu airport (October 1977). On 30 April 1980 six armed terrorists burst into the Iranian Embassy in London and took the staff hostage. The hostages were rescued by the SAS, and the terrorists killed, during a spectacular operation, much of which was seen live on television. This operation brought the regiment into the public eye, though both before and since it has officially shunned publicity. During the **Falklands War** the SAS took part in the successful re-capture of South Georgia from the Argentinians, intelligence gathering and the establishment of the beachhead at San Carlos. During the 1991 **Gulf War** SAS patrols were active behind Iraqi lines, particularly in operations to destroy Iraqi Scud missiles. It has also been involved in recent conflicts in Afghanistan and Iraq and in counter-terrorism measures following the bombings which took place in London on 7 July 2005.

Abbreviation **SAS**

Special Reserve *See* **reforms after the Boer War**

Spion Kop, battle of

(1900; *Boer Wars*) After the initial setbacks against the Boers, the British sent General Lord Frederick **Roberts** and General Lord **Kitchener** to South Africa to take command, while General Sir Redvers **Buller** retained command only of the Natal front. Buller launched a second attempt to relieve **Ladysmith** (19 January). A force commanded by General Sir Charles **Warren** captured the height of Spion Kop, 24 miles southwest of Ladysmith, but it was too steep for artillery to be mounted there. The Boers regained the hill (23 January) and Buller fell back across the Tugela river.

spontoon, espontoon

A weapon resembling a spear with a crosspiece. Spontoons were carried by officers until the **American War of Independence**, and by **infantry sergeants** from 1792 to 1830. By then the spontoon was not really regarded as a serious weapon but was sometimes useful to help sergeants keep their men in close formation in the stress of battle.

See also **pike**

[Via French from Italian *spontone*, from *punto* 'point']

Spurs, battle of the

(1513; *Anglo-French Wars*) The young Henry VIII, keen to renew the glories of the **Hundred Years' War**, led an army against France in 1513. Strengthened by a small force under the Holy Roman Emperor, he besieged Thérouanne (1 August). On 16 August a force of French cavalry misjudged its position and found itself confronted by the whole allied army. In the subsequent pursuit across the fields of Guinegate (modern Enguingatte) six standards and some high-ranking French nobles were captured. Although militarily insignificant, this skirmish gave Henry the victory he craved, the name 'battle of the Spurs' being a derisive reference to the main 'weapon' used by the French in their haste to flee. Thérouanne fell on 23 August and was razed to the ground. The other achievement of the campaign was to capture Tournai (23 September), which remained in English hands until 1518.

Also called **Guinegate, battle of**

squadron

Originally a relatively small body of men drawn up in a square, later a small force deployed for a particular purpose. Since the late 17th century, however, it has usually meant a body of **cavalry** of 100–200 men. Several squadrons, typically four, make up a cavalry **regiment** and the squadron in turn is divided into **troops**, usually two. The regiments in the modern Royal Armoured Corps are still divided in this way into squadrons.

[From Italian *squadrone* 'large squad', from assumed Vulgar Latin *exquadra* 'square']

staff

A group of officers based at the central headquarters of an army.

See also **staff officer**

staff captain

A **captain** serving on the **staff**

Staff College

The principal establishment in Britain to provide training for staff officers was founded in 1800 as the senior department of the **Royal Military College** (*see* **Royal Military Academy**). It became Staff College in 1858 and moved to a new building at Camberley, on the Sandhurst estate, in 1862. In 1998 it amalgamated with equivalent staff colleges in the Royal Naval and RAF to form the **Joint Service Command and Staff College**; this is now located at Shrivenham.

staff officer

1. In 1729, any **non-commissioned officer**

2. From 1777 to the present, an officer serving with a **general** or other commander at the headquarters of a **division** or **brigade**. The **general staff** was introduced into the British Army in 1906 and staff officers are usually experts in various fields such as logistics or intelligence.

Staffordshire Regiment (Prince of Wales's)

The **regiment**, which still exists, was formed (1959) by the amalgamation of the **South Staffordshire Regiment** and the **North Staffordshire Regiment**. It is due to unite with The Cheshire Regiment and The Worcestershire and Sherwood Foresters Regiment in 2007 to form The Mercian Regiment.

Staffordshire (1st) Regiment of Foot

The **regiment** was raised (1705) as Colonel Lillingston's Regiment of Foot. The name changed with the **colonel** until 1751 when it became the 38th Regiment of Foot. The name was further changed (1782) to the 38th (or 1st Staffordshire) Regiment of Foot.

In 1881 the regiment amalgamated with the **Staffordshire Volunteers** to become the **South Staffordshire Regiment**.

Staffordshire (2nd) Regiment of Foot

The **regiment** was raised (1758) by Colonel John Berrington as the 64th Regiment of Foot. The name was changed (1782) to the 64th (or 2nd Staffordshire) Regiment of Foot. In 1881 the regiment amalgamated with the 98th to become what was later known as the **North Staffordshire Regiment**.

Staffordshire Volunteers

The **regiment** was raised by Lieutenant-Colonel Lord Paget (1793) as the 80th Regiment of Foot (or Staffordshire Volunteers). The name remained unchanged until 1881 when the regiment amalgamated with the **Staffordshire (1st) Regiment of Foot** to become the **South Staffordshire Regiment**.

Stamford Bridge, battle of

(1066; *Norwegian Invasion of England*) After the English defeat at **Fulford** King Harold moved rapidly north and surprised the Norwegians, led by Harold Hardrada and Tostig, at Stamford Bridge, north of York. The Norwegians were defeated and Harold Hardrada and Tostig were killed. This was the last serious threat to England by the Scandinavians. Harold then moved south rapidly to meet the Normans at **Hastings**.

Standard, battle of the

(1138; *The Anarchy*) After 1135 England descended into civil war between King Stephen and the supporters of Henry I's daughter and chosen successor, Matilda (see **Anarchy, The**). In 1138 David I of Scotland three times invaded England, nominally in support of Matilda but also to conquer the northern English counties. Stephen countered the first invasion but, occupied with rebellion in the south, ignored the second, allowing the Scottish army to ravage Durham and northern Yorkshire unhindered. The third invasion was resisted by Archbishop Thurstan of York, who persuaded the barons and the people of Yorkshire to fight the invaders. On 29 August they made their stand at Northallerton around a carriage carrying the standards of saints associated with the north (hence the name 'battle of the Standard'). The Scots attacked, but their badly armed and undisciplined forces were routed by the English knights and archers within two hours. The victory preserved England from what was seen as a barbarian invasion and probably saved Stephen's throne; but David continued to occupy Cumbria and Northumberland and later extended his realm to include Durham and northern Lancashire.

standing army

A regular and permanent army, in contrast to one raised for a particular campaign. In the time of Charles II it consisted of the Household troops acting as the sovereign's bodyguard and paid for by the king. Later it was a national force financed by Parliament, held in readiness to face any emergency.

See also **Bill of Rights**

Starstreak High Velocity Missile *See* **anti-aircraft weapons**

Staunton, Francis French (1779?–1825)

Staunton was commissioned as an **ensign** in the Bombay Army (1798). He was promoted to **lieutenant** (1800) and **captain** (1807). He took part in the battle of **Seringapatam**. His most noted achievement was at the battle of **Korygaom**. He was made **aide-de-camp** to the governor-general and created **CB**. He was promoted to **major** (1819) and to **lieutenant-colonel** (1823).

steel helmet

Protective steel **helmets** were first issued by the French in 1915 and by the British in March 1916. They were not proof against a direct strike from a bullet but did give considerable protection against shrapnel, fragments or debris thrown up by artillery shells. Similar helmets, also sometimes known as 'tin hats', were worn during **World**

War II. Steel helmets have been replaced in recent years by more modern designs made of such artificial materials as **Kevlar**.

Steenkerke, battle of

(1692; *War of the Grand Alliance*) The French troops, commanded by the Duc de Luxembourg, had taken **Namur** (5 June) leaving their way open to Brussels. The Alliance forces, commanded by William III, made an all-night march and surprised the French at Steenkerke (2 August). After an initial success the Alliance forces were driven back, with the loss of 8,000 men.

Sten gun

A **submachine gun** used by British and Commonwealth forces during **World War II** and supplied to various Allies. It went out of use during the 1950s. The gun was light, cheap to manufacture and simple to maintain, but was not accurate and jammed readily. [Acronym from the surnames of R.V.V. Shepherd + H.J. Turpin, its designers + Enfield in Greater London, England, after Bren gun]

Stewart, Herbert (1843–85)

Stewart was born at Sparshot, Hampshire, and was educated at Winchester College (1854). He was commissioned as **ensign** in the 37th Foot (**North Hampshire Regiment of Foot**) and had been promoted to **captain** by 1868 when the **regiment** was in Bengal. He returned to England (1873) having exchanged to the 3rd Dragoon Guards. He entered the **Staff College** (1877). Stewart then served as **brigade major** of **cavalry** in Natal (1879) during the **Zulu War** and became military secretary to Sir Garnet **Wolseley** in Natal (18800), and was promoted to **brevet lieutenant-colonel** in the same year. He was captured by the Boers at **Majuba Hill** but was soon released. He spent a short time in Ireland before going to Egypt as brigade major of cavalry. For his services in Egypt he was promoted to **brevet colonel** and appointed **aide-de-camp** to the queen. He returned to Egypt, saw action at **El Teb** and in the expedition to relieve **Khartoum** when he commanded the column advancing through the desert. He was mortally wounded at **Abu Klea**. Just before his death he heard of his promotion to **major-general**.

Stirling, David (1915–90)

The creator of the **Special Air Service Regiment** (SAS). Stirling was an officer in the **Scots Guards** and transferred to the **commandos** (1940). While serving in the Middle East he submitted a plan for the formation of a special force to attack enemy airfields behind the German lines. The original plan was to drop by parachute on the targets, but this proved disastrous. A method of making wide sweeps through the desert using small groups of men with jeeps and lorries was adopted and proved very successful. Stirling was captured (1943), but by this time his units had destroyed at least 250 enemy aircraft. Stirling made four unsuccessful attempts to escape from various prison camps and was eventually sent to the top-security camp at Colditz Castle. He remained there until the end of the war.

Stirling Bridge, battle of

(1297; *English-Scottish Wars*) Edward I's intervention in Scotland provoked an uprising, led particularly by William Wallace. Edward sent the Earl of Surrey to put down the rebellion. The Scots were encamped at Stirling, which Surrey attempted to attack with a strong force. The English had to cross a narrow bridge over the Forth (11 September). Wallace laid an ambush at this bottleneck and wiped out the leading English troops. The English fell back, ultimately as far as the Tweed.

Stirlingshire Regiment

The **regiment** was raised (1787) by Colonel Robert **Abercromby** as the 75th (Highland) Regiment of Foot or Abercromby's Highlanders. The name was changed to the 75th Regiment of Foot (1807) and the 75th (Stirlingshire) Regiment of Foot (1862). The regiment served with Abercromby in India. It amalgamated with the 92nd in 1881, with the new regiment becoming the **Gordon Highlanders**.

stock

A type of stiff leather collar, buckled or tied at the back, worn as a standard part of uniform by **infantry** soldiers in the 18th century. It was designed to keep the head upright and help the soldier achieve a martial appearance. In reality it was desperately uncomfortable, restricted movement, and made it difficult for the soldier to aim his weapon accurately. A softer version was issued (1845) but the stiffened version was used again (1847). The stock was replaced (1862) by a leather tab which closed the opening of the collar.

[From Old English *stocc* 'tree trunk']

Stoke, battle of

(1487; *Wars of the Roses*) Following Henry VII's victory at **Bosworth**, a pretender to the throne appeared in 1486. In reality the boy was a commoner named Lambert Simnel, but he was passed off as Edward, Earl of Warwick and nephew of the Yorkist king Edward IV. Although it is doubtful whether anybody believed this claim, discontented Yorkists rebelled in his name and were equipped with a mercenary army by Margaret, Duchess of Burgundy and Edward IV's sister. This force landed in Ireland (May 1487), where it was welcomed and gathered more troops, and then crossed to England (June 1487). After some successful preliminary manoeuvring, it met the royal army under Henry VII at the village of East Stoke, near Newark (16 June). The King was victorious after three hours of fierce fighting. Most of the Yorkist leaders died in the battle, but Simnel was pardoned and put to work in the royal kitchens. The battle of Stoke ended the Wars of the Roses.

Stono Ferry, battle of

(1779; *American War of Independence*) The American commander in the South, Benjamin Lincoln, moved against Augusta (April) while the British General Augustus Prevost moved from Savannah to Charleston, which was defended by General William Moultrie. Lincoln returned to aid Moultrie and Prevost withdrew, leaving a rearguard of 900 at Stono Ferry. Moultrie with 1,200 men attacked the rearguard but was driven off. In spite of this victory Prevost abandoned his advance into South Carolina.

Stony Creek, battle of

(1813; *War of 1812*) To gain control of Lake Ontario an American force of 1,600 attacked York (now Toronto) (27 April) and returned to Niagara (8 May), forcing the British out of Fort George. The British **general**, John Vincent, fell back to Stony Creek at the western end of Lake Ontario where he made a stand with some 700 troops against 2,000 Americans. The Americans were defeated and fell back to Fort George.

Stony Point, battle of

(1779; *American War of Independence*) The British commander in New York, Sir Henry **Clinton**, sent a large force up the Hudson river (1 June) and captured the American fort at Stony Point where he left a garrison of 700 men commanded by Lieutenant-Colonel Henry Johnson. An American force of 1,350 commanded by General Anthony Wayne retook the fort (15 July). As it was near to New York, **Washington** ordered it to be dismantled and the Americans withdrew.

Stormberg, battle of

(1899; *Boer Wars*) A British force of 3,000 men commanded by General William Forbes Gatacre, moved from Cape Colony to Stormberg where the Boers had moved within 70 miles of Queenstown (10 December). Their guides misled them into an enemy ambush. 89 were killed and more than 600 taken prisoner. The British withdrew. Gatacre was dismissed for his mishandling of the situation.

Stow-on-the-Wold, battle of

(1646; *Civil War*) The last remaining force of Charles I was commanded by General Lord Jacob Astley. It was cornered by the Parliamentarians at Stow-on-the-Wold (26 March). After a brief fight Astley surrendered. Charles abandoned his headquarters at nearby Oxford (5 May) and surrendered to the Scottish army of General David Leslie at Newark.

stripe
1. *See* **chevron**

2. An indication of long service, or an indication of wounds received during wartime, worn on the left forearm.

See also **good conduct stripes**; **war service stripes**; **wound stripes**
[Probably from Middle Dutch or Middle Low German *stripe*]

Stuart, John (1759–1815)
Stuart was born in Georgia where his father was agent for Indian affairs. Stuart was educated at Westminster School and was commissioned as an **ensign** in the 3rd Foot (**East Kent Regiment**) (1778). He served in America and was present at the surrender of **Yorktown** where he was severely wounded. He was promoted to **lieutenant** (1782). He served at home for ten years and then went to Flanders with his **regiment**. He returned to England (1795) and was promoted to **brevet colonel** (1796). He was promoted to **brigadier-general** (1796) and commanded a force in Portugal. In 1798 he raised the Queen's German Regiment which went with him to Minorca (1799). The regiment was called the 97th Foot in 1808 and disbanded in 1818. From Minorca he went to Egypt (1801) as **brigadier-general** under Sir Ralph **Abercromby**. He then commanded the troops in Alexandria and was promoted (1802) to **major-general**. Stuart then commanded the home defence force (1803–05) until he sailed for the Mediterranean where he commanded the forces fighting the French in southern Italy. He won the victory at **Maida**. He was appointed colonel of the 74th Foot (**Foot, 74th (Highlanders)**). He was appointed commander of the land forces in the Mediterranean with the rank of **lieutenant-general** (1808), based at Messina. Due to tensions with the home government over the disposition of troops in the Mediterranean, Stuart resigned (1809) and returned home. He was appointed lieutenant-governor of Grenada (1811) and commander of the Western District (1813). He resigned through ill-health (1814).

subaltern
Any commissioned officer below the rank of **major**

submachine gun
A weapon capable of fully automatic fire but, unlike most machine guns, light enough to be carried, aimed and fired as an individual's personal weapon. Typically submachine guns use a simple blowback mechanism to achieve continuous firing. Submachine guns are also called machine carbines or machine pistols. They are short-range weapons, effective up to no more than 200 yards, and difficult to fire accurately to much less than that. The first true submachine gun was the German MP18, issued to troops in 1918. British forces used them extensively during **World War II**, but they have now largely disappeared from military service and been replaced by assault **rifles**.
See also **Sten gun**

substantive rank
The permanent rank in which an officer is confirmed, in contrast to a **brevet rank**. The appointment is published in the 'London Gazette', and he is said to be 'gazetted'. The title of such a rank may be used after the officer has retired from the army.

Sudan War (1881–99)
The misrule of the Sudan by Egypt led to a revolt (1881) led by the **Mahdi**. Britain was drawn into the conflict because Egypt was a British protectorate. By 1885 almost all the Anglo-Egyptians had been driven from the Sudan, but a concerted campaign of two-and-a-half years by General Horatio Herbert **Kitchener** finally brought peace. The Sudan was ruled as an Anglo-Egyptian condominium until 1956 when it became a republic.

Suez (1956)

In July 1956 Egypt nationalised the Suez Canal, which was largely owned by British and French interests and was regarded by both countries as of great strategic importance. To regain control, Britain and France reached a secret agreement with Israel (22–23 October): Israel would invade Egypt and an Anglo-French force would intervene, nominally to enforce a ceasefire but also to seize control of the Canal. Israel duly attacked (29 October) and advanced towards the Canal; and Britain and France issued an ultimatum demanding withdrawal, then bombed Egyptian airfields (31 October). On 5 November the 3rd battalion of the **Parachute Regiment** secured El Gamil airfield. The Anglo-French amphibious and airborne force landed, quickly overcame Egyptian resistance and moved to secure the Canal. Some 45,000 British troops were involved, of which 22 were killed. However, the operation met with international condemnation, especially from the USA and the USSR. US threats of economic sanctions forced Britain to accept a ceasefire (6 November), with which France reluctantly concurred. The Anglo-French force was withdrawn (December) and replaced by a UN **peacekeeping** force, in which Britain and France played no part. Although militarily successful, the Suez intervention was a political and diplomatic disaster; both Britain and France lost much of their traditional influence in the Middle East, and Britain's dependence on the USA was painfully exposed. The memory of the campaign has been downplayed in Britain: it is not listed on the battle honours of the regiments involved and a general service **medal** was issued for it only in 2004.

Suffolk Regiment

The **regiment** originated (1660) as the garrison company at Windsor Castle. It was commanded by Henry Howard, Duke of Norfolk, and when it was raised to regimental strength it was called the Duke of Norfolk's Regiment of Foot. The name changed with the **colonel** until 1751 when it was designated the 12th Regiment of Foot. The name changed further to the 12th (or the East Suffolk) Regiment of Foot (1782) and to the Suffolk Regiment (1881). It amalgamated with the Royal Norfolk Regiment in 1959 to form the 1st East Anglian Regiment (Royal Norfolk and Suffolk).

surcoat

A loose coat worn over armour during the Middle Ages. Later armorial bearings were displayed on it. From this practice is derived the term 'coat-of-arms'.
[From Old French *surcote* 'overcoat']

surface-to-air missile *abbreviation of* SAM

Surrey Regiment

The **regiment** was raised in Glasgow (1756) as the 2nd Battalion of the 31st Regiment of Foot. It became an independent regiment (1758) – the 70th Regiment of Foot. The named was changed (1782) to the 70th (or the Surrey) Regiment of Foot, to the 70th (or Glasgow Lowlands) Regiment of Foot (1813), to the 70th (or Surrey) Regiment of Foot (1825) and to the 70th (Surrey) Regiment (1855). In the 1881 reorganisation it merged with the 31st to become the **East Surrey Regiment**.

Sussex Regiment *See* **King's Own Scottish Borderers; Royal Sussex Regiment**

Sutherland Highlanders

The **regiment** was raised (1799) by General William Wemyss of Wemyss as the 93rd (Highland) Regiment of Foot. The name was changed (1861) to the 93rd (Sutherland Highlanders) Regiment of Foot. It merged with the 91st in 1881 to form the **Argyll and Sutherland Highlanders**.

sword

A weapon with a long blade, sharp on one or both edges, gripped behind a structure to protect the hand. There was no standard sword for the army, but during the 16th century the rapier was the most popular form. This was a long light sword with a cup for hand protection below the cross-piece. The length was a disadvantage when carrying other weapons such as a **pike** and a shorter weapon with a simple cut-and-thrust blade

developed during the 17th century. A sword with a short curved blade, known as a 'hanger', became popular in the latter part of the century. The blade was about 24 inches long. By the early 18th century the type of sword carried by a **regiment** was at the discretion of the **colonel** who also supplied them. With the introduction of the **bayonet** the swords carried by the **infantry** were considered an encumbrance by many regiments and they were not worn. During the same period the **cavalry** and **dragoons** carried a sword with a straight, single-edged blade and a basket hilt. The blade was about 32 inches long, but the pattern varied considerably from regiment to regiment. A Royal Warrant of 1768 laid down that the swords of each regiment should be uniform and that **sergeants, grenadiers** and the Royal Highlanders (**Black Watch**) were to carry swords, while **corporals** and **privates** of infantry regiments did not. Officers still carried swords and they became their principal weapon by the late 18th century when they stopped carrying **spontoons**. In 1788 a Board of General Officers laid down that all **light dragoons** were to carry a curved sword with a 36-inch blade while the **dragoon guards** and dragoons were to have straight-bladed swords with a half-basket hilt and a 45-inch blade. In 1796 a Royal Warrant dictated that officers in the infantry were to carry swords with brass guards with a grip of silver twisted wire and a straight cut-and-thrust blade 32 inches long. After this date various modifications were introduced to the design of cavalry and infantry swords, but uniformity was maintained. **Rifle** regiments of the early 19th century had sword-shaped **bayonets**, their equivalent command for 'fix bayonets' being 'fix swords'.
[From Old English *sweord*]

T

Taku, battle of (1860)

The attempt by the Western Powers to force trade concessions from China resulted in open aggression. One of the strongest points of the Chinese defences was a series of forts at Taku, at the mouth of the river Hai, which guarded the approaches to Tientsin (now Tianjin). An attack by a British gunboat flotilla and marines was repulsed (25 June 1859), but the forts were taken (27 August 1860) by an Anglo-French force of 17,000 commanded by General Sir James Hope **Grant** after a naval bombardment. Tientsin was opened to trade and Grant moved on to take Peking (now Beijing) (12 October).

Talavera, battle of

(1809; *Peninsular War*) The British **general** Sir Arthur Wellesley (**Wellington**) had driven the French, commanded by Marshal Nicolas **Soult**, out of Portugal and continued his advance into Spain up the Tagus valley. His 20,000-man British force was accompanied by a Spanish force of similar size, commanded by General Cuesta. When they reached Talavera supplies ran out. The French Marshal Claude Victor, with 50,000 men, moved in while Soult approached from the north. Victor attacked (28 July) not waiting for Soult to arrive. The Spaniards were not disciplined in set battles and retreated, leaving some 16,000 British to face 30,000 French. The French were thrown back with the loss of 7,300 men. Although victorious, Wellesley lost some 5,400 casualties and was too weak to face Soult. Victor withdrew towards Madrid, and Wellesley withdrew down the Tagus into Portugal. Soult was free to overrun south-west Spain, except Cadiz. Wellesley was created Viscount Wellington for his victory at Talavera.

Tamai, battle of

(1884; *Sudan War*) A British force of 4,000 attacked a Mahdist force commanded by Osman Digna (13 March). The Mahdists were defeated with the loss of 2,000 killed. The British lost 214 killed and wounded.

Tangier

Tangier was included in the dowry of Catherine of Braganza when she married Charles II. It was rented to the East India Company for £10 a year. It was garrisoned largely to maintain a naval base from which pirates could be attacked, and to prevent land attack by the Moors. The **Royal Dragoons** and the Queen's Regiment of Foot (**Queen's Royal Regiment (West Surrey)**) were raised specifically to garrison Tangier, and the earliest battle honour was awarded for Tangier.

Tangier Horse *See* **Royal Dragoons**

Tangier Regiment of Foot *See* **Queen's Royal Regiment (West Surrey)**

Tanjore, battle of

(1773; *British in India*) The fortress, defended by 20,000 men under the Rajah Lalijaji, was besieged by a British force commanded by General Joseph Smith (20 August). After the walls had been breached (16 September) the town was taken with little resistance.

tank

A heavily armoured fighting vehicle that moves on wheels running on an endless metal track. Tanks are usually armed with a **cannon** in a revolving turret and lighter automatic weapons. They were invented (1915) during **World War I** and were first used in large numbers in the battle of **Cambrai** (1917). These early tanks were equipped with light, forward-firing cannon and **machine guns**. World War I tanks were slow and lacked manoeuvrability but were greatly developed in the approach to **World War II**, in which they played a crucial part. They were the dominant weapons system in the early stages of the war in Europe but lost this pre-eminence as **anti-tank weapons** and techniques were improved later in the war. Since World War II tanks have been developed further and now typically have guns of 120mm calibre, are heavily armoured, weigh roughly 60 tons, and are propelled by diesel or gas-turbine engines at a speed of some 40 mph. The current main battle tank of the British Army is the **Challenger** 2.

[From the use of 'tank' as a codeword during manufacture]

Tank Corps *See* Royal Tank Regiment

Tarleton, Banastre (1754–1833)

Tarleton was born in Liverpool where his father was a merchant and mayor (1764). He was educated at Oxford and entered one of the inns of court. A **commission** was bought for him (1775) in the 1st King's Dragoon Guards with whom he sailed to America. He was present at the battle of **Charleston**, the capture of New York, the battle of White Plains and the capture of **Fort Washington**. As a **captain** in Harcourt's Horse he took part in the battle of the **Brandywine** and the captures of **Germantown** and Philadelphia. He was promoted to captain of the 79th Foot (1778). He moved to New York with **Clinton** where he was made **lieutenant-colonel** in command of the British Legion. When the legion was reorganised he became a **brevet major** and commanded Tarleton's 'Green Horse' which cut off the American communications, leading to the capture of **Charleston**. Tarleton's **cavalry** then played a decisive part in the taking of **Camden**. He then took part in all the major campaigns, finally being made prisoner at the fall of **Yorktown** and returning home on parole (1782). He was promoted to lieutenant-colonel of the Light Dragoons (1782) and became MP for Liverpool (1789–1806, 1807–12). He was on **half pay** (1783–88) during which time he wrote a history of his campaign in the southern parts of North America, and in which he criticised **Cornwallis**. Tarleton was promoted to **colonel** (1790) and to **major-general** (1794). He was promoted to **lieutenant-general** (1801) and commanded the Cork military district (1803) and the Severn military district (1803–18). He was promoted to **general** (1812). He held the colonelcy of the 22nd, 8th, 21st, and again the 8th Light Dragoons (**King's Royal Irish Hussars**) during the latter part of his life.

See also **Cowpens, battle of; Waxhaw Creek, battle of**

task force

A group made up from different branches of the armed forces to carry out a specific operation

tattoo

1. A drum beat to call troops into action

2. A military display, including marching, marching bands, military exercises and activities, presented as an entertainment

[From Dutch *taptoe*, literally 'tap to', a signal to shut off the tap of beer barrels at closing time in inns and taverns]

Tel-el-Kebir, battle of (1882)

A nationalist revolt in Egypt was led by Arabi Pasha. The British shelled and occupied Alexandria (July) and General Sir Garnet **Wolseley** landed with 17,000 men. This force moved inland and met the Egyptian Army of 22,000 at Tel-el-Kebir (13 September). The rebels were routed and Wolseley occupied Cairo (15 September). Arabi was captured and exiled. The revolt ended and the joint Anglo-French control of Egypt was abolished. Great Britain was thereafter the only protector.

Territorial Army

The **Territorial Force** of part-time soldiers was formed (1908) for home defence to decrease the number of regular soldiers and to increase the efficiency of the regular army. It superseded the **militia**. From 1921 it was called the Territorial Army and this force was required to serve overseas as well as at home. After **conscription** ended (1960), the Territorial Army was reorganised: whereas previously it had maintained full divisions, thereafter it provided units of **battalion** size or smaller that integrated with units of the regular Army. Its size was also reduced and has continued to decline. The Territorial Army has recently seen service in the **Iraq War** (2003) and its aftermath.

Abbreviation **TA**

Tewkesbury, battle of

(1471; *Wars of the Roses*) Having been defeated at **Barnet**, the Lancastrian Queen Margaret, wife of Henry VI, moved from Weymouth towards Wales to recruit more allies. The Yorkist Edward IV moved west to cut off the Lancastrians. The two forces met at Tewkesbury (4 May). The Lancastrian army was decisively defeated. The young Edward, Prince of Wales, was killed; the Lancastrian Edmund Beaufort, Duke of Somerset, was captured and beheaded. Margaret gave herself up, and on 22 May Henry VI, who was a prisoner in the Tower of London, was found dead. The only Lancastrian claimant to the throne was now the exiled 14-year-old Henry Tudor, Earl of Richmond.

The Highlanders (Seaforth, Gordons and Camerons)

The **regiment** was formed in 1994 by the union of the **Gordon Highlanders** and the The Queen's Own Highlanders (Seaforth and Camerons). It merged (2006) with The Royal Scots, The Royal Highland Fusiliers, The King's Own Scottish Borderers, The Black Watch and The Argyll and Sutherland Highlanders to form The **Royal Regiment of Scotland**.

The King's Regiment (Manchester and Liverpool)

The **regiment** was formed (1958) by the amalgamation of the **Manchester Regiment** and the **King's Regiment** (Liverpool). It is expected to unite (2006) with The King's Own Royal Border Regiment and The Queen's Lancashire Regiment to form The Duke of Lancaster's Regiment (King's, Lancashire and Border).

thermal imager

Any device that uses infrared radiation (heat) to create a visual image. All bodies emit infrared radiation in amounts that increase with temperature, and thermal imagers can thus be used to provide **night vision**. They have both advantages and disadvantages compared with **image intensifiers**: the latter rely on the presence of tiny amounts of light, whereas the former will work in its complete absence; however, the images produced by thermal imagers are not appropriate for some uses because the colours and intensities depend on heat and are very different from those of normal vision. Therefore, thermal imagers tend to be used for specialised purposes, especially **gunsights** (humans, being warm-blooded animals, stand out against most backgrounds unless countermeasures are taken), with image intensifiers being used for more general purposes. For example, the **Challenger** 2 tank's night vision capability is provided by a thermal imager for the gunner and commander and by an image intensifier for the driver.

The Royal Gloucestershire, Berkshire and Wiltshire Regiment

It was formed in 1994 by the amalgamation of The Duke of Edinburgh's Royal Regiment (Berkshire and Wiltshire) and the **Gloucestershire Regiment**. In 2007 it is expected to unite with The Devonshire and Dorset Light Infantry, The Light Infantry and The Royal Green Jackets, to form The Rifles.

The Troubles *See* **Northern Ireland**

Ticonderoga, battle of
1. (1758; *French and Indian War*) A French force of 3,600, commanded by the Marquis de **Montcalm**, was entrenched on a ridge in front of the fortress. A British force of 15,000, commanded by General Robert **Abercromby**, attacked without waiting for artillery support (8 July). They were repulsed with the loss of 1,944 killed and wounded. The 42nd Foot (**Black Watch**) lost nearly half their number. The fort fell (22 July 1759) to a force of 11,000 commanded by General **Amherst**.
2. (1777; *American War of Independence*) The British General John **Burgoyne** led a force of 7,700 British, Canadian, German and Indian troops from St. John's, Quebec, as part of an attack on Albany, New York. They attacked the American forces at Fort Ticonderoga (30 June) which was made untenable by the British bombardment from the nearby Mount Defiance. The garrison abandoned the fort (5 July) and Burgoyne continued to move south.

Tinchebray, battle of (1106)
Henry I became king of England 1100 on the death of his elder brother William II. However, his eldest brother, Robert, Duke of Normandy, who was absent on the First Crusade at William's death, disputed Henry's right to the throne. Robert invaded England in 1101 and received significant baronial support, but withdrew after agreeing to surrender his claim to England in return for an annual pension. Henry thereafter consolidated his hold on England while building up support in Normandy and undermining his brother's rule. He staged armed interventions in 1104 and 1105 and in 1106 besieged the castle of Tinchebray. Robert brought up his forces to break the siege, and battle was joined on 28 September. The fighting lasted about one hour and was decided by the charge of Henry's mounted reserve on the exposed flank of Robert's line. Henry thereafter ruled over Normandy; but Robert, who was captured in the battle, spent the rest of his life (until 1134) in captivity.

Tippermuir, battle of
(1644; *Civil War*) An army of Scots Royalists led by the Marquis of **Montrose** engaged a **Covenanter** army at Tippermuir outside Stirling (1 September). The 3,000-strong Royalist force destroyed the 5,000-strong Covenanter force, inflicting some 2,000 casualties.

Tipu Sahib (1749–99)
The son of **Haidar Ali** whom he succeeded as sultan of Mysore (1783). He supported the French against the British in India. On the conclusion of peace between France and Britain he agreed to a treaty (1784) which restored the pre-war *status quo*. In 1787 he sent ambassadors to France to ignite a war with Britain. When this failed he invaded Travancore which was protected by the British (1790–92). The British commanders Stuart and **Cornwallis** were supported by the Marathas and the Nizar, and Tipu was defeated. He was forced to surrender half his kingdom, pay a large indemnity and give his two sons as hostages. Tipu continued to intrigue with the French and was killed when **Seringapatam** was stormed by troops commanded by General **Harris**.

Tobruk, battle of
1. (January 1941; *World War II*) The British XIII Corps, commanded by General Sir Richard **O'Connor**, pressed westward across North Africa from **Bardia** and laid siege to Italian-held Tobruk (7 January). The 6th Australian and the 7th Armoured Divisions then led an assault on the town (21 January). Tobruk fell (22 January) and the Italian General Petassi Manella was taken prisoner with 25,000 men.
2. (March–November 1941; *World War II*) **Rommel's** first North African offensive began at El Agheila (24 March). He moved eastward rapidly, arriving at Tobruk (8 April). The garrison, largely the 9th Australian Division, commanded by General Morshead, beat back Rommel's attacks of 10–14 April and 30 April. The Axis offensive carried on eastward, reaching the Egyptian border (28 April). Tobruk, which

was supplied from the sea, held out for 240 days until it was relieved by the 8th Army's victory at **Sidi-Rezegh** (29 November).

3. (1942; *World War II*) During his second offensive across Libya **Rommel** forced the British 8th Army back into Egypt. The British General Neil Ritchie left 35,000 men, largely the 2nd South African Division, to hold Tobruk. Rommel captured Sidi Rezegh (17 June) and from there assaulted and took Tobruk, capturing 32,000 prisoners. Ritchie was dismissed. After the battle of **El Alamein**, the Axis forces retreated through Tobruk which they abandoned without a fight (13 November).

Tommy Atkins *See* **Atkins, Tommy**

Torch, Operation *See* **North-West Africa**

Torres Vedras

(1810; *Peninsular War*) After his victory at **Talavera** the duke of **Wellington** was forced to retreat into central Portugal and constructed massive defence works around Lisbon that were known as 'the lines of Torres Vedras'. This prevented the French from occupying Lisbon and ultimately forced their withdrawal from Portugal in early 1811.

Toulouse, battle of

(1814; *Peninsular War*) Having liberated Spain, **Wellington** moved into France and forced the French commander Marshal Nicolas **Soult** away from Bayonne, taking Bordeaux (12 March). Wellington then crossed the Garonne river (10 April) and a force, led by General Sir William Carr **Beresford**, took Toulouse. This was the last battle of the Peninsular War. **Napoleon** abdicated the next day and was exiled to Elba.

Tournai, battle of

(1709; *War of the Spanish Succession*) Peace negotiations between France and the Allies broke down (winter 1708–09). The Duke of **Marlborough** led an Allied army of 100,000 towards Paris. His way was barred by 90,000 French troops commanded by duc Claude de Villars in the city of Tournai. Marlborough, with Prince Eugene of Savoy, invested the city (27 June) which fell (3 September), the French suffering some 3,000 casualties. The Allies then moved on to Mons.

Townshend, Charles Vere Ferrers (1861–1924)

Townshend was educated at Cranleigh School, Kent, and entered the Royal Military College, Sandhurst. He received a **commission** in the Royal Marine Light Infantry (1881). He went to the Sudan and was present at the battles of **Abu Klea** and **Abu Kru**. He transferred to the Indian Army (1886), finally joining the Central India Horse. He saw service in the Himalayas and successfully defended Chitral (1895) until it was relieved. He then joined the Egyptian army (1896) and was promoted to **brevet lieutenant-colonel**. He commanded his battalion at **Atbara** and **Khartoum** and was awarded the DSO. He returned to India (1899) but then served in South Africa for a short time before returning home (1900) as a **major** in the **Royal Fusiliers (City of London Regiment)**. He transferred to the **King's Shropshire Light Infantry** (1906) and again went to India. He was promoted to substantive **colonel** (1908) and then went to South Africa as **brigadier-general** commanding Orange River Colony District (1909–11). He was promoted to **major-general** and went home to command the East Anglian Division of the **Territorial Army**. In 1913 he went to India to command the Jhanzi Brigade and then commanded the Rawalpindi Brigade. He then went to Mesopotamia with the 6th Indian Division. He was captured by the Turks at **Kut-al-Imara, battle of**. He held no further military appointments.

See also **Ctesiphon, battle of**

Townshend, George (1724–1807)

Townshend was the eldest son of George, Viscount Townshend. He was educated at St. John's College, Cambridge. He travelled on the Continent and joined the army there as a volunteer under the Duke of **Cumberland**, to whom he became **aide-de-camp**, and fought at **Culloden**. In 1748 he was promoted to **lieutenant-colonel** in the 1st Foot (**Royal Scots**). He quarrelled with Cumberland and retired from the army (1750).

When Cumberland retired in 1758, Townshend returned to the army as **colonel** and **aide-de-camp** to George II. He was appointed **brigadier-general** and went with **Wolfe** to **Quebec** (1759). When Wolfe was killed he took command of the army. He was appointed privy councillor (1760), promoted to **major-general** (1761) and appointed Master-General of the Ordnance (1763–67). Townshend was then made lord-lieutenant of Ireland (1767). His administration was radical and unpopular with Parliament and he was recalled as **Master-General of the Ordnance** (*see* **Ordnance, Board of**) (1773). After this his life was uneventful. He was promoted to **field marshal** (1796).

Towton, battle of
(1461; *Wars of the Roses*) The Yorkist King Edward IV moved north and defeated the Lancastrians at Ferrybridge in Yorkshire (28 March). The next day, the Yorkists, led by Richard Neville, Earl of Warwick, attacked Towton on a fortified hill. Favoured by a snowstorm and strong winds, the Yorkist archers attacked with impunity forcing the 20,000 Lancastrians to counter-attack down the hill, leaving their fortified position. Thousands were killed in hand-to-hand fighting. The Lancastrians were defeated and Queen Margaret fled to Scotland with the helpless King Henry VI.

train *See* artillery train; baggage train

trained bands
These were local forces derived from those levied in each shire in time of emergency. They were abolished when the **militia** was reformed during the reign of Charles II. *See also* **militia**

Travancore, battle of
(1789; *British in India*) The British lines were attacked by 15,000 Mysore troops under **Tipu Sahib** (28 December). The attack was repulsed with the loss of 2,000 Mysoris.

Trelawny's (Colonel Trelawny's Regiment of Foot) *See* Princess Charlotte of Wales's (or Hertfordshire) Regiment

Trenton, battle of
(1776; *American War of Independence*) The American commander, George **Washington**, had abandoned New York and moved across the Delaware river to cover the capital Philadelphia. The British, commanded by General Lord Charles **Cornwallis**, took up winter quarters at Trenton with 1,400 Hessian troops. Washington led 2,400 troops back across the frozen Delaware in a surprise attack (25 December). The German commander, Rall, was killed and Washington took prisoners back into Pennsylvania. Washington then re-crossed the Delaware (30–31 December) and took Trenton.

tricorn, tricorne
A hat with the brim turned up on three sides, worn by troops in the 18th century
[Directly or via French *tricorne* from Latin *tricornis* 'three-horned']

Trincomalee, battle of
(1767; *British in India*) A force of 12,000 British and Indian troops, commanded by Colonel Smith, surprised a 60,000-strong force of the armies of Hyderbad and Mysore commanded by **Haidar Ali**, as they rounded a hill. The British took advantage of the surprise and routed their opponents who lost 4,000 men and 64 guns. The British lost 150 killed and wounded.

Trinkitat, battle of *See* El Teb, battle of

troop
A sub-division of a **cavalry regiment**, broadly equivalent to an **infantry platoon**. When cavalry were mounted a troop might consist of 60–70 men; in the modern army a troop can include four to six tanks and their related personnel. Two or three troops usually make up a **squadron**.
[From French *troupe* 'group of people']

trooper
Formerly the lowest rank in the **cavalry**, and now in tank regiments.
See also **private**

Trooping the Colour
The ceremonial parading of the **colours** in front of the assembled troops. Originally this was carried out to ensure that the soldiers would recognise their colours in battle, but now it is a ceremony performed annually in front of the sovereign to express the loyalty of the regiments in the parade, which change each year.

tropical dress
A lightweight grey uniform was worn by the troops in **Tangier** at the time of Charles II. At the end of the 18th century a form of tropical dress was adopted by troops in the West Indies. It was not until the time of the **Indian Mutiny** that the lightweight khaki dress was introduced and it became used generally by the end of the 19th century.

Tucker, Charles (1838–1935)
Tucker was educated at Marlborough School and received a **commission** (1855) in the 22nd Foot (**Cheshire Regiment**). He was promoted to **captain** (1860) and transferred to the 80th Staffordshire Volunteers (later the 2nd **South Staffordshire Regiment**). When he died he was **colonel** of the South Staffordshire Regiment. He saw service in the Straits Settlements (now Malaysia) and in South Africa where his **regiment** played a prominent part in the battle of **Ulundi**. He was promoted to **lieutenant-colonel** (1879). In 1885 Tucker was appointed to command the Middlesex regimental district and by 1891 was colonel and then **brigadier-general** in Natal. He was promoted to **major-general** (1893) and went to India (1895) to command the Secunderabad district. He then commanded the 7th Division under Lord **Roberts** in South Africa (1899) where he served with distinction. He was promoted to **lieutenant-general** (1902) and appointed to command the Scottish district (1903). He retired in 1905.
See also **Karee, battle of**

tunic
A coat with skirts all around, thus giving protection to the chest and stomach. It replaced the coatee in 1855.
[Directly or via French *tunique* from Latin *tunica*]

Tunisia
(1942–43; *World War II*) The Anglo-American invasion of French **North-West Africa** (November 1942) prompted a build-up of Axis forces in Tunis and Bizerte. By November 1942 the German General Jürgen von Arnim commanded a force of 15,000 including the 10th Panzer Division. This force thwarted the Allies' aim of cutting off the rear of Field Marshal **Rommel** who was retreating from Libya. The advance by the British 1st Army, commanded by General Kenneth Anderson, was halted at Jefna (28 November) and the American II Corps was stopped at Sbeitla-Gafsa. The supreme commander **Eisenhower** assumed a defensive position on a line from the coast through Medjez-el-Bab to the Mareth Line in the south. On 19 February **Rommel's** Afrika Korps broke out of Faid and pushed back the American 1st Armored Division, but strong air support and a counter-attack by the British 6th Armoured Division restored the position. The British 8th Army breached the Mareth Line (26 March) and broke through the enemy's defences at Gabès (6 April). The two Allied forces from east and west then joined and moved to complete the occupation of Tunisia. The last of some 250,000 Axis forces surrendered (13 May). The battle for Tunisia ended the North African campaign.

UV

Ulundi, battle of
(1879; *Zulu War*) After the initial success of the Zulu uprising, the British in Natal launched a counter-offensive. 5,000 men led by General Lord Chelmsford and Sir Garnet **Wolseley** moved on the Zulu capital at Ulundi where they attacked and defeated 20,000 Zulus (4 July). Some 15,000 Zulus were killed while the British lost some 15 dead. The Zulu chief Cetshwayo was captured and the Zulu power was broken.

Vaal Krantz, battle of
(1900; *Boer Wars*) During his third attempt to relieve **Ladysmith** the British General Sir Redvers **Buller** crossed the Tugela river with 20,000 men and took Vaal Krantz (6 February). He held it for two days but was forced to fall back across the Tugela. This was the last major Boer victory.

vanguard
A group of soldiers moving in front of the main force.
See also **rearguard**
[Shortening of French *avant-garde* from *avant* 'before' + *garde* 'guard']

VC *abbreviation of* **Victoria Cross**

vedette
A mounted sentry or scout sent ahead of the main army to observe the enemy
[Via French from Italian *vedetta*, alteration (after *vedere* 'to see') of *veletta* from Spanish *vela* 'watch']

Venables, Robert (1612?–87)
Venables was born in Chester and joined the Parliamentary army at the beginning of the **Civil War**. By 1645 he was a **lieutenant-colonel** and was made governor of Liverpool (1648). He commanded a foot **regiment** (1648) which played a prominent part in the campaign in Ireland. He left Ireland (1654) to be **general** of the forces attacking the Spaniards in the West Indies. The fleet, commanded by Penn, sailed for Barbados, and Venables' troops were defeated in an attack on Hispaniola. His troops were ill-disciplined and poorly supplied, and Venables quarrelled with Penn. The force then attacked **Jamaica** which they took. Venables sailed home (1655) seriously ill. He was imprisoned, along with Penn, in the Tower (of London) for his failure in Hispaniola. He was released but held no further office under the Protectorate. At the Restoration he supported the king and was made governor of Chester.

Verdun, battle of
(1916; *World War I*) The German General Erich von **Falkenhayn** organised a massive assault on the Verdun sector of the **Western Front**, defended by the French 2nd Army, in an attempt to break the deadlock. A million Germans took part in a deliberate war of attrition to bleed the French white. The assault began on 21 February on an eight-mile front east of the Meuse river. The French **commander-in-chief**, Field Marshal Joseph **Joffre**, sent General Henri **Pétain** to take command at Verdun while Crown Prince Frederick Wilhelm commanded the German 5th Army. The last German attack was beaten back (11 July) and the front remained quiet until 24 October when the French, now commanded by General Robert **Nivelle**, counter-attacked. They counter-attacked again (15 December). The leadership of the French General Charles Mangin was outstanding in both these offensives. The fighting had ended by 18 December, with

little advantage being gained by either side. This was one of the longest and bloodiest conflicts of the war. The French lost 542,000 men and the Germans 434,000.

Verneuil, battle of

(1424; *Hundred Years' War*) The English army commanded by the Duke of Bedford had control of most of northern France when the French with their Scottish allies made a stand north of the river Loire, attacking the English at Verneuil. The attack by some 5,000 Scots and 10,000 French was repulsed by 9,000 English longbows. The French lost some 7,000 men, including most of the Scots. The Scots Earls of Douglas and Buchan were killed. This victory ranks with **Agincourt** as one of the major English victories during the Hundred Years' War and was the last attempt by the Scots to give aid to the French.

Vickers machine gun

The principal heavy **machine gun** used by British forces during the two world wars. Based on the Maxim design and manufactured by Vickers, it was introduced in 1912 and superseded only in the 1960s.

Victoria Cross

Britain's premier award for outstanding gallantry, instituted (January 1856) by Queen Victoria during the **Crimean War**. It can be awarded to all branches of the armed services irrespective of rank and also to civilians; posthumous awards have been permitted since 1902. Only 1,355 Victoria Crosses have been awarded (four to civilians).

Abbreviation **VC**

Villiers's (Colonel George Villiers's Regiment of Marines) *See* Huntingdonshire Regiment

Vimiero, battle of

(1808; *Peninsular War*) **Napoleon** had occupied Portugal and placed his brother Joseph on the throne of Spain (1808). The country rebelled and Britain sent an expeditionary force commanded by Sir Arthur Wellesley (**Wellington**) to Portugal. This force of 30,000 landed at Oporto (July) and moved towards Lisbon. The French General Andoche Junot moved out of Lisbon and met Wellesley's 7,000-man force at Vimiero (21 August). The French were defeated with the loss of 1,800 men and 13 guns. Instead of pursuing the victory, as Wellesley wished, more senior British **generals** arrived and agreed the Convention of Cintra (30 August). The French were allowed to evacuate Portugal and 26,000 French troops were transported back to France in British ships.

Vimy Ridge, battles of

(1915, 1917; *World War I*) A ridge 10 miles north of **Arras**. This was taken by the French (9 May 1915) and by the Canadian Corps of the British 1st Army (9 April 1917).

See also **Allenby, Edmund Henry Hynman**; **Artois-Loos, battle of**

Viscount Charlemont's Regiment of Foot *See* Herefordshire Regiment of Foot

Vitoria, battle of

(1813; *Peninsular War*) The defeat in Russia and the build-up of Allied forces compelled **Napoleon** to withdraw troops from Spain and Portugal. **Wellington** took advantage of the situation and moved from Portugal into northern Spain. King Joseph Bonaparte evacuated Madrid and fled across the Ebro river where he relied on a force of 66,000 commanded by Marshal Jourdan for protection. Wellington crossed the Ebro and outflanked the French at Vitoria (21 June). The French were defeated, losing 8,000 men and most of their artillery and transports. The Allies lost 5,000. The battle ended Napoleon's domination of Spain.

volunteers

Originally, troops raised locally in time of emergency at the instigation of a local dignitary. They may have been called to serve at home or overseas. For example, volunteers went to the Low Countries in the 16th century to support the Protestants against Catholic Spain. The **militia** was augmented by Volunteer Associations, raised on a local basis in times of emergency such as the threat caused by the Young Pretender (1745). In the latter half of the 18th century when tension with France increased, the local commanders of militia regiments raised volunteer companies attached to their regiments. After the French Revolution, when the need for home defence became urgent, local independent volunteer regiments were raised. During the period that followed, volunteer regiments were disbanded or re-formed depending on whether the country was at peace or under the threat of war. This situation existed until the position of the militia and volunteers was rationalised with the formation of the **Territorial Force** (*see* **Territorial Army**) in 1908, although many of the volunteer regiments still retain their titles. The volunteer forces of the British Army were expected to supply their own uniforms. This led to a wide diversity and originality, dictated by fashion and expense. From 1860, the brown, grey and black of civilian clothes were popular, being cheap and the cloths being made locally. In 1881 the volunteers were attached to the regular army and wore scarlet or green. After 1908 their dress was similar to that of the regular army.

See also **reforms after the Boer War**

W

Wakefield, battle of

(1460; *Wars of the Roses*) The Lancastrian Queen Margaret made two thrusts from Wales and Northern England into Yorkshire. Richard of York moved out of Sandal castle and met the Lancastrians at Wakefield (30 December). The Yorkists were severely defeated and Richard, his son Edmund, Earl of Rutland, and Richard Neville, Earl of Salisbury, were killed.

Wandiwash, battle of

(1760; *Seven Years' War*) The British had defended Madras (now Chennai) against the French in India and now went on the offensive. Lieutenant-Colonel Eyre **Coote** moved out to meet a Franco-Indian force, commanded by the Comte de Lally, at Wandiwash (22 January). The French were defeated and driven back to **Pondicherry**.

Warburg, battle of

(1760; *Seven Years' War*) Ferdinand, Duke of Brunswick, with strong support from Great Britain, held Westphalia when the French, commanded by the chevalier de Muy, moved towards Hanover. The two forces met at Warburg (31 July). The Allies' victory was due largely to the brilliance of the British cavalry commander the Marquis of **Granby**. The French lost some 3,000 men and were pushed back to the Rhine at Wesel.

See also **Blues and Royals; Dragoons, 1st; Dragoons, 2nd; Dragoons, 6th; Dragoon Guards, 1st; Dragoon Guards, 2nd; Dragoon Guards, 3rd; Dragoon Guards, 6th; Hussars, 7th; Hussars, 10th; Hussars, 11th**

War Department *See* **Cardwell reforms; Pitt's Reforms**

warhead

The payload of a **missile** containing explosive or other material such as a nerve gas

War in the Sind

During the 1840s the amirs of Sind, now a province of modern Pakistan, took a hostile attitude to the British during their war with Afghanistan, but instead of seeking their cooperation Charles **Napier** forced a treaty on the amirs and eradicated many of their fortresses. This led to open war in the Sind against the British.

See also **Afghan Wars**

War of 1812

This was an extension of the Napoleonic Wars. On 18 June 1812 the United States declared war on Great Britain. The supposed cause of the war was anger at Britain's interference with American shipping and trade in the course of Britain's blockade of Napoleon's empire. In reality 'war hawks' in the US Congress hoped to seize territory from British Canada. Despite the war's name, fighting continued until 1815. There were inconclusive battles along the US-Canadian frontier, a British invasion, soon withdrawn, of the **Baltimore** and Washington areas, and an American victory against another invasion at **New Orleans**. This last battle was actually fought after a treaty ending the war was signed at Ghent on 24 December 1814 due to the time taken for this news to reach the forces.

See also **Bladensburg, battle of; Burlington Heights, battle of; Chippewa river, battle of; Chrysler's Farm, battle of; Detroit, battle of; Fort Erie, battle of; Fort McHenry, battle of; Lundy's Lane, battle of; Plattsburg, battle of; Queenston Heights, battle of; Sackets Harbour, battle of; Stony Creek, battle of; Brock, Isaac**

Prevost, George

War Office

A Council of War (a committee of the Privy Council) was formed around 1620 and a Secretary of War is mentioned in 1642. The latter was probably a private secretary to the king, who then had complete control over the raising and maintenance of the army. The **Bill of Rights** and the **Mutiny Act** gave Parliament the right to raise an army, but the king still controlled it through the Secretary of War, who was not a member of the Cabinet. By 1704 the Secretary of War was a political appointee. He could be questioned by, but was not responsible to, Parliament. In 1783 the Secretary of War was made responsible to Parliament for voted expenditure, but command of the Army still remained with the king. Under Pitt (1785) the functions of feeding and equipping the troops were removed from the regimental **colonels** to the War Department. In 1793 a Secretary of State for War was appointed who was responsible to Parliament for military policy and the general conduct of operations. But he was frequently encumbered by the Secretary of State for the Colonies, allowing the **commander-in-chief** a free hand. The next set of changes were brought about by the **Cardwell reforms** after the **Crimean War**. Under Cardwell's War Office Act (1870) the Secretary of State for War became responsible for all army matters, and the commander-in-chief's office moved into the War Office. The commander-in-chief, the Duke of Cambridge, became the chief military adviser to the Secretary of State, who was assisted by a Permanent Under Secretary of State, a Parliamentary Under Secretary of State and a Financial Secretary.

See also **Cardwell reforms; reforms of the Duke of York; reforms after the Crimean War; reforms after the Boer War**

War Office Act (1870)

While Parliament controlled the raising, financing and discipline of the army under the **Bill of Rights** and other laws, its 'government, command and disposition' was still under the control of the sovereign. This anomaly was resolved by the War Office Act whereby the royal prerogative was exercised by the Secretary of State for War who was responsible to Parliament.

See also **War Office**

War of the Austrian Succession *See* **Austrian Succession, War of the**

War of the Grand Alliance *See* **Grand Alliance, War of the**

War of the Spanish Succession *See* **Spanish Succession, War of the**

warrant officer

A **non-commissioned officer** who has been given written authority for his rank

Warren, Charles (1840–1927)

Warren was born in Bengal, India, and educated at Cheltenham College, Sandhurst and Woolwich. He joined the **Royal Engineers** (1857) and took part in the Gibraltar survey (1859–65). He then served in Palestine (1867–70). By 1877 he had been surveying in the Orange Free State and had been awarded the **CGM**. During the Kaffir War (1877–78) he commanded the Diamond Fields Horse and was promoted to **brevet lieutenant-colonel**. Warren was appointed **commander-in-chief** Griqualand West (1879). He was chief instructor in military engineering at Chatham (1880–84) but in 1882 he went to Egypt and in 1884 to Bechuanaland (now Botswana). He was appointed chief commissioner of the Metropolitan Police (1886) but resigned (1888) after differences with the Home Office. He was then appointed to command in Singapore (1889–94). In 1894–97 he commanded the Thames district and was promoted to **lieutenant-general** (1897). He then commanded the 5th Division in Natal and was in command at **Spion Kop**. He took part in the relief of **Ladysmith** and then commanded an expedition sent to quell a rebellion in the north-west of the region. He returned home in 1900, was promoted to **general** (1904) and to colonel-commandant of the Royal Engineers (1905).

war service stripes

These were issued (January 1918) in recognition of service overseas. They were worn point upwards on the lower right arm. One red stripe was worn for service before 31 December 1914 and one blue one for each year afterwards. They were discontinued (1922) but brought back in February 1944 as red stripes to be worn singly or in groups of two, three or four.

Wars of the Roses (1455–85)

The Lancastrian King Henry VI was weak and suffered periods of insanity. This led to a power vacuum and a struggle between the Lancastrians (red rose) and Yorkists (white rose) led by Richard Plantagenet, 3rd Duke of York. The war began with the battle of **St. Albans** (1455). In 1461 Henry VI was deposed and Richard's son was crowned as Edward IV. Henry VI's wife Margaret continued the Lancastrian struggle in the interest of her son Edward, using help from France and Scotland. The former Yorkist commander Richard Neville, Earl of Warwick, changed sides and Henry VI was re-crowned king (1470). Edward IV then defeated the Lancastrians at the battle of **Tewkesbury** when Margaret was captured and her son Edward was killed. Henry VI died soon afterwards. Edward IV died (1483) and his 13-year-old son and successor Edward V was overthrown (and may have been killed) by his uncle Richard (Duke of Gloucester and third son of Richard Plantagenet), who became Richard III. The Wars of the Roses ended with the battle of **Bosworth**, where Richard III was killed and the Lancastrian Henry Tudor, Earl of Richmond, became Henry VII, and the battle of **Stoke**, where Henry defeated the Yorkist pretender Lambert Simnel.

Warwickshire Regiment of Foot *See* **Royal Warwickshire Fusiliers; South Wales Borderers**

Washington, George (1732–99)

Washington was born at Bridges Creek, Virginia and ultimately became heir to the family estates at Mount Vernon. He married Martha Custis, and the joint family estates made him one of the richest men in the colonies. He represented his county in the House of Burgesses and then represented Virginia in the Continental Congress (1774–75). He was elected **commander-in-chief** of the American forces during the **American War of Independence**. At the end of the war he returned to his estates at Mount Vernon. He presided over the convention of delegates from 12 states (the 13th state, Rhode Island, did not attend) that formulated the constitution when they met in Philadelphia (1787). Government under the constitution began (1789) with Washington as the first president. He served two terms until 1797, when, disillusioned with the new government, he retired from public life.

Waterloo, battle of

(1815; *French Wars*) Having fought at Ligny and **Quatre Bras** (16 June), **Napoleon** tried to deepen the wedge between the Anglo-Dutch army of the Duke of **Wellington** on the left and the Prussian Army of Field Marshal Gebhard von **Blücher** on the right, thus securing the road to Brussels. The French **marshal** Marquis Grouchy commanded 33,000 men on the right while Napoleon commanded 72,000 men at La Belle Alliance, facing 68,000 Allied troops commanded by Wellington across the Brussels road (18 June). A bloody and fruitless battle took place throughout the afternoon around the Château de Hougoumont on Wellington's right wing while a series of attacks, first by **infantry**, then **cavalry**, then infantry again, struck the Allied centre. The Anglo-Dutch lines held, and by late afternoon the two Prussian corps, commanded by General von Zieten and General Bülow, had come to their aid, threatening Napoleon's rear. The battle now hung in the balance and Marshal **Ney** led Napoleon's veteran Imperial Guard against Wellington's centre. The British held and the French fled as night approached back towards Paris, pursued by the British and Prussians. The French lost 26,000 killed or wounded, 9,000 captured and 9,000 missing. The Anglo-Dutch lost 15,000 and the Prussians 7,000. Napoleon returned to Paris and abdicated (7 July). Waterloo was one of the most decisive battles in history.

Wavell, Archibald Percival (1883–1950)

Wavell was educated at Winchester and Sandhurst (1900) and was **gazetted** to the **Black Watch**. He saw service in South Africa and then went to India (1903). He attended the **Staff College**, and lost an eye at the battle of **Ypres**, when he was awarded the **MC**. He then served as liaison officer to the Russians in Turkey and then in Palestine (1916) where he joined **Allenby's** staff as **brigadier-general** (1918). He served at the **War Office** and on the staff (1918–27). Wavell then commanded the 5th Division at Blackdown (1930) and then the 2nd Division at Aldershot. In 1937 he was given command in Palestine and Trans-Jordan and in 1939 was sent to form a new command in the Middle East. At the outbreak of **World War II** he was in command of the campaign in the North African desert and subsequently in **Greece** and **Crete**. He was replaced by **Auchinleck** and appointed **commander-in-chief** in India. He was in command in **Burma** (now Myanmar) during the early unsuccessful stages of the war with the Japanese but in 1943 Wavell was promoted to **field marshal** and appointed viceroy of India. He was in command during the troubles leading up to the partition of India until he was replaced as viceroy by Lord Mountbatten of Burma (1947). He had received decorations from eight countries and honorary degrees from six universities.

Waxhaw Creek, battle of

1780; *American War of Independence*) After the fall of Charleston to the British (12 May) the American **colonel** Abraham Burford withdrew his 350 men to North Carolina. He was pursued by several hundred mounted British commanded by Colonel Banastre **Tarleton** and overtaken at Waxhaw Creek (29 May). In spite of their surrendering, the British massacred the Americans, thus ending resistance in South Carolina.

weapons of mass destruction

Weapons that kill a very large number of people and in some cases have the potential to inflict lasting damage on the environment. They include nuclear weapons, chemical agents, such as nerve **gas** and the defoliant Agent Orange, and various types of lethal microorganisms, such as anthrax. Britain has conducted research into all three types; in particular, British scientists contributed to the American atomic bombs that were dropped on Japan in 1945, although it was not until 1952 that Britain successfully tested its own atomic bomb. Weapons of mass destruction can be used both as tactical weapons against military forces in battle and also as strategic weapons against the enemy's civilian population and economic capacity. They are also suitable for use by terrorists, because great destructive power can be carried in a small and easily concealed device. In fact, examples of their use are comparatively few, and then on a small scale: the threat of large-scale use is considered so terrible that strategy evolves to prevent it. For example, from the 1950s the basic strategy of the Cold War was the doctrine of Mutually Assured Destruction: both sides had sufficient nuclear capacity to destroy the other, and both made it clear that they would do so if attacked with nuclear weapons. The main aim of policy therefore became to prevent this happening, while maintaining it as a credible threat and not conceding an advantage to the other side. With the end of the Cold War, the emphasis shifted to preventing the proliferation of these weapons, and in particular their acquisition by so-called 'rogue states' or by terrorists. Evidence that Iraq was developing weapons of mass destruction was a major diplomatic issue in the 1990s, and was the principal justification for the **Iraq War** 2003). This position was undermined when investigations following the overthrow of Saddam Hussein's regime failed to find any such weapons or a current capability to produce them.

Abbreviation WMD

webbing

Stout webbing replaced leather for soldiers' equipment after the **Boer War**

Wellesley, Arthur *See* **Wellington, 1st Duke of**

Wellington, 1st Duke of (1769–1852)

Wellesley was born in Dublin and was the brother of Lord Richard Wellesley governor-general of India. He joined the army (1787) and served in India where he became governor of Mysore and defeated the **Marathas**. He was knighted (1804) and was elected as an MP (1806). He was Irish secretary (1807) and in the same year defeated the Danes at Copenhagen. He took command during the **Peninsular War** and defeated the French at **Talavera, Salamanca** and **Toulouse**. For his part in this campaign he was created Duke of Wellington. His greatest victory was at **Waterloo**. He joined the government as **Master-General of the Ordnance** (*see* **Ordnance Board of**) (1818); was constable of the Tower (of London) (1826); **Commander-in-Chief** (1827); and Tory prime minister (1828–30). His objection to parliamentary reform brought down his government. Wellington was foreign secretary under Peel (1834–35) and retired from public life (1846).

Also known as **Wellesley, Arthur**; *See also* **Argaon, battle of**; **Assaye, battle of**

wellington boot

A leather boot which came to just below the knee. It was worn generally at the end of the **Crimean War** and then by **infantry** officers in full dress.
[After the 1st Duke of Wellington (1769–1852), who favoured it]

Welsh Guards

A **regiment** of **Foot Guards** raised (1915) by George V from a nucleus of Welshmen serving in the other regiments of **Foot Guards**

Welsh Regiment

The **regiment** was raised as an invalid unit at Chelsea (1719) as Colonel Fielding's Regiment of Foot. It changed its name with its **colonels** until it became the Royal Invalids (41st Regiment of Foot) (1747). The name was changed again (1751) to the 41st Regiment of Foot or Invalids and to 41st (Royal Invalids) Regiment of Foot (1782). In 1787 it became the 41st Regiment of Foot and in 1831 the 41st (The Welsh) Regiment of Foot. In the 1881 reorganisation the 41st was merged with the 69th **South Lincolnshire Regiment** with the new regiment remaining titled as the Welsh Regiment. The Welsh Regiment joined with the **South Wales Borderers** in 1969 to form the **Royal Regiment of Wales**.

West African Frontier Force

The force was established (1900) when the army of the Royal Niger Company was taken over by the Crown. Its chief function was to deal with the intrusion of Moslems from the north into northern Nigeria. It was renamed (1928) the **Royal West African Frontier Force**. Initially its strength was kept sufficient to deal with local situations but was increased, especially during **World War II** when it served overseas. It was disbanded in 1960.

Western Front

The area of land in western Europe where the Allied and German armies confronted each other during **World War I**. Moving little between late 1914 and 1918, it ran from the coast of Belgium through Belgium and northern France to Rheims, Verdun and the Swiss border. It was the scene of the war's heaviest and most prolonged fighting.

West Essex Regiment of Foot

The **regiment** was raised (1755) by Lord Manners as the 58th Regiment of Foot. It became the 56th Regiment of Foot (1757) and the 56th (or West Essex) Regiment of Foot (1782). It was amalgamated as part of the **Essex Regiment** in 1881.

West Lancashire Regiment *See* **East Lancashire Regiment**

West Middlesex Regiment

The **regiment** was raised (1755) as the 59th Regiment of Foot and was re-numbered the 57th Regiment of Foot (1757). It was re-named the 57th (or West Middlesex

Regiment of Foot (1782). It was amalgamated with the **East Middlesex Regiment of Foot** in 1881 to form the **Middlesex Regiment**.

See also **Albuera, battle of**

Westmorland Regiment

The **regiment** was raised (1755) as the 57th Regiment of Foot. It was re-named the 55th Regiment of Foot (1757) and the (Westmorland) Regiment of Foot (1782). It was nick-named 'The Two Fives'. In 1881 it was amalgamated with the **Cumberland Regiment** to form the **Border Regiment**.

West Norfolk Regiment of Foot

The **regiment** was raised (1745) by Lieutenant-Colonel John Campbell as the 56th Regiment of Foot. It was re-named as the 54th Regiment of Foot (1757) and in 1782 it became the 54th (or West Norfolk) Regiment of Foot. In 1881 it merged with the 39th to form the **Dorsetshire Regiment of Foot**.

Weston, Aylmer Gould Hunter (1864–1940)

Weston was educated at Wellington College and the **Royal Military Academy**. He received a **commission** in the **Royal Engineers** (1884) and served in India where he commanded the Bengal Sappers with the Waziristan Field Force (1894–95). He was made **brevet major**, then served with **Kitchener** in Egypt (1896) and entered the **Staff College** (1898). In 1899 he commanded the first mounted engineers in South Africa, carrying out many daring operations. He was awarded the DSO and was made brevet **lieutenant-colonel** (1900). Weston then returned home and was appointed general staff officer, Eastern Command (1904–08) and then **colonel** and chief general staff officer Scottish Command (1908). In 1911 he was made assistant director of military training at the **War Office**. In 1914 he was **brigadier-general** in command of the 11th Infantry Brigade at Colchester. He took his **brigade** to France (1914) and was promoted to **major-general** for its part in the battles of **Le Cateau** and on the Aisne. In 1915 he commanded the 29th Division during its landing at Cape Helles in the **Gallipoli** campaign. In this campaign he was promoted to temporary **lieutenant-general** commanding the VIII Corps. He returned with the corps to France and was confirmed as lieutenant-general. He retired in 1920 and became Colonel Commandant of the Royal **Artillery** (1921).

West Suffolk Regiment of Foot

The **regiment** was raised (1756) as the 2nd Battalion of the 8th Foot (**King's Regiment (Liverpool)**). It became independent (1758) as the 63rd (or the West Suffolk) Regiment of Foot and amalgamated with the 96th Regiment of Foot (1881).

West Surrey Regiment *See* Queen's Royal Regiment (West Surrey)

West Wall *See* Siegfried Line

West Yorkshire Regiment

The **regiment** was raised (1685) as Colonel Sir Edward **Hales's** Regiment of Foot. The name was changed with the **colonel** until 1751 when it was designated the 14th Regiment of Foot. In 1782 it became the 14th (or the Bedfordshire) Regiment of Foot; in 1876 the 14th (Buckinghamshire) (Prince of Wales's Own) Regiment of Foot; and in 1881 the Prince of Wales's Own (West Yorkshire Regiment). In 1920 it was re-named the West Yorkshire Regiment (the Prince of Wales's Own) and by an amalgamation in 1958 became part of the **Prince of Wales's Own Regiment of Yorkshire**.

Wexford, battle of

(1649; *Civil War*) Having massacred the Royalist garrison at **Drogheda**, **Cromwell** moved into the south-east of Ireland and attacked the seaport of Wexford. The garrison could not hold out and the town fell (11 October). The defenders were massacred and the town sacked.

wheellock

A mechanism for firing the priming charge in a **musket** or similar weapon. It was developed about 1515. A piece of flint or iron pyrites was held firmly in a clamp and a milled iron wheel fixed firmly against it which was rotated by hand. The resulting spark ignited the charge and fired the gun. It was replaced by the **flintlock**.

Whish, William Sampson (1787–1853)

Whish was born at Northwold and received a **commission** in the Bengal Artillery (1804). He was promoted to **captain** (1807) and commanded the rocket troop of horse artillery during the **Maratha Wars** (1817–18). By 1821 he had been promoted to **major** and then to **lieutenant-colonel** for distinguished service in the field (1826) when commanding the Karnal and Sirhind division of artillery. By 1841 he had been promoted to **major-general** and went home on leave until the end of 1847. Whish was given command of the Punjab Division (1848) and was in command at **Multan**. He transferred to command the Bengal Division. He was promoted to **lieutenant-general** (1851) and died in London while on leave.

White, George Stuart (1835–1912)

White was born at Whitehall (Co. Antrim) and entered Sandhurst. He joined the 27th Foot (**Inniskilling Regiment of Foot**) and served in India during the **Indian Mutiny**. He transferred to the 92nd Foot (**Gordon Highlanders**), and as a **major** distinguished himself at Charasia during the **Afghan War** (1879). He was awarded the **Victoria Cross** and promoted to **brevet colonel**. He then commanded his **regiment** at home before serving as assistant **paymaster general** in Egypt (1884–85). White then commanded a **brigade** in Burma (now Myanmar) (1885–89). He was promoted to **major-general** (1889). He was then given command at Quetta (India) and was largely responsible for the pacification of Baluchistan. He replaced Sir Frederick **Roberts** as **commander-in-chief** in India. In 1897 he was Quartermaster-General at the **War Office**. At the outbreak of the **Boer War** (1899) White took command in Natal where he undertook the defence of **Ladysmith**. He returned home after the siege and was appointed governor of Gibraltar. He was promoted to **field marshal** (1905).

white flag

This has been used as a sign of truce since early times. It was usually carried or accompanied by a trumpeter, who was considered noncombatant and immune from capture.

Whitelock, John (1757–1833)

Whitelock was born in Wiltshire and educated at Marlborough College. Through influence, he was commissioned **ensign** in the 14th Foot (**West Yorkshire Regiment**) (1778). He was promoted to **lieutenant** (1780) and went to Jamaica (1782). He transferred to the 36th Foot (**Herefordshire Regiment of Foot**) (1784) and was promoted to **major** in the 60th Foot (**King's Royal Rifle Corps**) (1788). He returned to the West Indies and was promoted to **lieutenant-colonel** in the 13th Foot (**Somerset Light Infantry**), serving in Jamaica (1791). He took part in the campaign against the French in San Domingo. After further service in the West Indies he returned home. Whitelock was promoted to **major-general** (1798) and to **lieutenant-general** (1805). In 1799 he was lieutenant-general of Portsmouth and in 1805 inspector-general of recruiting. He was then appointed to command a force sent to re-take **Buenos Aires**. The expedition was a failure and Whitelocke was court-martialled (1808). He was found guilty and cashiered. He spent the rest of his life in retirement, mainly at Bristol.

white phosphorus

A type of phosphorus used since **World War I** to create smoke screens and, more controversially, as an incendiary or anti-personnel weapon. It is the most effective smoke-screen agent known, producing large amounts of smoke very quickly as it burns on contact with air, and is especially suitable for small weapons such as hand grenades. However, this smoke is toxic to humans and phosphorus itself can produce serious burns. Regarded in some quarters as a chemical weapon, the use of white phosphorus as an incendiary or anti-personnel weapon is of dubious legality under various international agreements, and the British Army employs it only to create smoke screens.

Wills, Charles (1666–1741)

Wills was born in Cornwall and was appointed **subaltern** in Colonel Thomas Erle's Regiment of Foot (disbanded in 1698) and served in Ireland. He was then appointed **captain** in the 19th Foot (**Green Howards**) (1691) and served in Flanders. In 1694 he was appointed **major** in Colonel Saunderson's Foot and was promoted to **lieutenant-colonel** (1697). The **regiment** was disbanded and Wills was made lieutenant-colonel in Viscount Charlemont's Foot (36th Foot, later the **Herefordshire Regiment of Foot**) in Ireland. The regiment went to the West Indies where Wills commanded the attacks on the French in Guadeloupe (1705). Wills went to Spain as quartermaster-general (1705–10). He was promoted to **brigadier-general** (1707) and to **major-general** (1709). He fought at Almenara and Saragossa (now Zaragoza), was captured at **Brihuega** but was allowed to return home. Wills was in command in Cheshire when **Preston** was taken by the Jacobites (1715). He, with General Carpenter, was responsible for the relief of the town and the surrender of the Jacobites. He was promoted to **lieutenant-general**. Wills was appointed **colonel** of the 3rd Foot (**East Kent Regiment**) (1716), governor of Portsmouth (1717), lieutenant-general of Ordnance (1718), KB (1725), colonel of the 1st Foot Guards (**Grenadier Guards**) (1726) and **general** commanding the foot (1739).

Willshire, Thomas (1789–1862)

Willshire was born in Halifax, Nova Scotia. He enlisted in the 38th Foot (**Staffordshire (1st) Regiment of Foot**). He joined the **regiment** in the West Indies (1798) and came with it to England (1800), and went to school. He was promoted to **captain** (1804). The regiment took part in the attack on **Buenos Aires**. It then went to Portugal where it was present at the battles of **Roliça**, **Vimiero** and **Corunna**. In 1812 the 38th Foot went again to the Peninsula and Willshire commanded the light company at **Salamanca**, **Vitoria** and **San Sebastian**. He was promoted to **brevet lieutenant-colonel**. Willshire went to the Netherlands (1815) and then served on the staff in Paris. He then went to the Cape and was involved in the battles with the Kaffirs. The 38th went to Calcutta (now Kolkata) (1822) and Willshire was made **major** without purchase in the 46th Foot (**South Devonshire Regiment of Foot**), then lieutenant-colonel without purchase in the 2nd Foot (**Queen's Royal Regiment (West Surrey)**), based at Poona (1827). He was promoted to brevet **colonel** (1837) and commanded the infantry in Bombay (now Mumbai). He served in the First **Afghan War** and was created baronet (1840) for his part in the capture of **Khelat**. He returned home (1840) and was appointed commandant at Chatham (1841–46). Willshire was promoted to **major-general** (1846), colonel of the 51st Foot (**Yorkshire West Riding (2nd) Light Infantry Regiment**) (1849), **lieutenant-general** (1854) and **general** (1861).

Wiltshire Regiment of Foot

The **regiment** was raised (1756) as the 2nd Battalion of the 4th **King's Own Royal Regiment (Lancaster)**, becoming independent (1758) as the 62nd Regiment of Foot. In 1782 it became the 62nd (or Wiltshire) Regiment of Foot. A new Wiltshire Regiment was formed (1881) by the amalgamation of the 62nd and the 99th **Duke of Edinburgh's Regiment of Foot**. It was known initially as the Duke of Edinburgh's (Wiltshire Regiment), changing its title (1920) to the Wiltshire Regiment (Duke of Edinburgh's). It became part of the **Duke of Edinburgh's Royal Regiment (Berkshire and Wiltshire)** in 1959.

Winchester, battle of

(1141; *The Anarchy*) Following her victory at **Lincoln** and the capture of King Stephen, Matilda tried to establish her authority over England but succeeded only in alienating powerful people whose support she needed. One such was Henry, Bishop of Winchester, and Matilda and Robert, Earl of Gloucester and her principal commander, besieged his castle at Winchester (August 1141). However, they were surrounded by an army under Stephen's queen (also called Matilda) and Geoffrey de Mandeville, Earl of Essex. Robert's forces began to fight their way out of the city on 14 September. They were partially successful: Matilda and others escaped, but Robert was captured while attempting to delay the pursuit. This defeat marked the end of Matilda's realistic hopes of making herself Queen of England.

Windham, Charles Ash (1810–70)
Windham was born in Norfolk, educated at Sandhurst and received a **commission** in the **Coldstream Guards** in which **regiment** he was promoted to **lieutenant-colonel** by 1846. He served in Canada (1838–42) and returned to England, retiring on half pay in 1849. At the outbreak of the **Crimean War** Windham was promoted to **colonel** and made an assistant quartermaster-general with the 4th Division. He was present at the battles of the **Alma** and **Balaclava**. He was given command of the 2nd Brigade of the 2nd Division and led the assault on the **Redan**. He was promoted to **major-general** and commanded the British troops occupying **Sebastopol** (now Sevastopol). He was highly praised on his return home. Windham then went to India and was in command at **Cawnpore** (now Kanpur) during the second siege (1857). He then moved to command the Lahore Division, returning to England in 1861. He was appointed colonel of the 46th Foot (**South Devonshire Regiment of Foot**) (1861), promoted to **lieutenant-general** (1863) and commanded the troops in Canada (1867–70).
See also **Pandu Naddi, battle of**

Wingate, Orde Charles (1903–44)
Wingate was born in India and educated at Charterhouse and the **Royal Military Academy**, Woolwich. He was commissioned in the Royal **Artillery** (1923) and served in the Sudan and Libya (1923–28). He served as an intelligence officer in Palestine (1928–33) and organised patrols which specialised in **commando** tactics. He led the Ethiopian-Sudanese force which took Addis Ababa from the Italians (1941). He was sent to India to organise a special force called the Chindits who, during February–May 1943, entered Japanese-held Burma (now Myanmar) and, receiving their supplies by air, conducted effective guerrilla operations against the occupying Japanese forces. Having crossed the Irrawaddy river in an attempt to cut Japanese communications, they found that progress was impossible and were forced to return to India. In March 1944 Wingate was given command of a second Chindit operation to invade central **Burma** and succeeded in cutting the Mandalay–Myitkyina railway. Soon after this he was killed in an air crash.

wings
Originally wings were pieces of cloth worn to cover the shoulder seam of the sleeveless jacket worn during the 18th century. Later they were worn by **flank companies** like the **grenadiers** and **light infantry**.

WMD *abbreviation of* **weapons of mass destruction**

Wolfe, James (1727–59)
Wolfe was born at Westerham vicarage, Kent, the eldest son of General Edward Wolfe. He received a **commission** in the 44th Foot (**East Essex Regiment**) but changed to the 12th Foot (**Suffolk Regiment**) (1742) and went to Flanders. He fought at **Dettingen**. He obtained a company in the 4th Foot (**King's Own Royal Regiment (Lancaster)**) and was appointed **brigade major** (1745). The **regiment** returned home and fought the Jacobites at **Falkirk** and **Culloden**. Wolfe returned to the Netherlands (1747) as brigade major in Mordaunt's **brigade** and was wounded at **Lauffeld**. On his return he was promoted to **major** in the 20th Foot (**East Devonshire Regiment**) (1749) and to **lieutenant-colonel** (1750). He was on garrison duty in Scotland (1749–57). The regiment then took part in the abortive assault on Rochefort (1757). Wolfe was then given command of the brigade, under Jeffrey **Amherst**, that was largely responsible for the capture of **Louisbourg** (1758). Wolfe then led the expedition which captured

Quebec. Wolfe was killed during the action, as was the French commander, Marquis de **Montcalm**. He was buried at Greenwich.

Wolseley, Garnet Joseph (1833–1913)

Born in Co. Dublin, Ireland, Wolseley was the son of an army **major**. He entered the army as a 2nd **lieutenant** (1852) and served in **Burma** (now Myanmar), the **Crimean War** and the **Indian Mutiny**. He was wounded and lost the sight in one eye. At the age of 25 he was made **lieutenant-colonel** (the youngest in the army) and sailed for China (1860). In 1861 he was sent to Canada to improve its defences against America and led the Red river expedition (1870). In 1871 he was made assistant **adjutant-general** at the **War Office**. He was sent to West Africa (1873) to subdue the **Ashanti**, resulting in his destroying **Kumasi**. He went to South Africa (1875) to negotiate with the colonists and was given command in South Africa during the **Zulu War** (1879). He returned to the War Office as Quartermaster-General (1880) and then as Adjutant-General (1882). He was sent to Egypt (1882) to suppress a local uprising when he seized the Suez Canal and defeated Arabi Pasha at **Tel-el-Kebir** (13 September). In 1884 he organised an expedition to relieve General Charles **Gordon** in **Khartoum**. The advance party arrived (28 January 1885) two days after the city had fallen and Gordon had been killed. Wolseley then commanded the troops in Ireland (1890–94), was made **field marshal** and **commander-in-chief** (1895–99). He was responsible for many reforms in the Army, and for the efficient mobilisation of forces for the **Boer War**. He is also remembered as the 'very model of a modern major-general' in the Gilbert and Sullivan operetta 'The Pirates of Penzance'.

women soldiers in the British Army

A Women's Army Auxiliary Corps was raised (1917) for noncombatant duties during **World War I**. It was re-named Queen Mary's Army Auxiliary Corps (1918) and disbanded (1919). A similar Auxiliary Territorial Service was formed (1938) and was re-named (1949) the **Women's Royal Army Corps** (WRAC). Since the 1960s women have played an increasing role in the army and in 1992 the WRAC was disbanded and its members transferred to other corps; the largest part amalgamated with the **Royal Army Pay Corps** to form the Staff and Personnel Branch of the **Adjutant General's Corps**. Women were thus fully integrated into the Army for all training and noncombat purposes; however, they are still not used in combat roles.

Women's Royal Army Corps *See* women soldiers in the British Army

Women's Transport Service *See* First Aid Nursing Yeomanry

Wood, Henry Evelyn (1838–1919)

Wood was born at Cressing and was educated at Marlborough College. He joined the Navy (1852) as a midshipman and served in the Naval Brigade in the **Crimea**. He was present at the battles of **Inkermann** and **Sebastopol** (now Sevastopol) and was wounded at the **Redan**. He was then commissioned as a **cornet** in the 13th Light Dragoons (**Hussars, 13th**) but transferred to the 17th Lancers (1857) and served in India. He was awarded the **Victoria Cross** for his part in an encounter at Sindhara 1859). He was promoted to **captain** (1861). He transferred to the 73rd Foot (**Perthshire Regiment**) (1862) and attended the **Staff College**. He passed out (1864) and held several staff appointments before taking part in the **Ashanti War** as **brevet lieutenant-colonel** (1873). He was promoted to brevet **colonel** and created CB. Wood then served on the staff before going with his **regiment** to South Africa (1878) where he commanded a column during the **Zulu War**. He returned to command at Chatham 1882) and was promoted to **major-general**. In 1882 he went to Egypt and became **commander-in-chief** of the Egyptian Army. He returned home (1896) and then held some appointments. Wood was promoted to **lieutenant-general** (1891), was appointed Quartermaster-General (1893) and promoted to **general** (1895). In 1897 he was made Adjutant-General. In 1901 he was appointed commander of the II Corps and was created **field marshal** in 1903.

See also **Kambula, battle of**

Woolwich

Formerly a town and now part of London on the south bank of the river Thames. The site of the Royal Dockyard and military storage depots from the 16th century, facilities were established to manufacture ordnance (1696) and artillery (1717) that expanded throughout the 18th century. These were controlled by the Board of **Ordnance**. In 1805 the complex was renamed the Royal **Arsenal**, with the **Royal Military Academy** moving there in 1808. Employing over 72,000 people in World War I, the Royal Arsenal subsequently declined and the last manufacturing facility was closed in 1967; it ceased to be a military establishment in 1994. (The Royal Military Academy had moved to Sandhurst in 1947.) The Royal Artillery barracks and museum are also at Woolwich.

Worcester, battle of

(1651; *Civil War*) In spite of being defeated at **Dunbar**, the Scots crowned Charles II king at Scone (1 January). Oliver **Cromwell** led the English army into Edinburgh and moved on to Perth. The Scottish General David Leslie led 16,000 Scots in a counter-invasion of England. Cromwell, having cut off the Scots from their base, marched in pursuit. The 20,000 veterans of the **New Model Army** caught up with 10,000 Royalists at Worcester. The Royalist army was destroyed (3 September) and Charles II spent six weeks in hiding before escaping to France.

Worcestershire and Sherwood Foresters Regiment (29th/45th Foot)

The **regiment** was formed (1970) by the amalgamation of the **Worcestershire Regiment** and the **Sherwood Foresters**. It is due to unite (2007) with The Cheshire Regiment and The Staffordshire Regiment to form The Mercian Regiment.

Worcestershire Regiment

The **regiment** was raised (1694) as Colonel Farrington's Regiment of Foot. It was reduced to **cadre** status (1698) but was revived (1702) as Brigadier-General Farrington's Regiment of Foot. The name was changed with the **colonel** until 1751 when it became the 29th Regiment of Foot. In 1782 the name was again changed to the 29th (or the Worcestershire) Regiment of Foot. The Worcestershire Regiment was formed (1881) by the amalgamation of the 29th Foot and the 36th **Herefordshire Regiment of Foot**.

See also **Worcestershire and Sherwood Foresters Regiment (29th/45th Foot)**

World War I (1914–18)

The arms race and hostile alliances in Europe erupted into war, triggered by the assassination of the Austrian Archduke Franz Ferdinand at Sarajevo (28 June 1914). The Austro-Hungarian Empire under Emperor Franz Josef declared war on Serbia (28 July) and Russia under Nicholas II mobilised (30 June) to support Serbia. Germany under Wilhelm II, allied with Austria and Italy as the Triple Alliance, declared war on Russia (1 August) and on France (3 August). France, Great Britain and Russia were joined in the Triple Entente. Germany declared war on Belgium (4 August) and Great Britain came to Belgium's aid on the same day. Italy refused to help Austria and Germany, who were joined by Turkey (2 November) and Bulgaria (14 October 1915). Montenegro joined the Allies (France, Belgium, Russia, Serbia and Great Britain) (5 August 1914) as did Japan (23 August 1914), Italy (23 May 1915), Romania (27 August 1915), Portugal (9 March 1916), USA (6 April 1917) and Greece (27 June 1917). Russia left the war (3 March 1918). Bulgaria surrendered (29 September 1918) followed by Turkey (31 October 1918) and Austria-Hungary (3 November 1918). Battered by Allied offensives on the Western Front, the German Army collapsed in the late summer and autumn of 1918. Kaiser Wilhelm II abdicated (9 November) and the armistice was signed (11 November 1918). The subsequent Treaty of Versailles stored up many grievances which helped cause **World War II**.

See also **Amiens, battle of; Antwerp, battle of; Ardennes, battle of; Arras, battle of; Artois-Loos, battle of; Baghdad, battle of; Cambrai, battle of; Cambrai-St Quentin, battle of; Ctesiphon, battle of; Gallipoli, battle of; Gaza, battles of; Kut** al-Imara, battle of; Le Cateau, battle of; Loos, battle of; Lys river, battle of; Marne river, battle of; Megiddo, battle of; Messines, battle of; Mons, battle of; Neuve-Chapelle, battle of; Passchendaele, battle of; Ramadi, battle of; Salonika, battle of; Sharqat, battle of; Somme, battle of; Vimy Ridge, battles of; Ypres, battle of; Allenby, Edmund Henry Hynman; Byng, Julian Hedworth George; Falkenhayn, Erich Georg Anton Sebastian von; Foch, Ferdinand; French, John Denton Pinkstone; Gough, Hubert de la Poer; Haig, Douglas; Hindenburg, Paul von; Horne, Henry Sinclair; Joffre, Joseph-Jacques-Césaire; Kitchener, Horatio Herbert; Ludendorff, Erich; Maude, Frederick Stanley; Moltke, Helmuth Johannes Ludwig von; Murray, Archibald James; Nivelle, Robert Georges; Pétain, Henri-Philippe; Rawlinson, Henry Seymour; Smith-Dorrien, Horace; barbed wire; gas; Hindenburg Line; machine gun; tank

World War II (1939–45)

Adolf Hitler became chancellor of Germany (30 January 1933) and during the next six years carried out a policy of German rearmament and territorial expansion. He remilitarised the Rhineland (1936), carried out the Anschluss with Austria (March 1938) and occupied Czechoslovakia (October 1938 and March 1939). Germany invaded Poland (1 September 1939) and Great Britain and France declared war on Germany (3 September 1939). The Germans overran Poland by October 1939, and in 1940 Denmark, Norway, Holland, Belgium and France capitulated. Italy declared war on France and Britain shortly before France's surrender. Britain stood alone until Germany, having occupied Yugoslavia and Greece, invaded its former ally, Russia (June 1941). In December 1941 Japan attacked the US base at Pearl Harbor and British possessions in the Pacific. Germany and Italy declared war on the USA (10 December 1941) and China joined the Allies. Allied victories in North Africa and Sicily drove Italy out of the war (8 September 1943). The Allied invasion of Europe (D-Day) on 6 June 1944 decided the fate of Hitler's Germany which was now squeezed from the west, from Russia and from Italy. Germany surrendered (8 May 1945). The early victories of Japanese in the Pacific were halted (June 1942) at the battle of Midway and the largely American forces swept across the Central and Southwest Pacific. Similarly Japan's early victories in Malaya and **Burma** (now Myanmar) were halted after fierce fighting by mainly British Empire forces, which in turn won major victories in 1944–45. The dropping of the two atomic bombs on Hiroshima and Nagasaki (August 6 and 9 1945) determined the Japanese surrender (14 August 1945).

See also **Alam Halfa, battle of; Anzio, battle of; Ardennes, battle of; Arnhem, battle of; Bardia, battle of; Beda Fomm, battle of; Burma campaigns; Caen, battle of; Cassino, battle of; Crete, battle of; Dieppe, battle of; Dodecanese Islands, battle of; Dunkirk, battle of; East Africa; East Indies; El Alamein, battle of; Falaise Gap, battle of; Flanders; France; Gazala, battle of; Germany; Gothic Line; Greece; Gustav Line; Habbaniya, battle of; Hong Kong; Imphal, battle of; Italy, South; Madagascar, battle of; Malaya; Mandalay, battle of; Mareth Line, battle of; Medenine, battle of; Mersa-Matruh, battle of; Normandy; North-West Africa; Norway; Po Valley, battle of; Salerno, battle of; Sangro, battle of; Sicily, battle of; Sidi Barrani, battle of; Sidi-Rezegh, battle of; Singapore, battle of; Sollum-Halfaya Pass, battle of; Tobruk, battle of; Tunisia; Alexander, Harold Rupert Leofric George; Auchinleck, Claude John Eyre; Cunningham, Alan Gordon; Eisenhower, Dwight David; Freyberg, Bernard Cyril; Graziani, Rodolfo; Kesselring, Albert; Leese, Oliver William Hargreaves; Montgomery, Bernard Law; O'Connor, Richard Nugent; Patton, George Smith; Platt, William; Rommel, Erwin; Rundstedt, Karl Rudolf Gerd von; Slim, William Joseph; Wavell, Archibald Percival; Bren gun; commando; Siegfried Line; Sten gun**

wound stripes

These were introduced in August 1916 to be worn in recognition of wounds received on active service. They were in the form of a short strip of gold braid worn upright on the left arm. They became obsolete in 1922 but were reintroduced in 1944 to become obsolete again after **World War II**.

WRAC *See* **women soldiers in the British Army**

YZ

Yamashita, Tomoyuki (1885–1946)
Born in Kochi, Japan, Yamashita graduated from the Army Academy (1905) and the Army War College (1916) to become an officer for the Army General Staff. He became the highest ranking **general** in the air force of the Imperial Army. He played a large part in planning the invasion of the Thai and Malay peninsulas (1941–42) and obtained the surrender of the British in **Singapore**. He then commanded a training base in Manchuria until 1944, when he commanded the defence of the Philippines. His forces were defeated but he held out until the general surrender of the Japanese (August 1945). Yamashita was tried for war crimes, of which he was convicted, and hanged in Manila.
Also known as **The Tiger of Malaya**

yeomanry
The volunteer **cavalry**. They had to purchase their own uniforms which were consequently very varied.
See also **reforms after the Boer War**

Yeomen of the Guard *See* regular army

York, Duke of (Frederick Augustus) (1763–1827)
The second son of King George III, Frederick was **gazetted** as **colonel** in the army (1780) and went to Hanover, Austria and Prussia to study military tactics. He was appointed **colonel** of the 2nd Horse Grenadier Guards (2nd Life Guards) (1782); **lieutenant-general** and colonel of the **Coldstream Guards** (1784). In 1793 he went to Flanders as **commander-in-chief** of the British forces, and after a disastrous campaign returned to England. In 1795 George III promoted him to **field marshal** and commander-in-chief of the Army. He returned to Holland (1799) and at the end of the campaign signed the treaty of **Alkmaar** which allowed the British to leave Holland on condition that 7,000 French prisoners were released. He was later forced to resign as commander-in-chief (1809) after revelations that his mistress, Mary Anne Clarke, had trafficked in officers' **commissions**, almost certainly without the duke's knowledge. However the duke became commander-in-chief again in 1811 and held the post until his death. By the standards of the time the duke was a generally efficient army administrator as commander-in-chief, but his indecisive generalship in the field is remembered in the song The Grand Old Duke of York.
Also known as **Duke of York and Albany**; *See also* **Bergen op Zoom, battle of 2**; re-forms of the Duke of York

York and Lancaster Regiment
The **regiment** was raised (1794) as the 84th Regiment of Foot and was re-named the 84th (York and Lancaster) Regiment of Foot in 1809. It became simply the York and Lancaster Regiment (1881) by the amalgamation of the 65th **Yorkshire North Riding Regiment of Foot (2nd)** and the 84th. The regiment was disbanded in 1968.

Yorkshire North Riding Regiment *See* Green Howards, The

Yorkshire North Riding Regiment of Foot (2nd)
The **regiment** was raised (1756) as the 2nd Battalion of the 12th Regiment of Foot. It became independent (1758) as the 65th Regiment of Foot. In 1782 it was re-named the 65th (2nd Yorkshire, North Riding) Regiment of Foot. It became part of the **York and Lancaster Regiment** in 1881.

Yorkshire Regiment (14th/15th, 19th, and 33rd/76th Foot)

The **regiment** is due to be formed (2007) by the union of The Prince of Wales's Own Regiment of Yorkshire, the Green Howards and The Duke of Wellington's Regiment (West Riding)

Yorkshire West Riding (2nd) Light Infantry Regiment

The 51st (2nd Yorkshire West Riding) The King's Own Yorkshire Light Infantry Regiment began when Colonel Robert Napier raised the 53rd Regiment of Foot, known as Napier's Regiment of Foot (1755). It was re-numbered as the 51st Regiment of Foot (1757) and became the 51st (2nd Yorkshire West Riding) Regiment of Foot. It was designated the 51st (2nd Yorkshire West Riding) Regiment of Foot (Light Infantry) (1809) and the 51st (2nd Yorkshire West Riding) The King's Own Yorkshire Light Infantry Regiment (1821). It was one of the infantry **regiments** which fought at **Minden**. It merged with the 105th in 1881 to form the **King's Own Yorkshire Light Infantry**.

Yorkshire West Riding Regiment of Foot, 1st *See* Duke of Wellington's Regiment

Yorktown, siege of

(1781; *American War of Independence*) Major-General Lord Charles **Cornwallis** withdrew his 8,000 man force from Virginia to Yorktown which had a deep water harbour and could be provisioned from the sea. However, the Royal Navy lost its superiority at sea to the French at the battle of the Virginia Capes (5–9 September) and Cornwallis was isolated. Meanwhile General **Washington** concentrated an American-French force of 17,300 and invested Yorktown (28 September). The Americans had superior artillery and the British were short of ammunition and suffered an outbreak of smallpox. These factors contributed to Cornwallis's lack of spirit in defending Yorktown. By 14 October two key redoubts had fallen and the British position was untenable. Cornwallis surrendered (19 October). Five days later **Clinton** arrived in Chesapeake Bay with 7,000 reinforcements, but realising that he was too late, returned to New York. This was the last major engagement of the war. Peace negotiations opened (April 1782) which concluded in the United States being granted independence (September 1783).

Ypres, battle of

1. (1914; *World War I*) The German 4th and 6th Armies attacked the **British Expeditionary Force** commanded by Field Marshal Sir John **French** and the French IX and XVI Corps commanded by General Joseph **Joffre** at Ypres in an attempt to capture the Channel ports (18 October–30 November). The German drive was halted but with appalling casualties on both sides. The British lost some 58,155, the French 50,000 and the Germans 130,000.

2. (1915; *World War I*) The Germans wanted to eliminate the Allied salient at Ypres as it was a threat to Brussels and was an inconvenient bulge in the battle line. A victory would also renew the threat to the Channel ports. This was the first time that the Germans used poison **gas** in the West. However, the large British casualties were due not so much to the gas but to the superior German **artillery**. The Germans made small advances but did not eliminate the Ypres salient. The British lost 59,275, the French some 10,000 and the Germans 35,000.

3. (1917; *World War I*) The 1917 third battle of Ypres is also sometimes known as the battle of **Passchendaele**, though in strict military usage this term is confined to the very last stage of the campaign. General **Haig's** main plan for 1917 was for an all-out attack on the German positions in Flanders. He hoped to make a decisive breakthrough but in any case to continue the process of attrition of the German forces which he believed had been started effectively on the **Somme**. Preliminary operations at **Arras** and **Messines** were fairly successful but when the main attack began (31 July) progress was slow. Bad weather turned much of the terrain around Ypres into a huge marsh; many soldiers simply drowned in the mud. Despite this Haig continued the offensive, sticking to his strategy of keeping up remorseless pressure on the Germans and, critics would say, almost ruining the British Army in the process. Meticulous planning by General **Plumer** achieved some advances in the later stages of the battle before it was wound down in early November. More than 300,000 men on each side became casualties.

Zulu War (1879)

The British annexed the Transvaal (1877) and the boundary of King Cetshwayo of the Zulus was adjusted in his favour on condition that he disbanded his army. To enforce this, British troops invaded Zulu territory. The Zulus achieved a stunning victory at **Isandlwana** but then were held at **Rorke's Drift** and defeated at **Kambula** and **Ulundi**.

See also **Wolseley, Garnet Joseph**

Chronological List of Battles

851	Aclea	Danish Invasion of Britain	871	Ashdown	Danish Invasion of Britain

10th Century

937	Brunanburh				

11th Century

1016	Ashingdon		1066	Stamford Bridge	Norwegian Invasion of England
1066	Fulford	Norwegian Invasion of England	1093	Alnwick	English-Scottish Wars
1066	Hastings	Norman Conquest of England			

12th Century

1106	Tinchebray		1138	The Standard	The Anarchy
1119	Brémule	Anglo-French War	1141	Lincoln	The Anarchy

13th Century

1214	Bouvines		1265-66	Kenilworth	Barons' Wars
1215	Rochester	Barons' Wars	1266	Chesterfield	Barons' War
1217	Lincoln	Barons' Wars	1296	Berwick upon Tweed	English-Scottish Wars
1224	Bedford	Barons' Wars			
1264	Lewes	Barons' Wars	1296	Dunbar	English-Scottish Wars
1264	Northampton	Barons' Wars	1297	Stirling Bridge	English-Scottish Wars
1264	Rochester	Barons' Wars			
1265	Axholme	Barons' Wars	1298	Falkirk	English-Scottish Wars
1265	Evesham	Barons' Wars			

14th Century

1306	Methven	English-Scottish Wars	1346	Neville's Cross	English-Scottish Wars
1307	Loudon Hill	English-Scottish Wars			
1314	Bannockburn	English-Scottish Wars	1356	Poitiers	Hundred Years' War
1319	Myton	English-Scottish Wars	1364	Auray	Hundred Years' War
1322	Boroughbridge		1367	Najera	Hundred Years' War
1322	Byland	English-Scottish Wars	1370	Pont Valain	Hundred Years' War
1333	Halidon Hill	English-Scottish Wars	1372	Chizai	Hundred Years' War
1346-47	Calais	Hundred Years' War	1388	Otterburn	English-Scottish Wars
1346	Crécy	Hundred Years' War	1399	Ravenspur	

15th Century

1403	Shrewsbury	Baronial War	1450	Formigny	Hundred Years' War
1408	Bramham Moor	Baronial War	1453	Castillon	Hundred Years' War
1415	Agincourt	Hundred Years' War	1455	St Albans	Wars of the Roses
1415	Harfleur	Hundred Years' War	1459	Ludford Bridge	Wars of the Roses
1418-19	Rouen	Hundred Years' War	1459	Blore Heath	Wars of the Roses
1421	Beaugé	Hundred Years' War	1460	Northampton	Wars of the Roses
1423	Cravant	Hundred Years' War	1460	Sandwich	Wars of the Roses
1424	Verneuil	Hundred Years' War	1460	Wakefield	Wars of the Roses
1428-29	Orleans	Hundred Years' War	1461	Ferrybridge	Wars of the Roses
1429	Jargeau	Hundred Years' War	1461	Mortimer's Cross	Wars of the Roses
1429	Patay	Hundred Years' War			
1449	Rouen	Hundred Years' War			

15th Century (cont.)

1461	St Albans	Wars of the Roses	1471	Barnet	Wars of the Roses
1461	Towton	Wars of the Roses	1471	Ravenspur	Wars of the Roses
1464	Hedgeley Moor	Wars of the Roses	1471	Tewkesbury	Wars of the Roses
			1485	Bosworth	Wars of the Roses
1464	Hexham	Wars of the Roses	1487	Stoke	Wars of the Roses
1469	Banbury	Wars of the Roses			

16th Century

1513	Flodden	English-Scottish Wars	1544	Boulogne	Anglo-French War
1513	The Spurs	Anglo-French War	1547	Pinkie	English-Scottish Wars
1542	Solway Moss	English-Scottish Wars	1558	Calais	

17th Century

1640	Newburn	Bishops' Wars	1646	Stow-on-the-Wold	Civil War
1642	Brentford	Civil War			
1642	Edgehill	Civil War	1648	Preston	Civil War
1643	Adwalton Moor	Civil War	1649	Drogheda	Civil War
			1649	Wexford	Civil War
1643	Braddock Down	Civil War	1650	Carbiesdale	Civil War
			1650	Dunbar	Civil War
1643	Chalgrove Field	Civil War	1651	Worcester	Civil War
			1655	Jamaica	
1643	Grantham	Civil War	1658	The Dunes	
1643	Lansdowne	Civil War	1679	Bothwell Bridge	Scottish Covenanters' Revolt
1643	Newbury	Civil War			
1643	Roundway Down	Civil War	1679	Drumclog	Scottish Covenanters' Revolt
1644	Aberdeen	Civil War	1685	Sedgemoor	Monmouth's Rebellion
1644	Alresford	Civil War	1689	Killiecrankie	Jacobite Rebellions
1644	Cheriton	Civil War	1689	Londonderry	Jacobite Rebellions
1644	Cropredy Bridge	Civil War	1690	Boyne	Irish Resistance to William and Mary
1644	Lostwithiel	Civil War	1690	Fleurus	War of the Grand Alliance
1644	Marston Moor	Civil War	1690	Port Royal	King William's War
1644	Newbury	Civil War	1691	Aughrim	
1644	Tippermuir	Civil War	1691	Limerick	Jacobite Rebellions
1645	Alford	Civil War	1692	Namur	War of the Grand Alliance
1645	Auldearn	Civil War			
1645	Inverlochy	Civil War	1692	Steenkerke	War of the Grand Alliance
1645	Kilsyth	Civil War			
1645	Langport	Civil War	1695	Namur	War of the Grand Alliance
1645	Naseby	Civil War			
1645	Philiphaugh	Civil War			

18th Century

1704	Blenheim	Spanish Succession, War	1708	Oudenarde	Spanish Succession, War
1704	Donauwörth	Spanish Succession, War	1709	Malplaquet	Spanish Succession, War
1704	Gibraltar	Spanish Succession, War	1709	Tournai	Spanish Succession, War
1705	Barcelona	Spanish Succession, War	1710	Brihuega	Spanish Succession, War
1706	Ramillies	Spanish Succession, War	1710	Port Royal	Queen Anne's War
1707	Almanza	Spanish Succession, War	1715	Preston	Jacobite Rebellions
1708	Lille	Spanish Succession, War			

Year	Battle	War
1715	Sheriffmuir	Jacobite Rebellions
1743	Dettingen	War of the Austrian Succession
1745	Carlisle	Jacobite Rebellions
1745	Fontenoy	War of the Austrian Succession
1745	Louisbourg	King George's War
1745	Prestonpans	Jacobite Rebellions
1746	Culloden Moor	Jacobite Rebellions
1746	Falkirk	Jacobite Rebellions
1746	Madras	War of the Austrian Succession
1747	Bergen op Zoom	War of the Austrian Succession
1747	Lauffeld	War of the Austrian Succession
1751	Arcot	British in India
1752	Bahur	British in India
1753	Golden Rock	British in India
1755	Beauséjour	French and Indian War
1756	Calcutta	Seven Years' War
1756	Oswego	French and Indian War
1757	Hastenbeck	Seven Years' War
1757	Plassey	Seven Years' War
1758	Louisbourg	French and Indian War
1758-59	Madras	Seven Years' War
1758	Ticonderoga	French and Indian War
1759	Masulipatam	Seven Years' War
1759	Minden	Seven Years' War
1759	Niagara	French and Indian War
1759	Quebec	French and Indian War
1760	Montreal	French and Indian War
1760	Quebec	French and Indian War
1760	Sainte Foy	French and Indian War
1760	Wandiwash	Seven Years' War
1760	Warburg	Seven Years' War
1761	Pondicherry	Seven Years' War
1762	Havana	Seven Years' War
1762	Manila	Seven Years' War
1762	Martinique	Seven Years' War
1763	Morshedabad	British in India
1763	Oondwa Nullah	British in India
1764	Buxar	British in India
1767	Trincomalee	British in India
1771	Bemis Heights	American War of Independence
1773	Tanjore	British in India
1775	Aras	Maratha Wars
1775	Bunker Hill	American War of Independence
1775	Lexington	American War of Independence
1775	and Concord	Independence
1775	Quebec	American War of Independence
1776	Brooklyn	American War of Independence
1776	Fort Washington	American War of Independence
1776	Long Island	American War of Independence
1776	Trenton	American War of Independence
1777	Bemis Heights	American War of Independence
1777	Bennington	American War of Independence
1777	Brandywine	American War of Independence
1777	Danbury	American War of Independence
1777	Fort Mercer & Fort Miffin	American War of Independence
1777	Freeman's Farm	American War of Independence
1777	Germantown	American War of Independence
1777	Paoli	American War of Independence
1777	Saratoga	American War of Independence
1777	Ticonderoga	American War of Independence
1778	Monmouth	American War of Independence
1778	Savannah	American War of Independence
1779-83	Gibraltar	American War of Independence
1779	Paulus Hook	American War of Independence
1779	Savannah	American War of Independence
1779	Stono Ferry	American War of Independence
1779	Stony Point	American War of Independence
1780	Ahmadabad	Maratha Wars
1780	Bassein	Maratha Wars
1780	Camden	American War of Independence
1780	Charleston	American War of Independence

Year	Battle	War		Year	Battle	War
1780	Deeg	Maratha Wars		1781	Porto Novo	British in India
1780	Gwalior	Maratha Wars		1781	Yorktown	American War of Independence
1780	King's Mountain	American War of Independence		1783	Mangalore	British in India
1780	Perembacum	British in India		1789	Travancore	British in India
1780	Waxhaw Creek	American War of Independence		1790	Calicut	
1781	Cowpens	American War of Independence		1791	Arikera	British in India
1781	Eutaw Springs	American War of Independence		1791	Bangalore	British in India
1781	Guilford Courthouse	American War of Independence		1791	Savandroog	British in India
1781	Negapatam			1792	Seringapatam	British in India
1781	Pollicore	British in India		1799	Alkmaar	French Wars
1781-82	Minorca	American War of Independence		1799	Bergen op Zoom	French Revolutionary Wars
				1799	Malavilly	British in India
				1799	Seringapatam	British in India
				1799	Sidassir	British in India

19th Century

Year	Battle	War		Year	Battle	War
1801	Alexandria	French Revolutionary Wars			Heights	War of 1812
1803	Agra	Maratha Wars		1812	Salamanca	Peninsular War
1803	Aligarh	Maratha Wars		1813	Burlington Heights	War of 1812
1803	Argaon	Maratha Wars		1813	Castella	Peninsular War
1803	Assaye	Maratha Wars		1813	Chrysler's Farm	War of 1812
1803	Delhi	Maratha Wars		1813	Nive	Peninsular War
1803	Laswari	Maratha Wars		1813	Nivelle	Peninsular War
1804	Deeg	Maratha Wars		1813	Sackets Harbour	War of 1812
1804	Delhi	Maratha Wars		1813	San Sebastian	Peninsular War
1804	Farrukhabad	Maratha Wars		1813	Sorauren	Peninsular War
1805	Bhurtpore	Maratha Wars		1813	Stony Creek	War of 1812
1806	Blueberg	French Wars		1813	Vitoria	Peninsular War
1806	Buenos Aires	French Wars		1814	Baltimore	War of 1812
1806	Cape Town	French Wars		1814	Bladensburg	War of 1812
1806	Maida	French Wars		1814	Lake Champlain	War of 1812
1807	Montevideo	French Wars		1814	Chippewa river	War of 1812
1808	Roliça	Peninsular War		1814	Fort Erie	War of 1812
1808	Vimiero	Peninsular War		1814	Fort McHenry	War of 1812
1809	Corunna	Peninsular War		1814	Lundy's Lane	War of 1812
1809	Oporto	Peninsular War		1814	Orthez	Peninsular War
1809	Talavera	Peninsular War		1814	Plattsburg	War of 1812
1810	Bussaco	Peninsular War		1814	Toulouse	Peninsular War
1811	Albuera	Peninsular War		1815	New Orleans	War of 1812
1811	Barossa	Peninsular War		1815	Quatre Bras	French Wars
1811	Fuentes de Oñoro	Peninsular War		1815	Waterloo	French Wars
1811	Sabugal	Peninsular War				
1812	Badajoz	Peninsular War				
1812	Ciudad Rodriga	Peninsular War				
1812	Detroit	War of 1812				
1812	Queenston					

1817	Bhurtpore	Maratha Wars
1817	Fort Sitabaldi	Maratha Wars
1817	Kirkee	Maratha Wars
1817	Mahidpur	Maratha Wars
1818	Chanda	Maratha Wars
1818	Korygaom	Maratha Wars
1819	Asirghar	Maratha Wars
1824	Accra	Ashanti War
1824	Kamarut	Burma campaigns
1824	Kemendine	Burma campaigns
1824	Kokein	Burma campaigns
1825	Accra	Ashanti War
1826	Dodowah	
1839	Ghazni	Afghan War I
1839	Khelat	Afghan War I
1842	Gandamak	Afghan War I
1842	Ghoaine	Afghan War I
1842	Jellalabad	Afghan War I
1842	Kabul	Afghan War I
1842	Khojah	Afghan War I
1843	Hyderabad	British War in the Sind
1843	Maharajpur	Sikh Wars
1843	Meanee	War in the Sind
1845	Ferozeshah	Sikh Wars
1845	Mudki	Sikh Wars
1846	Aliwal	Sikh Wars
1846	Sobraon	Sikh Wars
1848	Boomplaats	
1848	Multan	Sikh Wars
1848	Ramnagar	Sikh Wars
1849	Chilianwala	Sikh Wars
1849	Gujurat	Sikh Wars
1854	Alma	Crimean War
1854	Balaclava	Crimean War
1854	Inkerman	Crimean War
1854-55	Sebastopol	Crimean War
1855	Chernaya river	Crimean War
1855	Redan	Crimean War
1857	Agra	Indian Mutiny
1857	Aong	Indian Mutiny
1857	Cawnpore	Indian Mutiny
1857	Delhi	Indian Mutiny
1857	Goraria	Indian Mutiny
1857-58	Lucknow	Indian Mutiny
1857	Maharajpur	Indian Mutiny
1857	Nujufghur	Indian Mutiny
1857	Onao	Indian Mutiny
1857	Pandu Naddi	Indian Mutiny
1857	Pandu Naddi	Indian Mutiny
1858	Azimghur	Indian Mutiny
1858	Banda	Indian Mutiny
1858	Betwa	Indian Mutiny
1858	Gaulauli	Indian Mutiny
1858	Gwalior	Indian Mutiny
1858	Jhansi	Indian Mutiny
1858	Kalpi	Indian Mutiny
1858	Kotah	Indian Mutiny
1858	Musa Bagh	Indian Mutiny
1860	Taku	
1864	Gate Pah	Maori War
1868	Magdala	
1873	Kumasi	Ashanti War
1874	Amoaful	Ashanti War
1878	Peiwar Pass	Afghan War II
1879	Isandlwana	Zulu War
1879	Kambula	Zulu War
1879	Rorke's Drift	Zulu War
1879	Sherpur	Afghan War II
1879	Ulundi	Zulu War
1880	Ahmed Khel	Afghan War II
1880	Bronkhorst Spruit	Boer Wars
1880	Kandahar	Afghan War II
1880	Maiwand	Afghan War II
1881	Ingogo	Boer Wars
1881	Laing's Nek	Boer Wars
1881	Majuba Hill	Boer Wars
1882	Tel-el-Kebir	
1883	El Obeid	Sudan War
1884	El Teb	Sudan War
1884-85	Khartoum	Sudan War
1884	Tamai	Sudan War
1885	Abu Klea	Sudan War
1885	Abu Kru	Sudan War
1885	Hashin	Sudan War
1885	Kirbekan	Sudan War
1893	Bulawayo	
1896	Ferkah	Sudan War
1896	Kumasi	Ashanti War
1897	Dargai	North-West Frontier
1898	Atbara	Sudan War
1898	Omdurman	Sudan War
1899	Belmont	Boer Wars
1899	Colenso	Boer Wars
1899	Farquhar's Farm	Boer Wars
1899-1900	Kimberley	Boer Wars
1899-1900	Ladysmith	Boer Wars
1899-1900	Mafeking	Boer Wars
1899	Magersfontein	Boer Wars
1899	Modder river	Boer Wars
1899	Rietfontein	Boer Wars
1899	Stormberg	Boer Wars

20th Century

Year	Battle	War	Year	Battle	War
1900	Bloemfontein	Boer Wars	1918	Marne river	World War I
1900	Johannesburg	Boer Wars	1918	Megiddo	World War I
1900	Karee	Boer Wars	1918	Sharqat	World War I
1900	Paardeberg	Boer Wars	1918	Somme	World War I
1900	Peking	Boxer Rebellion	1940	Dunkirk	World War II
1900	Pieter's Hill	Boer Wars	1940	Sidi Barrani	World War II
1900	Reddersberg	Boer Wars	1941	Bardia	World War II
1900	Sanna's Post	Boer Wars	1941	Beda Fomm	World War II
1900	Senekal	Boer Wars	1941	Crete	World War II
1900	Spion Kop	Boer Wars	1941	Habbaniya	World War II
1900	Vaal Krantz	Boer Wars	1941	Sidi-Rezegh	World War II
1914	Antwerp	World War I	1941	Sollum-Halfaya Pass	World War II
1914	Ardennes	World War I	1941	Tobruk	World War II
1914	Le Cateau	World War I	1941	Tobruk	World War II
1914	Marne river	World War I	1942	Alam Halfa	World War II
1914	Mons	World War I	1942	Dieppe	World War II
1914	Ypres	World War I	1942	El Alamein	World War II
1915	Artois-Loos	World War I	1942	Gazala	World War II
1915	Ctesiphon	World War I	1942	Madagascar	World War II
1915-16	Gallipoli	World War I	1942	Mersa-Matruh	World War II
1915	Kut-al-Imara	World War I	1942	Singapore	World War II
1915	Loos	World War I	1942	Tobruk	World War II
1915-18	Salonika	World War I	1943	Dodecanese Islands	World War II
1915	Neuve-Chapelle	World War I	1943	Mareth Line	World War II
1915	Vimy Ridge	World War I	1943	Medenine	World War II
1915	Ypres	World War I	1943	Salerno	World War II
1916	Somme	World War I	1943	Sangro	World War II
1916	Verdun	World War I	1943	Sicily	World War II
1917	Arras	World War I	1944	Antwerp	World War II
1917	Baghdad	World War I	1944	Anzio	World War II
1917	Cambrai	World War I	1944-45	Ardennes	World War II
1917	Gaza	World War I	1944	Arnhem	World War II
1917	Messines	World War I	1944	Caen	World War II
1917	Passchendaele	World War I	1944	Cassino	World War II
1917	Ramadi	World War I	1944	Falaise Gap	World War II
1917	Vimy Ridge	World War I	1944	Imphal	Burma campaigns
1917	Ypres	World War I	1944	Kohima	World War II
1918	Amiens	World War I	1945	Mandalay	World War II
1918	Cambrai-St. Quentin	World War I	1945	Po Valley	World War II
1918	Lys river	World War I	1982	Goose Green	Falklands War

Chronological List of Dates of Birth of Military Figures

16th Century

1577?-1663	O'Brien, Daniel	1599-1658	Cromwell, Oliver
1592-1676	Newcastle, Earl of	1599?-1685	Dalyell, Thomas

17th Century

1608-1670	Monck, George	1658-1735	Peterborough, Earl of
1612-1671	Fairfax, Thomas	1661-1707	Cutts, John
1612?-1687	Venables, Robert	1666-1741	Wills, Charles
1619-1682	Rupert, Prince	1670-1734	Berwick, Duke of
1621-1650	Montrose, Marquis of	1678-1766	Noailles, Adrien Maurice, 3rd Duke of
1630-1703	Ginkel, Godbert de		
1640-1692	Mackay, Hugh	1679-1741	Dormer, James
1640?	Baillie, William	1683-1760	George II
1648-1720	Massue, Henri de	d.1692	Lanier, John
1649-1685	Monmouth, Duke of	d.1693	Sarsfield, Patrick
1649-1689	Dundee, Viscount	d.1695	Hales, Edward
1650-1722	Marlborough, 1st Duke of	1696-1750	Saxe, Hermann-Maurice

18th Century

1705-1782	Campbell, John, 4th Earl of Loudoun	1738-1805	Cornwallis, Charles
		1738?-1795	Clinton, Henry
1712-1759	Montcalm, Louis Joseph, Marquis de	1740-1827	Abercromby, Robert
		1742-1819	Blücher, Gebbard Leberecht von
1715-1774	Johnson, William		
1716-1785	Sackville, George	1744-1808	Lake, Gerard
1717-1790	Eliott, George Augustus	1745-1799	Hartley, James
1717-1797	Amherst, Jeffrey	1746-1829	Harris, George
1718-1759	Prideaux, John	1748-1843	Graham, Thomas
1718-1784	Haviland, William	1749-1799	Tipu Sahib
1719?-1794	Murray, James	1750?-1834	Doyle, John
1721-1765	Cumberland, Duke of (William Augustus)	1753-1828	Cameron, Alan
		1754-1833	Tarleton, Banastre
1721-1770	Granby, Marquis of	1756-1822	Auchmuty, Samuel
1721-1787	Draper, William	1757-1829	Baird, David
1721-1787	Gage, Thomas	1757-1833	Whitelock, John
1722-1792	Burgoyne, John	1758-1815	Picton, Thomas
1724-1807	Townshend, George	1759-1815	Stuart, John
1724-1808	Carleton, Guy	d.1760	Cope, John
1724-1758	Howe, George Augustus	1761-1809	Moore, John
1725-1774	Clive, Robert	1763-1827	York, Duke of (Frederick Augustus)
1726-1805	Munro, Hector		
1726-1782	Monckton, Robert	1764-1812	Craufurd, Robert
1726-1783	Coote, Eyre	1764-1843	Hislop, Thomas
1727-1759	Wolfe, James	1766-1814	Ross, Robert
1728?-1806	Gates, Horatio	1767-1816	Prevost, George
1728-1782	Haidar Ali	1768-1847	Doveton, John
1729-1807	Grey, Charles	1768-1854	Beresford, William Carr
1729-1814	Howe, William	1768-1854	Paget, Henry William
1732-1799	Washington, George	1769-1812	Brock, Isaac
1734-1801	Abercromby, Ralph	1769-1815	Ney, Michel
1737-1812	Musgrave, Thomas	1769-1821	Napoleon Bonaparte

1769-1843	Campbell, Archibald	1784-1853	Godwin, Henry Thomas
1769-1851	Soult, Nicolas-Jean de Dieu	1786-1872	Pollock, George
		1787-1853	Whish, William Sampson
1769-1852	Wellington, 1st Duke of	1787-1860	Smith, Harry George Wakelyn
1770?-1824	McCarthy, Charles		
1772-1828	Congreve, William	1787-1867	Menshikov, Aleksandr Sergeyevich, Prince
1772-1842	Hill, Rowland		
1772-1854	Drummond, Gordon	1788-1855	Raglan, Lord
1774-1850	Cambridge, 1st Duke of	1789-1862	Willshire, Thomas
1779?-1825	Staunton, Francis French	1792-1863	Campbell, Colin
		1792-1868	Simpson, James
1779-1869	Gough, Hugh	1793-1883	England, Richard
1781-1844	Keane, John	1795-1857	Havelock, Henry
1782-1842	Elphinstone, William George Keith	1797-1868	Cardigan, 7th Earl of
		1798-1853	Pretorius, Andries Wilhelmus Jacobus
1782-1845	Nott, William		
1782-1845	Sale, Robert Henry	1799-1857	Barnard, Henry William
1782-1853	Napier, Charles James	1799-1871	Scarlett, James York
d.1783	Goddard, Thomas		

19th Century

1800-1860	Roberts, Henry Gee	1839-1908	Buller, Redvers Henry
1800-1888	Lucan, Lord	1840-1927	Warren, Charles
1801-1885	Rose, Hugh Henry	1843-1885	Stewart, Herbert
1803-1863	Outram, James	1844-1885	Mahdi, the
1806-1857	Lawrence, Henry Montgomery	1845-1932	Methuen, Paul Sanford
		1847-1934	Hindenburg, Paul von
1808-1875	Grant, James Hope	1848-1916	Moltke, Helmuth Johannes Ludwig von
1810-1870	Windham, Charles Ash		
1810-1890	Napier, Robert	1850-1916	Kitchener, Horatio Herbert
1811-1881	Eyre, Vincent	1851-1929	Foch, Ferdinand
1821-1857	Nicholson, John	1852-1925	French, John Denton Pinkstone
1825-1904	Kruger, Stephanus Johannes Paulus		
		1852-1931	Joffre, Joseph-Jacques-Césaire
1826-1878	Greathed, William Wilberforce Harris	1853-1947	Hamilton, Ian Standish Monteith
1826?-1884	Cetshwayo		
1830-1883	Hicks, William	1855-1940	Lake, Percy Henry Noel
1831-1900	Joubert, Petrus (Piet) Jacobus	1856-1924	Nivelle, Robert Georges
		1856-1934	Rundle, Henry Macleod Leslie
1832-1914	Roberts, Frederick Sleigh		
1833-1913	Wolseley, Garnet Joseph	1856-1951	Pétain, Henri-Philippe
1833-1885	Earle, William	1857-1921	Nixon, John Eccles
1833-1885	Gordon, Charles George	1857-1932	Plumer, Herbert Charles Onslow
1834-1902	Scott, Francis Cunningham		
1834-1913	Prendergast, Harry North Dalrymple	1857-1941	Baden-Powell, Robert Stephenson Smyth
		1858-1930	Smith-Dorrien, Horace
1835-1912	White, George Stuart	1860-1945	Murray, Archibald James
1838-1919	Wood, Henry Evelyn		
1838-1935	Tucker, Charles		

19th Century (cont.)

1861-1922	Falkenhayn, Erich Georg Anton Sebastian von	1875-1953	Rundstedt, Karl Rudolf Gerd von
1861-1924	Townshend, Charles Vere Ferrers	1882-1955	Graziani, Rodolfo
		1883-1950	Wavell, Archibald Percival
1861-1928	Haig, Douglas	1883-1963	Brooke, Alan Francis
1861-1929	Horne, Henry Sinclair	1884-1981	Auchinleck, Claude John Eyre
1861-1936	Allenby, Edmund Henry Hynman	1885-1945	Patton, George Smith
1861-1970	Slim, William Joseph	1885-1946	Yamashita, Tomoyuki
1862-1919	Botha, Louis	1885-1960	Kesselring, Albert
1862-1930	Mahon, Bryan Thomas	1885-1975	Platt, William
1862-1935	Byng, Julian Hedworth George	1887-1966	Percival, Arthur Ernest
		1887-1976	Montgomery, Bernard Law
1864-1917	Maude, Frederick Stanley	1887-1983	Cunningham, Alan Gordon
1864-1925	Rawlinson, Henry Seymour	1888-1935	Lawrence, Thomas Edward
		1889-1963	Freyberg, Bernard Cyril
1864-1940	Weston, Aylmer Gould Hunter	1889-1981	O'Connor, Richard Nugent
		1890-1969	Eisenhower, Dwight David
1865-1937	Ludendorff, Erich	1891-1944	Rommel, Erwin
1865-1951	Birdwood, William Riddell	1891-1969	Alexander, Harold Rupert Leofric George
1870-1931	Cobbe, Alexander Stanhope	1891-1970	Slim, William Joseph
		1894-1978	Leese, Oliver William Hargreaves
1870-1950	Smuts, Jan Christiaan		
1870-1963	Gough, Hubert de la Poer		

20th Century

1903-1944	Wingate, Orde Charles	1915-1990	Stirling, David